CHAPTER 79

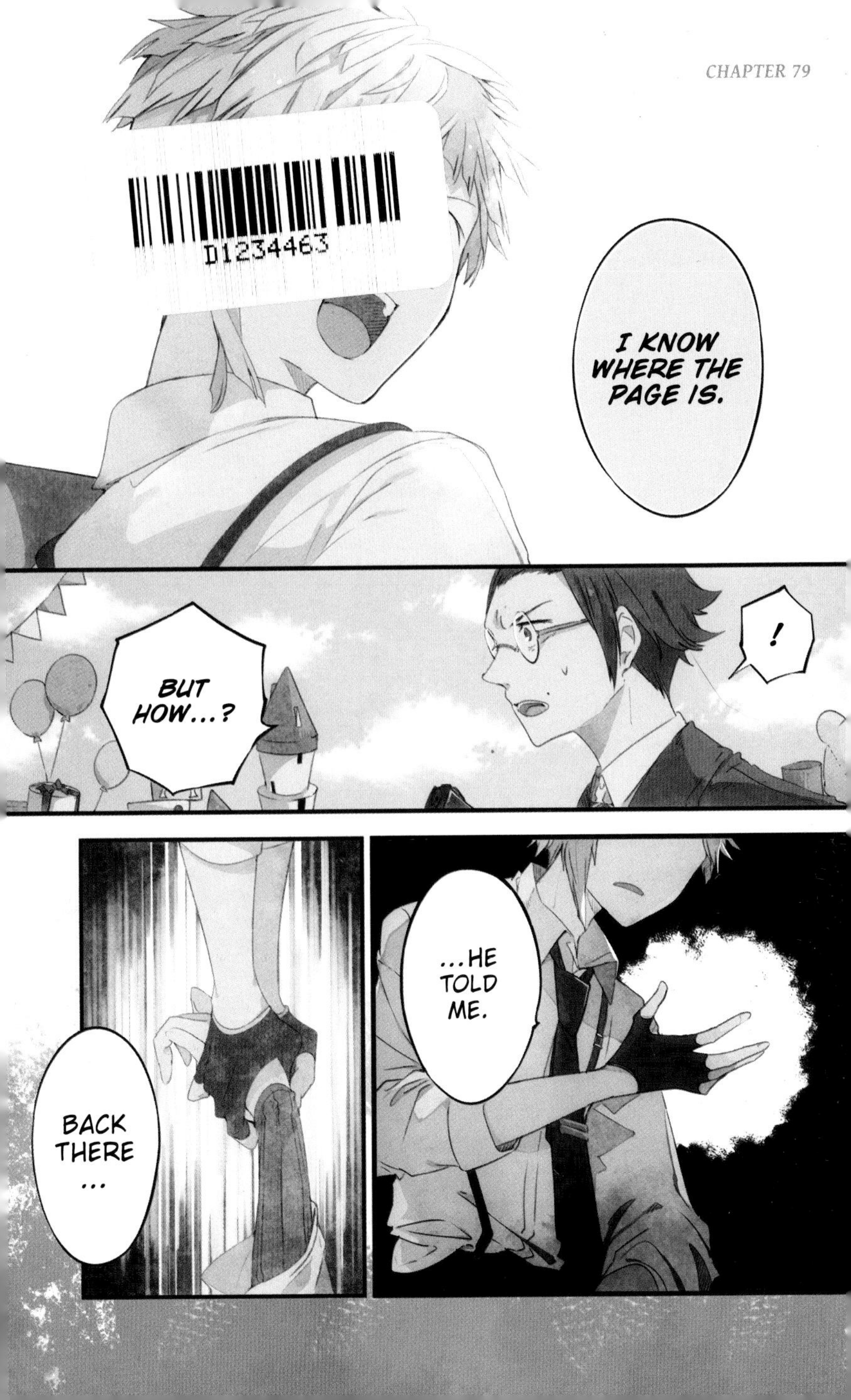
I KNOW WHERE THE PAGE IS.
!
BUT HOW...?
...HE TOLD ME.
BACK THERE ...

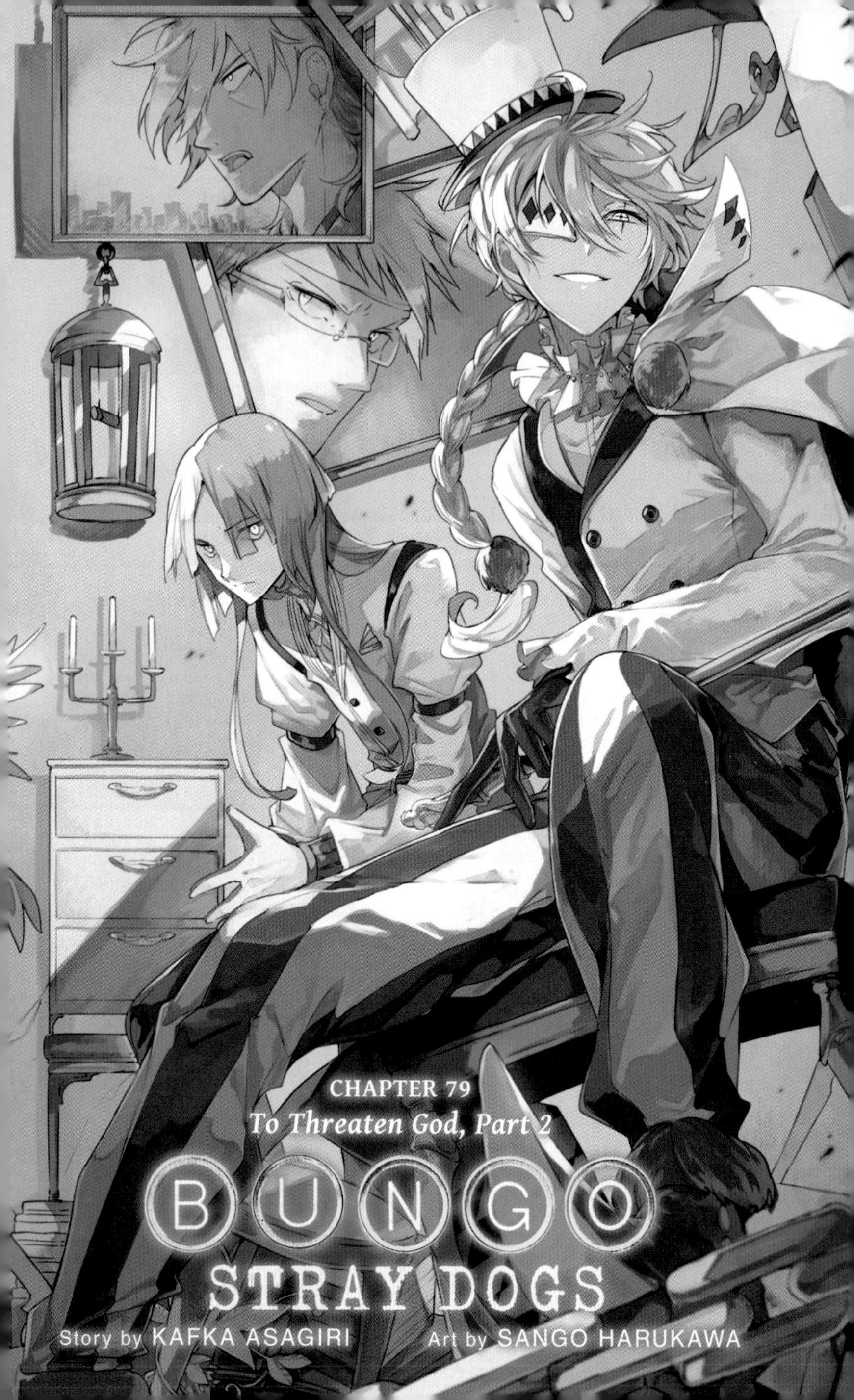
CHAPTER 79
To Threaten God, Part 2
BUNGO
STRAY DOGS
Story by KAFKA ASAGIRI
Art by SANGO HARUKAWA

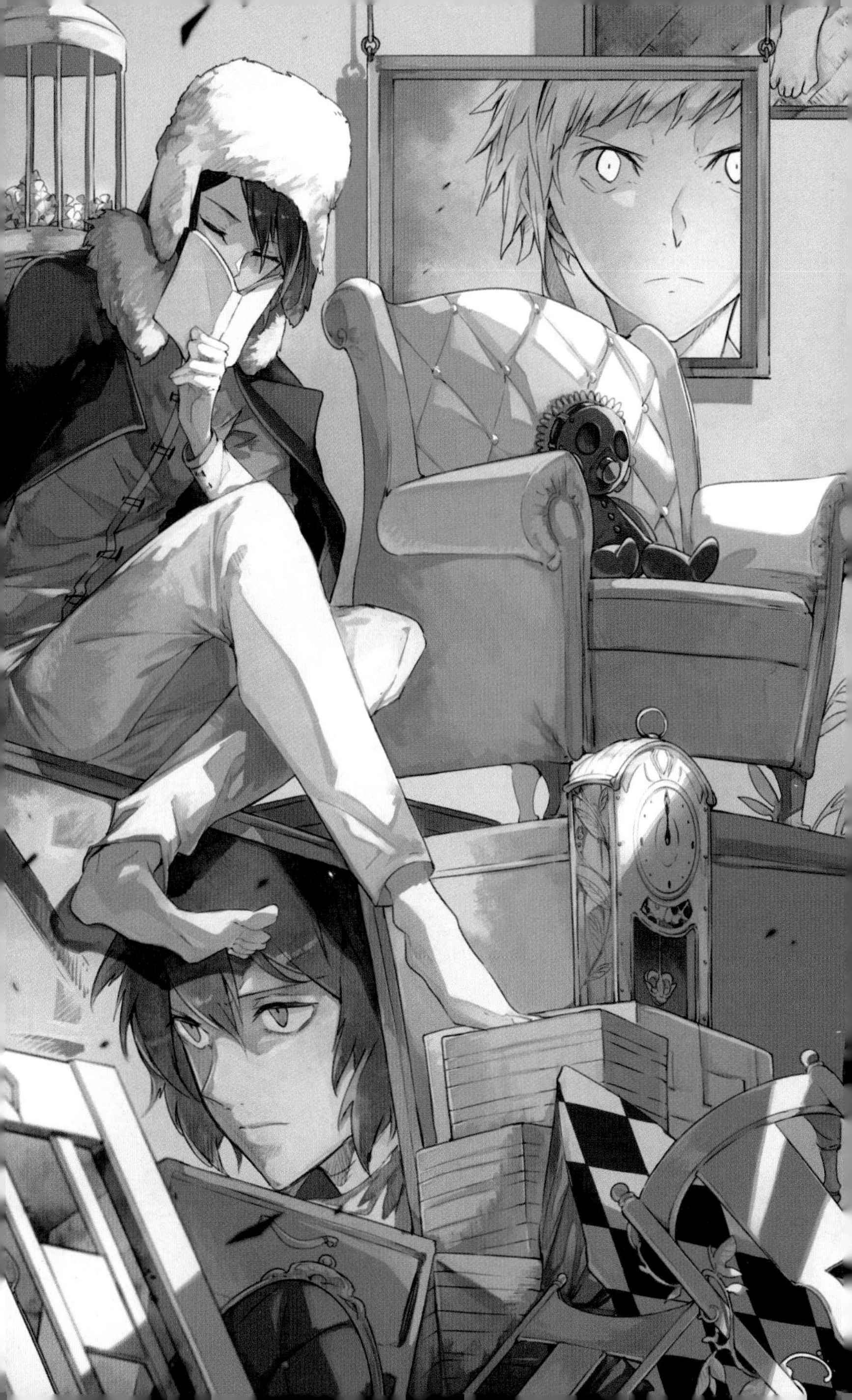

TABLE of CONTENTS

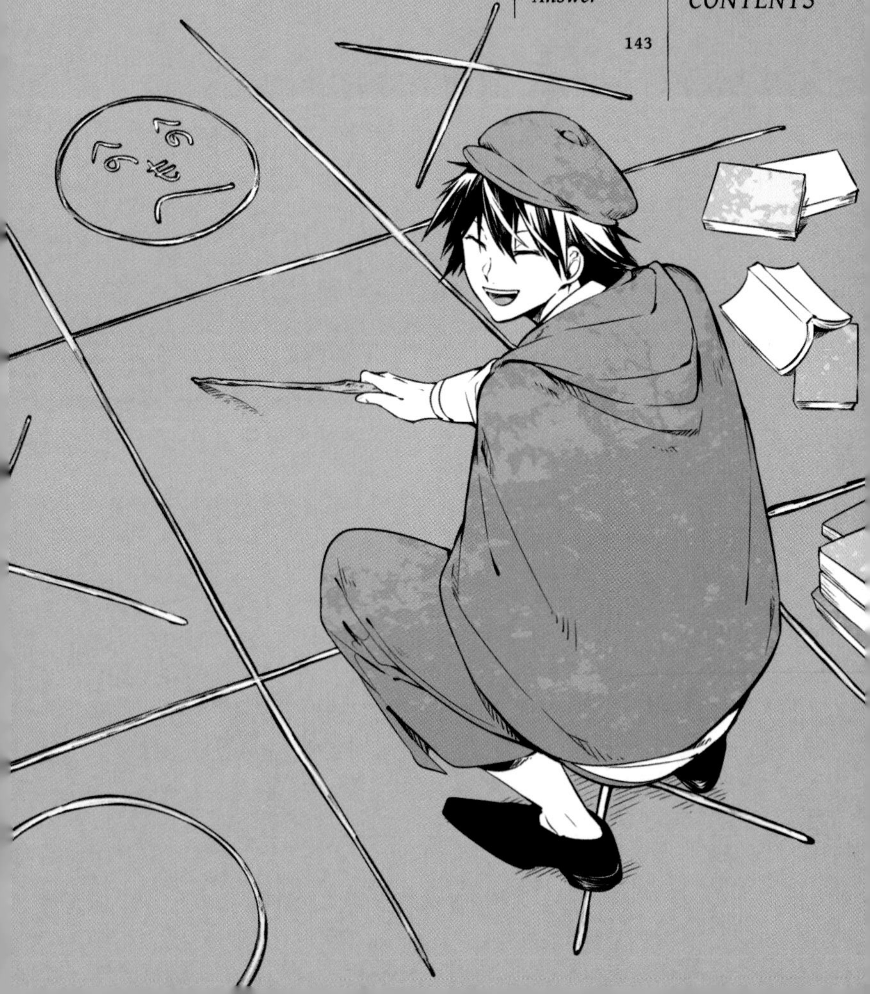

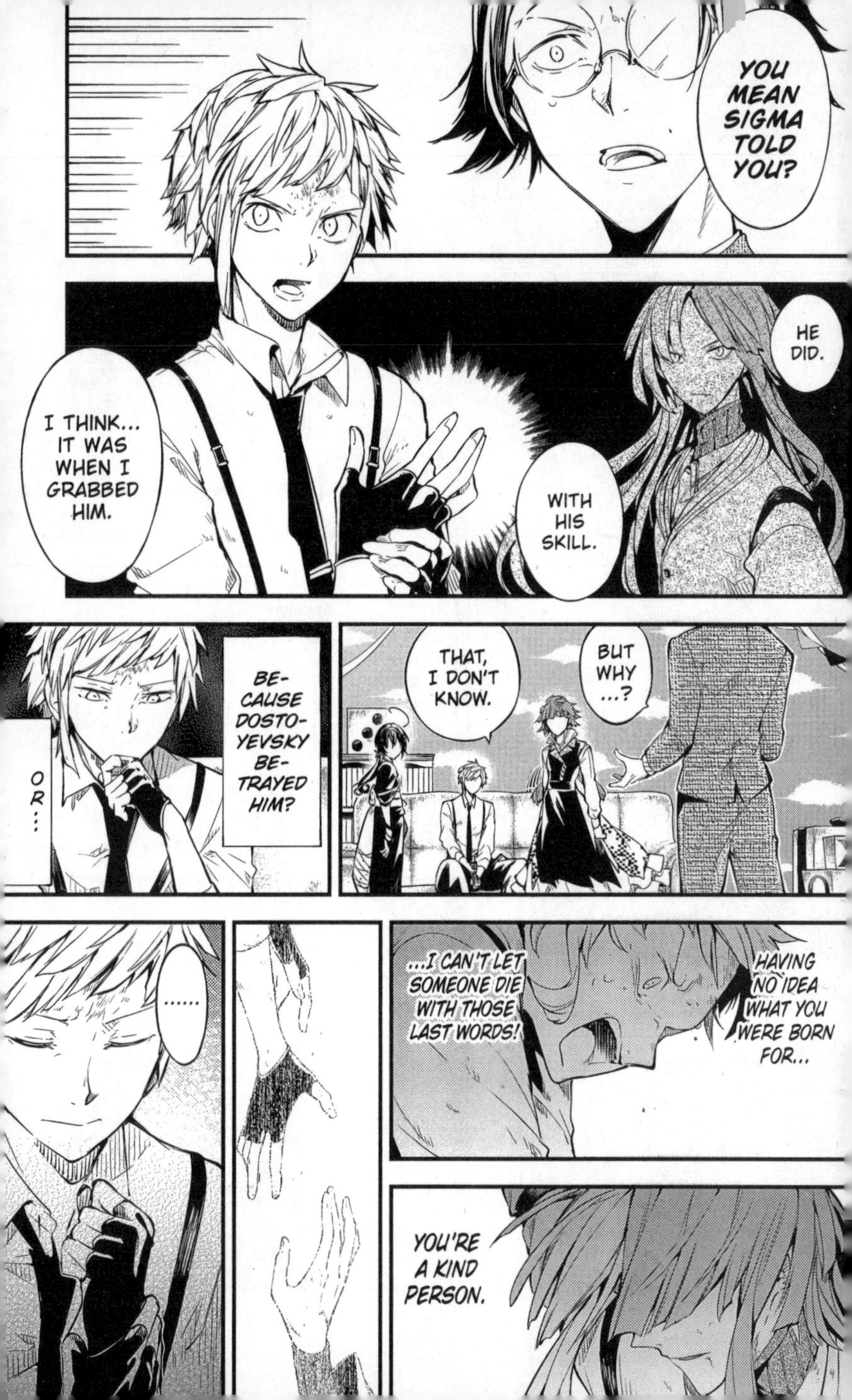
YOU MEAN SIGMA TOLD YOU?
HE DID.
WITH HIS SKILL.
I THINK... IT WAS WHEN I GRABBED HIM.
BUT WHY ...?
THAT, I DON'T KNOW.
BE-CAUSE DOSTO-YEVSKY BE-TRAYED HIM?
OR...
HAVING NO IDEA WHAT YOU WERE BORN FOR...
...I CAN'T LET SOMEONE DIE WITH THOSE LAST WORDS!
YOU'RE A KIND PERSON.
......

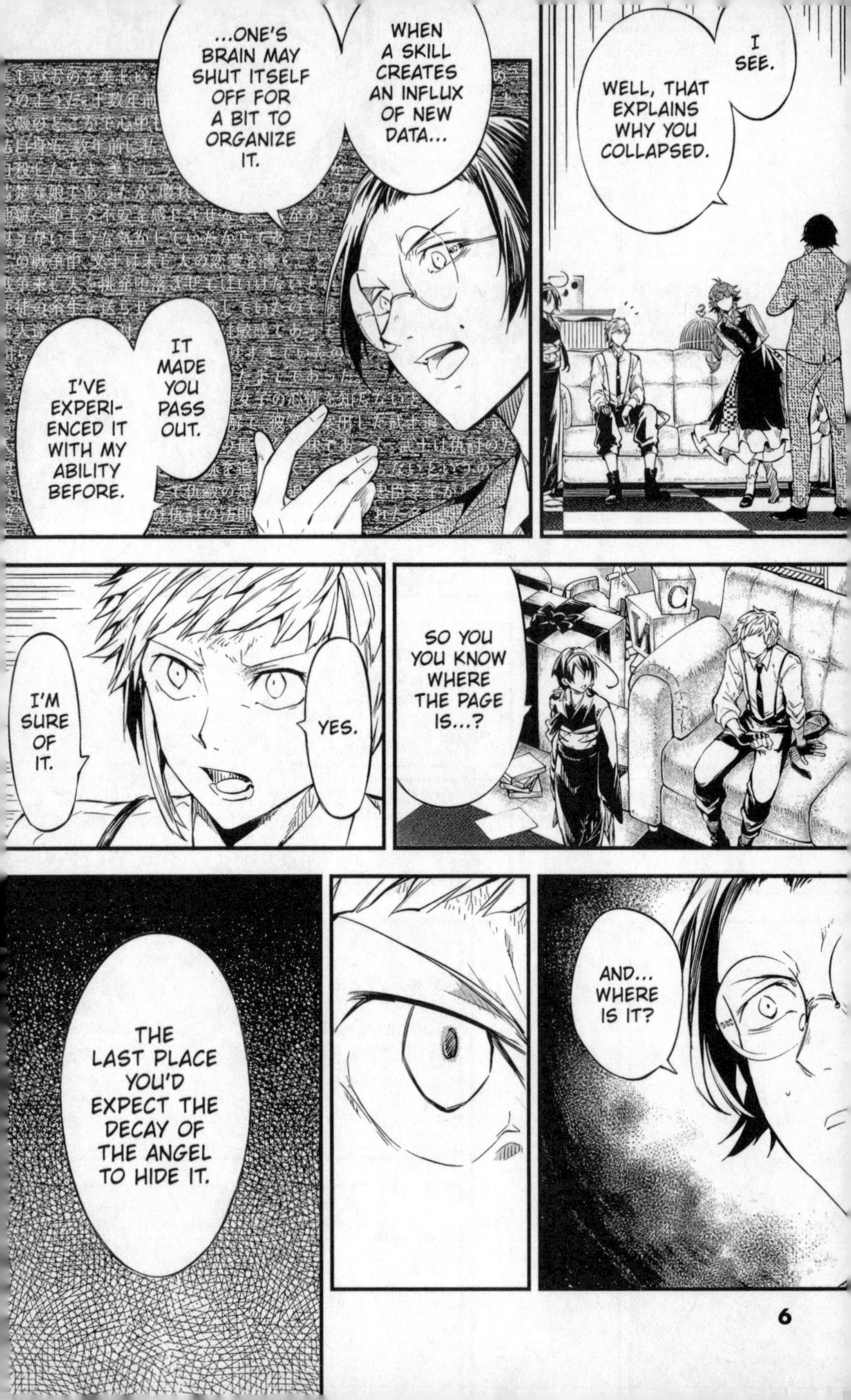
I SEE.
WELL, THAT EXPLAINS WHY YOU COLLAPSED.
WHEN A SKILL CREATES AN INFLUX OF NEW DATA...
...ONE'S BRAIN MAY SHUT ITSELF OFF FOR A BIT TO ORGANIZE IT.
IT MADE YOU PASS OUT.
I'VE EXPERI-ENCED IT WITH MY ABILITY BEFORE.
SO YOU YOU KNOW WHERE THE PAGE IS...?
YES.
I'M SURE OF IT.
AND... WHERE IS IT?
THE LAST PLACE YOU'D EXPECT THE DECAY OF THE ANGEL TO HIDE IT.

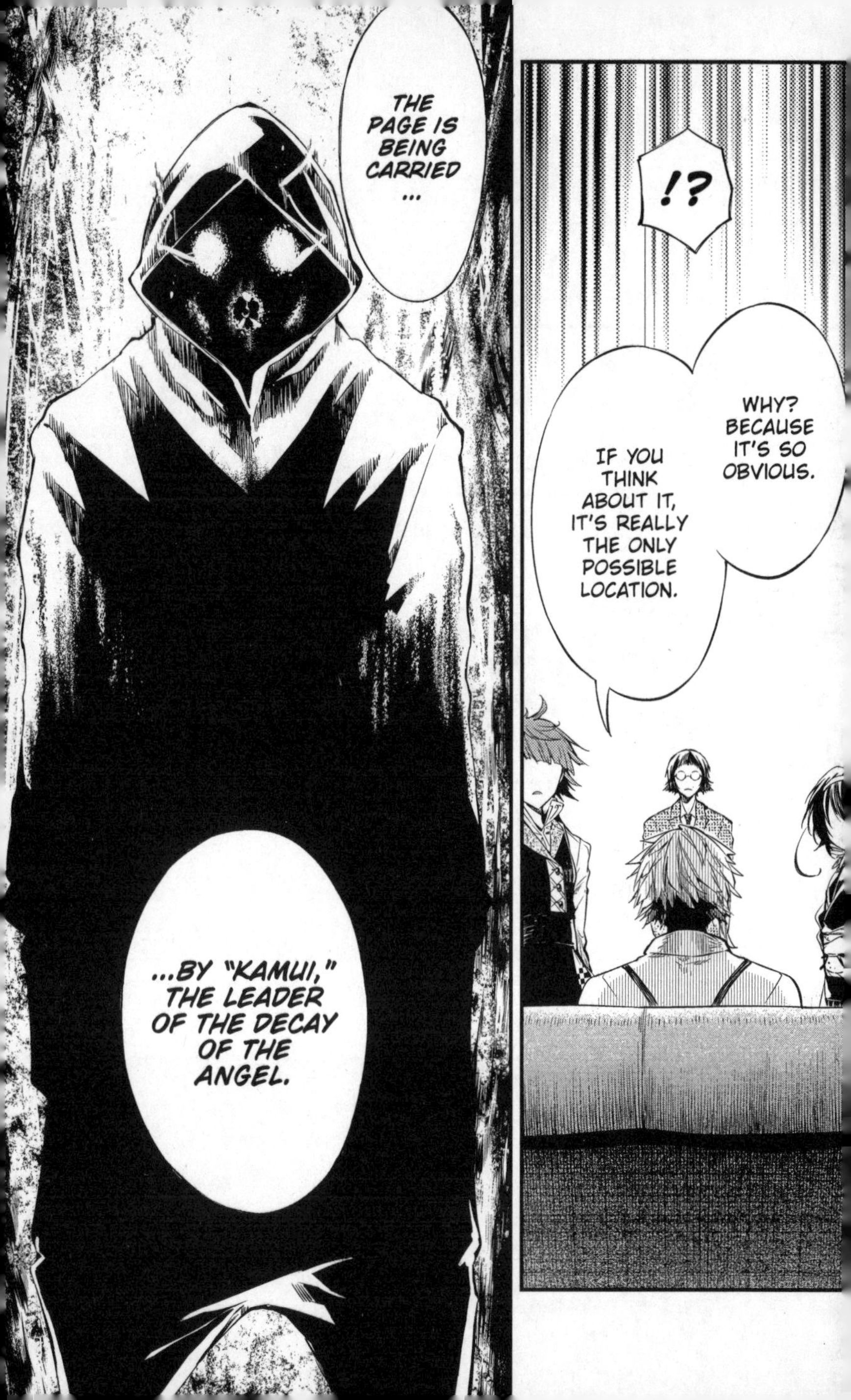
!?
WHY? BECAUSE IT'S SO OBVIOUS.
IF YOU THINK ABOUT IT, IT'S REALLY THE ONLY POSSIBLE LOCATION.
THE PAGE IS BEING CARRIED ...
...BY "KAMUI," THE LEADER OF THE DECAY OF THE ANGEL.

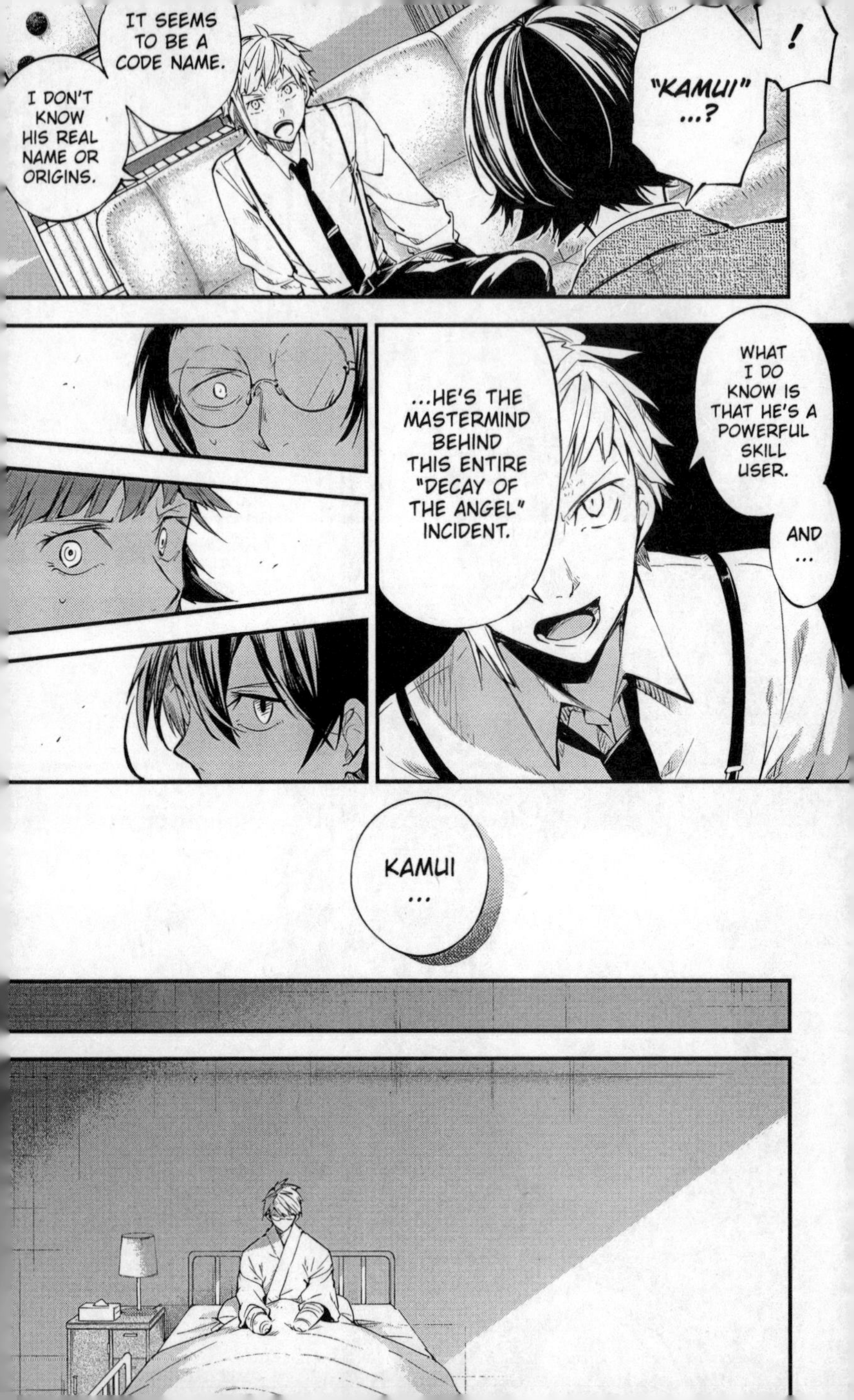
!
"KAMUI" ...?
IT SEEMS TO BE A CODE NAME.
I DON'T KNOW HIS REAL NAME OR ORIGINS.
WHAT I DO KNOW IS THAT HE'S A POWERFUL SKILL USER.
AND ...
...HE'S THE MASTERMIND BEHIND THIS ENTIRE "DECAY OF THE ANGEL" INCIDENT.
KAMUI ...

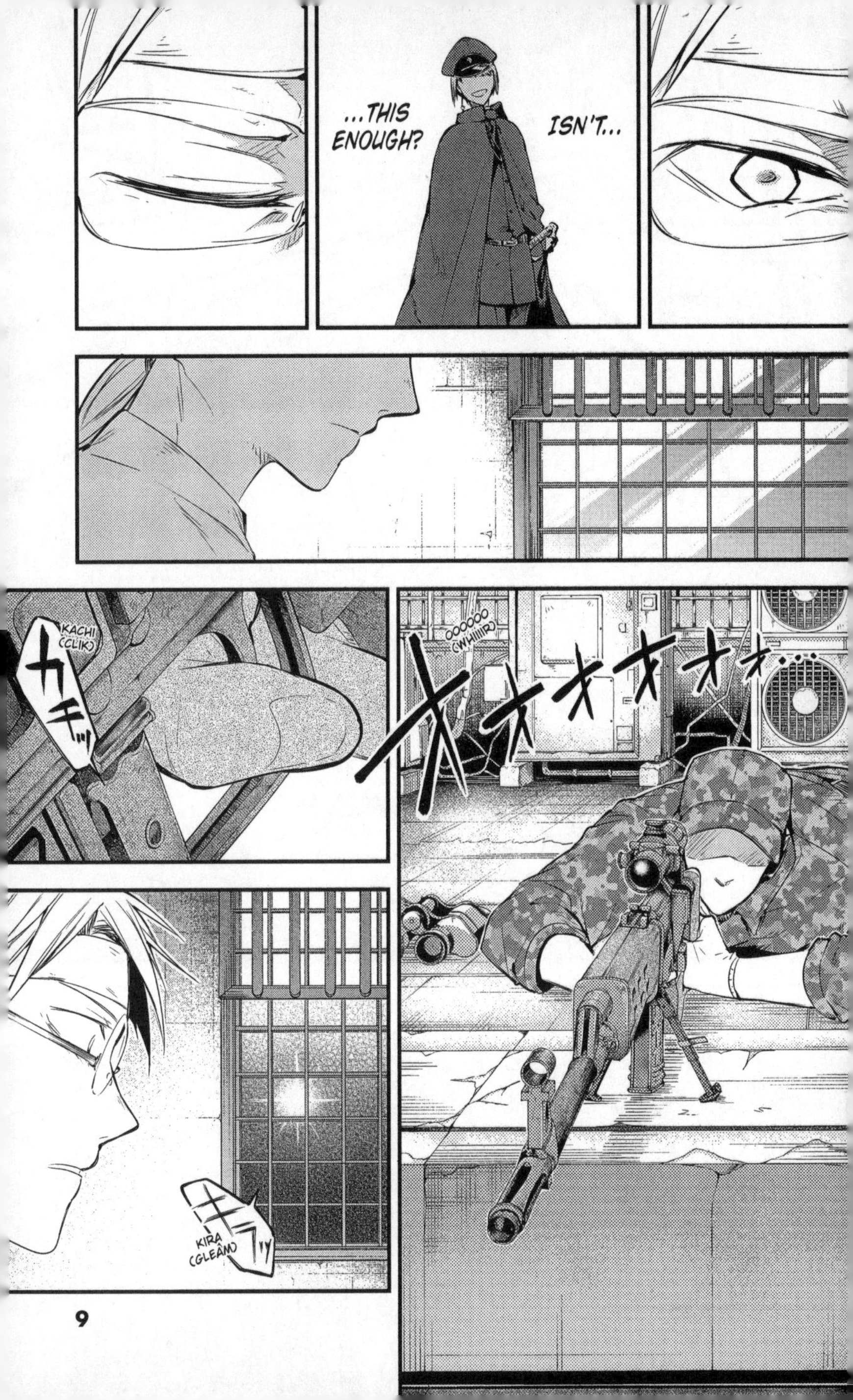
ISN'T...
...THIS ENOUGH?
OOOOOO (WHIIIIR)
オオオオオォ…
KACHI (CLIK)
カチッ
KIRA (GLEAM)
キラッ

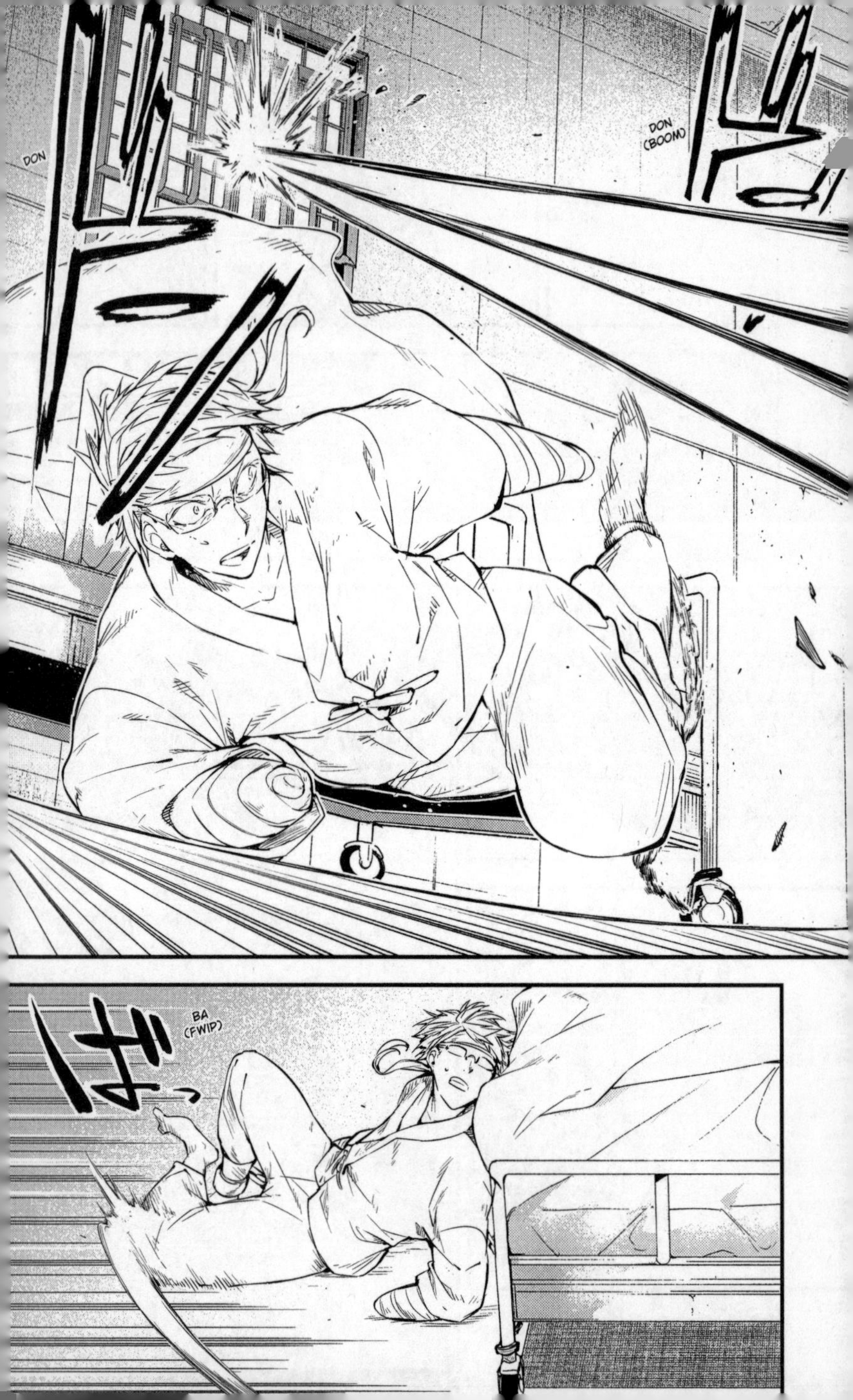
ドンッ
DON (BOOM)
ドン
DON
ばっ
BA (FWIP)

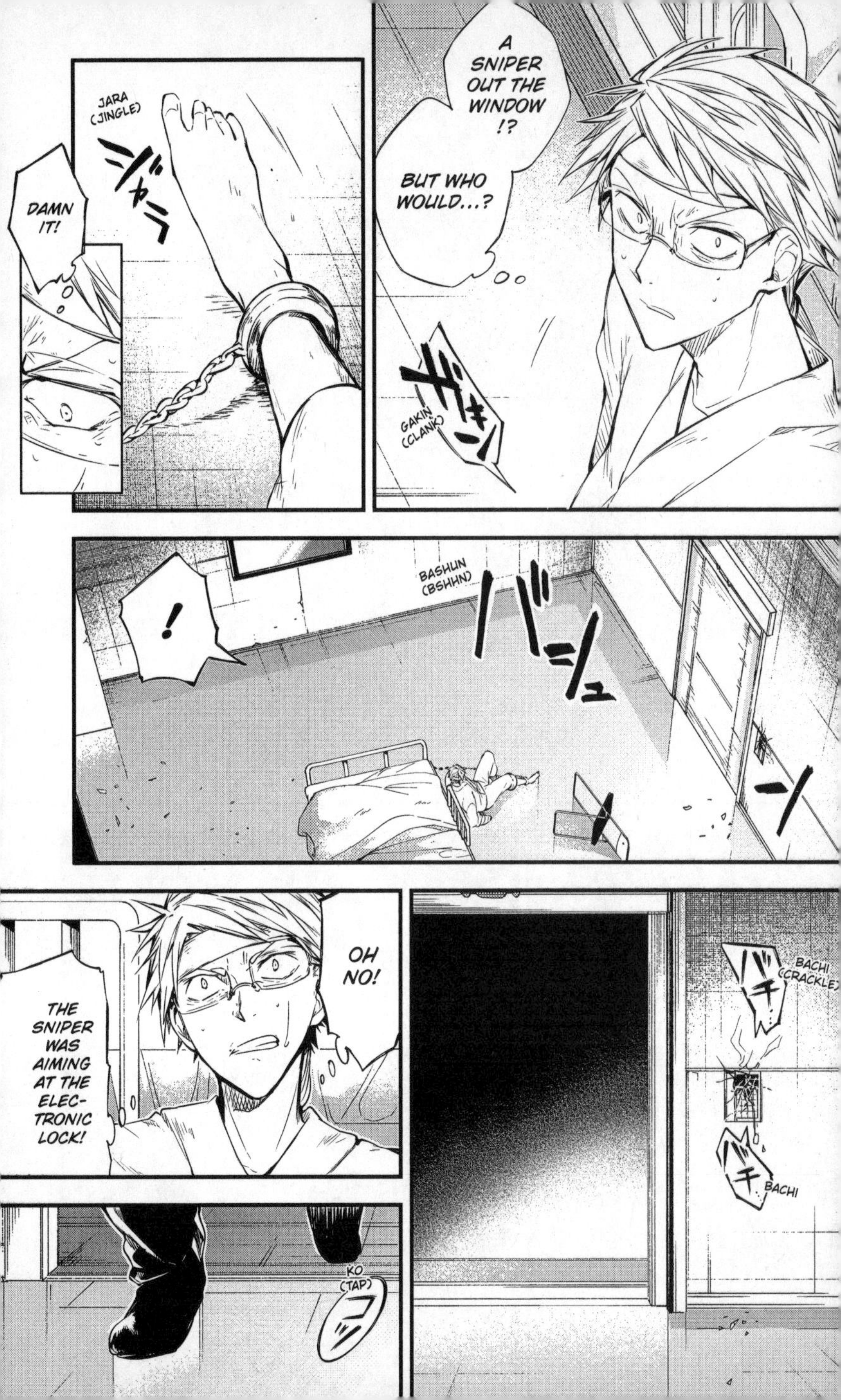
A SNIPER OUT THE WINDOW !?
BUT WHO WOULD...?
GAKIN (CLANK)
JARA (JINGLE)
DAMN IT!
BASHUN (BSHHN)
!
BACHI (CRACKLE)
BACHI
OH NO!
THE SNIPER WAS AIMING AT THE ELEC-TRONIC LOCK!
KO (TAP)

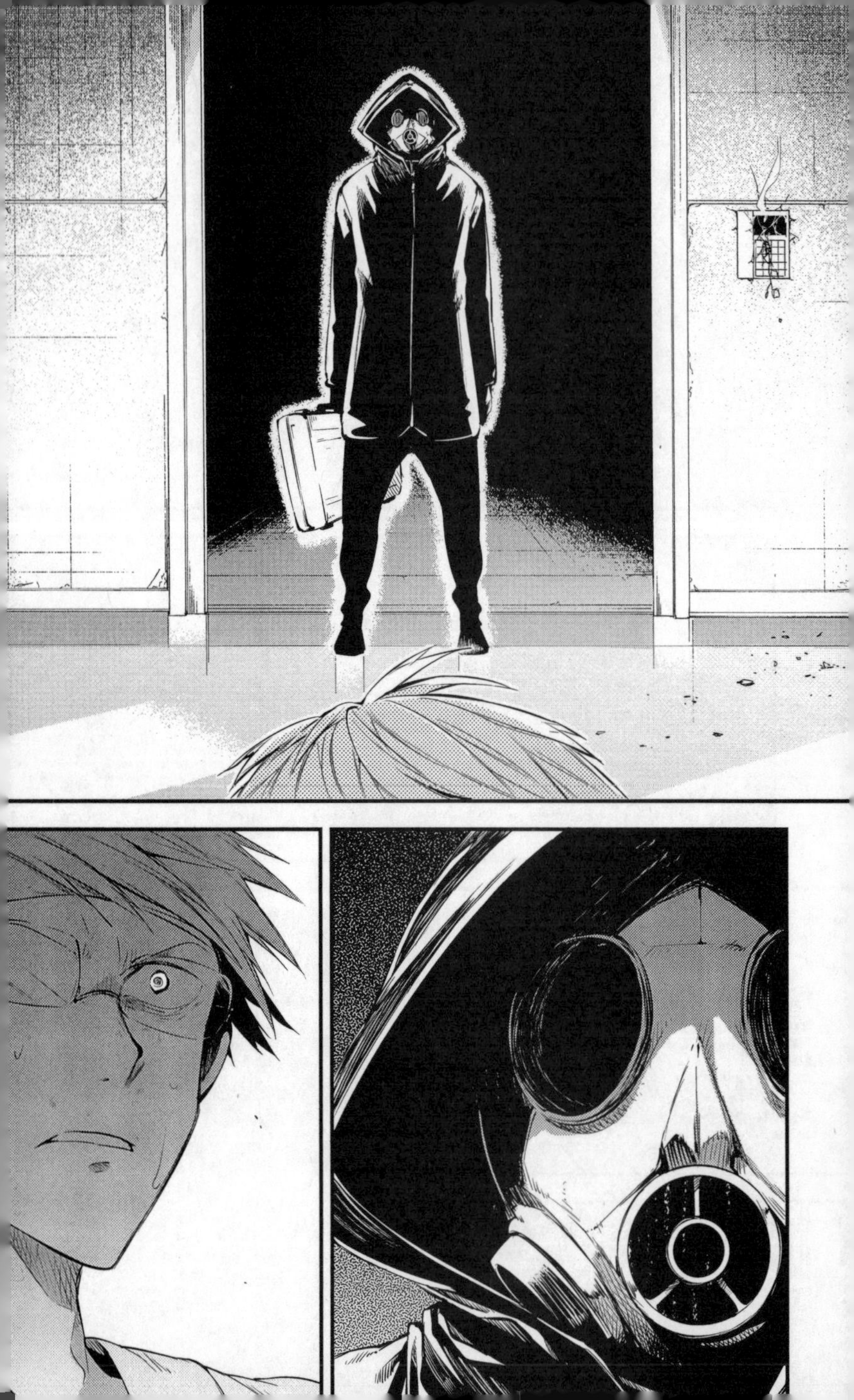

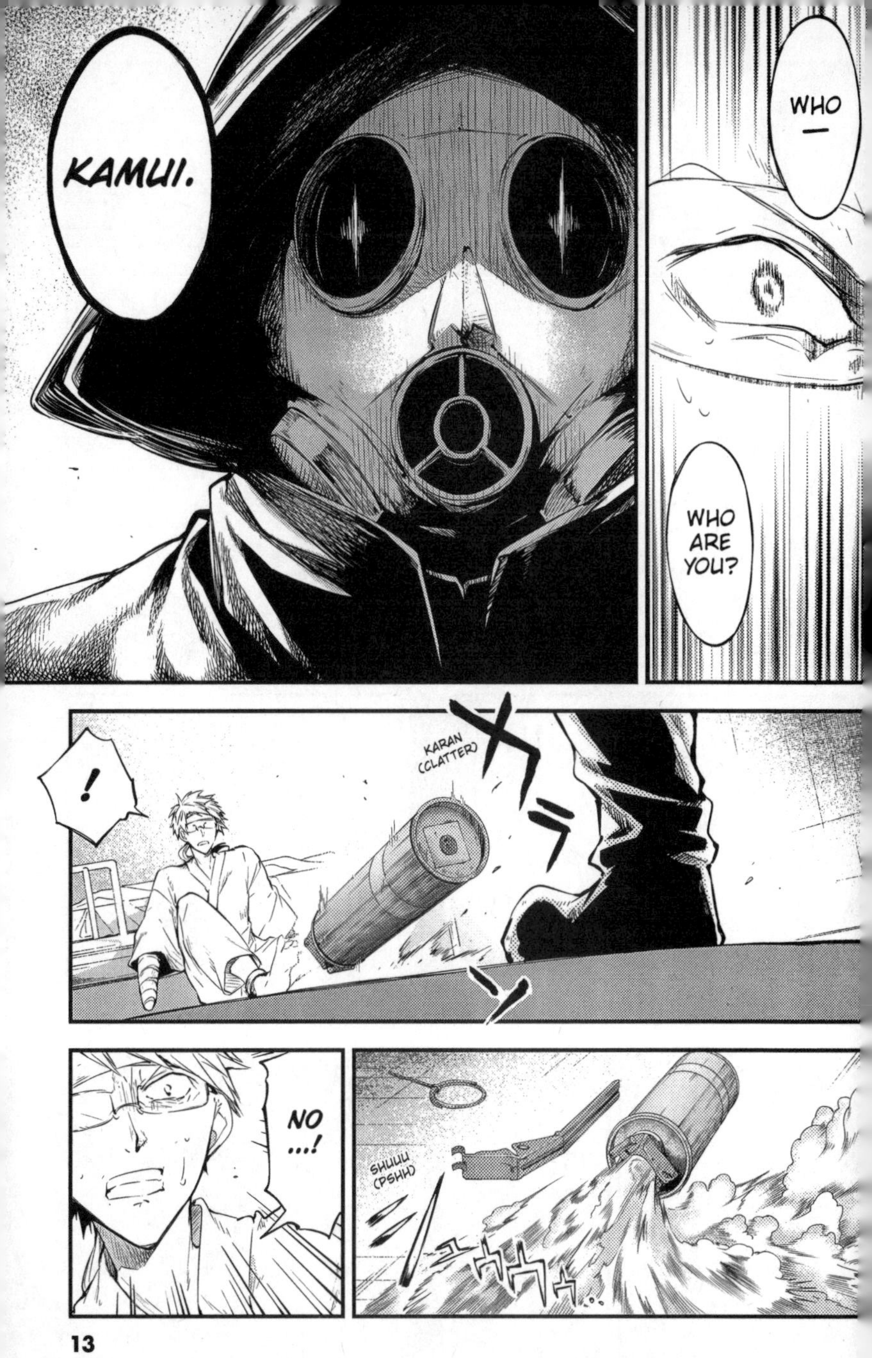
WHO —
WHO ARE YOU?
KAMUI.
KARAN (CLATTER)
!
SHUUU (PSHH)
NO ...!

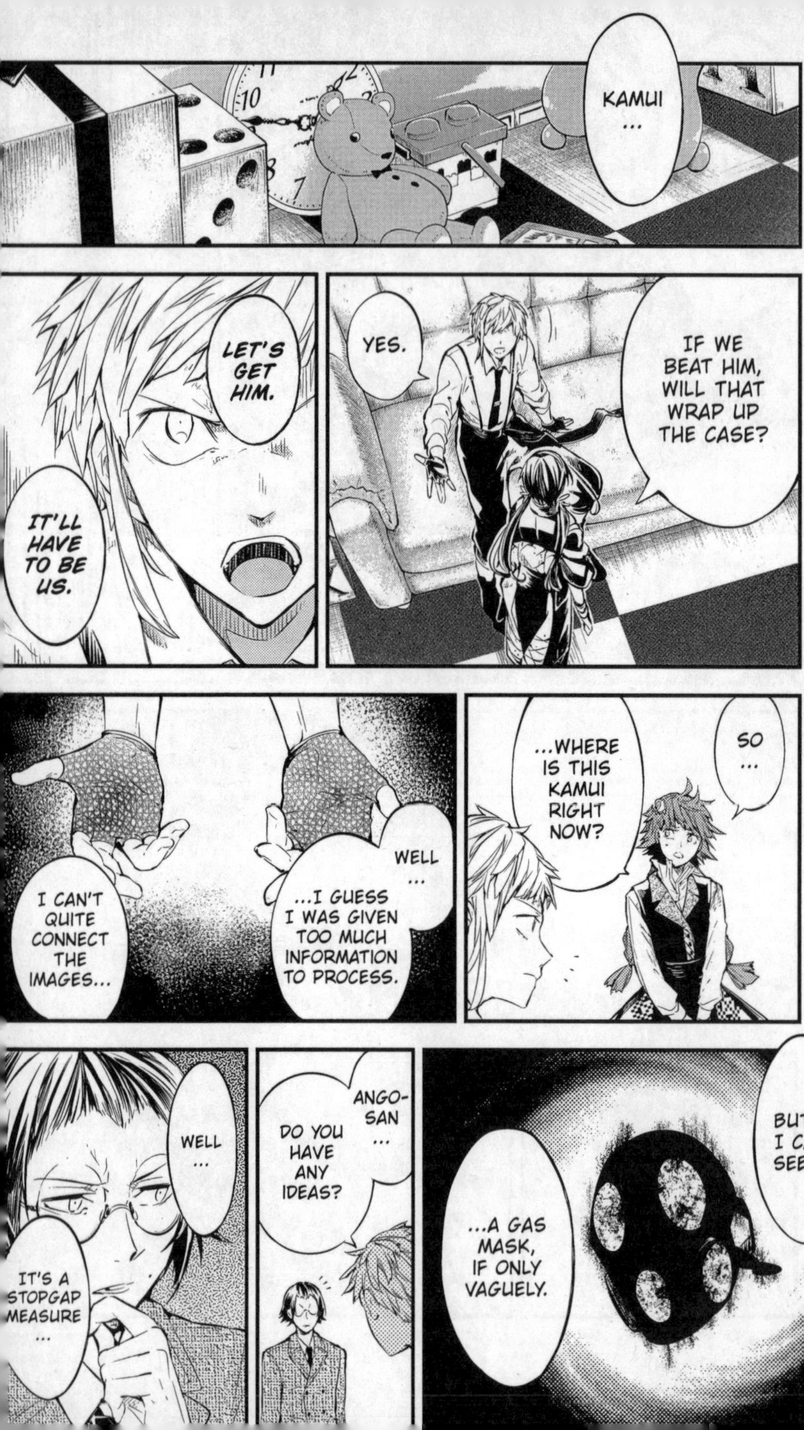
KAMUI ...
IF WE BEAT HIM, WILL THAT WRAP UP THE CASE?
YES.
LET'S GET HIM.
IT'LL HAVE TO BE US.
SO ...
...WHERE IS THIS KAMUI RIGHT NOW?
WELL ...
...I GUESS I WAS GIVEN TOO MUCH INFORMATION TO PROCESS.
I CAN'T QUITE CONNECT THE IMAGES...
BUT... I CAN SEE...
...A GAS MASK, IF ONLY VAGUELY.
ANGO-SAN ...
DO YOU HAVE ANY IDEAS?
WELL ...
IT'S A STOPGAP MEASURE ...

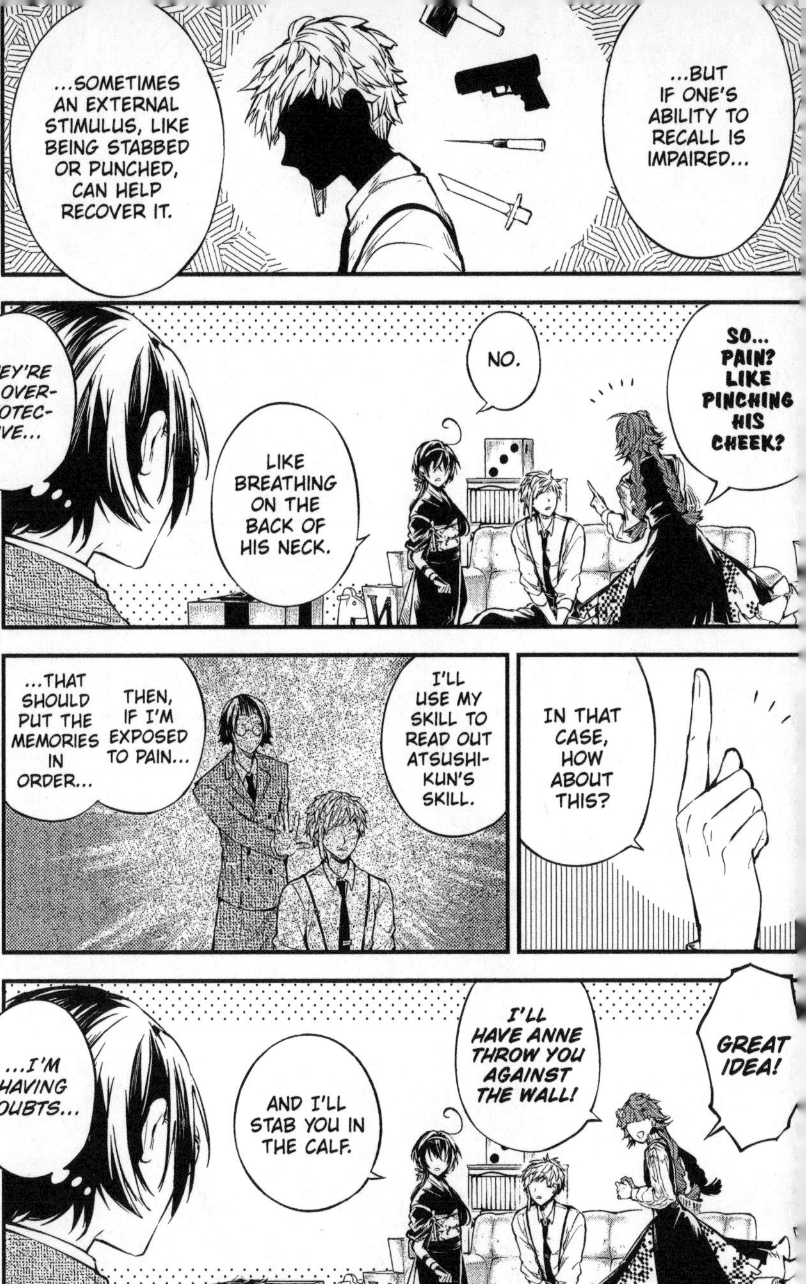
...BUT IF ONE'S ABILITY TO RECALL IS IMPAIRED...
...SOMETIMES AN EXTERNAL STIMULUS, LIKE BEING STABBED OR PUNCHED, CAN HELP RECOVER IT.
SO... PAIN? LIKE PINCHING HIS CHEEK?
NO.
LIKE BREATHING ON THE BACK OF HIS NECK.
THEY'RE SO OVER-PROTEC-TIVE...
IN THAT CASE, HOW ABOUT THIS?
I'LL USE MY SKILL TO READ OUT ATSUSHI-KUN'S SKILL.
THEN, IF I'M EXPOSED TO PAIN...
...THAT SHOULD PUT THE MEMORIES IN ORDER...
GREAT IDEA!
I'LL HAVE ANNE THROW YOU AGAINST THE WALL!
AND I'LL STAB YOU IN THE CALF.
...I'M HAVING DOUBTS...

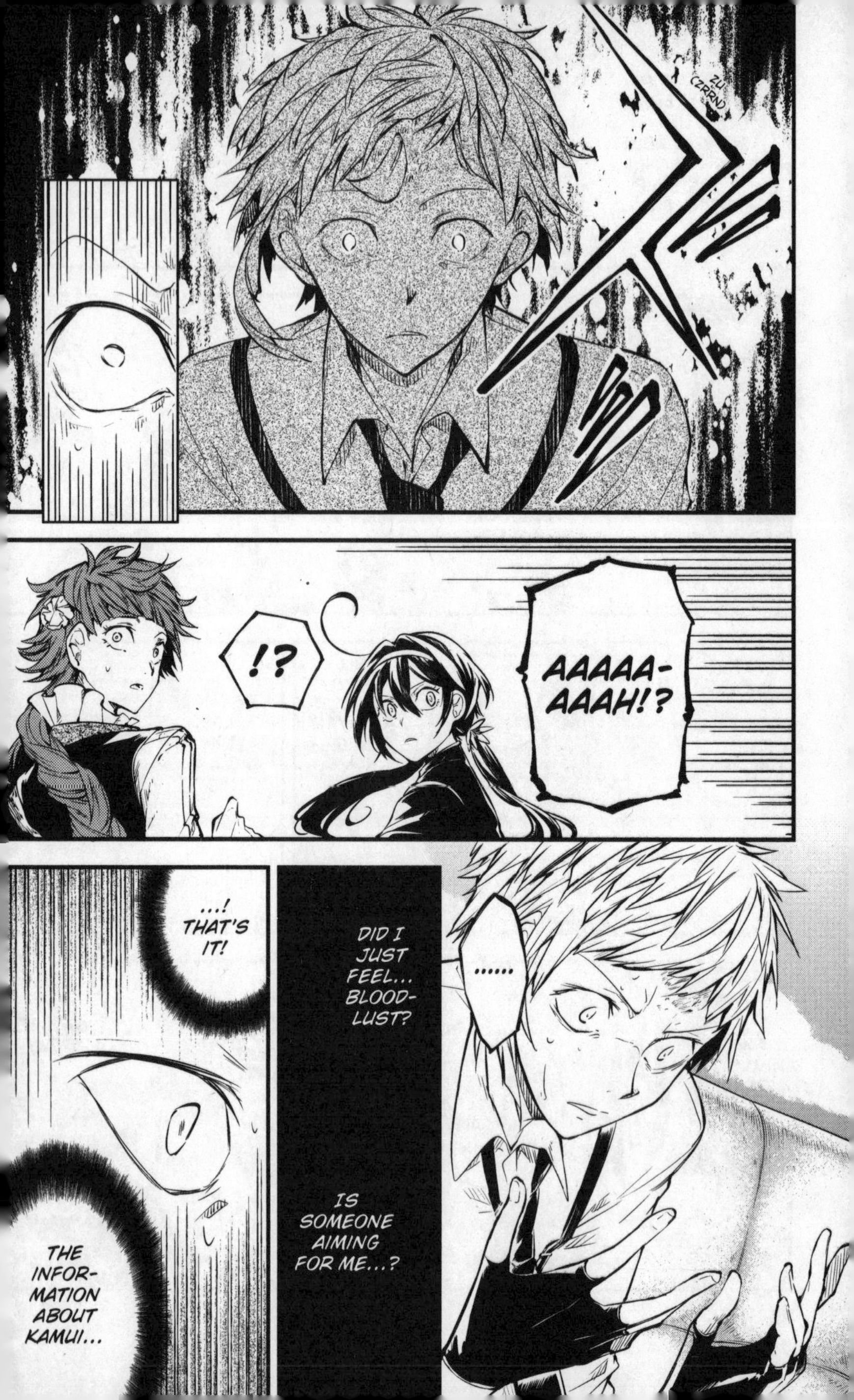
ZU (ZRRND)
AAAAA-AAAH!?
!?
......
DID I JUST FEEL... BLOOD-LUST?
IS SOMEONE AIMING FOR ME...?
...! THAT'S IT!
THE INFOR-MATION ABOUT KAMUI...

GASHI
(GRAB)

HUH?

WE HAVE TO GET OUT OF HERE NOW!

ANGO-SAN...

I KNOW WHERE KAMUI IS.

ARE YOU OKAY !?

GURA
(CRUMPLE)

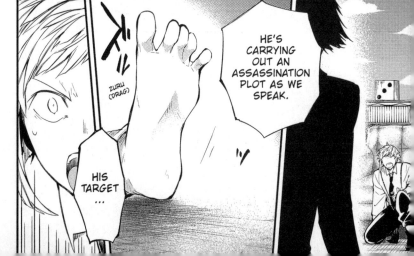

HE'S CARRYING OUT AN ASSASSINATION PLOT AS WE SPEAK.

HIS TARGET ...

ZURU
(DRAG)

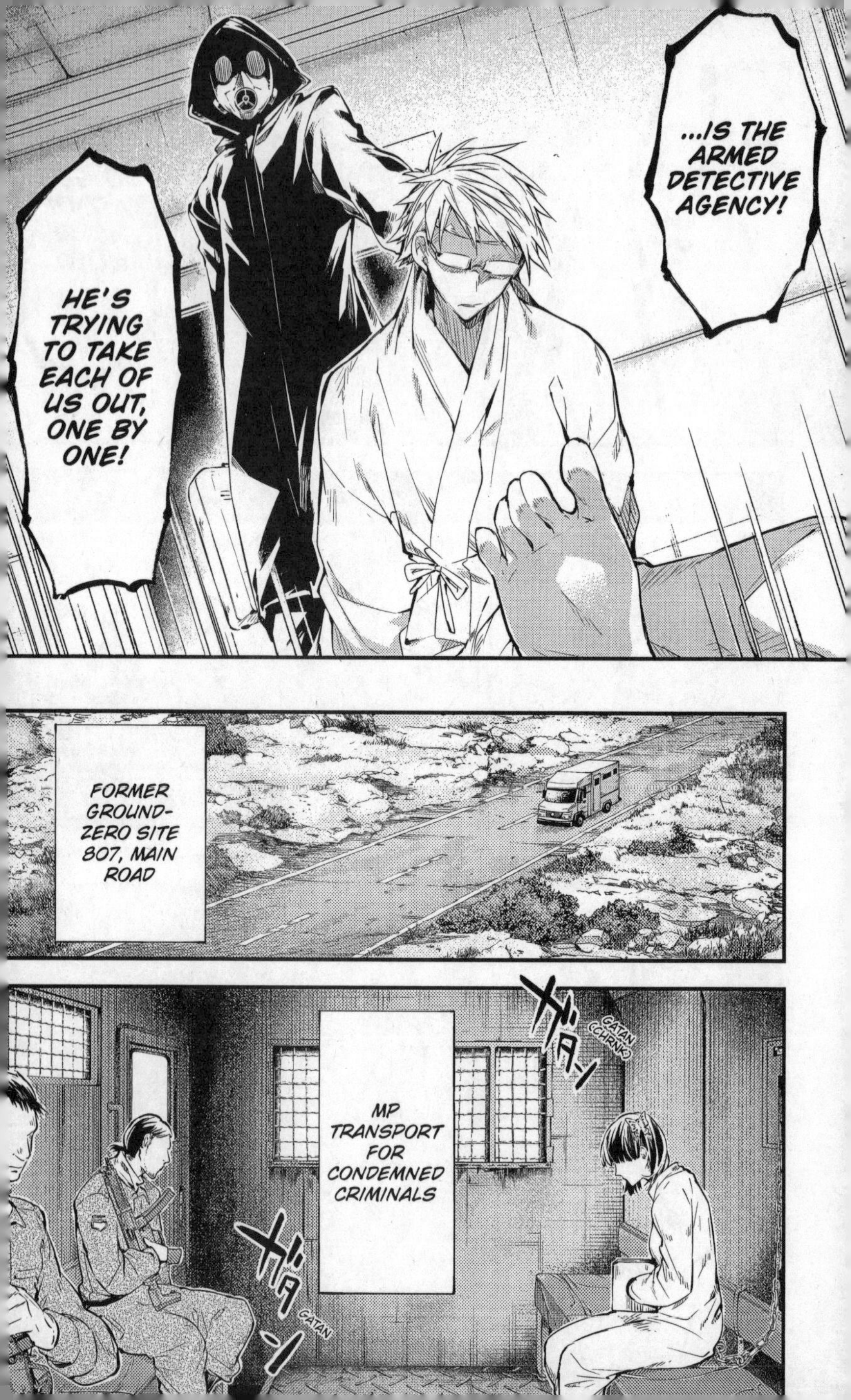
...IS THE ARMED DETECTIVE AGENCY!
HE'S TRYING TO TAKE EACH OF US OUT, ONE BY ONE!
FORMER GROUND-ZERO SITE 807, MAIN ROAD
GATAN (CHRNK)
MP TRANSPORT FOR CONDEMNED CRIMINALS
GATAN

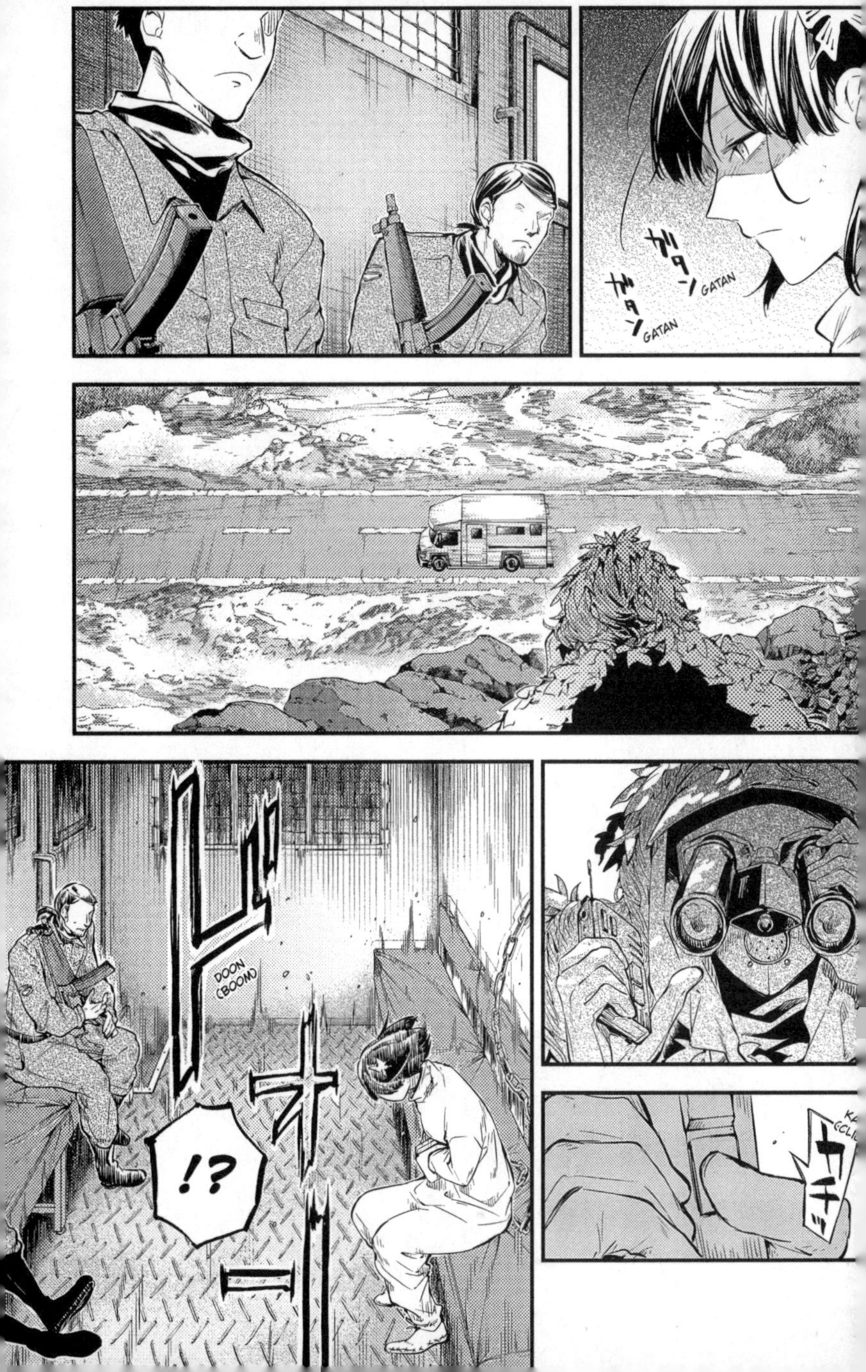
ガタン
GATAN
ガタン
GATAN
カチッ
ドン
DOON (BOOM)
!?

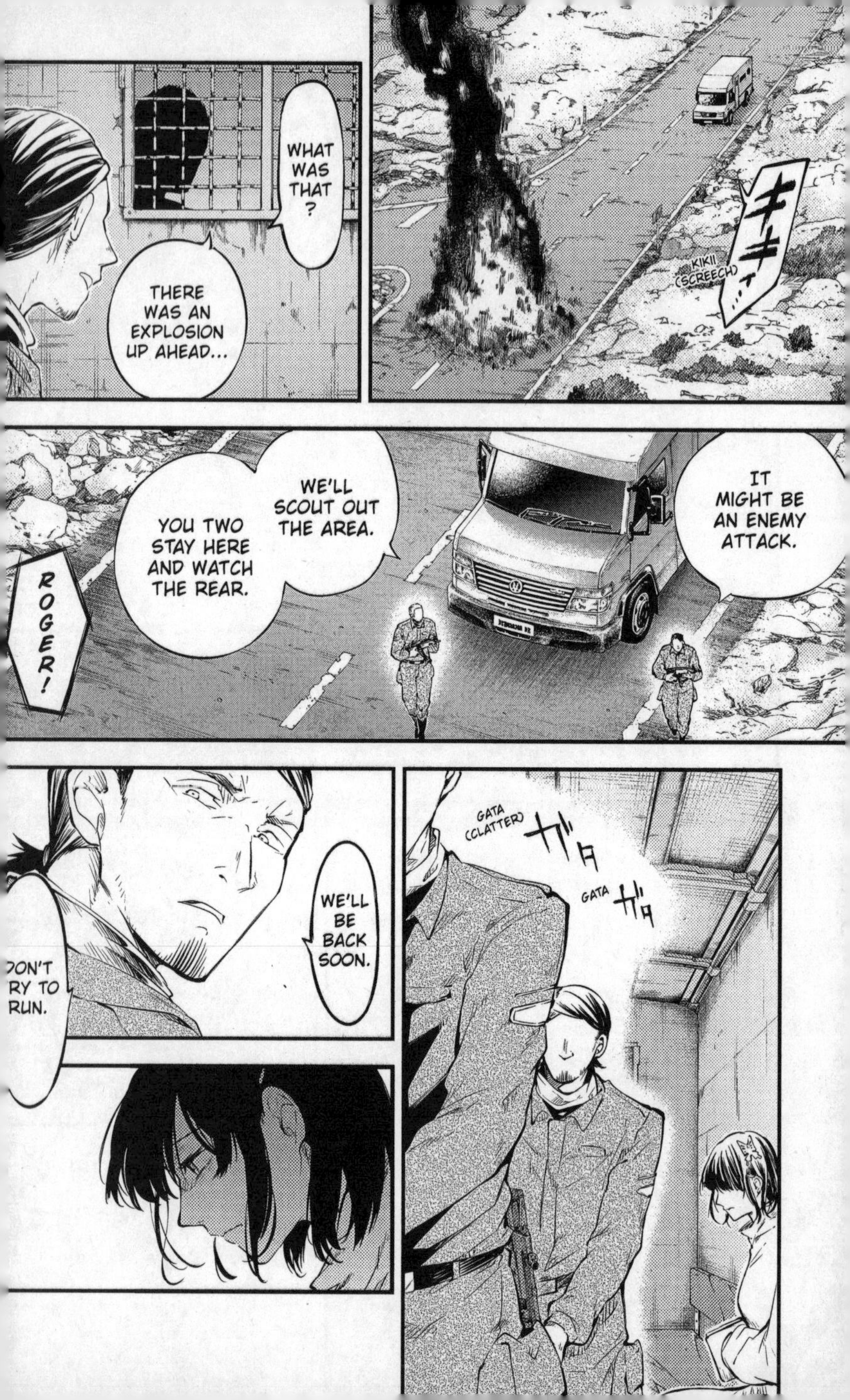
KIKII (SCREECH)
WHAT WAS THAT?
THERE WAS AN EXPLOSION UP AHEAD...
IT MIGHT BE AN ENEMY ATTACK.
WE'LL SCOUT OUT THE AREA.
YOU TWO STAY HERE AND WATCH THE REAR.
ROGER!
GATA (CLATTER)
GATA
WE'LL BE BACK SOON.
DON'T RY TO RUN.

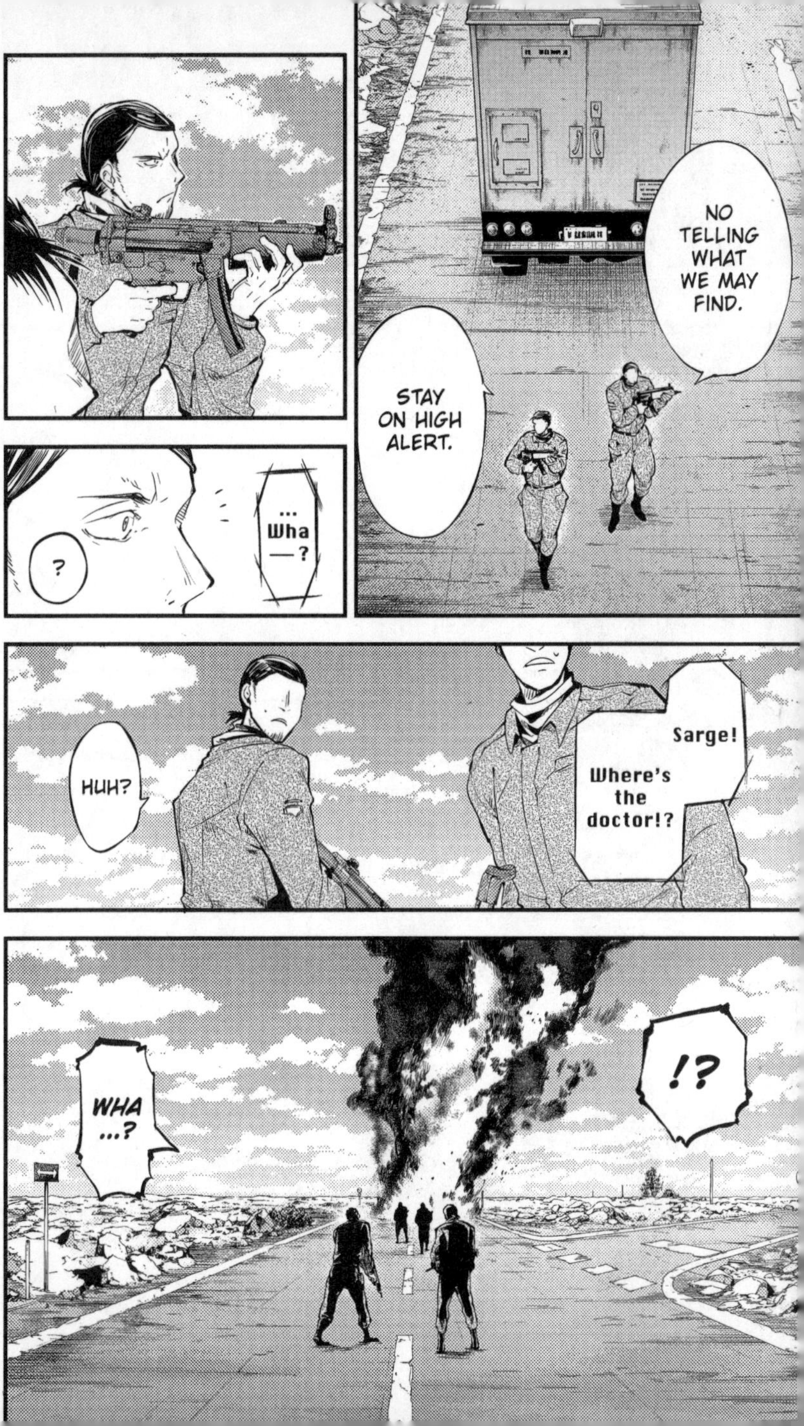
NO TELLING WHAT WE MAY FIND.
STAY ON HIGH ALERT.
... Wha—?
?
Sarge! Where's the doctor!?
HUH?
!?
WHA ...?

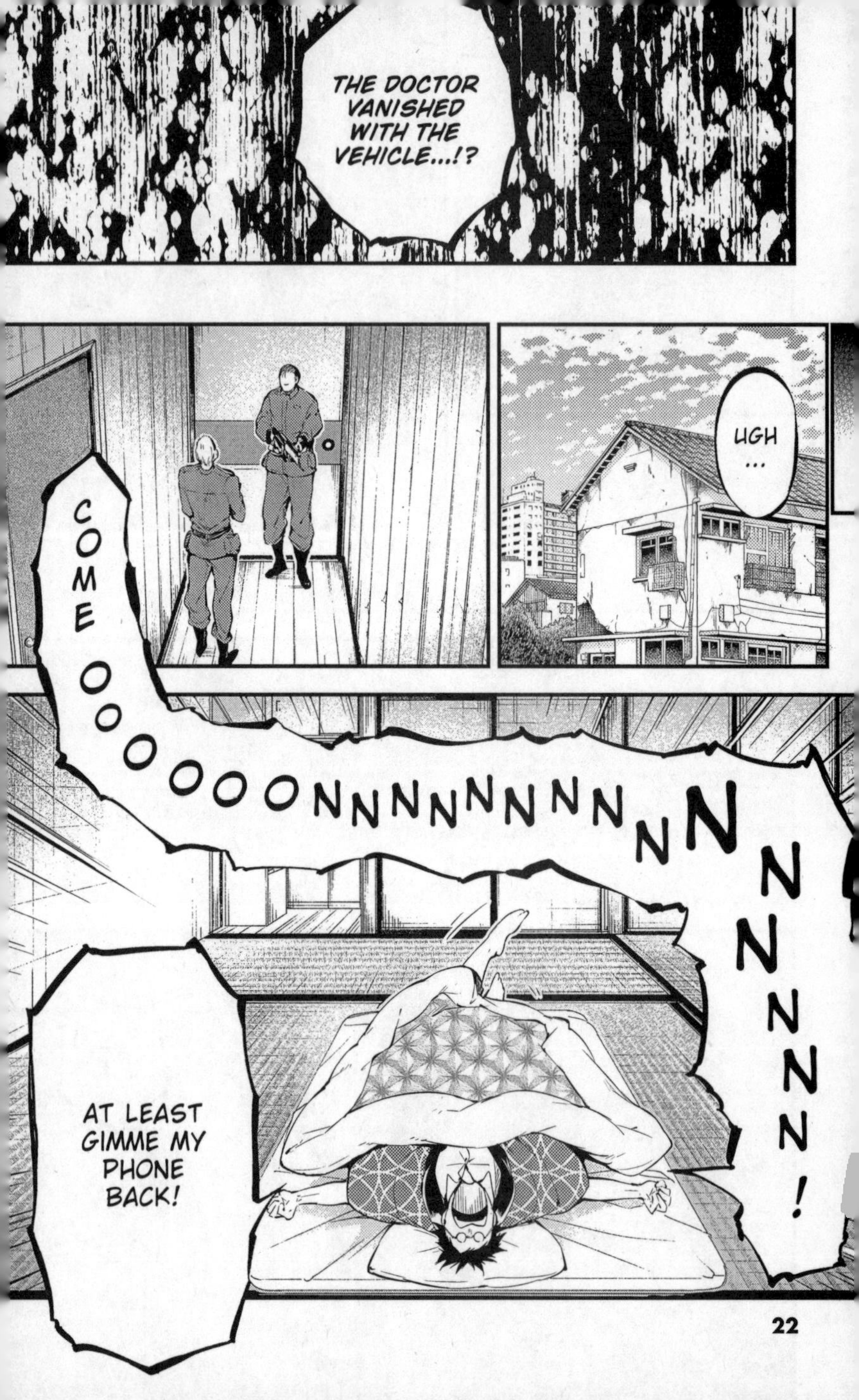
THE DOCTOR VANISHED WITH THE VEHICLE...!?
UGH ...
COME OOOOOONNNNNNNNNNNNNNN!
AT LEAST GIMME MY PHONE BACK!

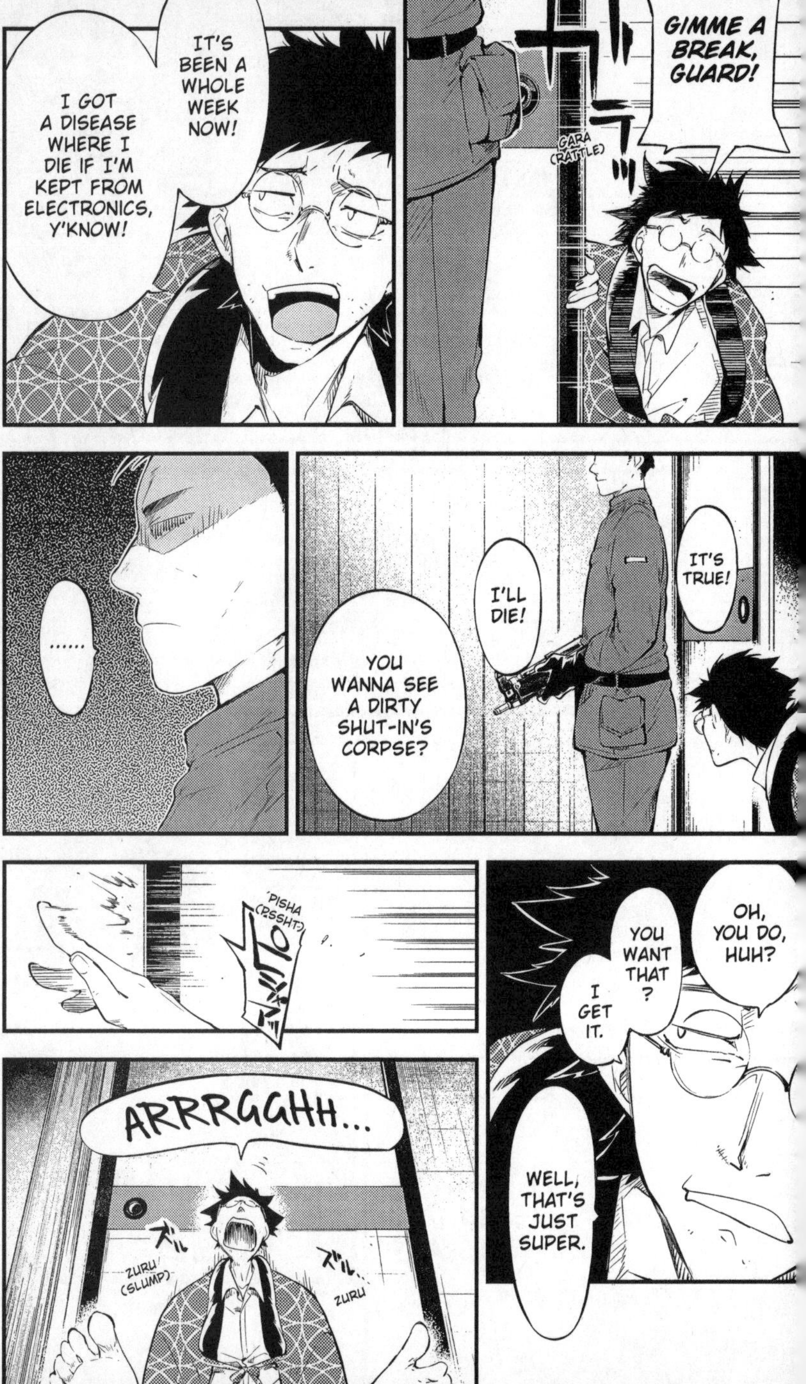
GARA (RATTLE)
GIMME A BREAK, GUARD!
IT'S BEEN A WHOLE WEEK NOW!
I GOT A DISEASE WHERE I DIE IF I'M KEPT FROM ELECTRONICS, Y'KNOW!
IT'S TRUE!
I'LL DIE!
YOU WANNA SEE A DIRTY SHUT-IN'S CORPSE?
......
OH, YOU DO, HUH?
YOU WANT THAT?
I GET IT.
WELL, THAT'S JUST SUPER.
PISHA (PSSHT)
ARRRGGHH...
ZURU (SLUMP)
ZURU

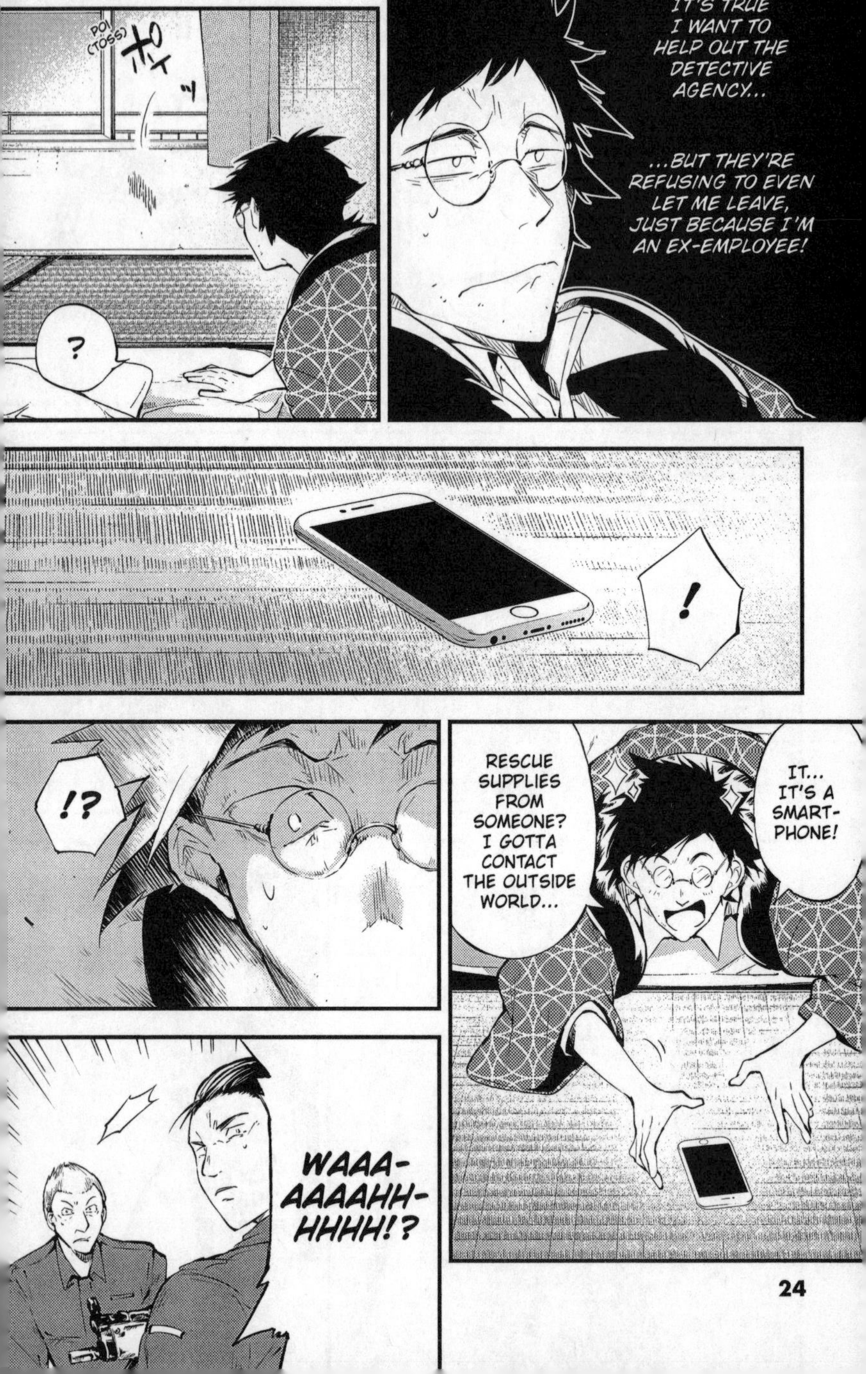
IT'S TRUE I WANT TO HELP OUT THE DETECTIVE AGENCY...
...BUT THEY'RE REFUSING TO EVEN LET ME LEAVE, JUST BECAUSE I'M AN EX-EMPLOYEE!
ポイッ
POI (TOSS)
?
!
IT... IT'S A SMART-PHONE!
RESCUE SUPPLIES FROM SOMEONE? I GOTTA CONTACT THE OUTSIDE WORLD...
!?
WAAA-AAAAHH-HHHH!?

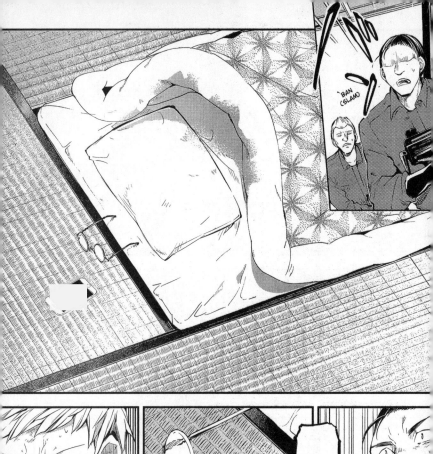

BAN (SLAM)

ONE BY ONE...

...THEY'RE BEING RUBBED OUT...

FUKU-
ZAWA.

GET
OUT.

26

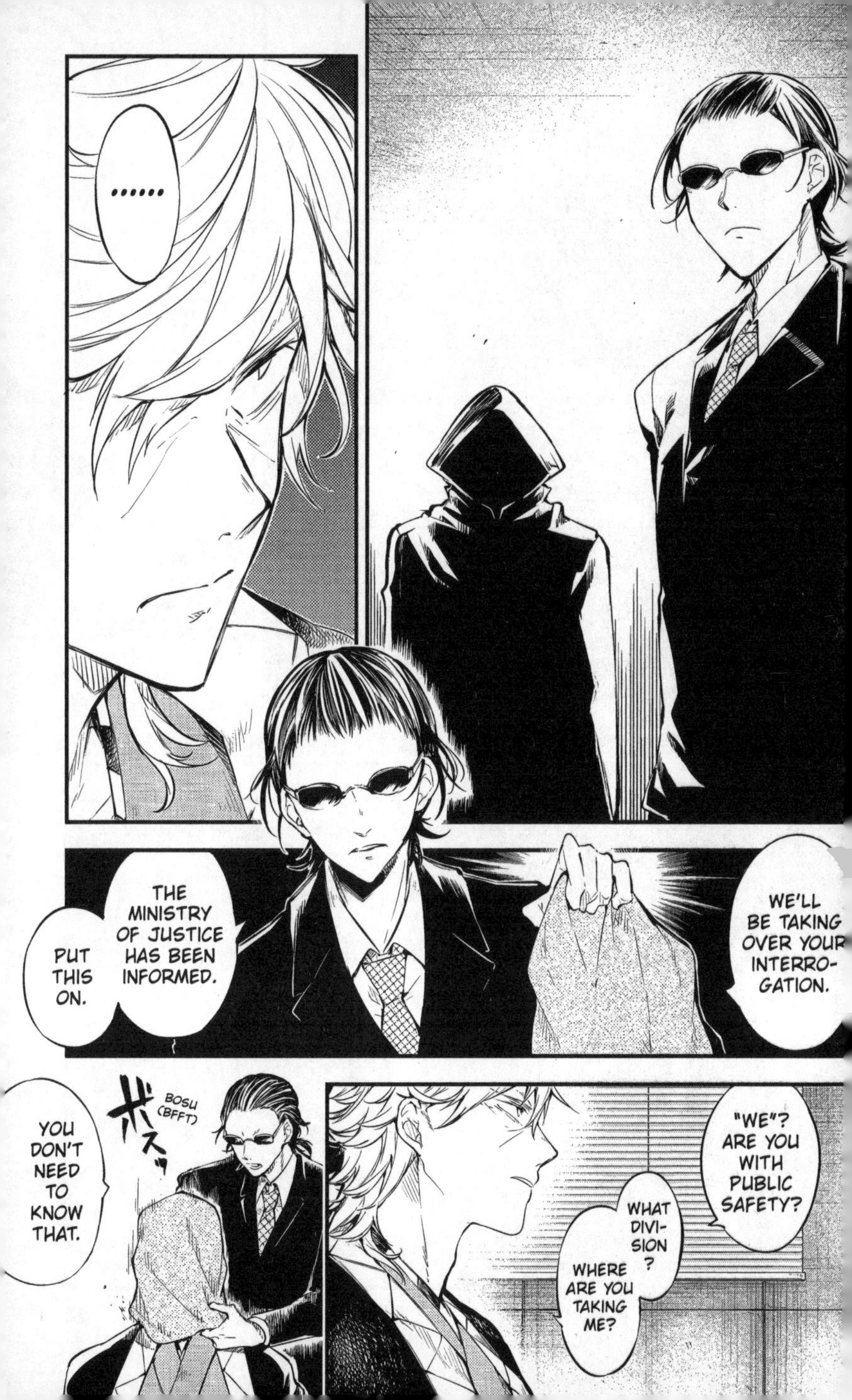
......
WE'LL BE TAKING OVER YOUR INTERROGATION.
THE MINISTRY OF JUSTICE HAS BEEN INFORMED.
PUT THIS ON.
"WE"? ARE YOU WITH PUBLIC SAFETY?
WHAT DIVISION?
WHERE ARE YOU TAKING ME?
ボスッ
BOSU (BFFT)
YOU DON'T NEED TO KNOW THAT.

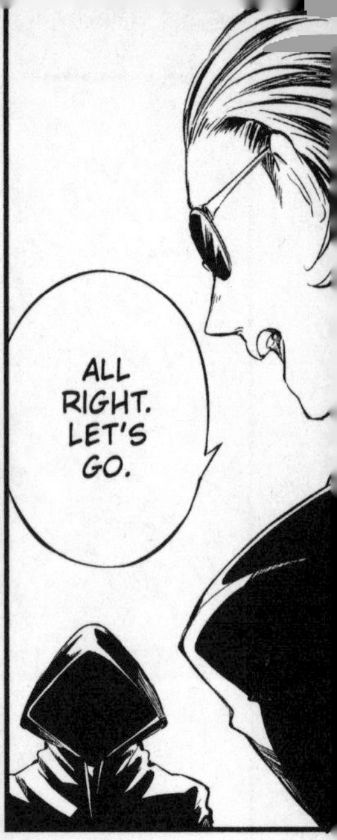
ALL RIGHT. LET'S GO.
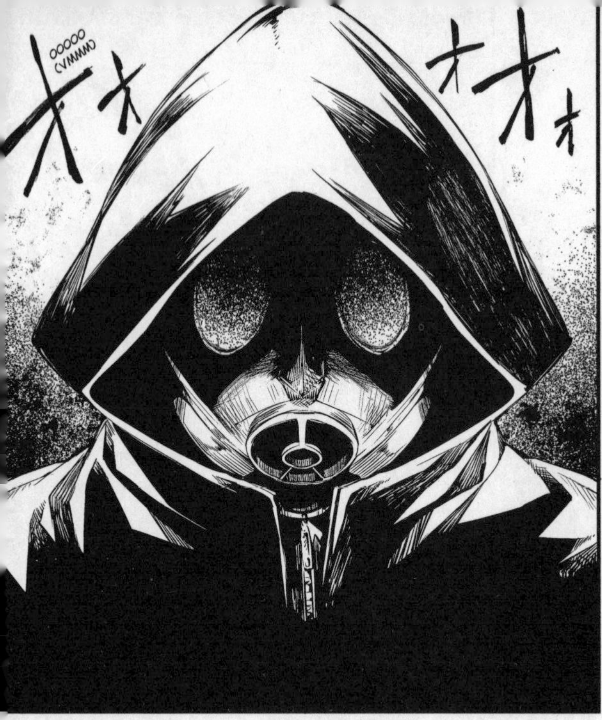
OOOOO (VMMMM)
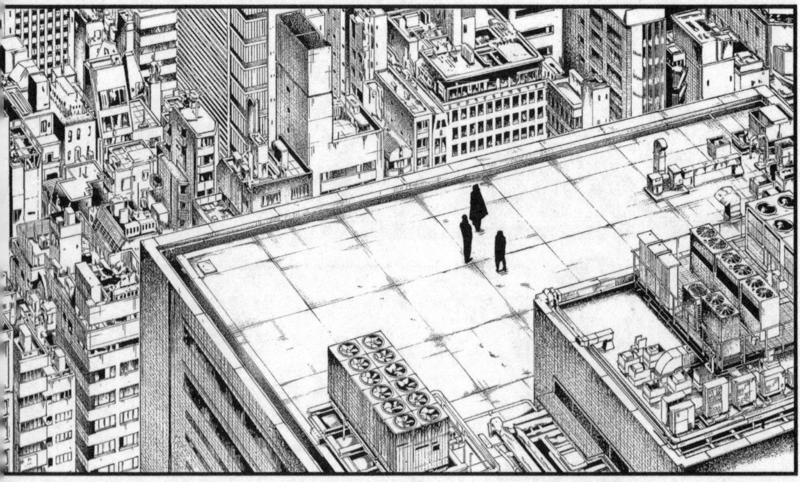

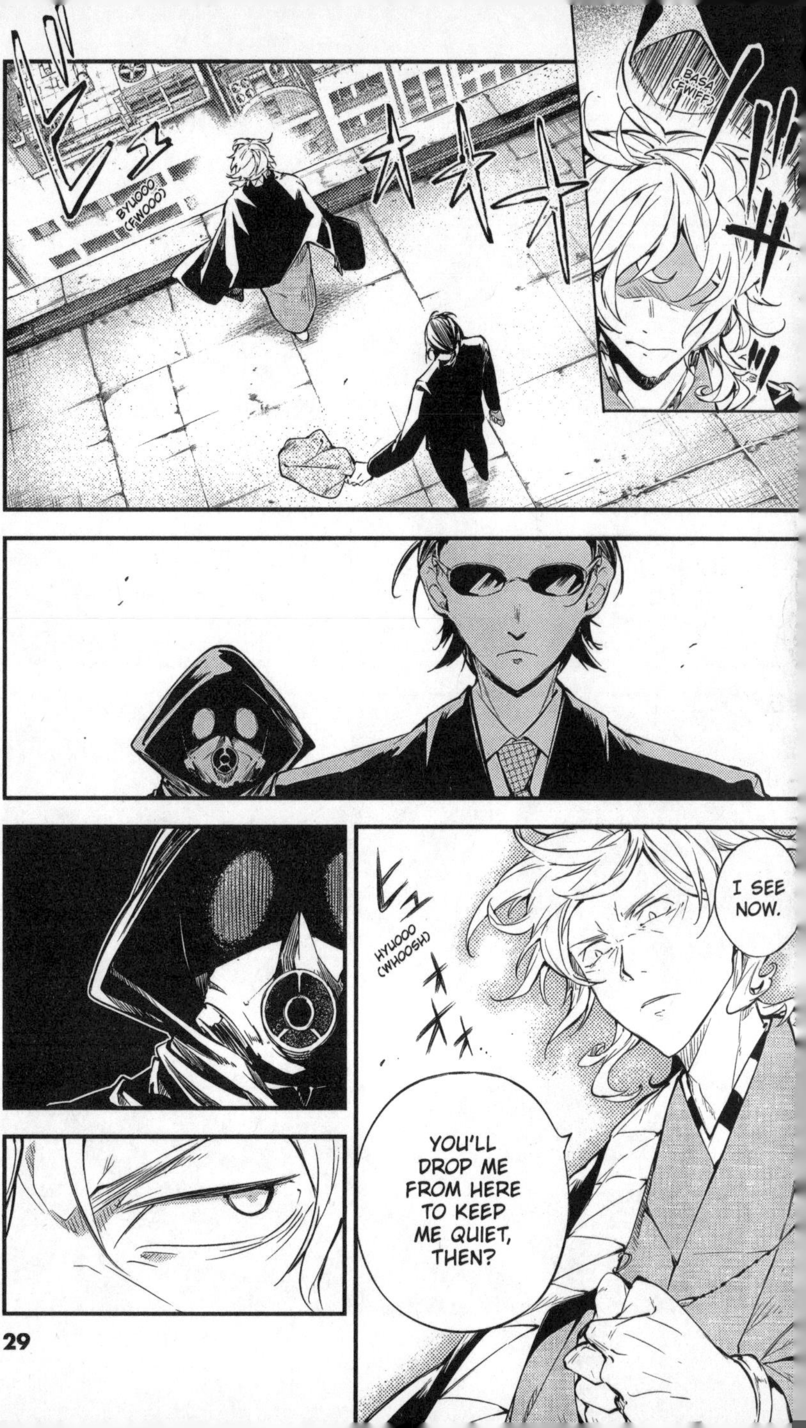
BASA (FWIFF)
BYUOOO (FWOOO)
I SEE NOW.
HYUOOO (WHOOSH)
YOU'LL DROP ME FROM HERE TO KEEP ME QUIET, THEN?

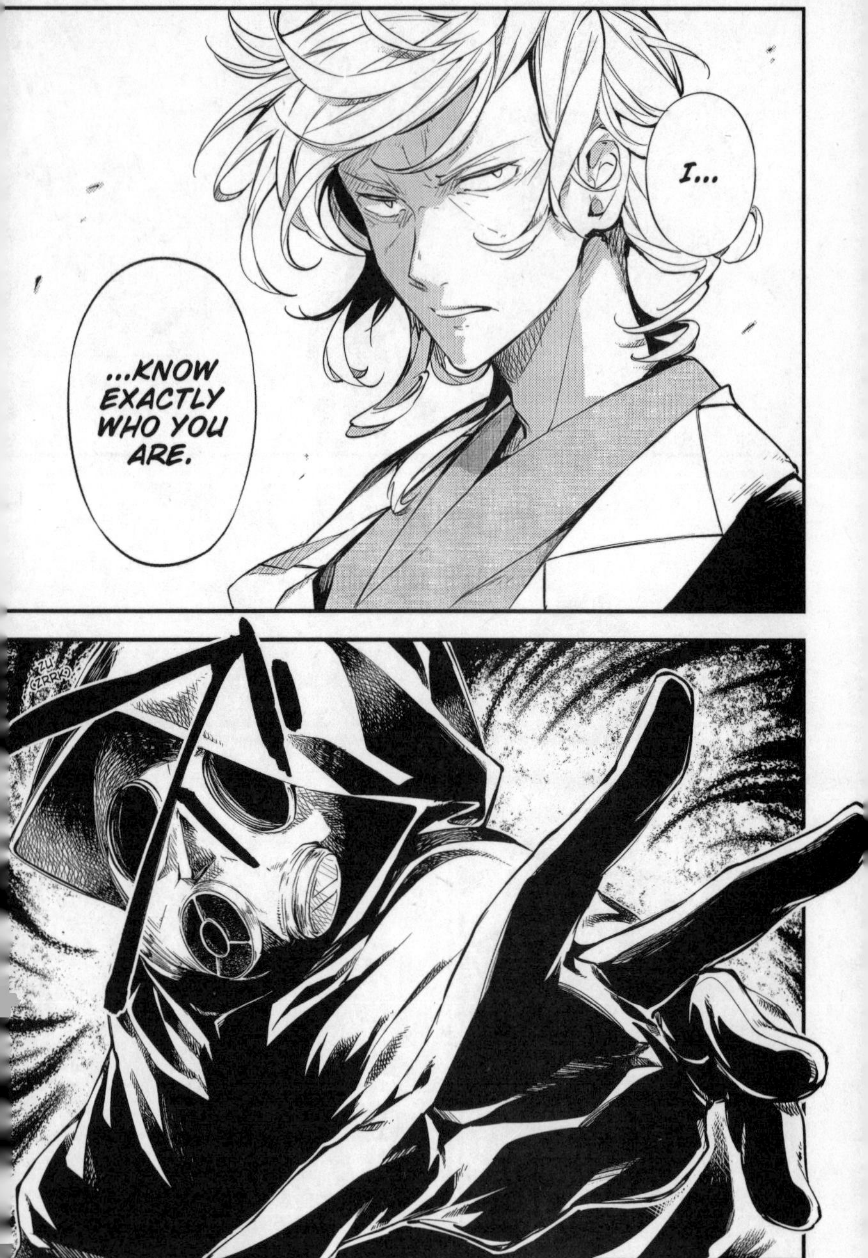
I...
...KNOW EXACTLY WHO YOU ARE.
ZU (ZRRK)

ANGO SAKAGUCHI

SKILL: **Discourse on Decadence**
Reads the "memories" left inside objects.

AGE: *25*

BIRTH DATE: *October 20*

HEIGHT: *178cm*

WEIGHT: *63kg*

BLOOD TYPE: *A*

LIKES: *Antiques, memories, materialism*

DISLIKES: *Working overtime, all-nighters, betrayal*

BUNGO
STRAY DOGS

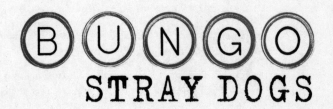

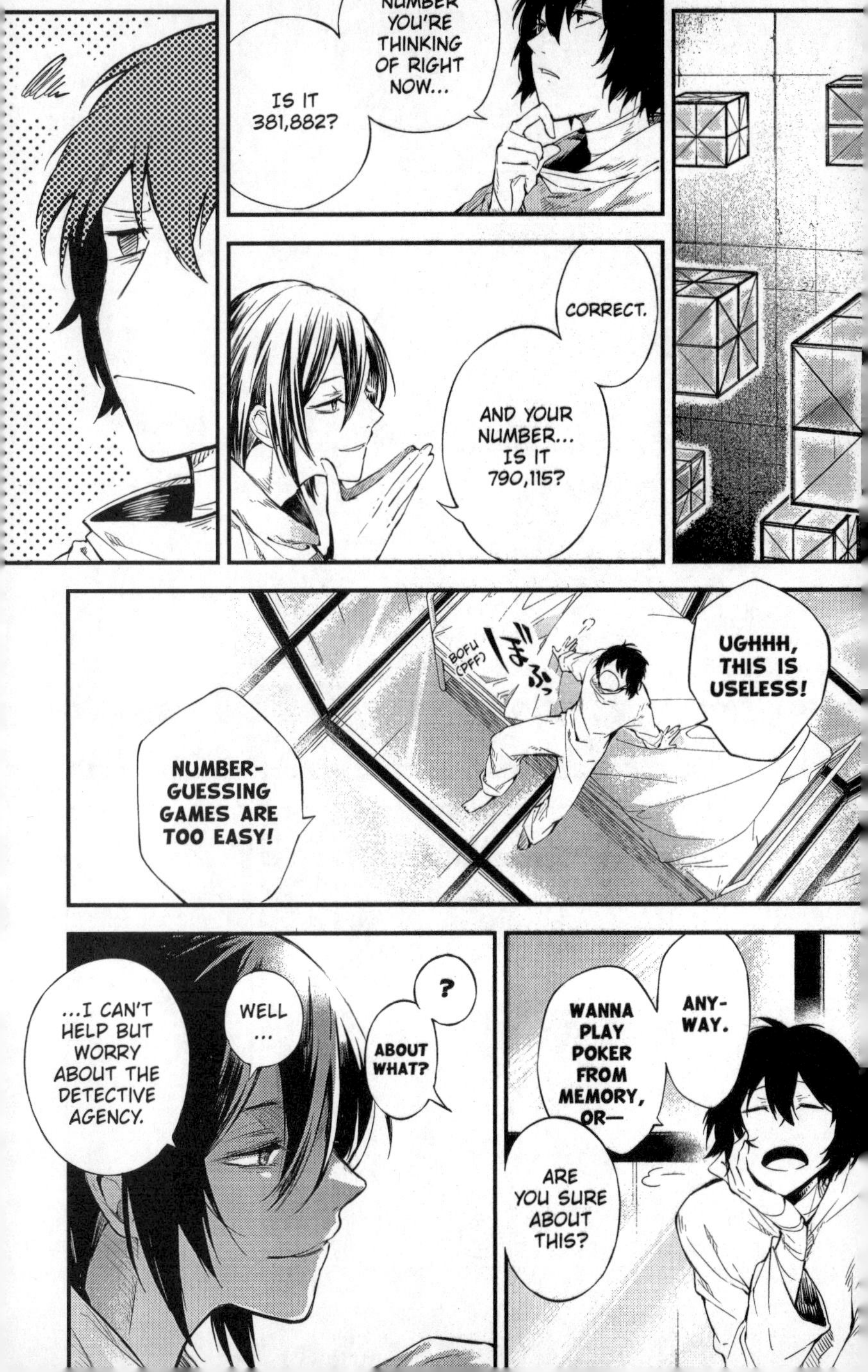
THE NUMBER YOU'RE THINKING OF RIGHT NOW...
IS IT 381,882?
CORRECT.
AND YOUR NUMBER... IS IT 790,115?
UGHHH, THIS IS USELESS!
BOFU (PFF)
NUMBER-GUESSING GAMES ARE TOO EASY!
ANY-WAY.
WANNA PLAY POKER FROM MEMORY, OR—
ARE YOU SURE ABOUT THIS?
?
ABOUT WHAT?
WELL...
...I CAN'T HELP BUT WORRY ABOUT THE DETECTIVE AGENCY.

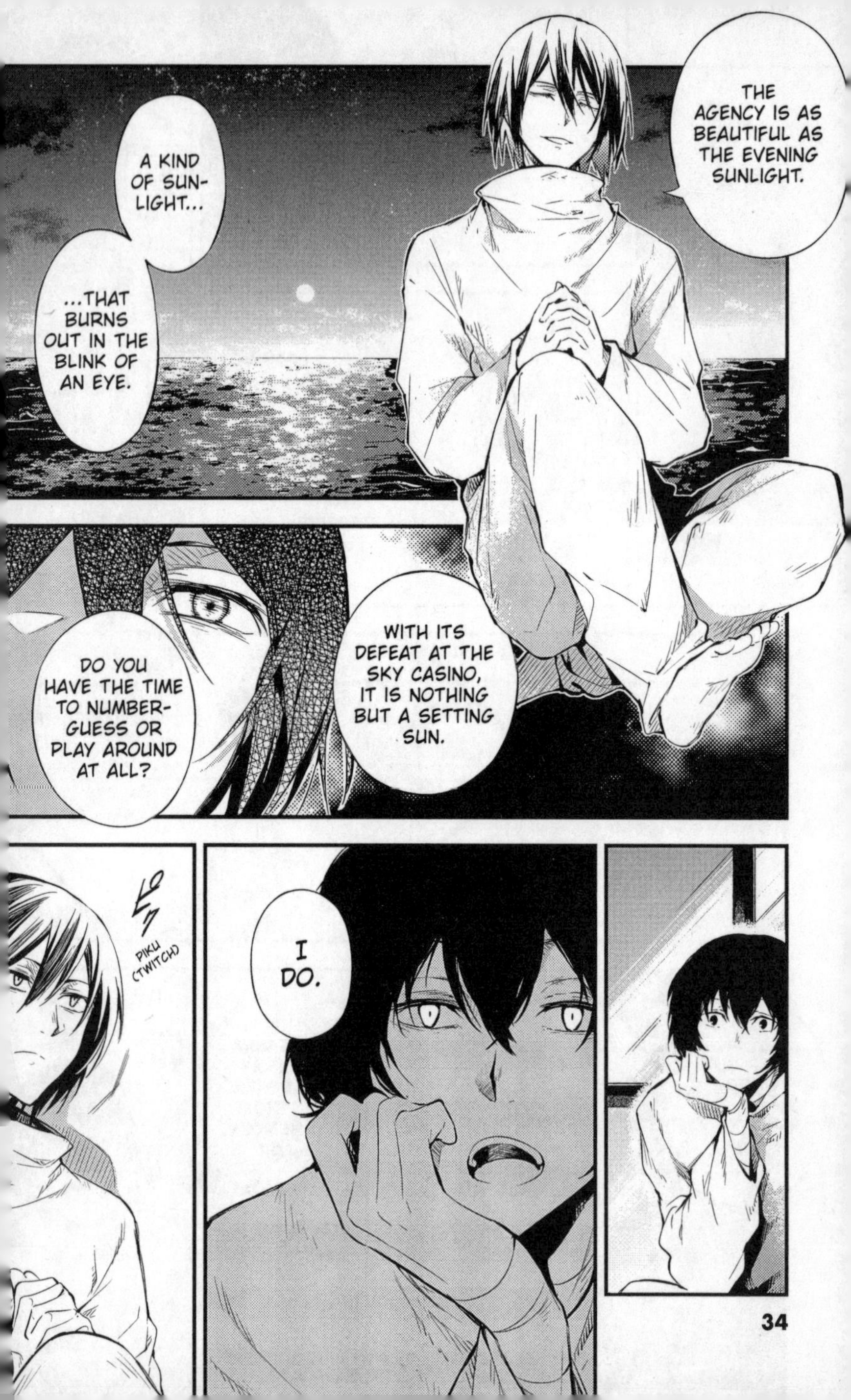
THE AGENCY IS AS BEAUTIFUL AS THE EVENING SUNLIGHT.
A KIND OF SUN-LIGHT...
...THAT BURNS OUT IN THE BLINK OF AN EYE.
WITH ITS DEFEAT AT THE SKY CASINO, IT IS NOTHING BUT A SETTING SUN.
DO YOU HAVE THE TIME TO NUMBER-GUESS OR PLAY AROUND AT ALL?
I DO.
PIKU (TWITCH)

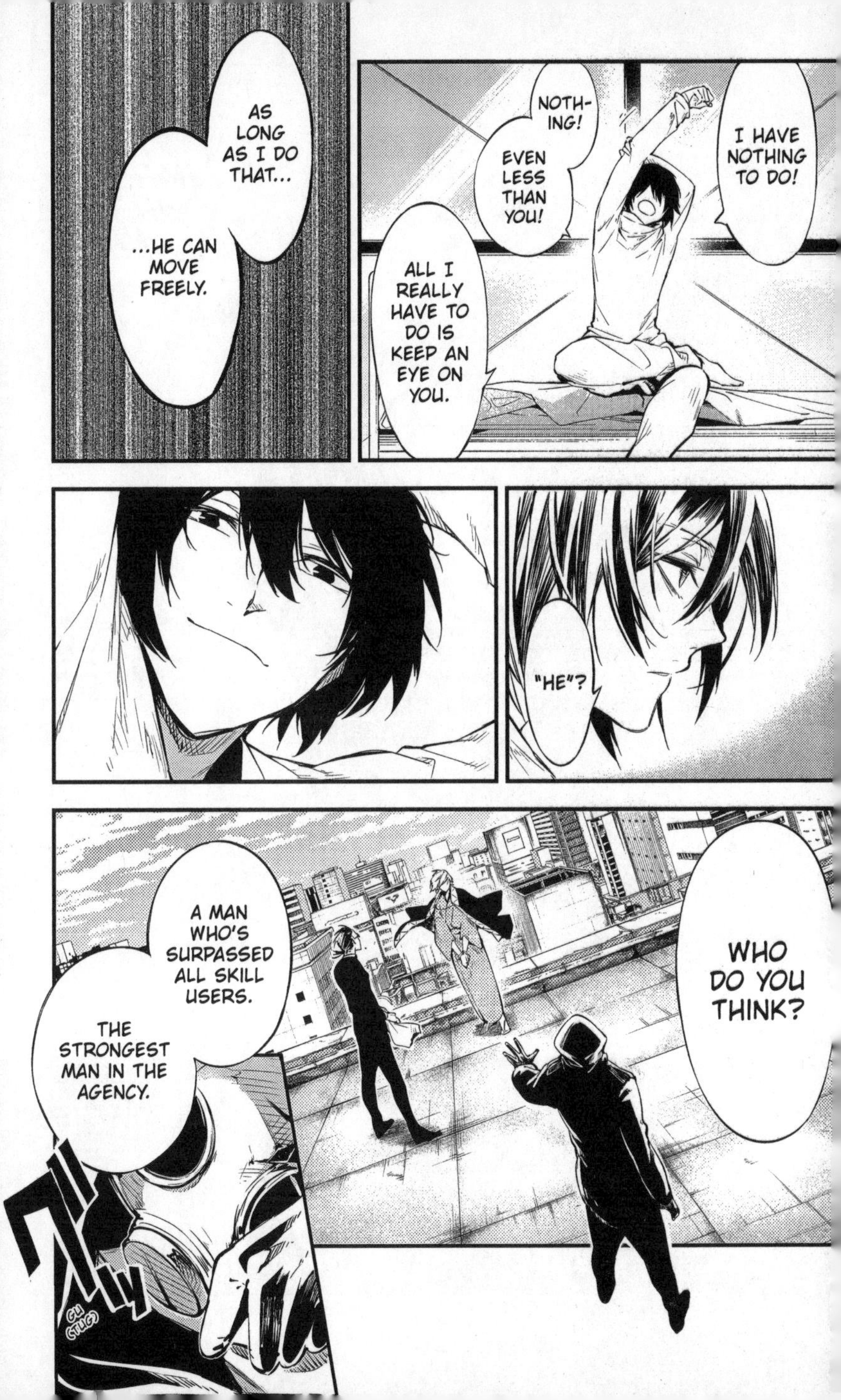
I HAVE NOTHING TO DO!
NOTHING!
EVEN LESS THAN YOU!
ALL I REALLY HAVE TO DO IS KEEP AN EYE ON YOU.
AS LONG AS I DO THAT...
...HE CAN MOVE FREELY.
"HE"?
WHO DO YOU THINK?
A MAN WHO'S SURPASSED ALL SKILL USERS.
THE STRONGEST MAN IN THE AGENCY.
GU (TUG)

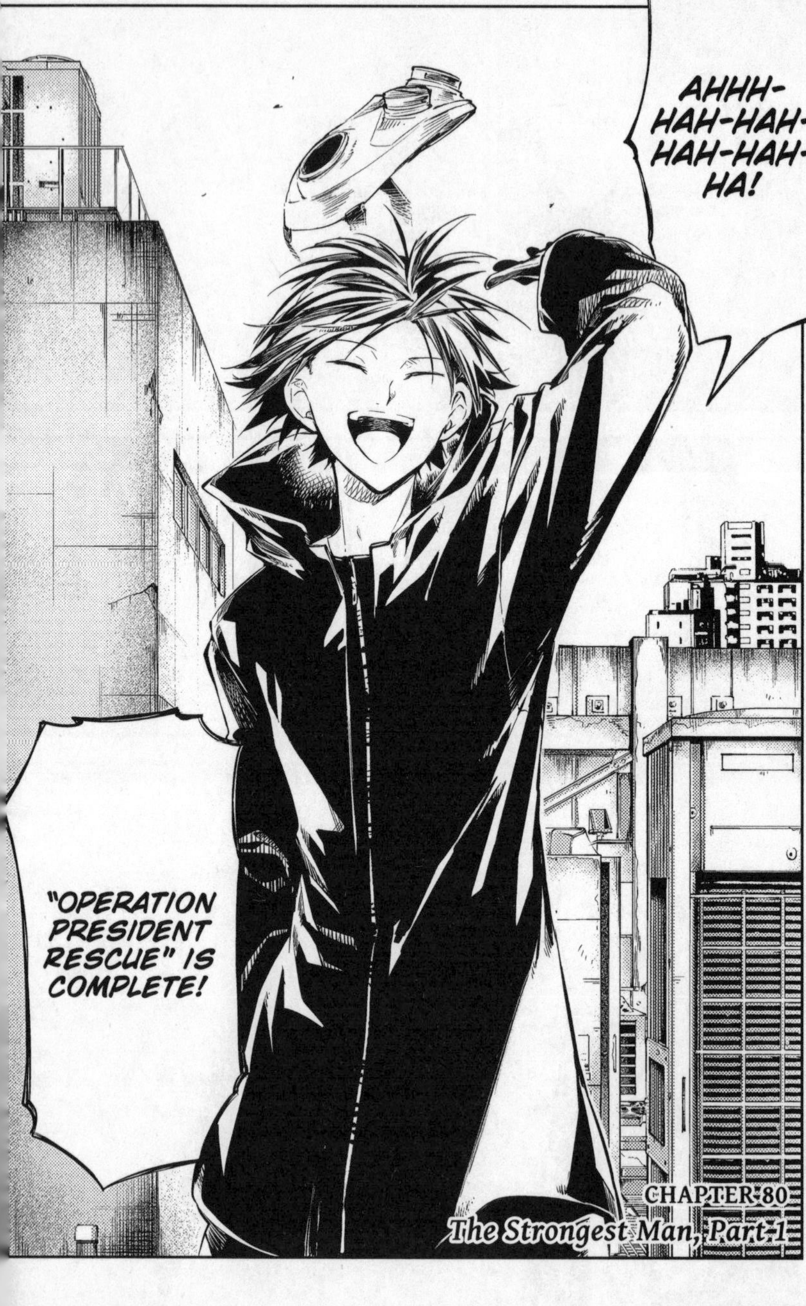
AHHH-HAH-HAH-HAH-HAH-HA!
"OPERATION PRESIDENT RESCUE" IS COMPLETE!

CHAPTER 80
The Strongest Man, Part 1

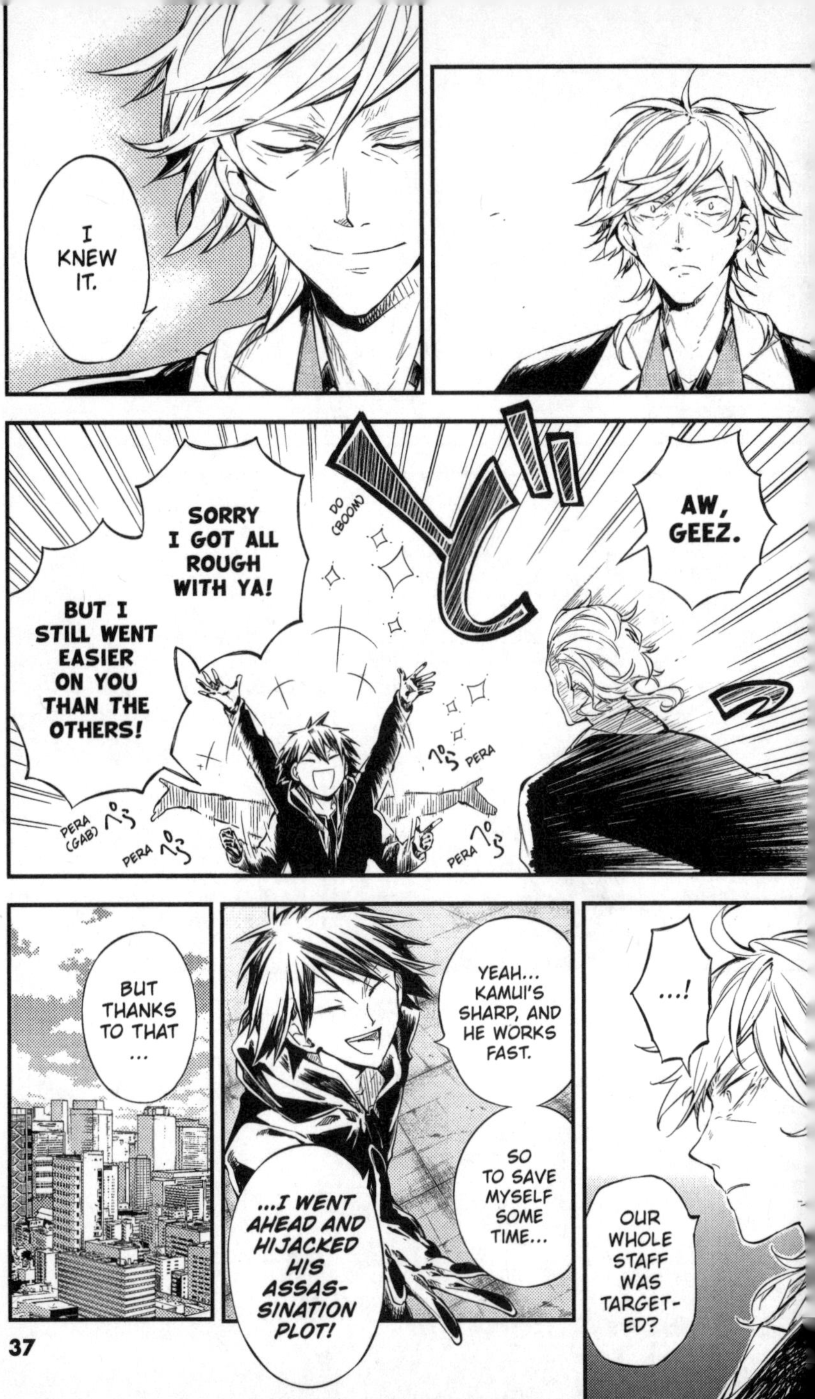
I KNEW IT.
AW, GEEZ.
DO (BOOM)
SORRY I GOT ALL ROUGH WITH YA!
BUT I STILL WENT EASIER ON YOU THAN THE OTHERS!
PERA
PERA
PERA (GAB)
PERA
...!
OUR WHOLE STAFF WAS TARGET-ED?
YEAH... KAMUI'S SHARP, AND HE WORKS FAST.
SO TO SAVE MYSELF SOME TIME...
...I WENT AHEAD AND HIJACKED HIS ASSAS-SINATION PLOT!
BUT THANKS TO THAT ...

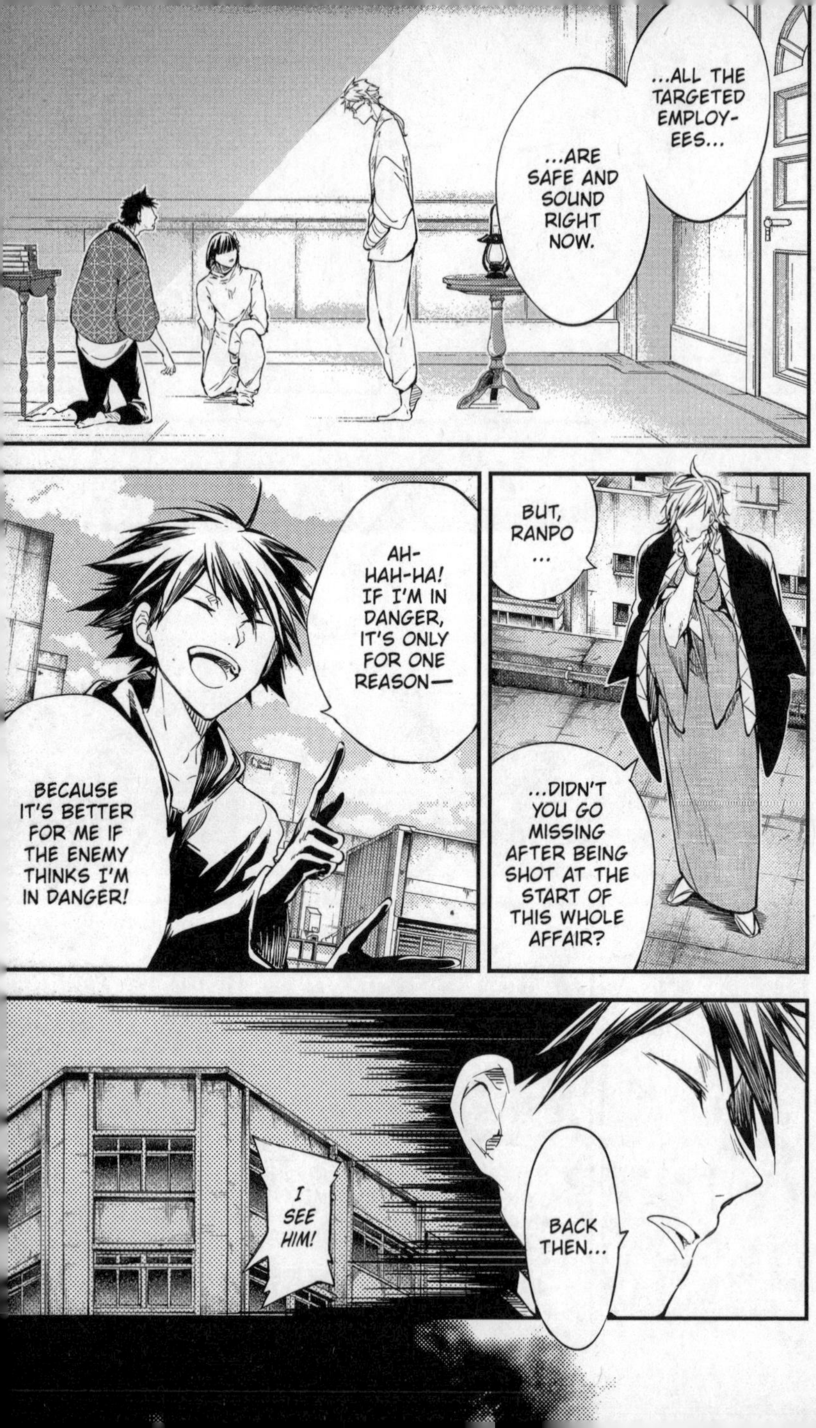
...ALL THE TARGETED EMPLOY-EES...
...ARE SAFE AND SOUND RIGHT NOW.
BUT, RANPO ...
...DIDN'T YOU GO MISSING AFTER BEING SHOT AT THE START OF THIS WHOLE AFFAIR?
AH-HAH-HA! IF I'M IN DANGER, IT'S ONLY FOR ONE REASON—
BECAUSE IT'S BETTER FOR ME IF THE ENEMY THINKS I'M IN DANGER!
BACK THEN...
I SEE HIM!

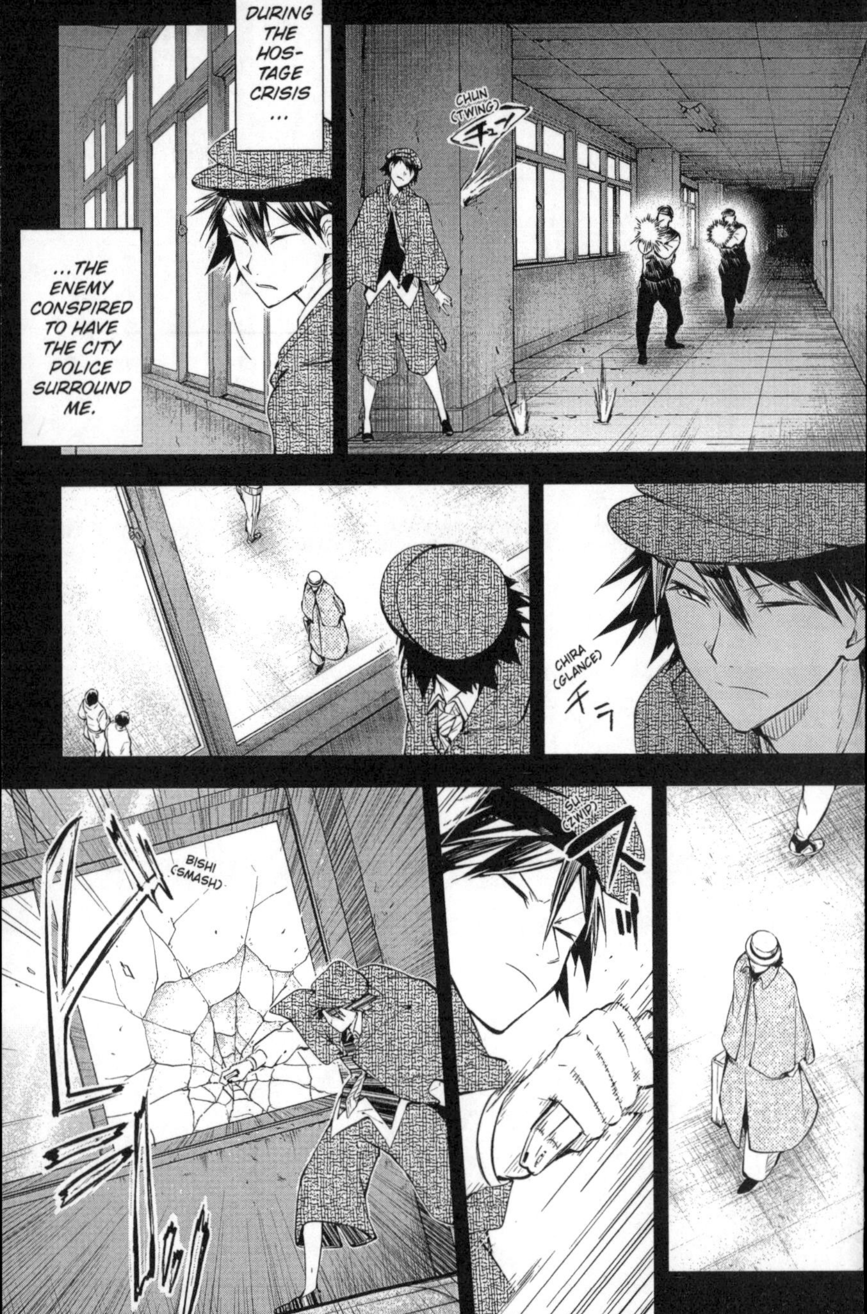
DURING THE HOS-TAGE CRISIS ...
CHUN (TWING)
チュン
...THE ENEMY CONSPIRED TO HAVE THE CITY POLICE SURROUND ME.
CHIRA (GLANCE)
チラ
SU (ZWIP)
BISHI (SMASH)

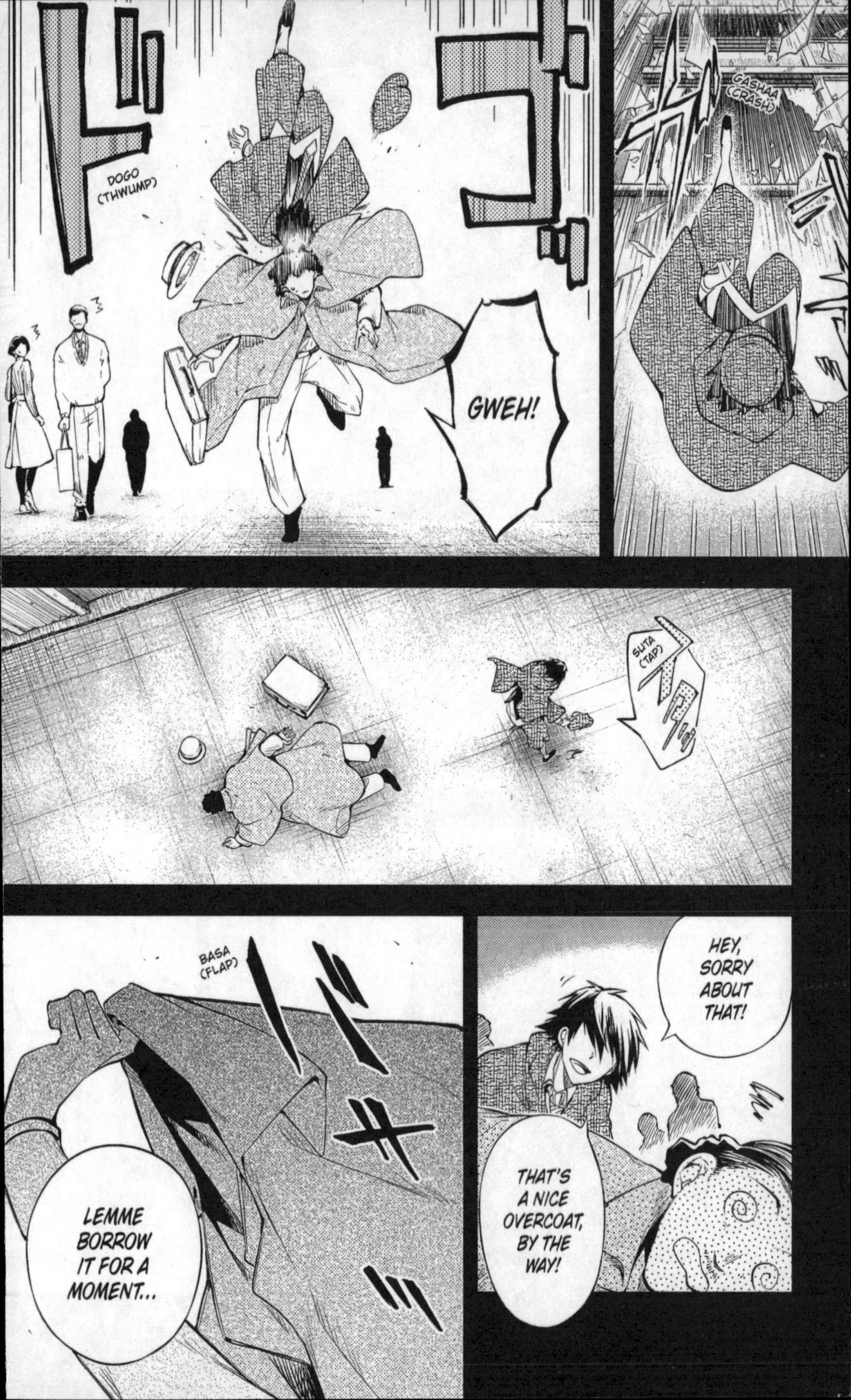
GASHAA (CRASH)
DOGO (THWUMP)
GWEH!
SUTA (TAP)
HEY, SORRY ABOUT THAT!
THAT'S A NICE OVERCOAT, BY THE WAY!
BASA (FLAP)
LEMME BORROW IT FOR A MOMENT...

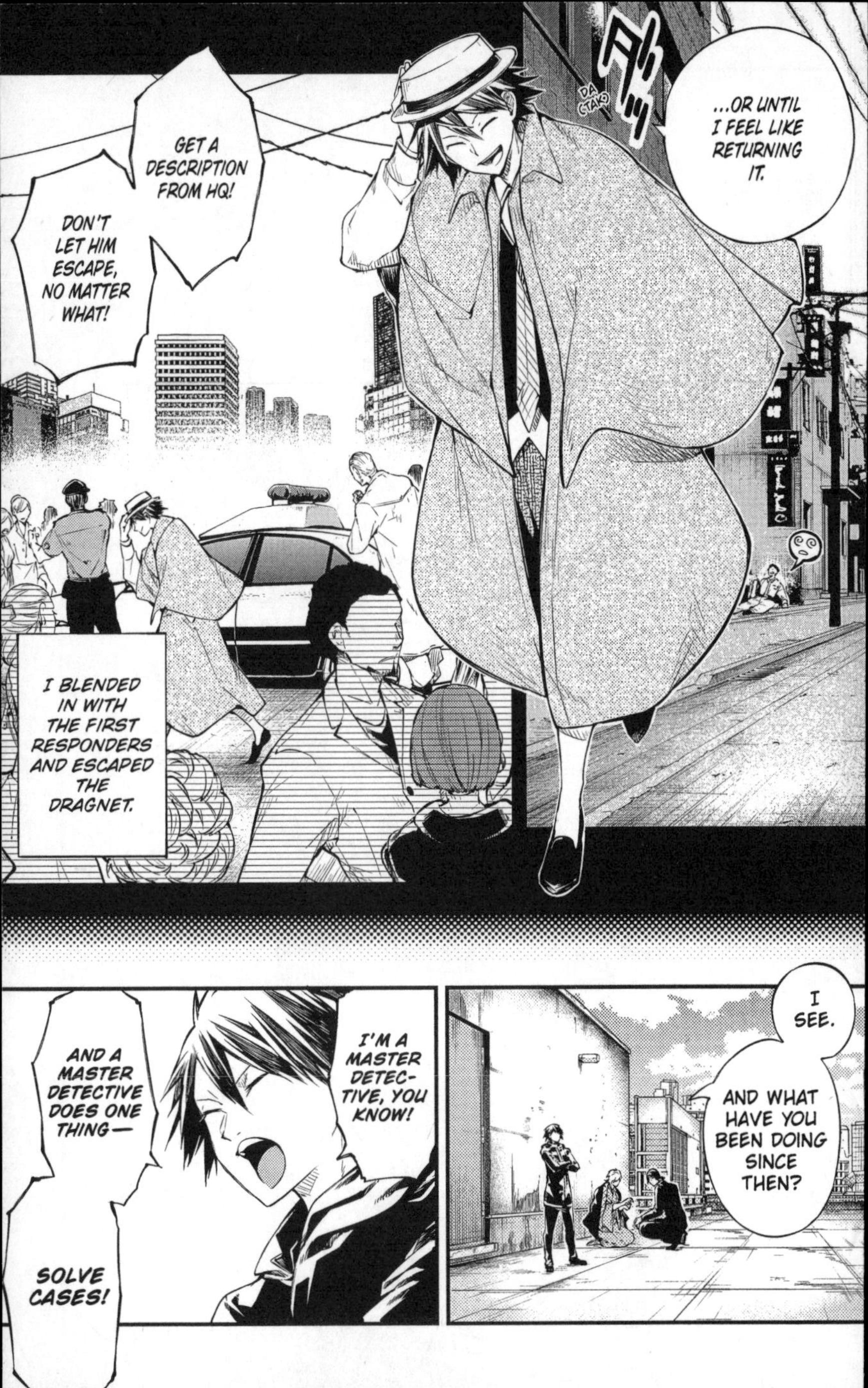
DA (TAK)
...OR UNTIL I FEEL LIKE RETURNING IT.
GET A DESCRIPTION FROM HQ!
DON'T LET HIM ESCAPE, NO MATTER WHAT!
I BLENDED IN WITH THE FIRST RESPONDERS AND ESCAPED THE DRAGNET.
I SEE.
AND WHAT HAVE YOU BEEN DOING SINCE THEN?
I'M A MASTER DETECTIVE, YOU KNOW!
AND A MASTER DETECTIVE DOES ONE THING—
SOLVE CASES!

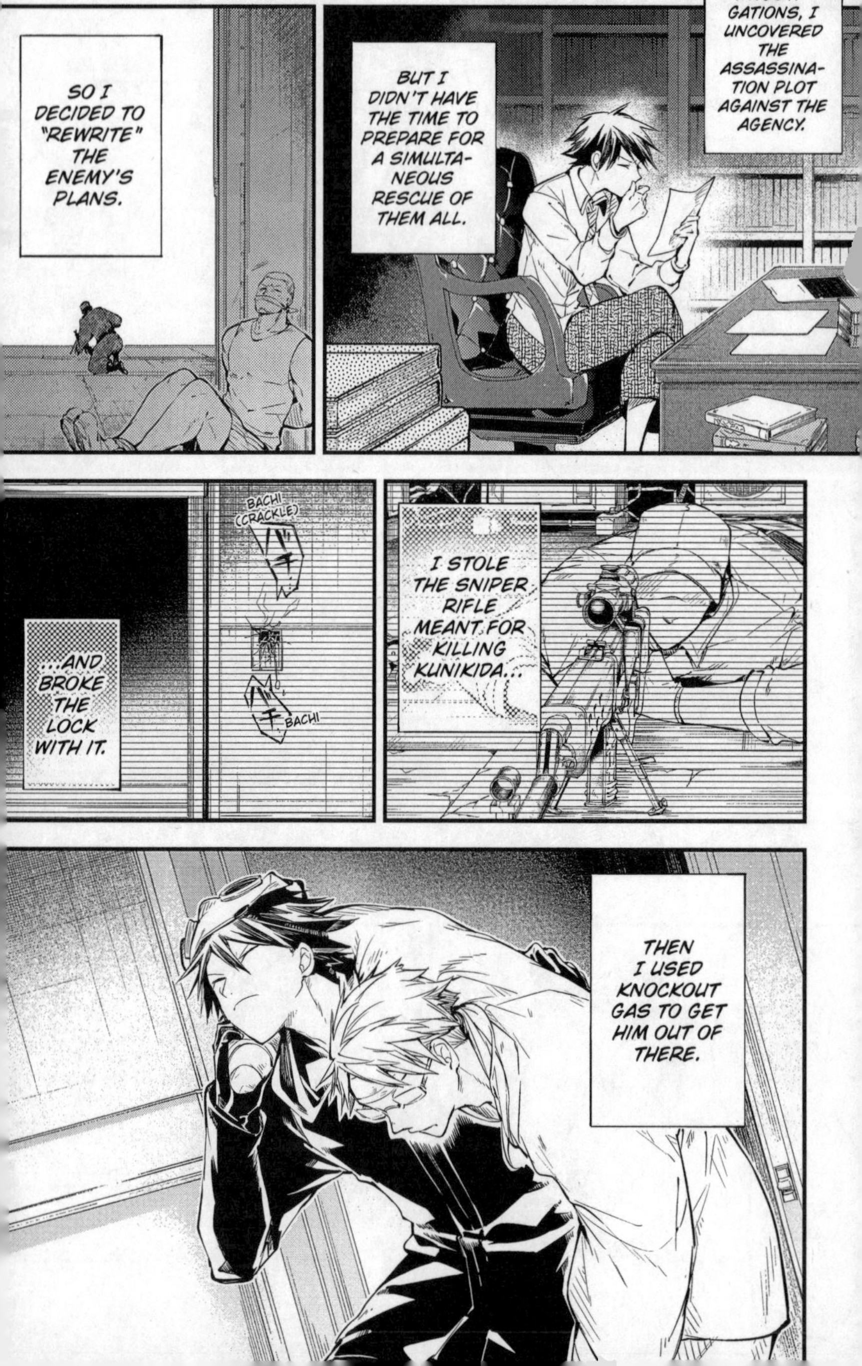
IN MY INVESTIGATIONS, I UNCOVERED THE ASSASSINATION PLOT AGAINST THE AGENCY.
BUT I DIDN'T HAVE THE TIME TO PREPARE FOR A SIMULTANEOUS RESCUE OF THEM ALL.
SO I DECIDED TO "REWRITE" THE ENEMY'S PLANS.
I STOLE THE SNIPER RIFLE MEANT FOR KILLING KUNIKIDA...
BACHI (CRACKLE)
BACHI
...AND BROKE THE LOCK WITH IT.
THEN I USED KNOCKOUT GAS TO GET HIM OUT OF THERE.

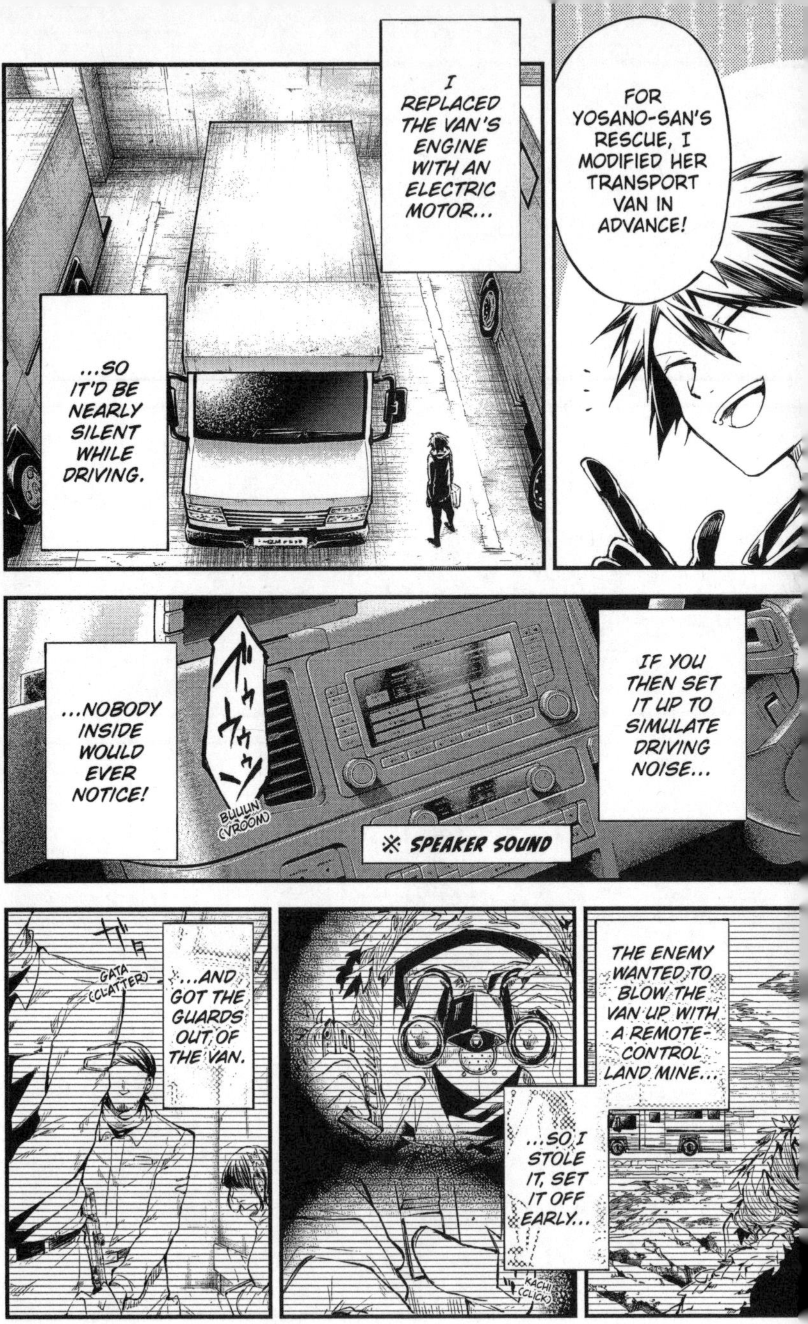
FOR YOSANO-SAN'S RESCUE, I MODIFIED HER TRANSPORT VAN IN ADVANCE!
I REPLACED THE VAN'S ENGINE WITH AN ELECTRIC MOTOR...
...SO IT'D BE NEARLY SILENT WHILE DRIVING.
IF YOU THEN SET IT UP TO SIMULATE DRIVING NOISE...
※ SPEAKER SOUND
BUUUN (VROOM)
...NOBODY INSIDE WOULD EVER NOTICE!
THE ENEMY WANTED TO BLOW THE VAN UP WITH A REMOTE-CONTROL LAND MINE...
...SO I STOLE IT, SET IT OFF EARLY...
KACHI (CLICK)
GATA (CLATTER)
...AND GOT THE GUARDS OUT OF THE VAN.

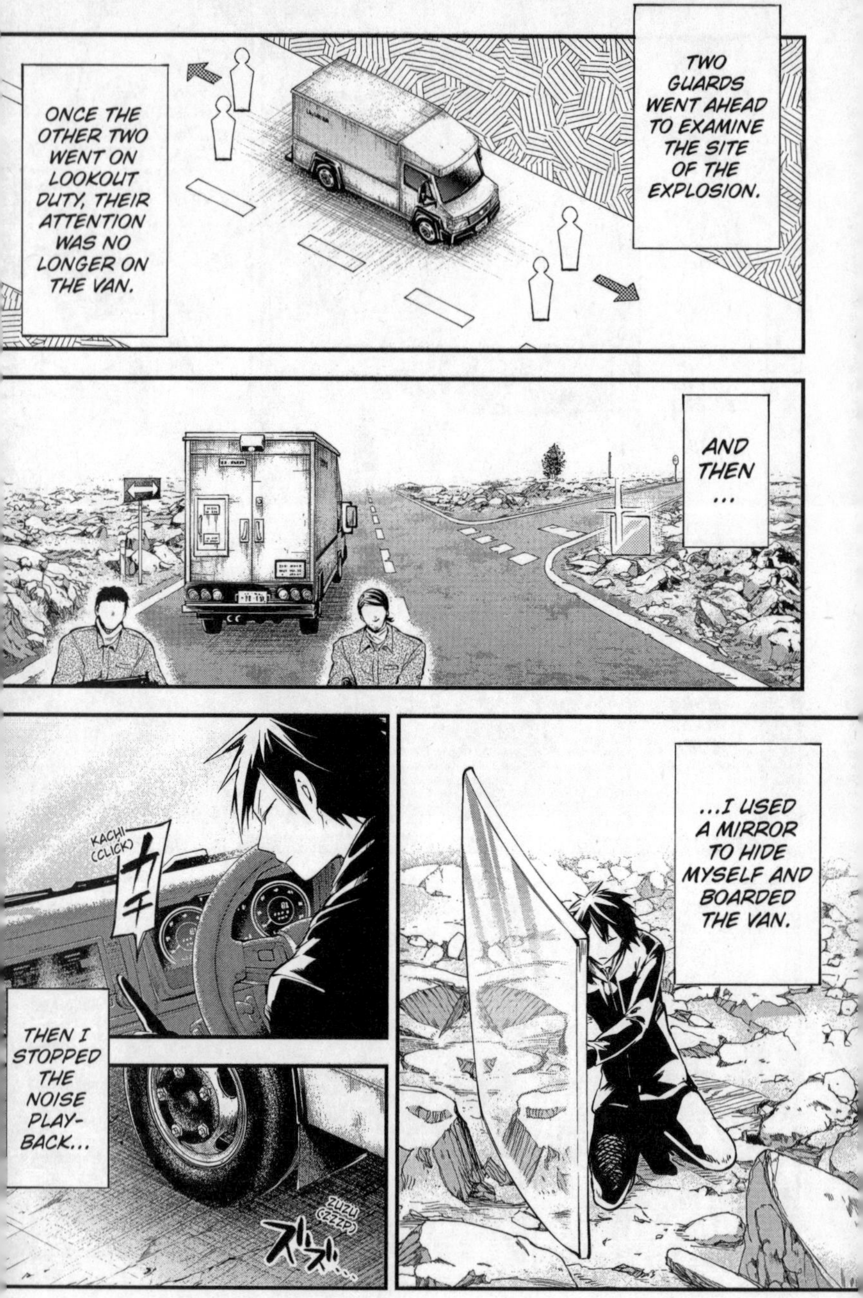
TWO GUARDS WENT AHEAD TO EXAMINE THE SITE OF THE EXPLOSION.
ONCE THE OTHER TWO WENT ON LOOKOUT DUTY, THEIR ATTENTION WAS NO LONGER ON THE VAN.
AND THEN ...
...I USED A MIRROR TO HIDE MYSELF AND BOARDED THE VAN.
KACHI (CLICK)
カチ
THEN I STOPPED THE NOISE PLAY-BACK...
ZUZU (ZZZP)
ズズ...

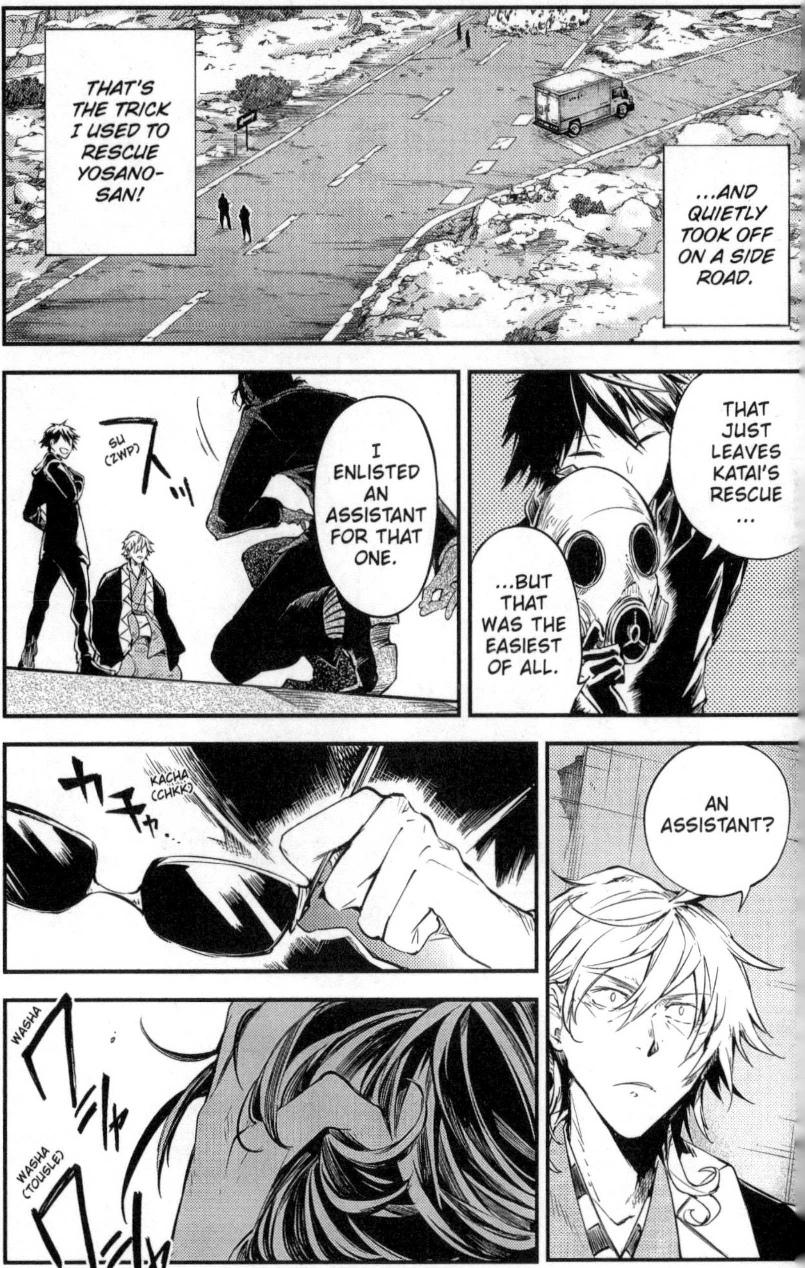
...AND QUIETLY TOOK OFF ON A SIDE ROAD.
THAT'S THE TRICK I USED TO RESCUE YOSANO-SAN!
THAT JUST LEAVES KATAI'S RESCUE ...
...BUT THAT WAS THE EASIEST OF ALL.
I ENLISTED AN ASSISTANT FOR THAT ONE.
SU (ZWP)
AN ASSISTANT?
KACHA (CHKK)
WASHA
WASHA (TOUSLE)

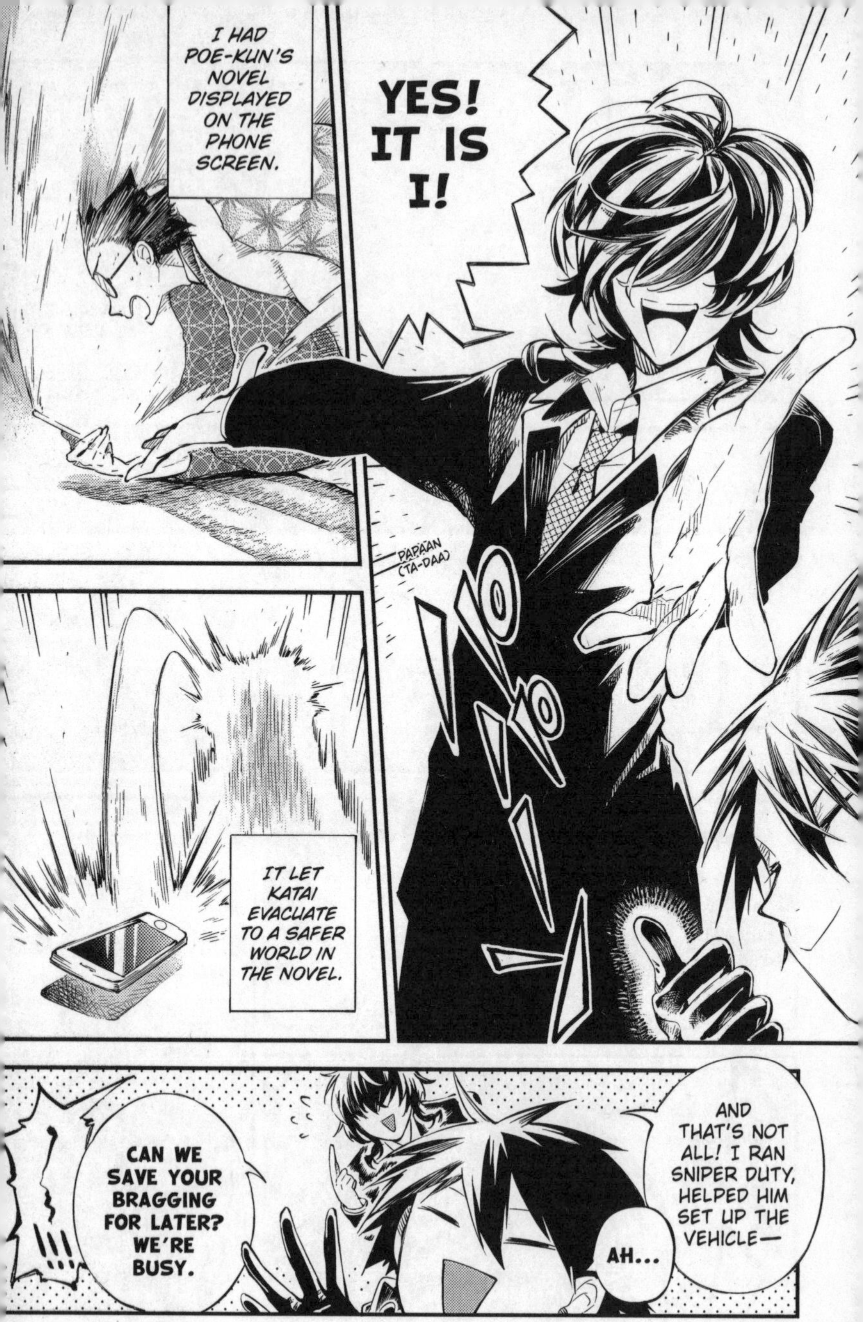
YES! IT IS I!
PAPAAN (TA-DAA)
I HAD POE-KUN'S NOVEL DISPLAYED ON THE PHONE SCREEN.
IT LET KATAI EVACUATE TO A SAFER WORLD IN THE NOVEL.
AND THAT'S NOT ALL! I RAN SNIPER DUTY, HELPED HIM SET UP THE VEHICLE—
AH...
CAN WE SAVE YOUR BRAGGING FOR LATER? WE'RE BUSY.
!!!

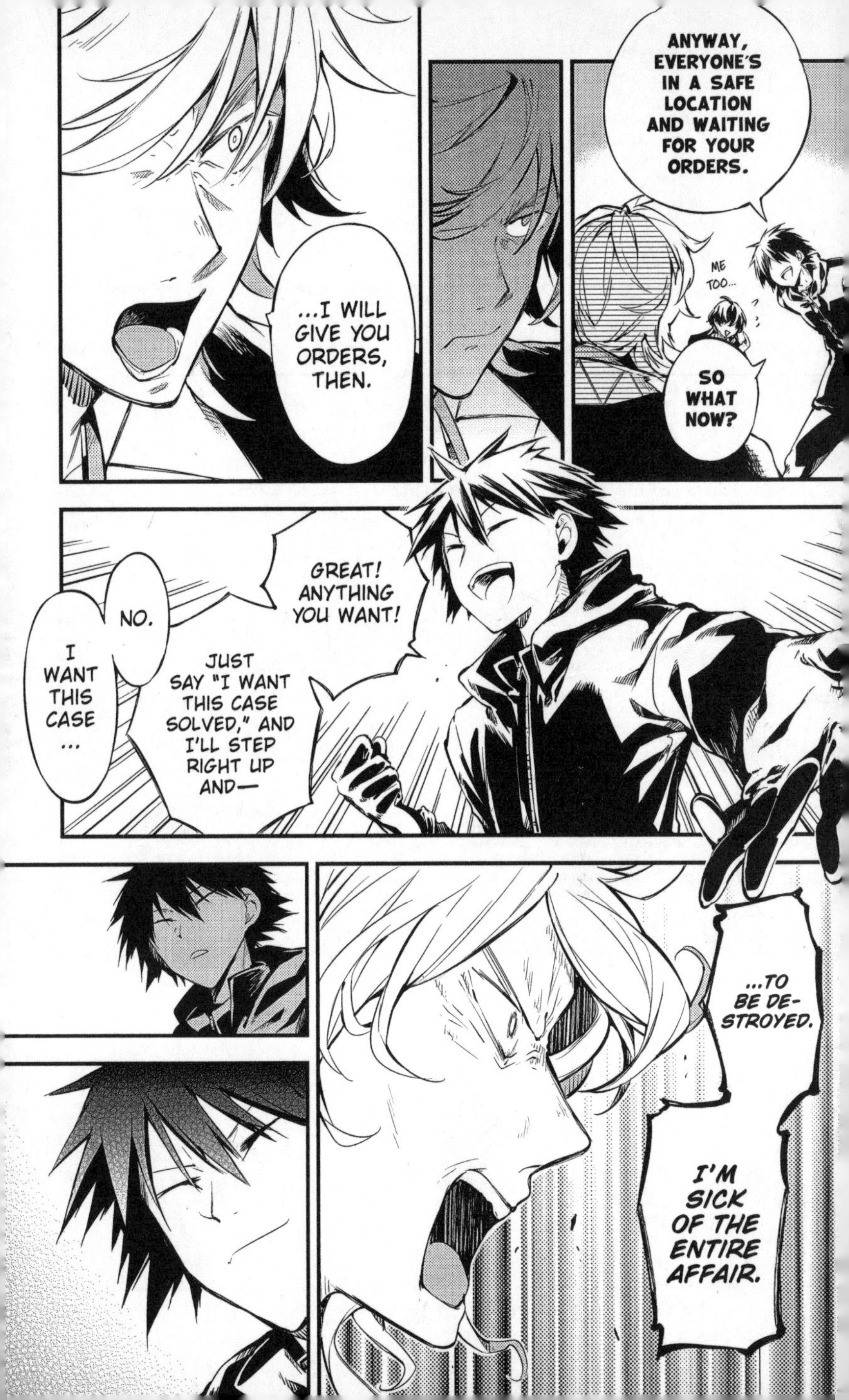
ANYWAY, EVERYONE'S IN A SAFE LOCATION AND WAITING FOR YOUR ORDERS.
ME TOO...
SO WHAT NOW?
...I WILL GIVE YOU ORDERS, THEN.
GREAT! ANYTHING YOU WANT!
JUST SAY "I WANT THIS CASE SOLVED," AND I'LL STEP RIGHT UP AND—
NO.
I WANT THIS CASE ...
...TO BE DE-STROYED.
I'M SICK OF THE ENTIRE AFFAIR.

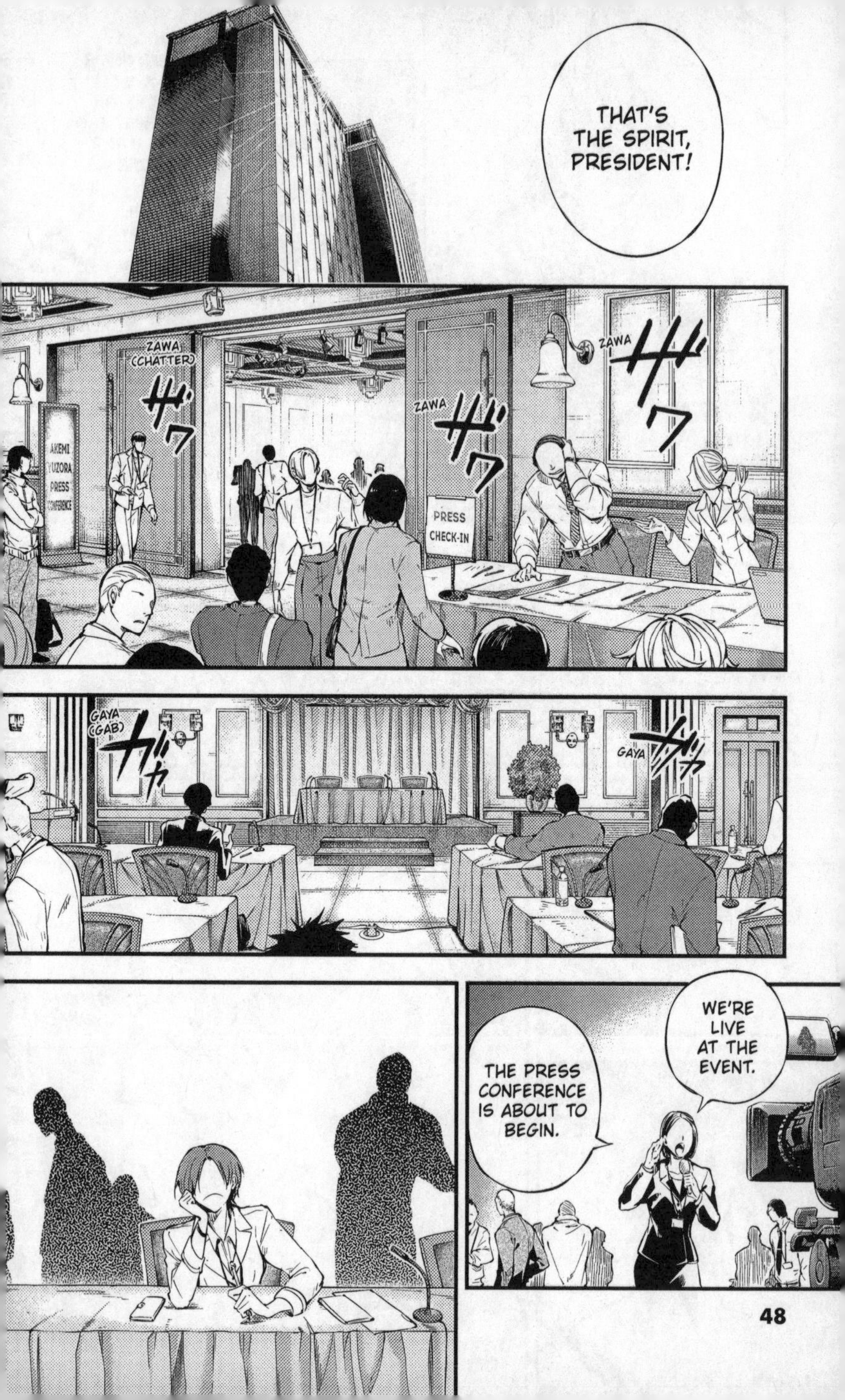
THAT'S THE SPIRIT, PRESIDENT!
ZAWA
ザワ
ZAWA
ザワ
PRESS CHECK-IN
ZAWA (CHATTER)
ザワ
AKEMI YUZORA PRESS CONFERENCE
GAYA
ガヤ
GAYA (GAB)
ガヤ
WE'RE LIVE AT THE EVENT.
THE PRESS CONFERENCE IS ABOUT TO BEGIN.

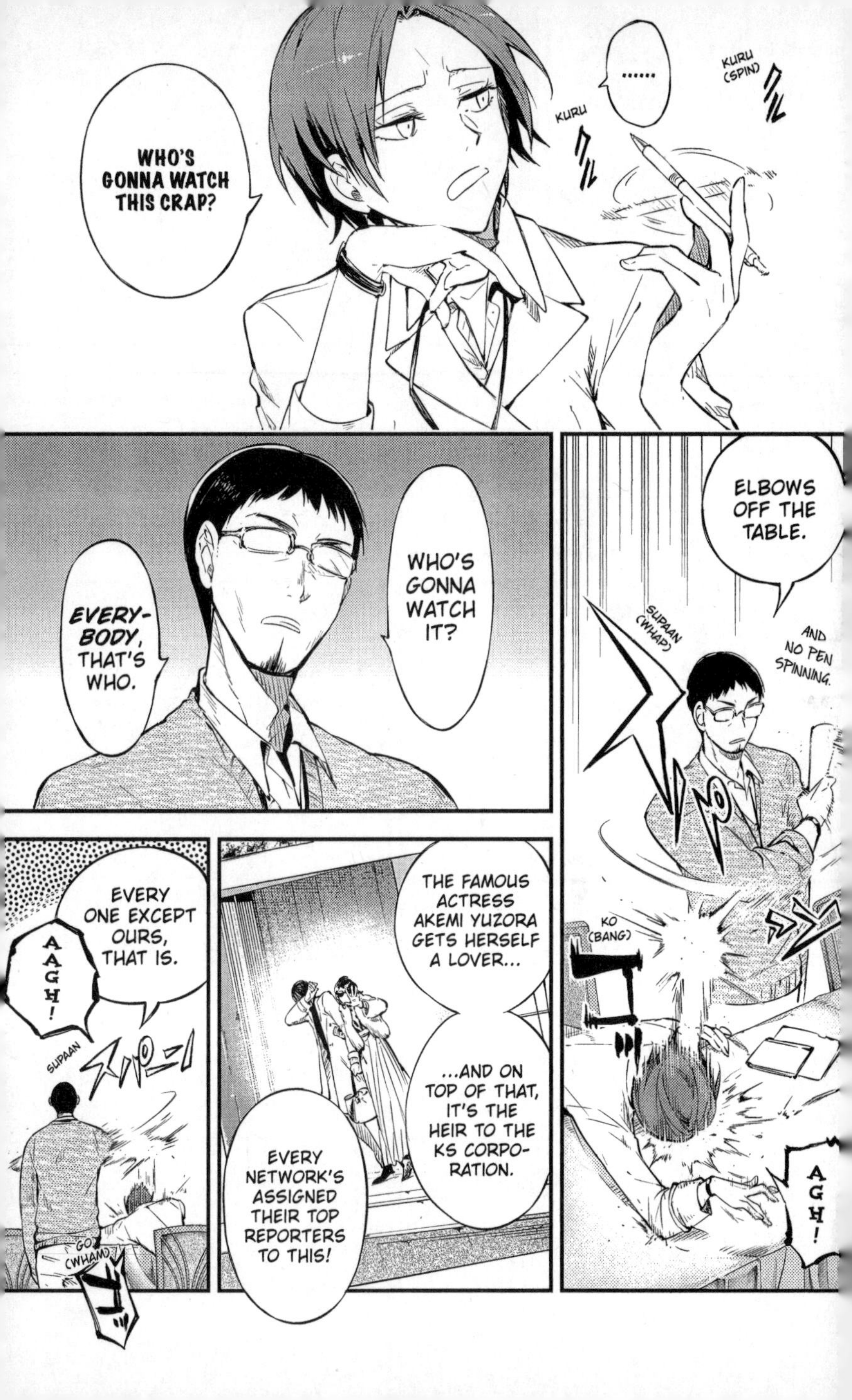

KURU (SPIN)
......
KURU
WHO'S GONNA WATCH THIS CRAP?
ELBOWS OFF THE TABLE.
SUPAAN (WHAP)
AND NO PEN SPINNING.
KO (BANG)
AGH!
WHO'S GONNA WATCH IT?
EVERY-BODY, THAT'S WHO.
THE FAMOUS ACTRESS AKEMI YUZORA GETS HERSELF A LOVER...
...AND ON TOP OF THAT, IT'S THE HEIR TO THE KS CORPO-RATION.
EVERY NETWORK'S ASSIGNED THEIR TOP REPORTERS TO THIS!
EVERY ONE EXCEPT OURS, THAT IS.
AAGH!
SUPAAN
GO (WHAM)

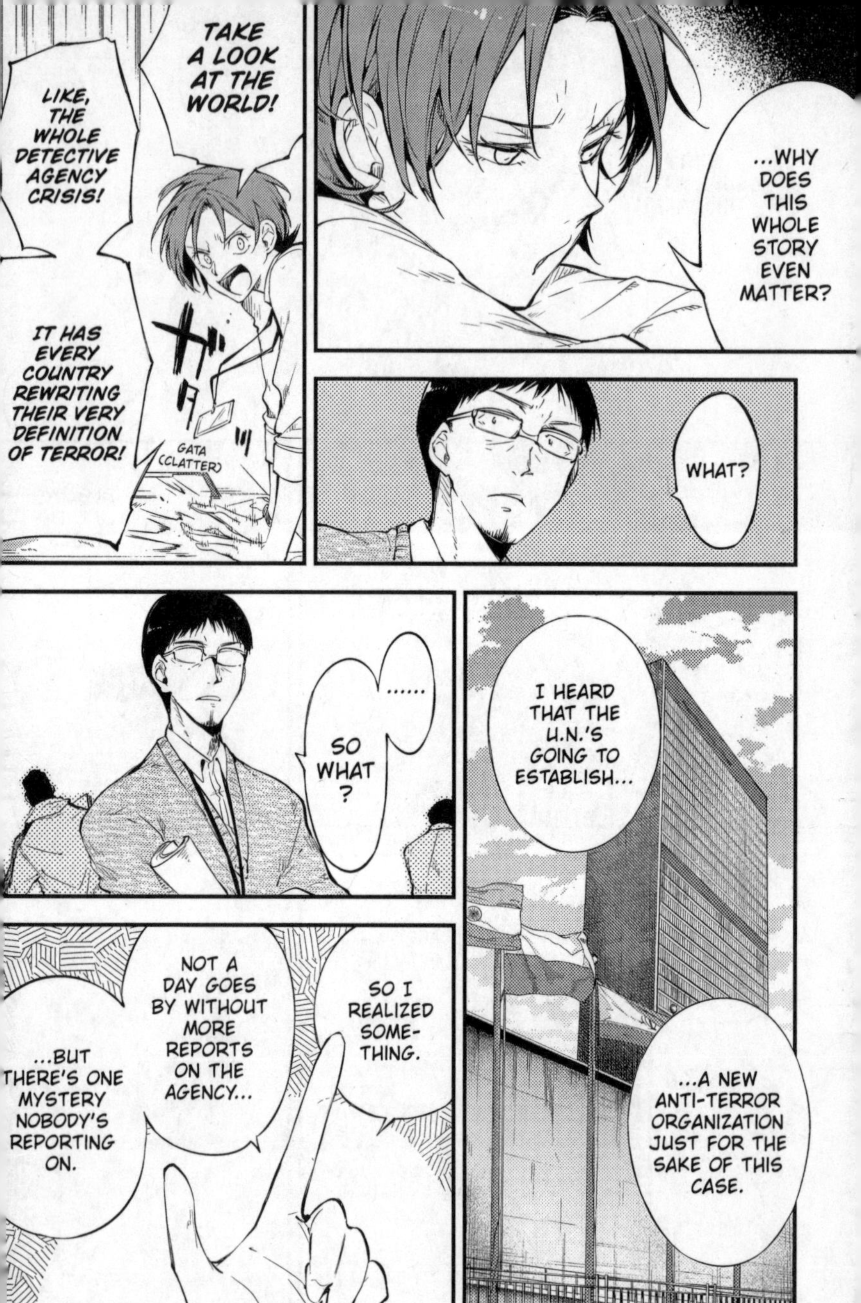
...WHY DOES THIS WHOLE STORY EVEN MATTER?
WHAT?
TAKE A LOOK AT THE WORLD!
LIKE, THE WHOLE DETECTIVE AGENCY CRISIS!
IT HAS EVERY COUNTRY REWRITING THEIR VERY DEFINITION OF TERROR!
GATA (CLATTER)
I HEARD THAT THE U.N.'S GOING TO ESTABLISH...
...A NEW ANTI-TERROR ORGANIZATION JUST FOR THE SAKE OF THIS CASE.
......
SO WHAT?
SO I REALIZED SOME-THING.
NOT A DAY GOES BY WITHOUT MORE REPORTS ON THE AGENCY...
...BUT THERE'S ONE MYSTERY NOBODY'S REPORTING ON.

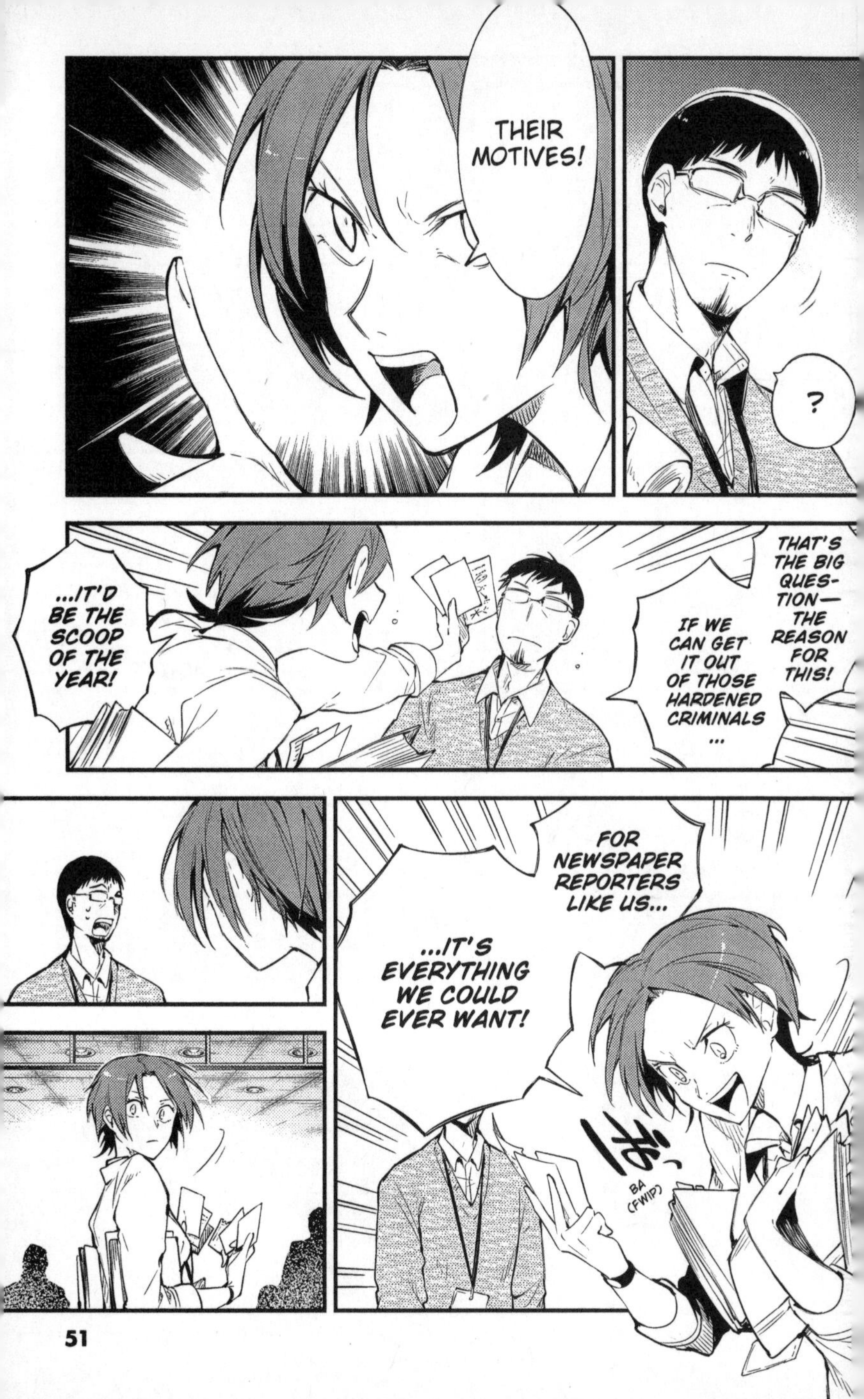
?
THEIR MOTIVES!
THAT'S THE BIG QUES-TION—THE REASON FOR THIS!
IF WE CAN GET IT OUT OF THOSE HARDENED CRIMINALS...
...IT'D BE THE SCOOP OF THE YEAR!
FOR NEWSPAPER REPORTERS LIKE US...
...IT'S EVERYTHING WE COULD EVER WANT!
ばっ
BA (FWIP)

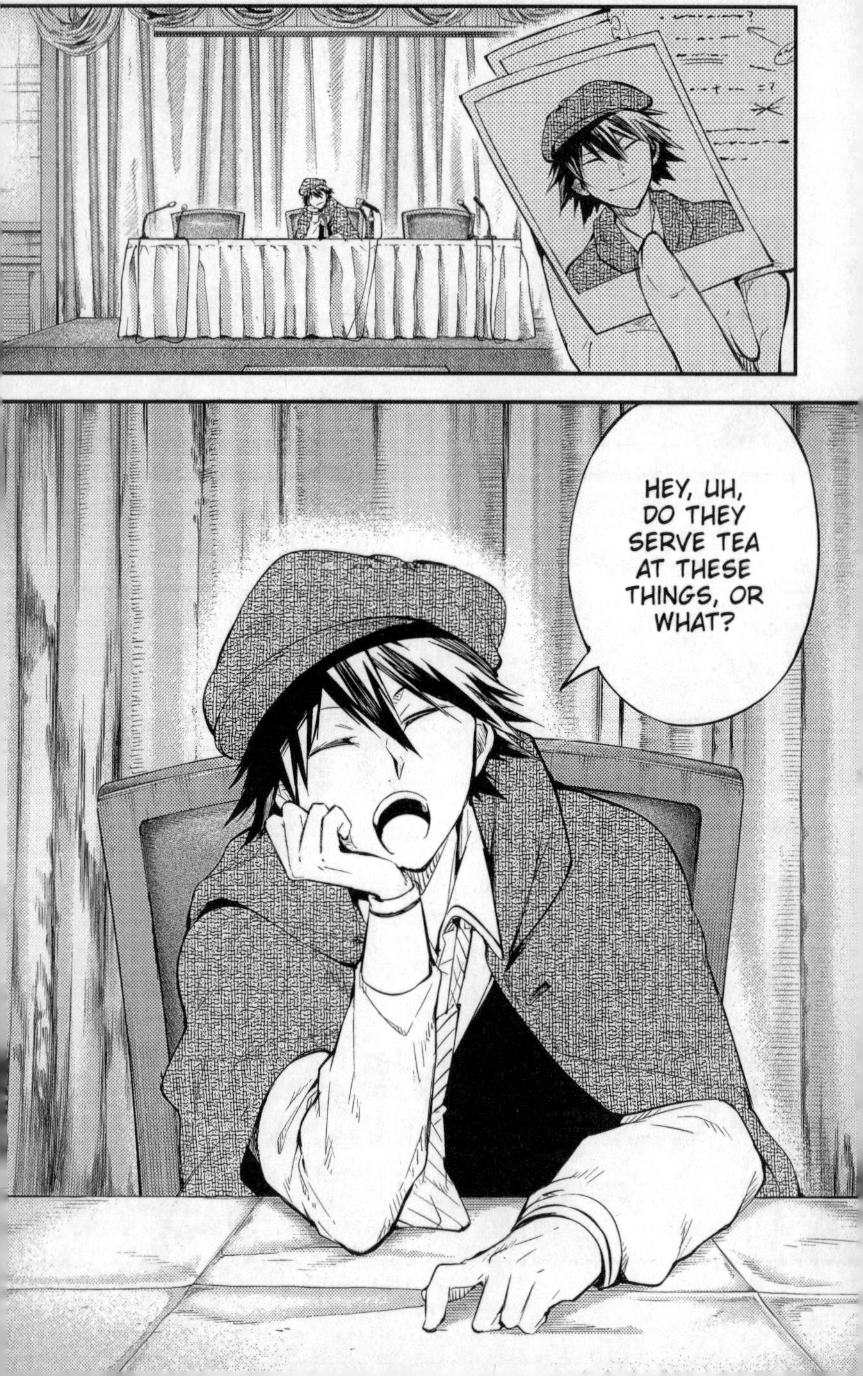
HEY, UH, DO THEY SERVE TEA AT THESE THINGS, OR WHAT?

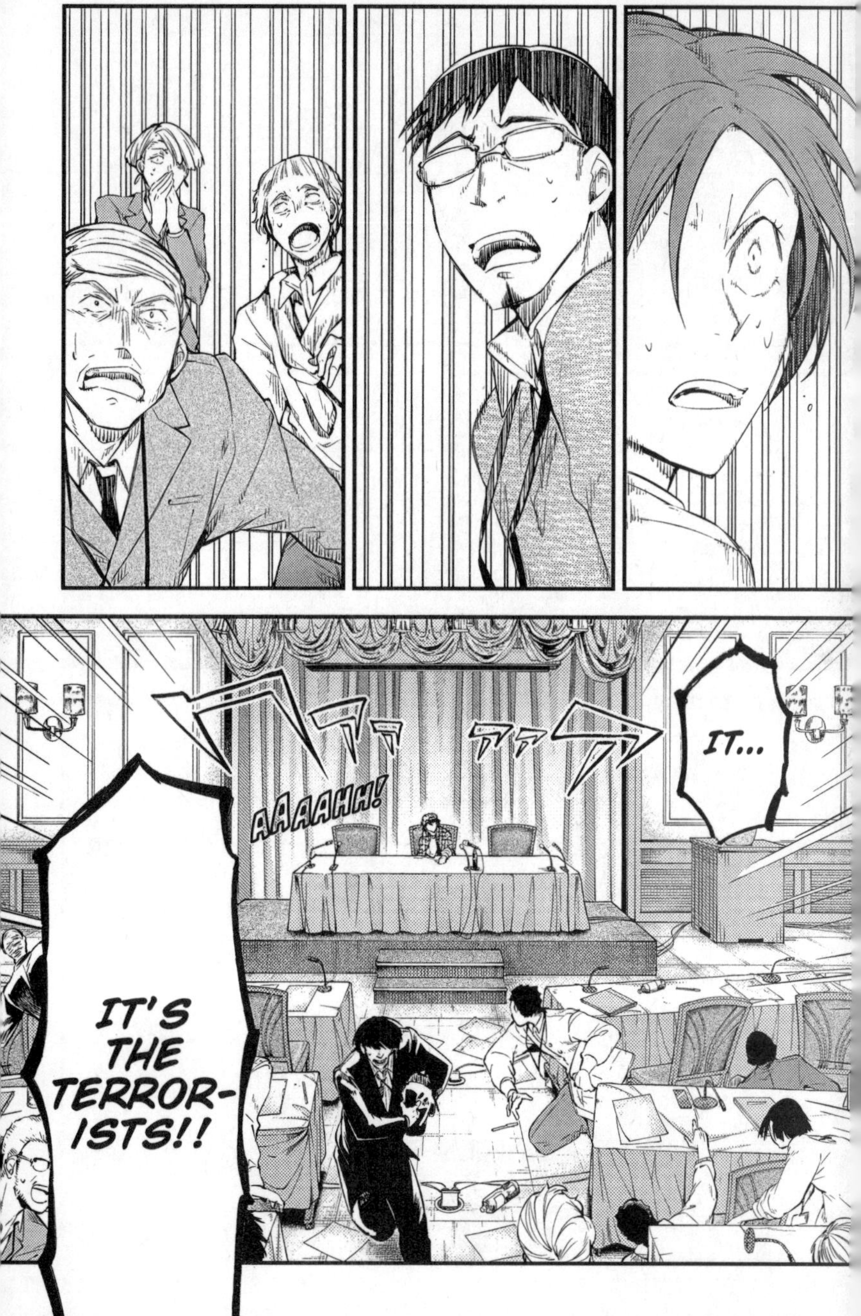
IT...
AAAAHH!
IT'S THE TERROR-ISTS!!

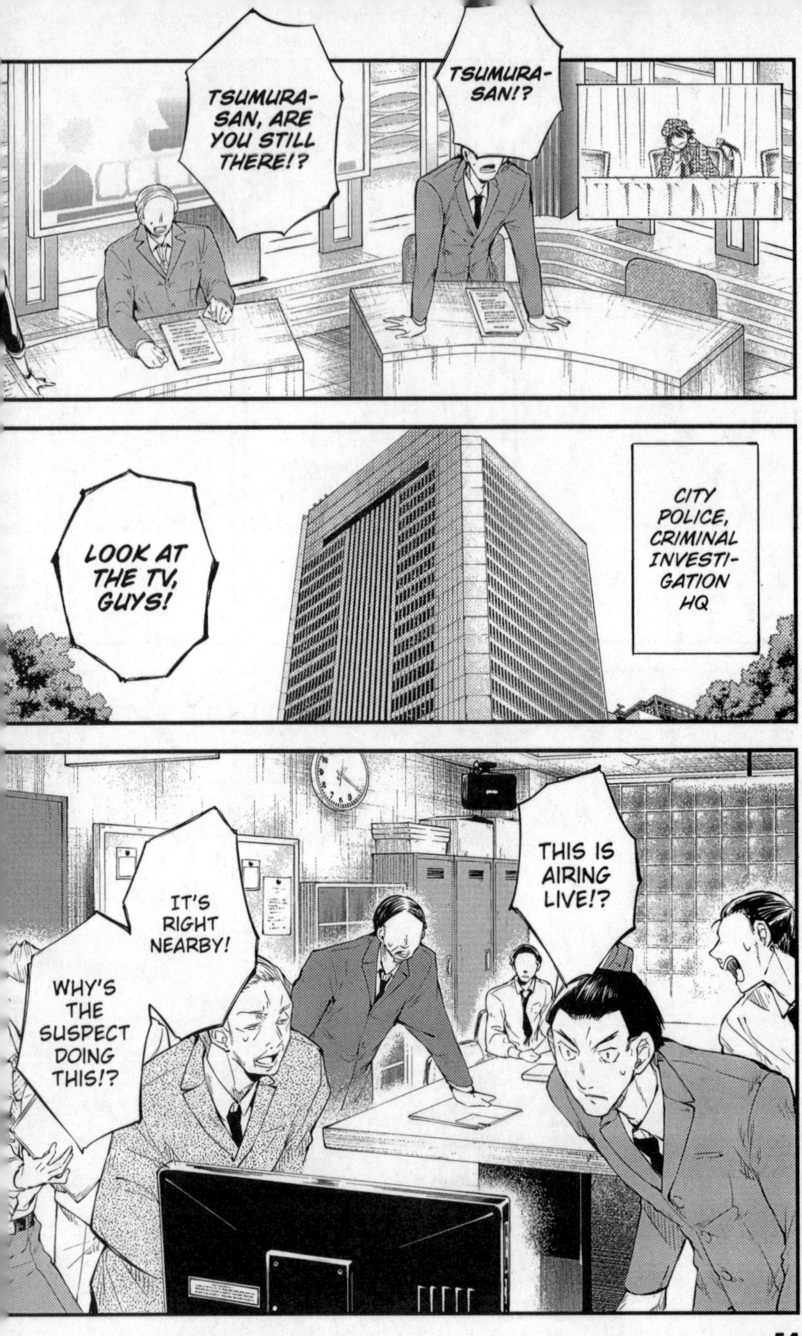
TSUMURA-SAN!?
TSUMURA-SAN, ARE YOU STILL THERE!?
CITY POLICE, CRIMINAL INVESTIGATION HQ
LOOK AT THE TV, GUYS!
THIS IS AIRING LIVE!?
IT'S RIGHT NEARBY!
WHY'S THE SUSPECT DOING THIS!?

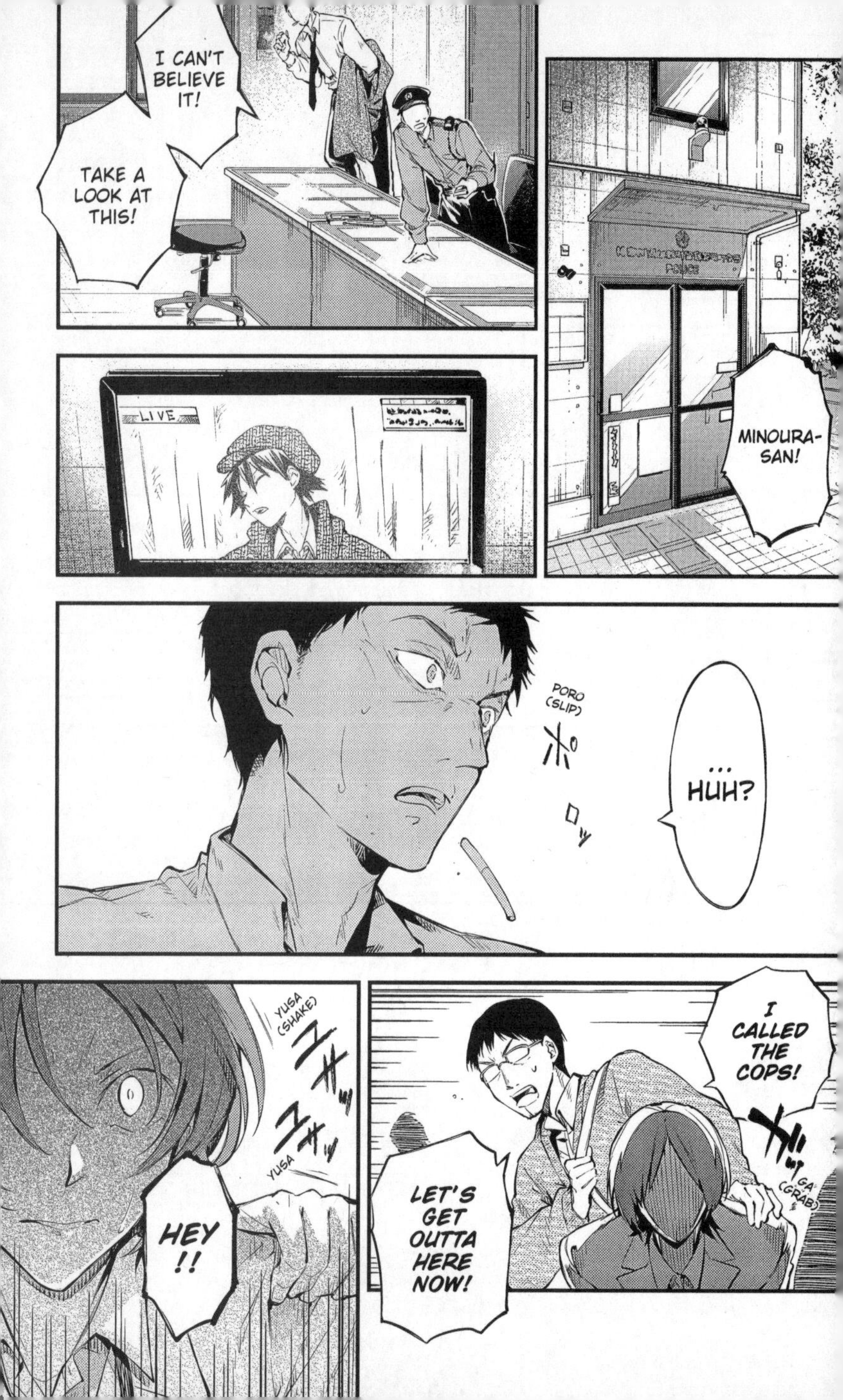
MINOURA-SAN!
I CAN'T BELIEVE IT!
TAKE A LOOK AT THIS!
LIVE
... HUH?
PORO (SLIP)
I CALLED THE COPS!
GA' (GRAB)
LET'S GET OUTTA HERE NOW!
YUSA (SHAKE)
YUSA
HEY !!

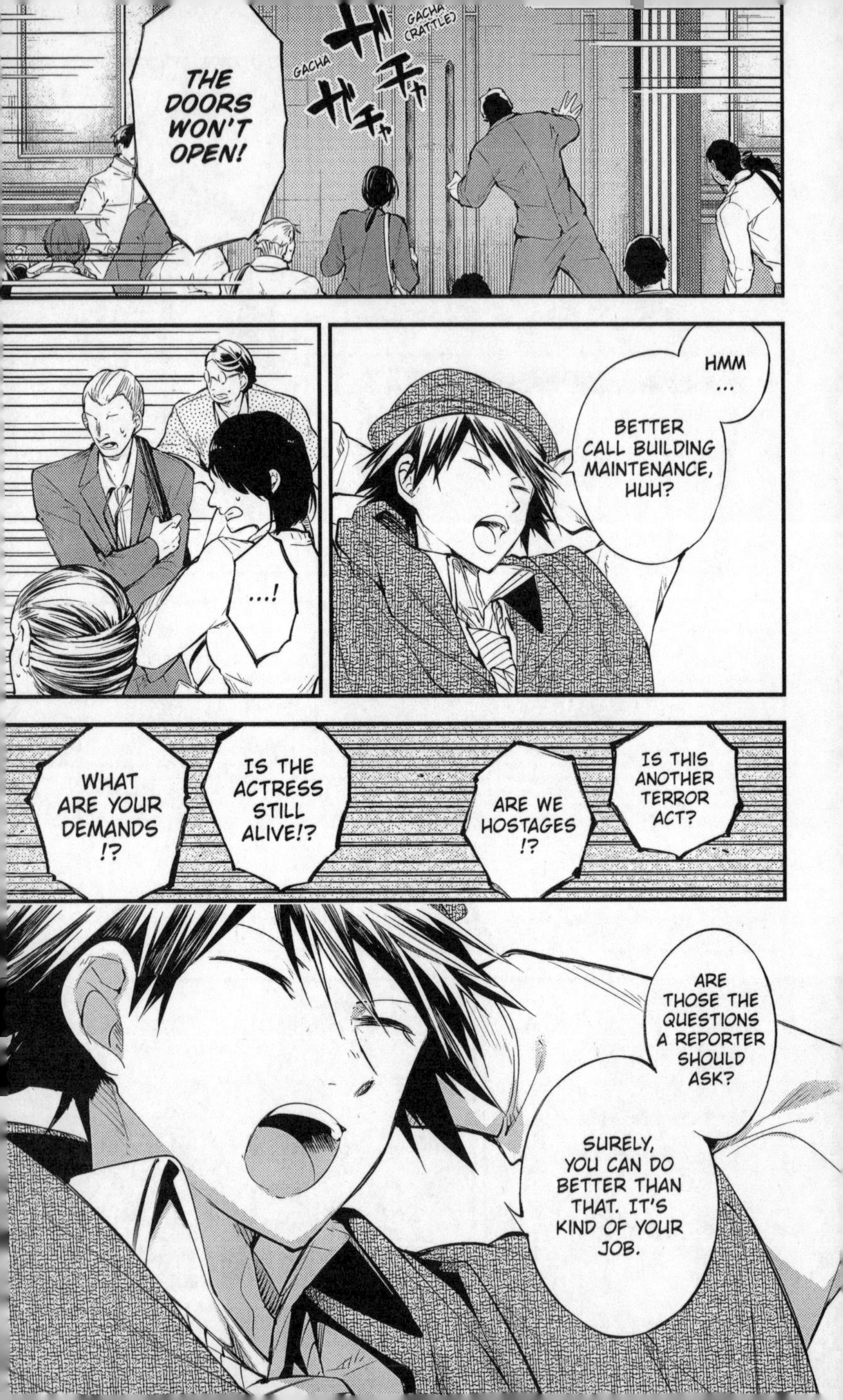
GACHA (RATTLE)
ガチャ
GACHA
ガチャ
THE DOORS WON'T OPEN!
HMM ...
BETTER CALL BUILDING MAINTENANCE, HUH?
...!
IS THIS ANOTHER TERROR ACT?
ARE WE HOSTAGES !?
IS THE ACTRESS STILL ALIVE!?
WHAT ARE YOUR DEMANDS !?
ARE THOSE THE QUESTIONS A REPORTER SHOULD ASK?
SURELY, YOU CAN DO BETTER THAN THAT. IT'S KIND OF YOUR JOB.

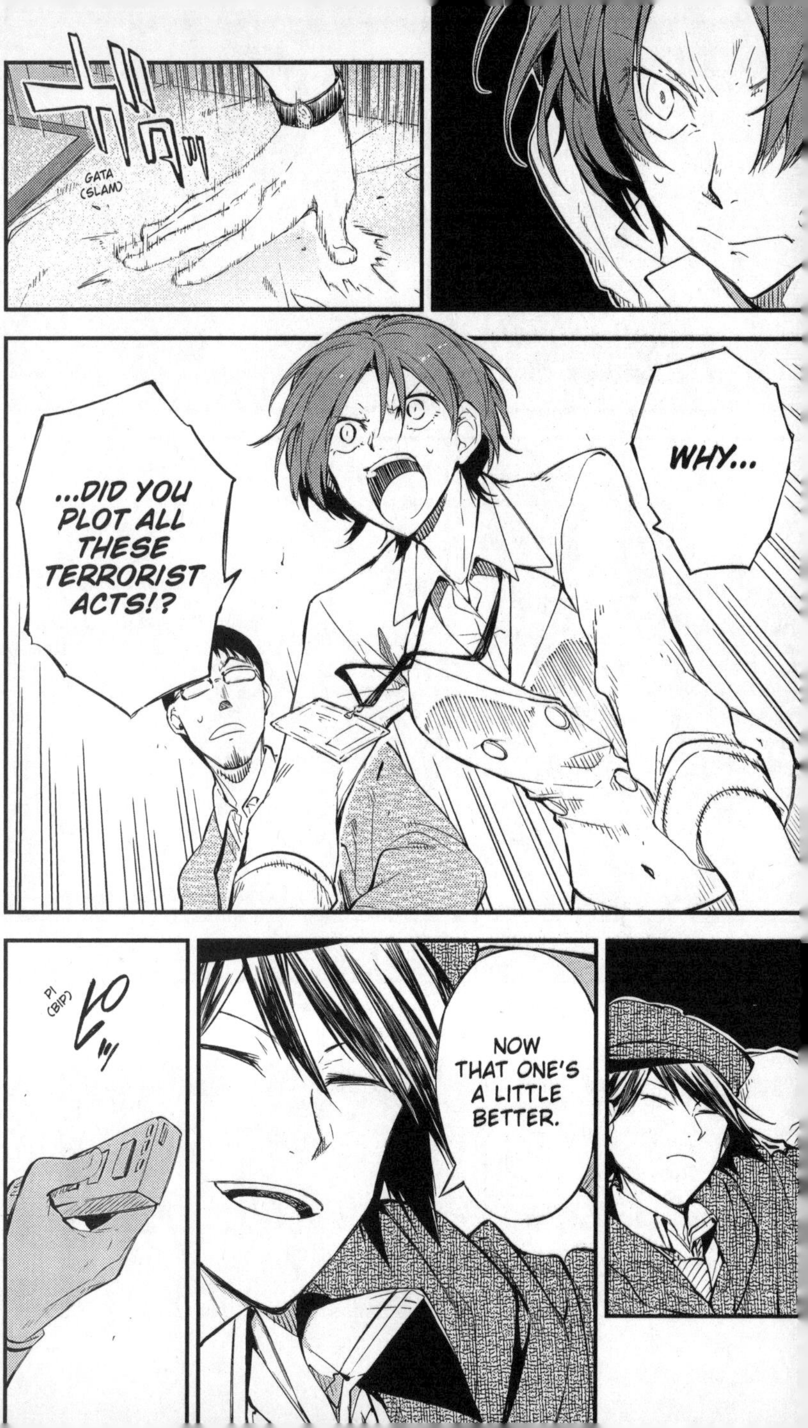
GATA
(SLAM)
WHY...
...DID YOU PLOT ALL THESE TERRORIST ACTS!?
NOW THAT ONE'S A LITTLE BETTER.
PI
(BIP)

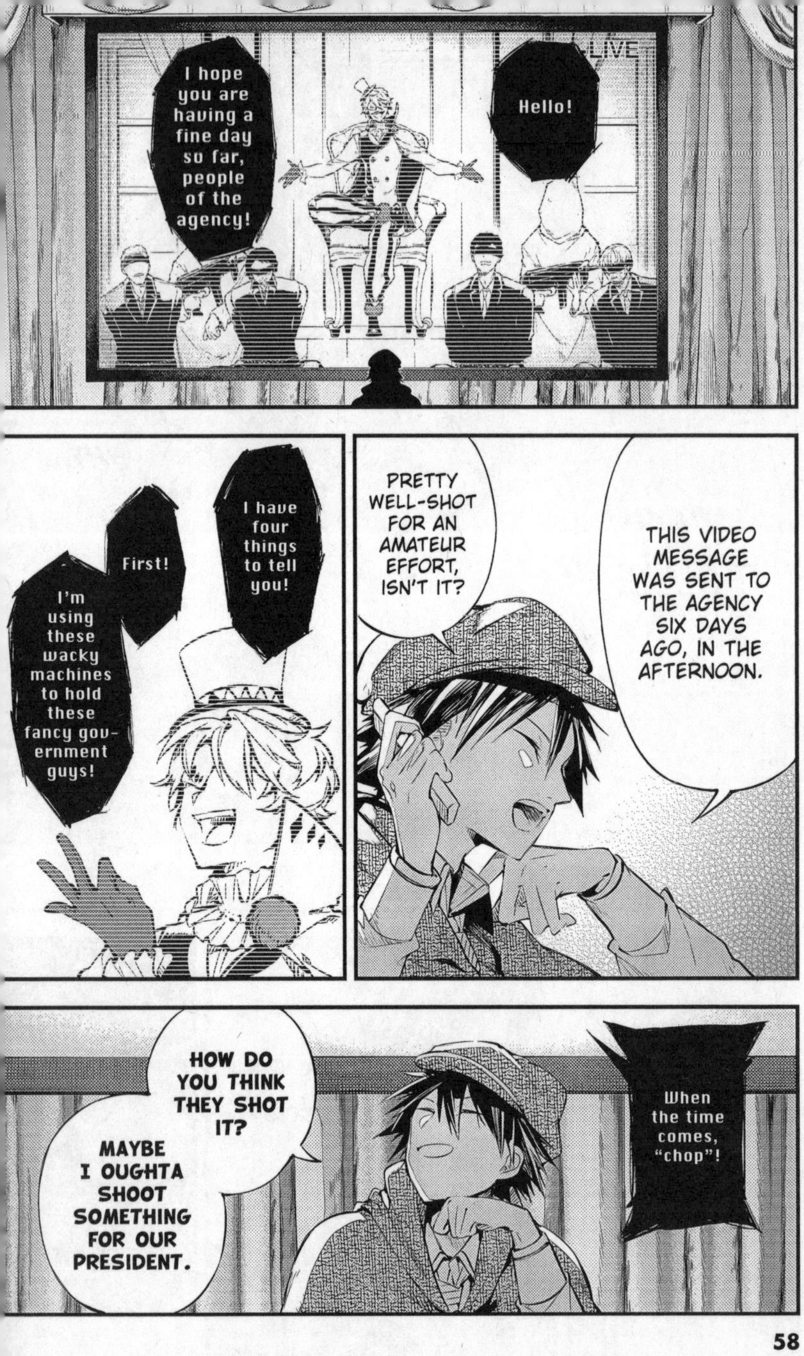
LIVE
Hello!
I hope you are having a fine day so far, people of the agency!
THIS VIDEO MESSAGE WAS SENT TO THE AGENCY SIX DAYS AGO, IN THE AFTERNOON.
PRETTY WELL-SHOT FOR AN AMATEUR EFFORT, ISN'T IT?
I have four things to tell you!
First!
I'm using these wacky machines to hold these fancy gov-ernment guys!
When the time comes, "chop"!
HOW DO YOU THINK THEY SHOT IT?
MAYBE I OUGHTA SHOOT SOMETHING FOR OUR PRESIDENT.

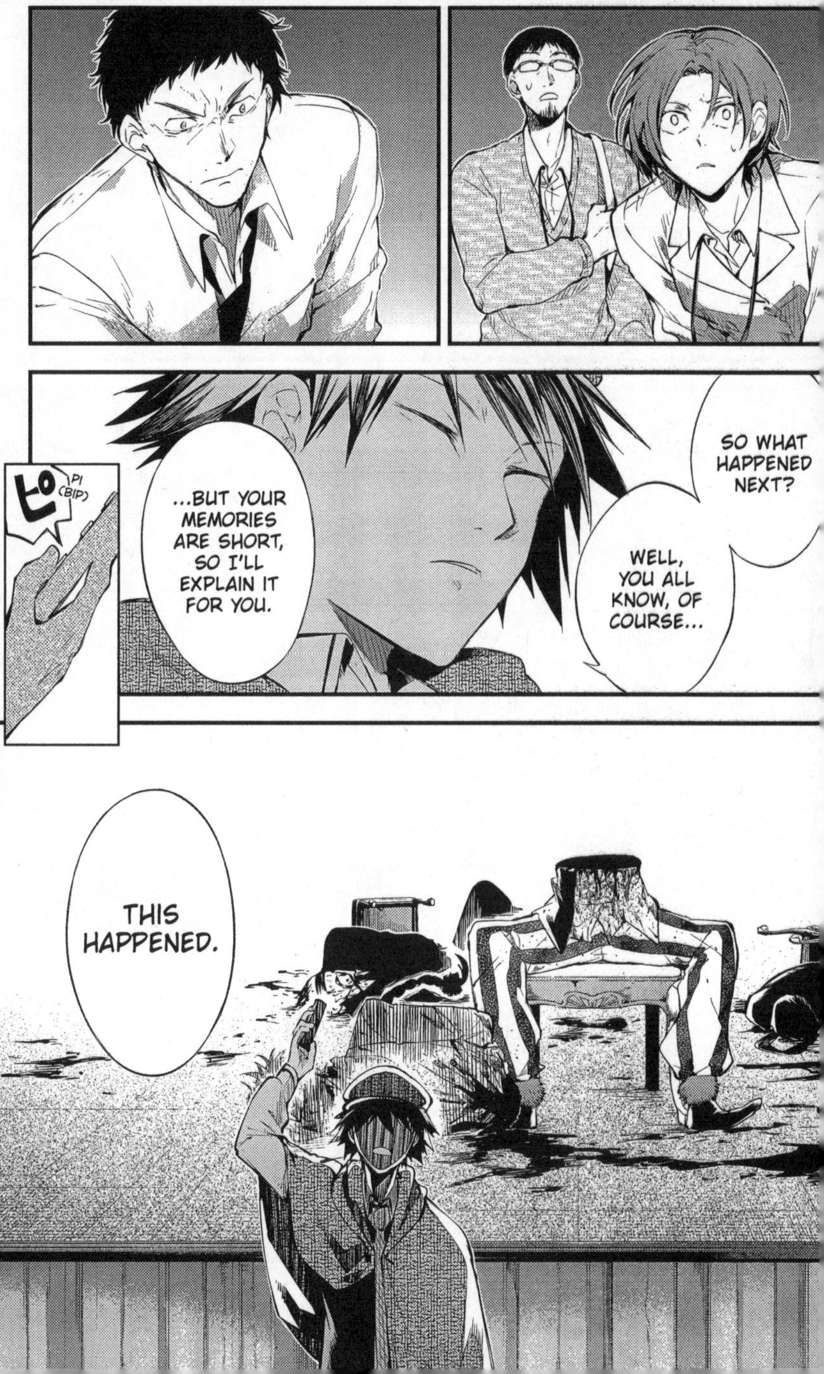
SO WHAT HAPPENED NEXT?
WELL, YOU ALL KNOW, OF COURSE...
...BUT YOUR MEMORIES ARE SHORT, SO I'LL EXPLAIN IT FOR YOU.
ピ
PI (BIP)
THIS HAPPENED.

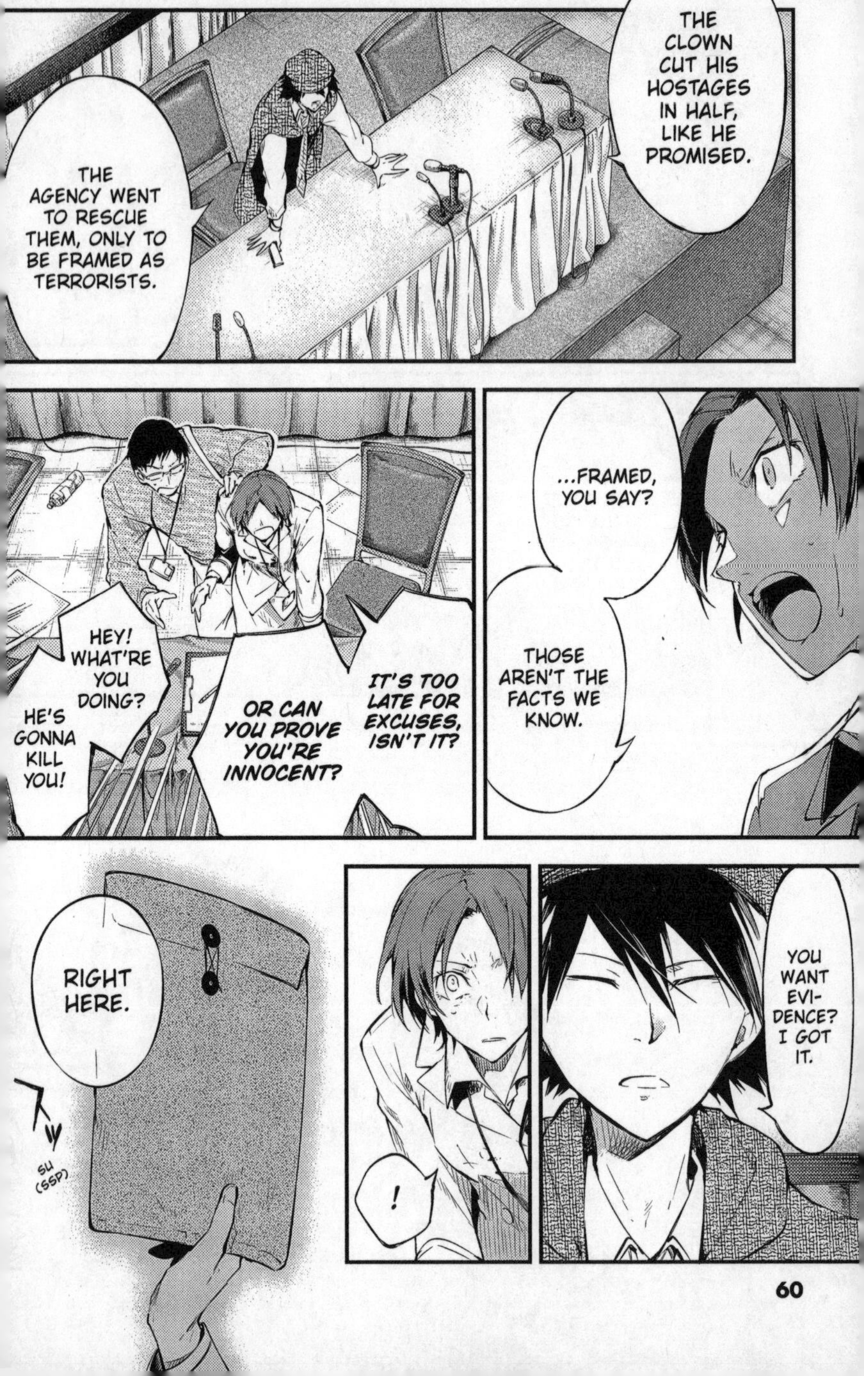
THE CLOWN CUT HIS HOSTAGES IN HALF, LIKE HE PROMISED.
THE AGENCY WENT TO RESCUE THEM, ONLY TO BE FRAMED AS TERRORISTS.
...FRAMED, YOU SAY?
THOSE AREN'T THE FACTS WE KNOW.
IT'S TOO LATE FOR EXCUSES, ISN'T IT?
OR CAN YOU PROVE YOU'RE INNOCENT?
HEY! WHAT'RE YOU DOING?
HE'S GONNA KILL YOU!
YOU WANT EVI-DENCE? I GOT IT.
!
RIGHT HERE.
SU (SSP)

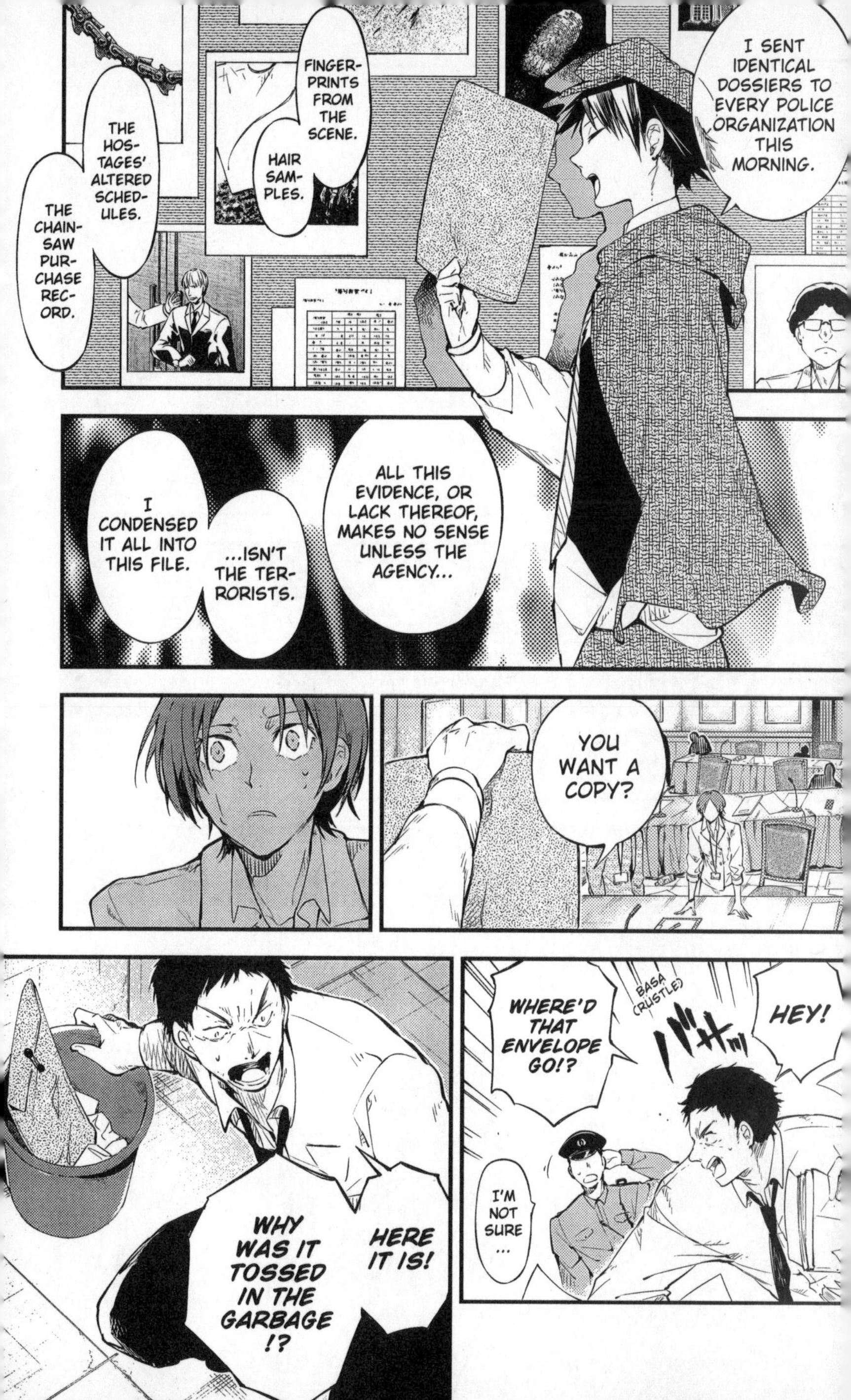
I SENT IDENTICAL DOSSIERS TO EVERY POLICE ORGANIZATION THIS MORNING.
FINGER-PRINTS FROM THE SCENE.
HAIR SAM-PLES.
THE HOS-TAGES' ALTERED SCHED-ULES.
THE CHAIN-SAW PUR-CHASE REC-ORD.
ALL THIS EVIDENCE, OR LACK THEREOF, MAKES NO SENSE UNLESS THE AGENCY...
...ISN'T THE TER-RORISTS.
I CONDENSED IT ALL INTO THIS FILE.
YOU WANT A COPY?
HEY!
BASA (RUSTLE)
WHERE'D THAT ENVELOPE GO!?
I'M NOT SURE ...
HERE IT IS!
WHY WAS IT TOSSED IN THE GARBAGE !?

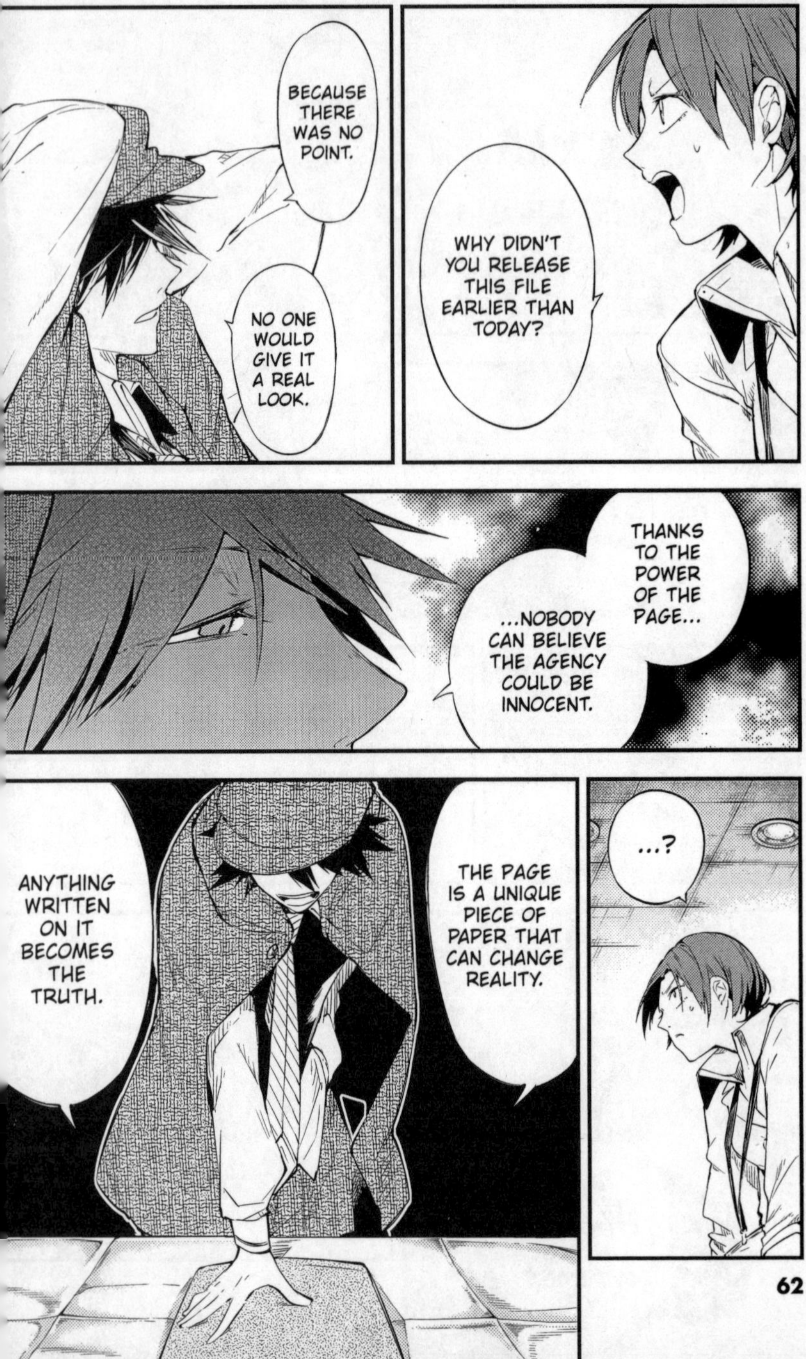
WHY DIDN'T YOU RELEASE THIS FILE EARLIER THAN TODAY?
BECAUSE THERE WAS NO POINT.
NO ONE WOULD GIVE IT A REAL LOOK.
THANKS TO THE POWER OF THE PAGE...
...NOBODY CAN BELIEVE THE AGENCY COULD BE INNOCENT.
...?
THE PAGE IS A UNIQUE PIECE OF PAPER THAT CAN CHANGE REALITY.
ANYTHING WRITTEN ON IT BECOMES THE TRUTH.

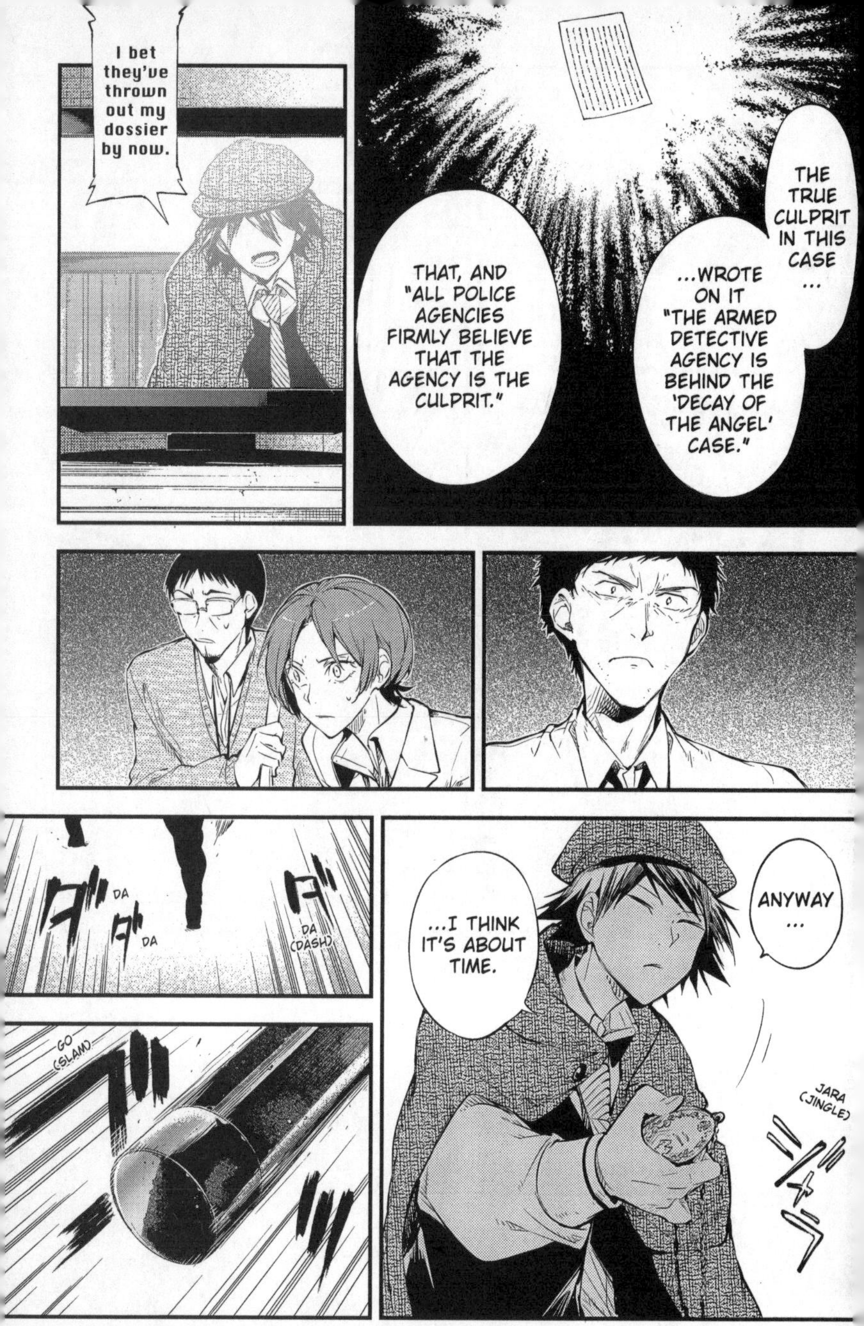
THE TRUE CULPRIT IN THIS CASE ...
...WROTE ON IT "THE ARMED DETECTIVE AGENCY IS BEHIND THE 'DECAY OF THE ANGEL' CASE."
THAT, AND "ALL POLICE AGENCIES FIRMLY BELIEVE THAT THE AGENCY IS THE CULPRIT."
I bet they've thrown out my dossier by now.
ANYWAY ...
...I THINK IT'S ABOUT TIME.
JARA (JINGLE)
DA
DA
DA (DASH)
GO (SLAM)

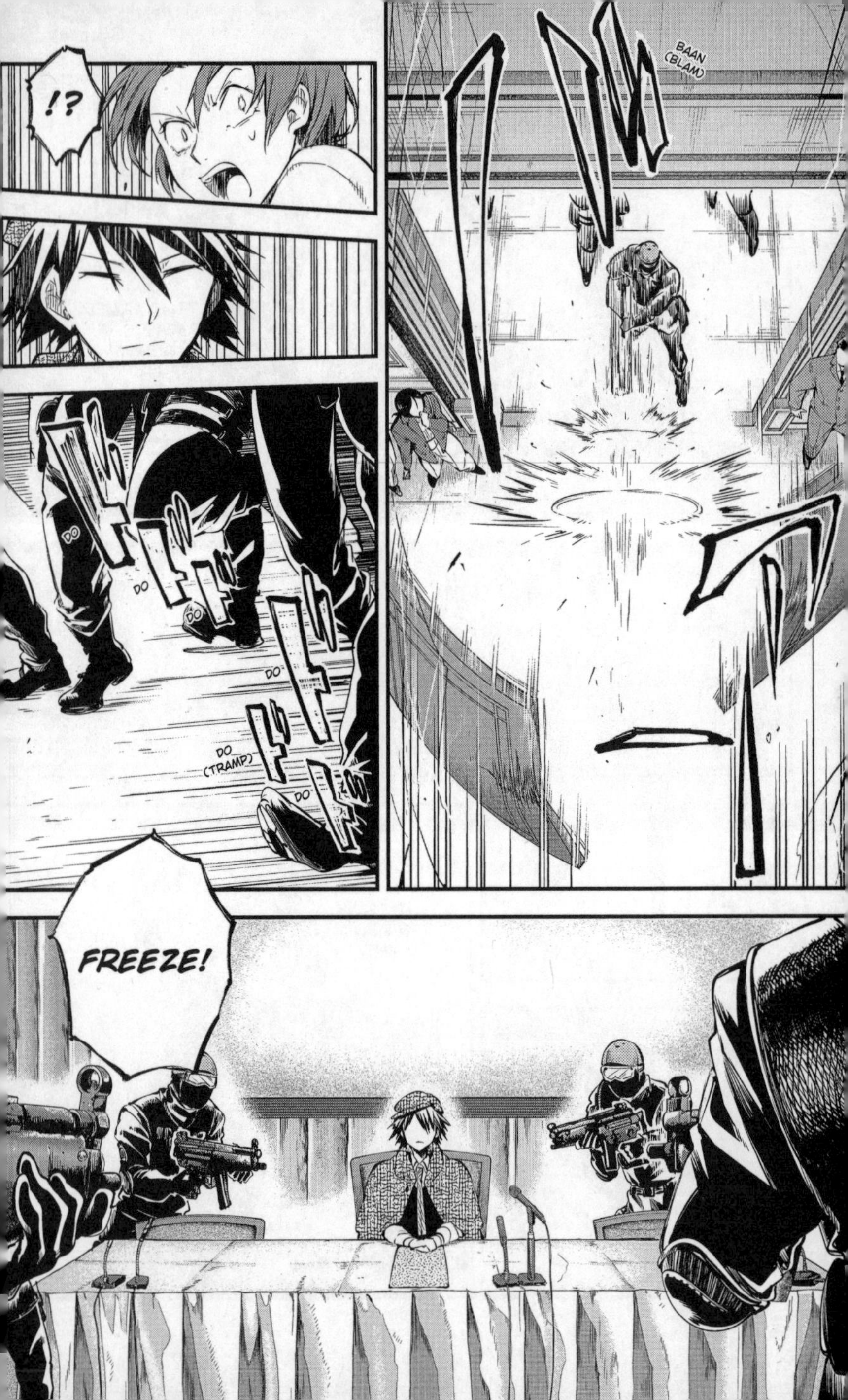
BAAN
(BLAM)
!?
DO
DO
DO
DO
(TRAMP)
DO
FREEZE!

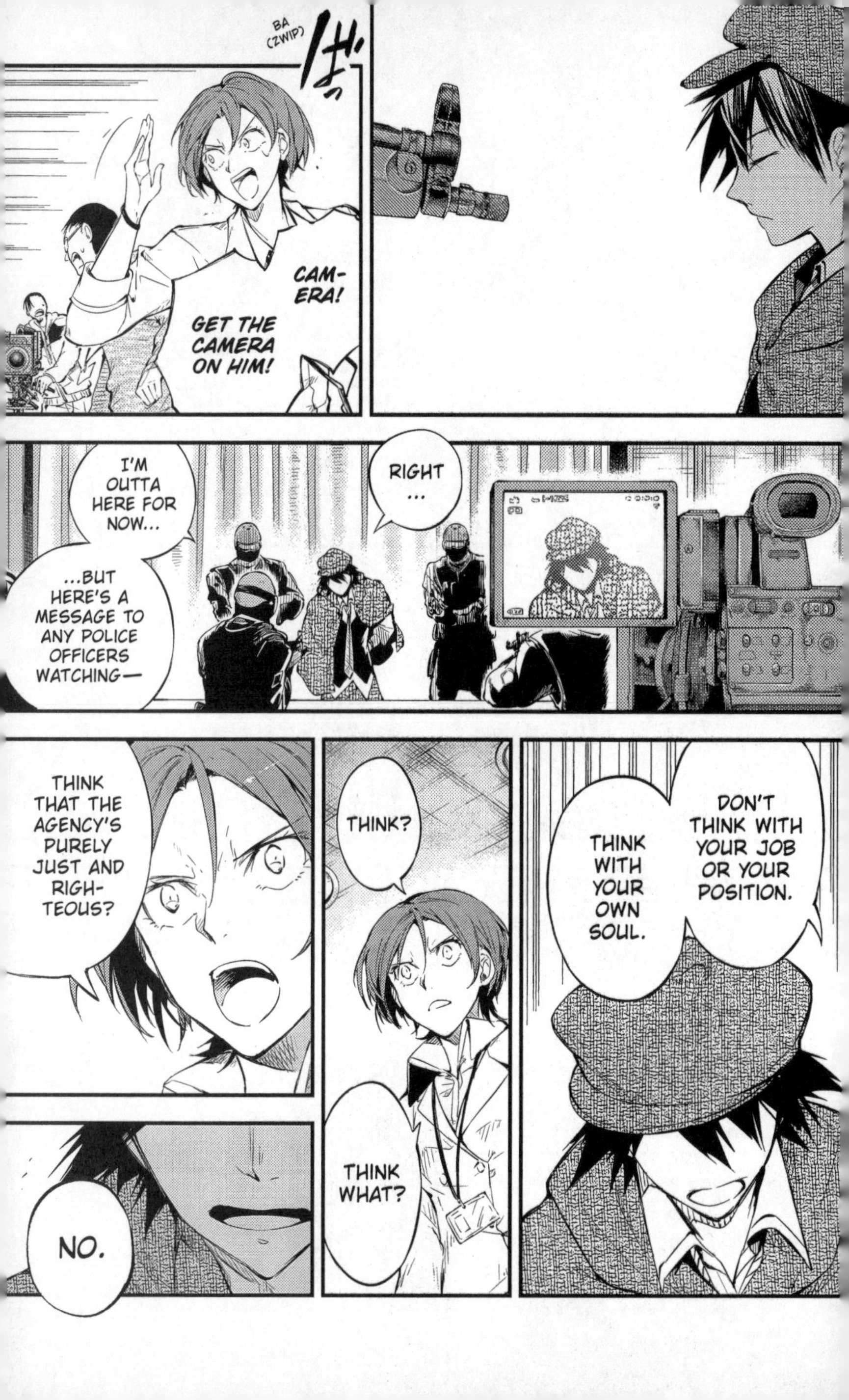
BA (ZWIP)
CAM-ERA!
GET THE CAMERA ON HIM!
RIGHT ...
I'M OUTTA HERE FOR NOW...
...BUT HERE'S A MESSAGE TO ANY POLICE OFFICERS WATCHING—
DON'T THINK WITH YOUR JOB OR YOUR POSITION.
THINK WITH YOUR OWN SOUL.
THINK?
THINK WHAT?
THINK THAT THE AGENCY'S PURELY JUST AND RIGH-TEOUS?
NO.

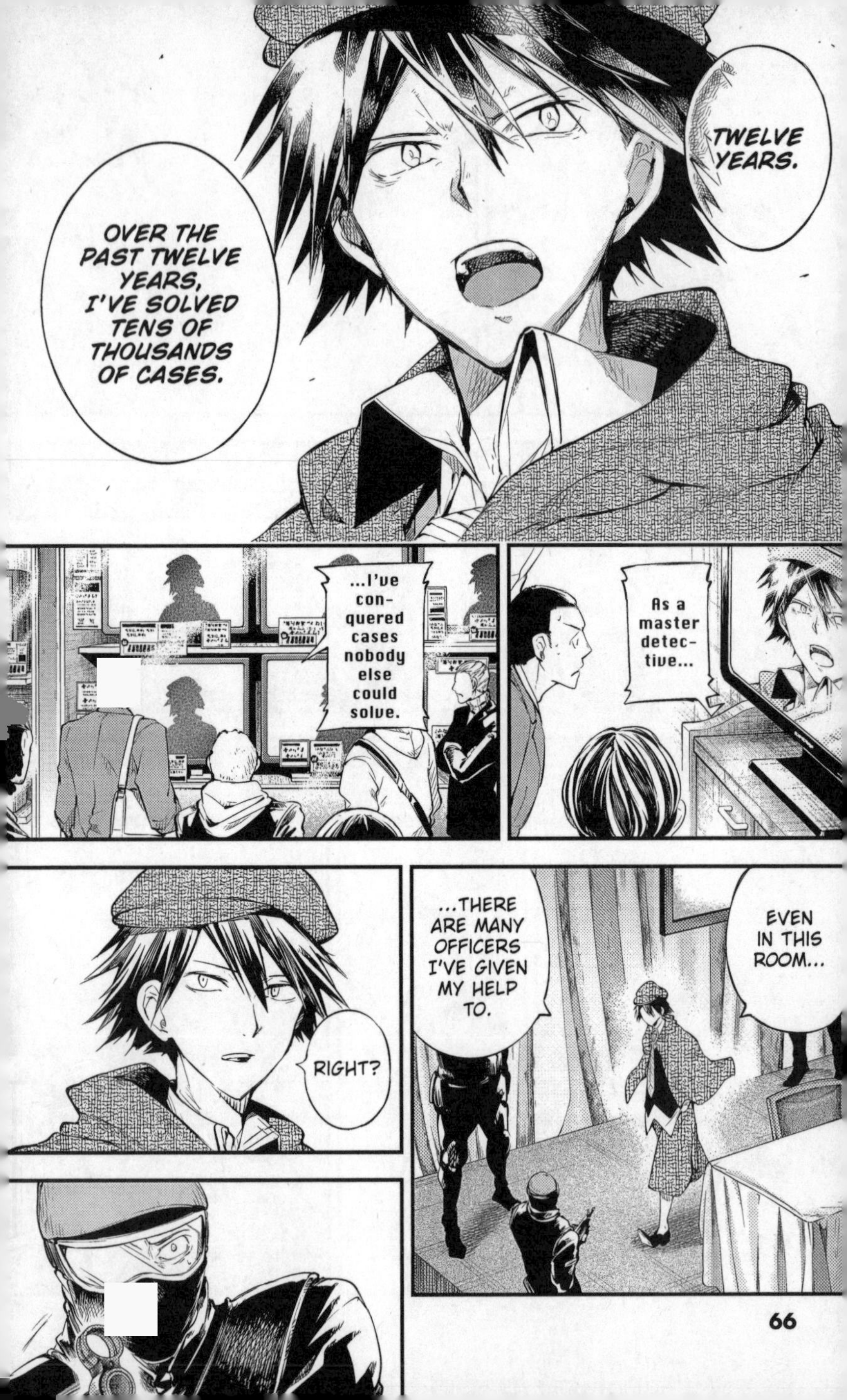
TWELVE YEARS.
OVER THE PAST TWELVE YEARS, I'VE SOLVED TENS OF THOUSANDS OF CASES.
As a master detective...
...I've conquered cases nobody else could solve.
EVEN IN THIS ROOM...
...THERE ARE MANY OFFICERS I'VE GIVEN MY HELP TO.
RIGHT?

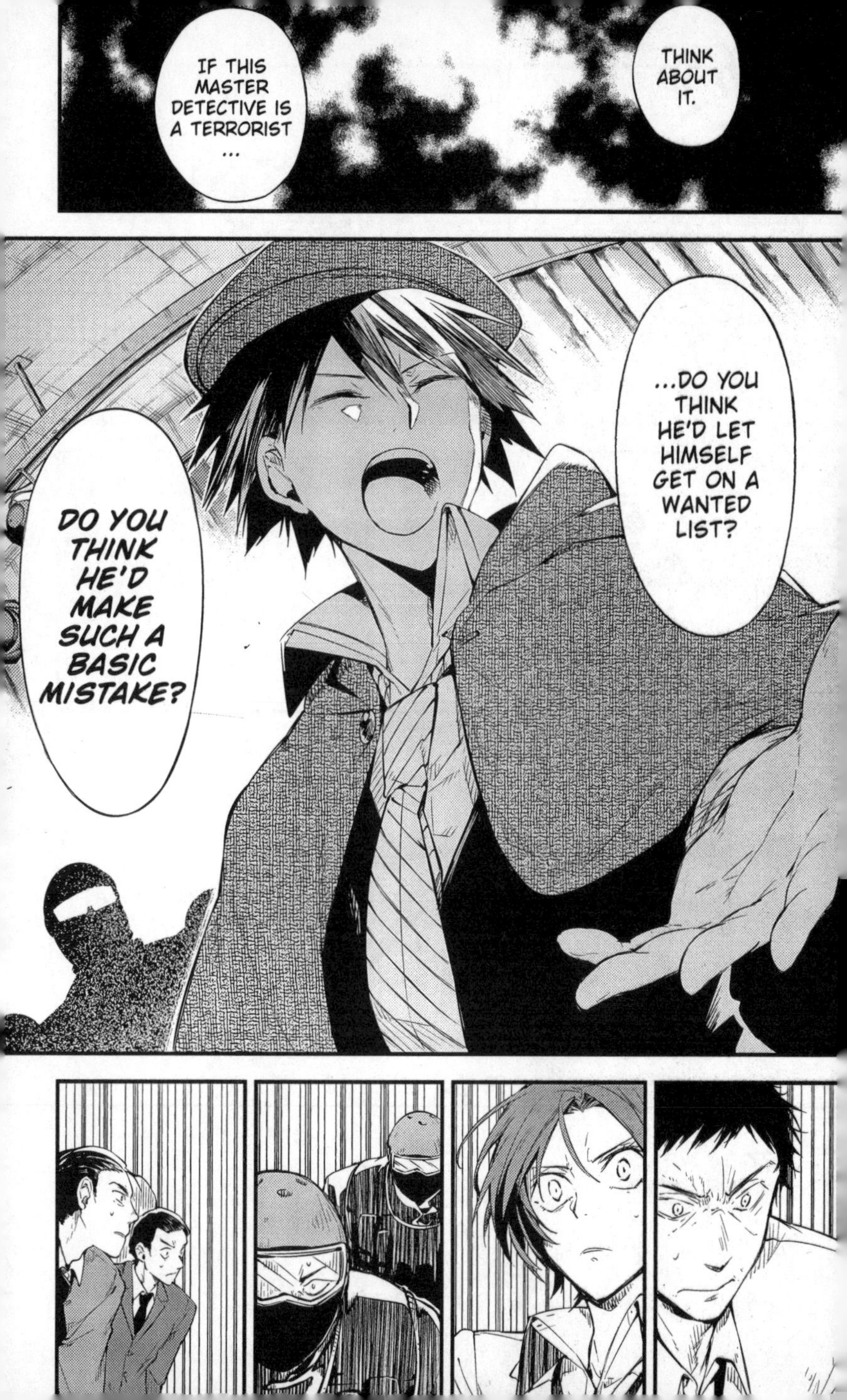
THINK ABOUT IT.
IF THIS MASTER DETECTIVE IS A TERRORIST...
...DO YOU THINK HE'D LET HIMSELF GET ON A WANTED LIST?
DO YOU THINK HE'D MAKE SUCH A BASIC MISTAKE?

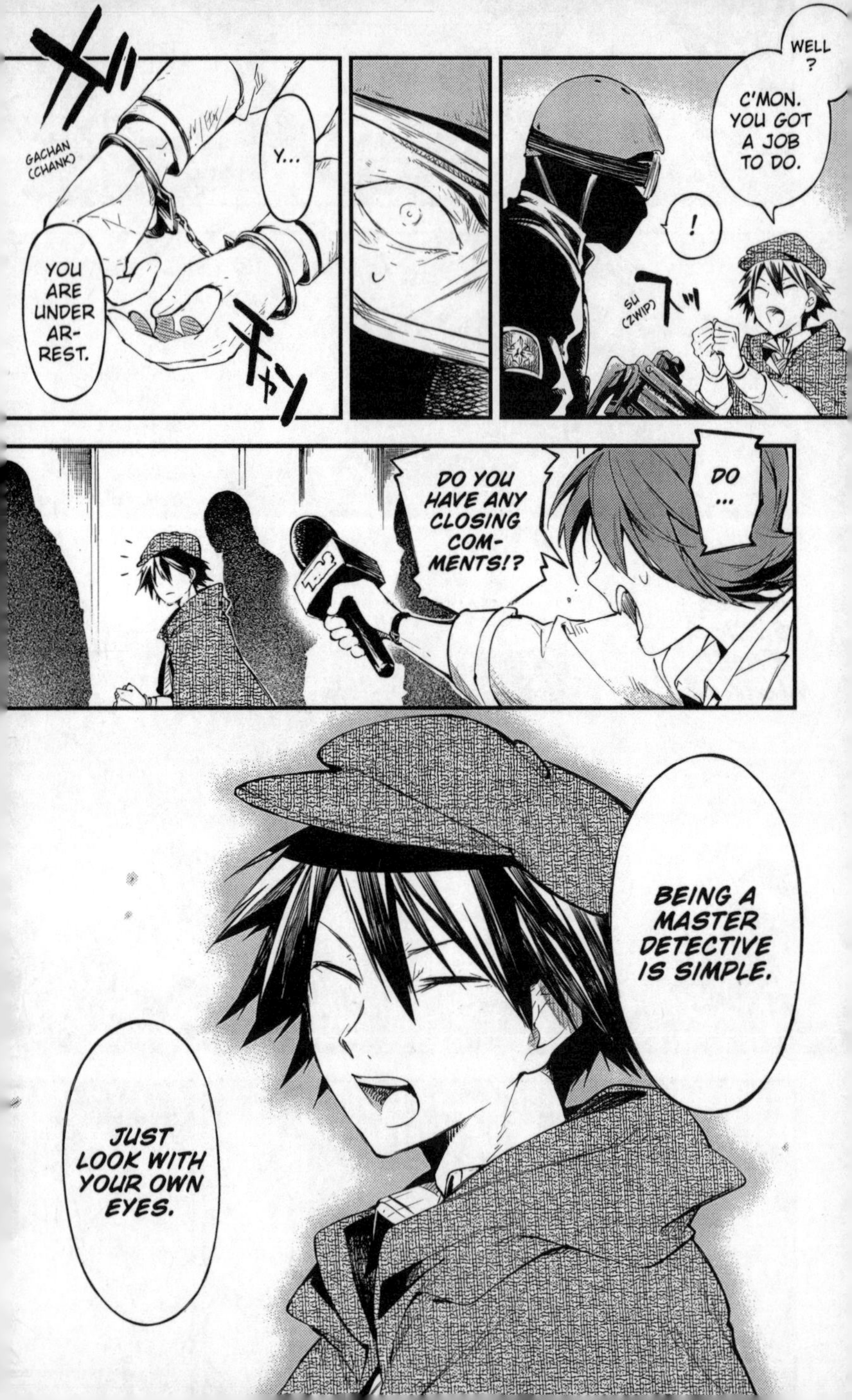
WELL ?
C'MON. YOU GOT A JOB TO DO.
!
SU (ZWIP)
Y...
GACHAN (CHANK)
YOU ARE UNDER AR- REST.
DO ...
DO YOU HAVE ANY CLOSING COM- MENTS!?
BEING A MASTER DETECTIVE IS SIMPLE.
JUST LOOK WITH YOUR OWN EYES.

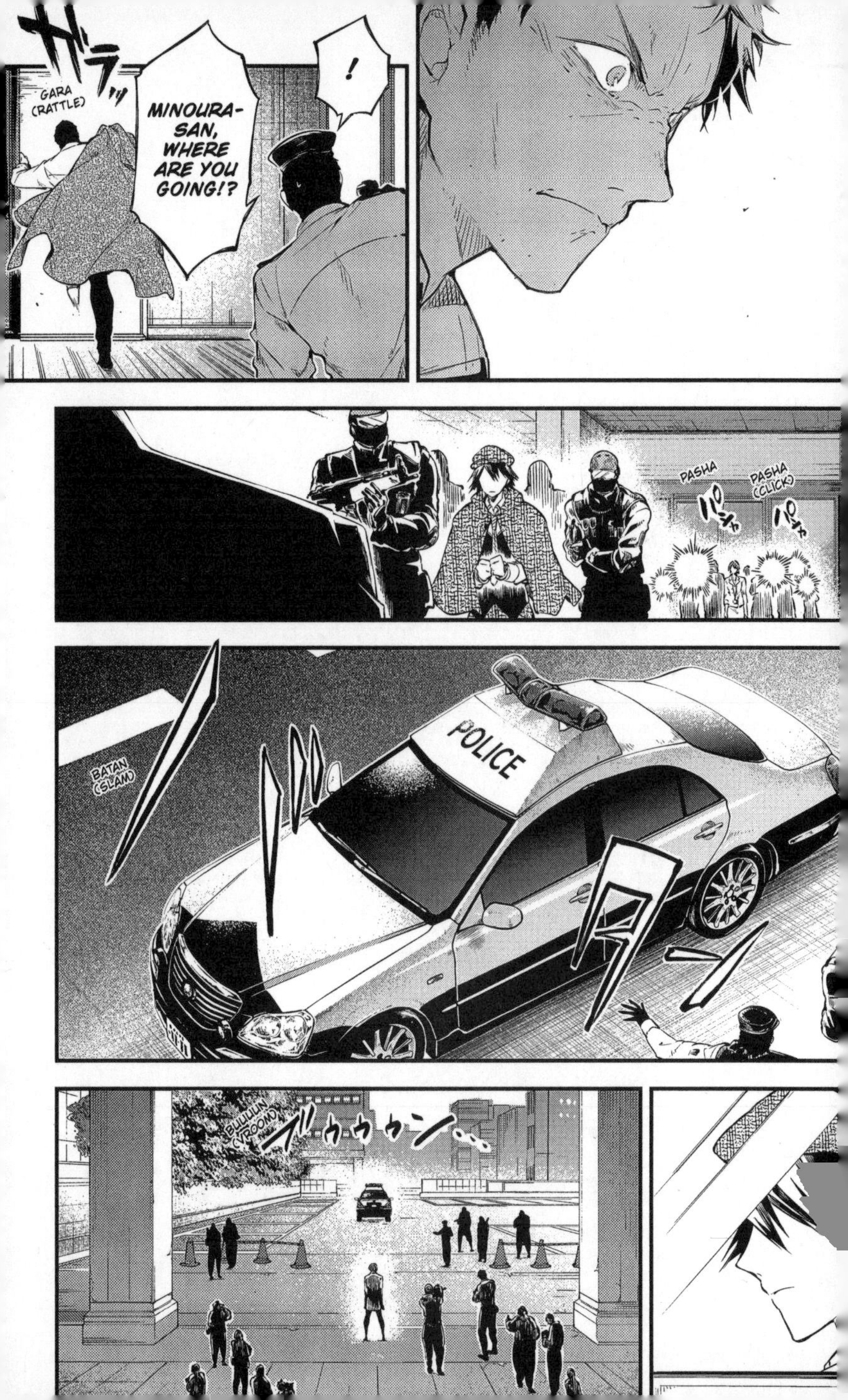
!
MINOURA-SAN, WHERE ARE YOU GOING!?
ガラッ
GARA (RATTLE)
PASHA (CLICK)
パシャ
PASHA
パシャ
POLICE
BATAN (SLAM)
BUUUUN (VROOM)
ブゥゥゥン…

BUNGO
STRAY DOGS

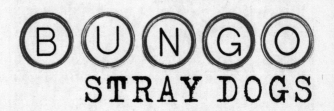

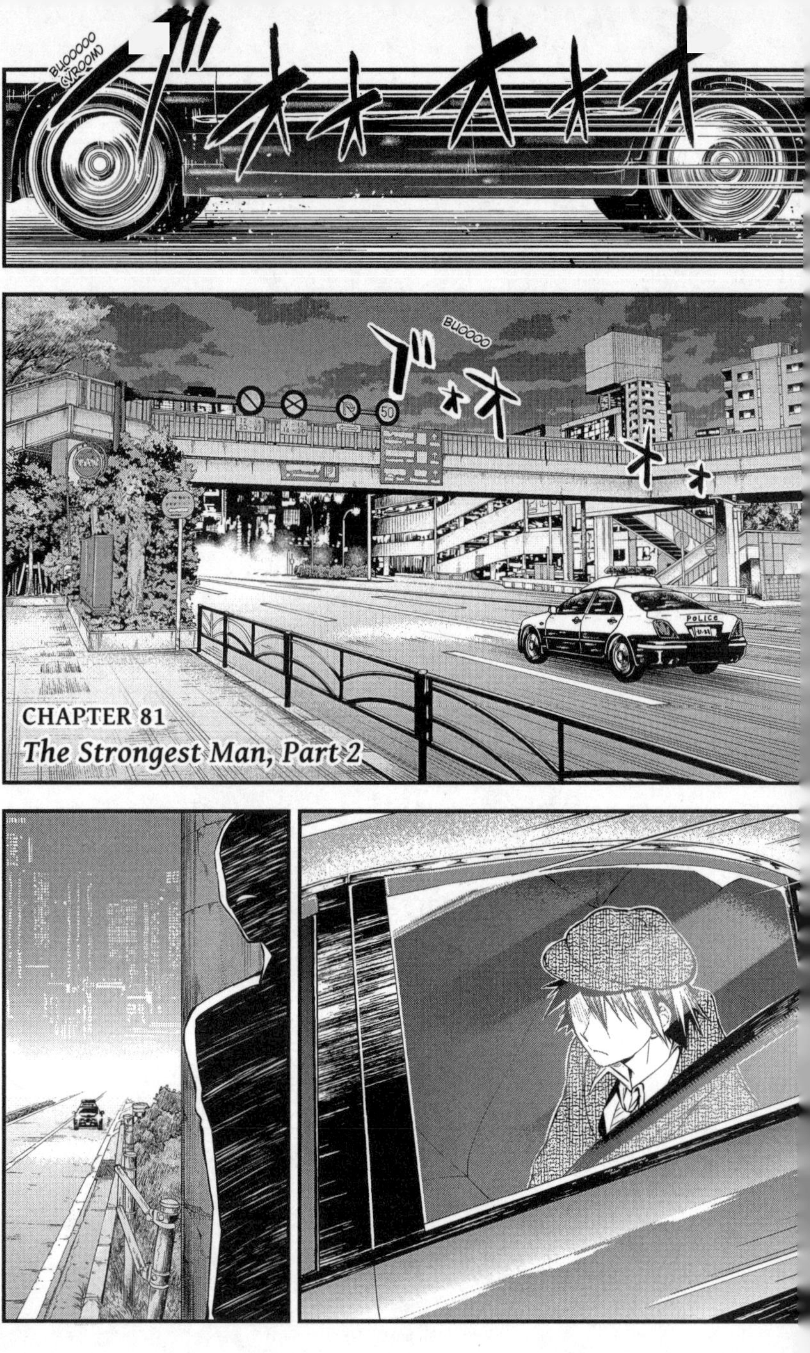
BUOOOOO (VROOM)
BUOOOO
CHAPTER 81
The Strongest Man, Part 2

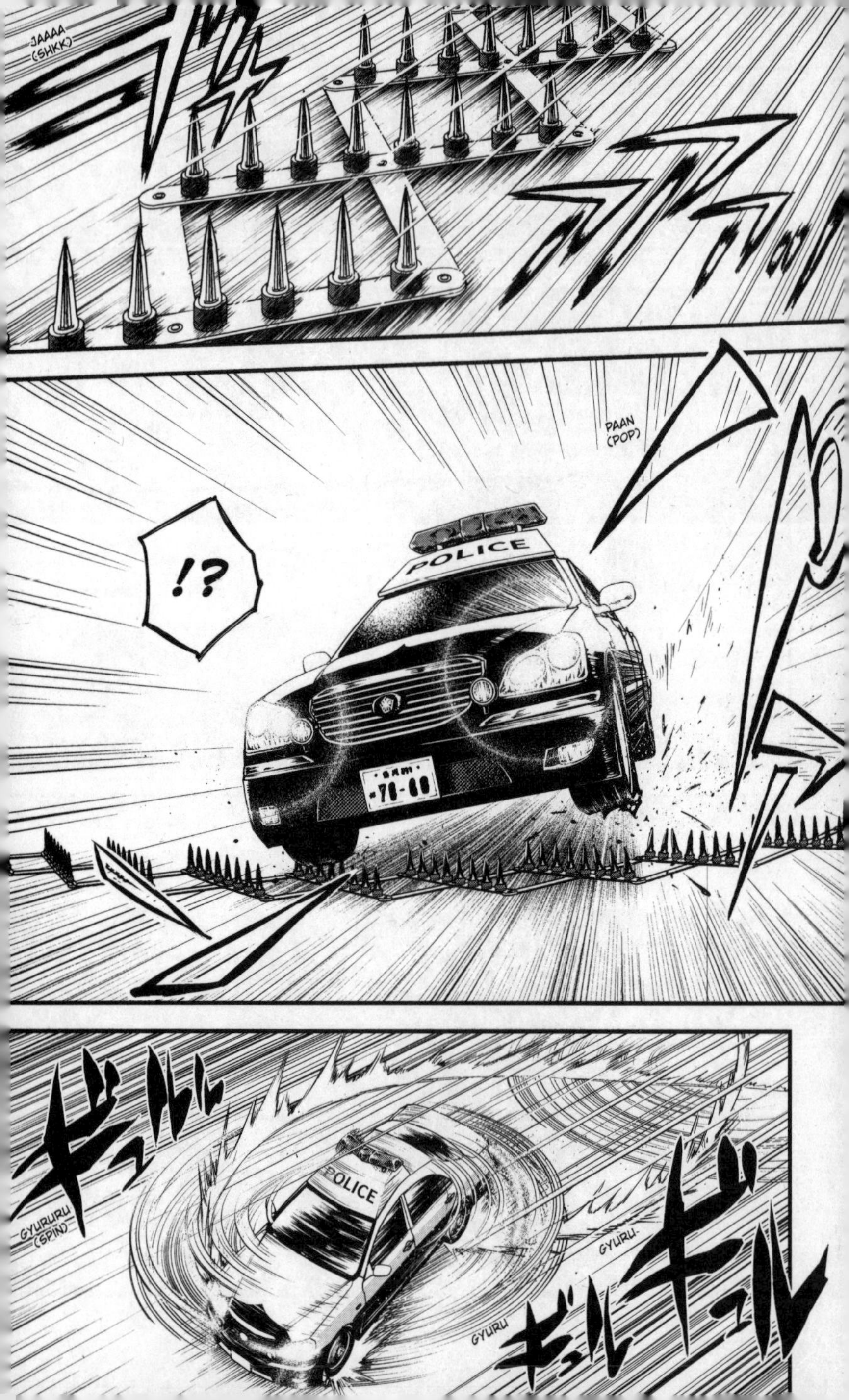
JAAAA
(SHKK)
PAAN
(POP)
!?
GYURU-
GYURU
GYURURU
(SPIN)

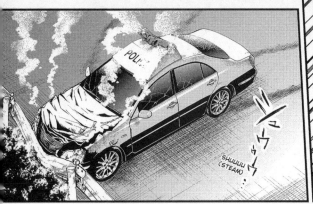

SHUUUU
(STEAM)

DOON
(BOOM)

GACHA
(GACHAK)

OOH
...

OUT OF THE CAR.

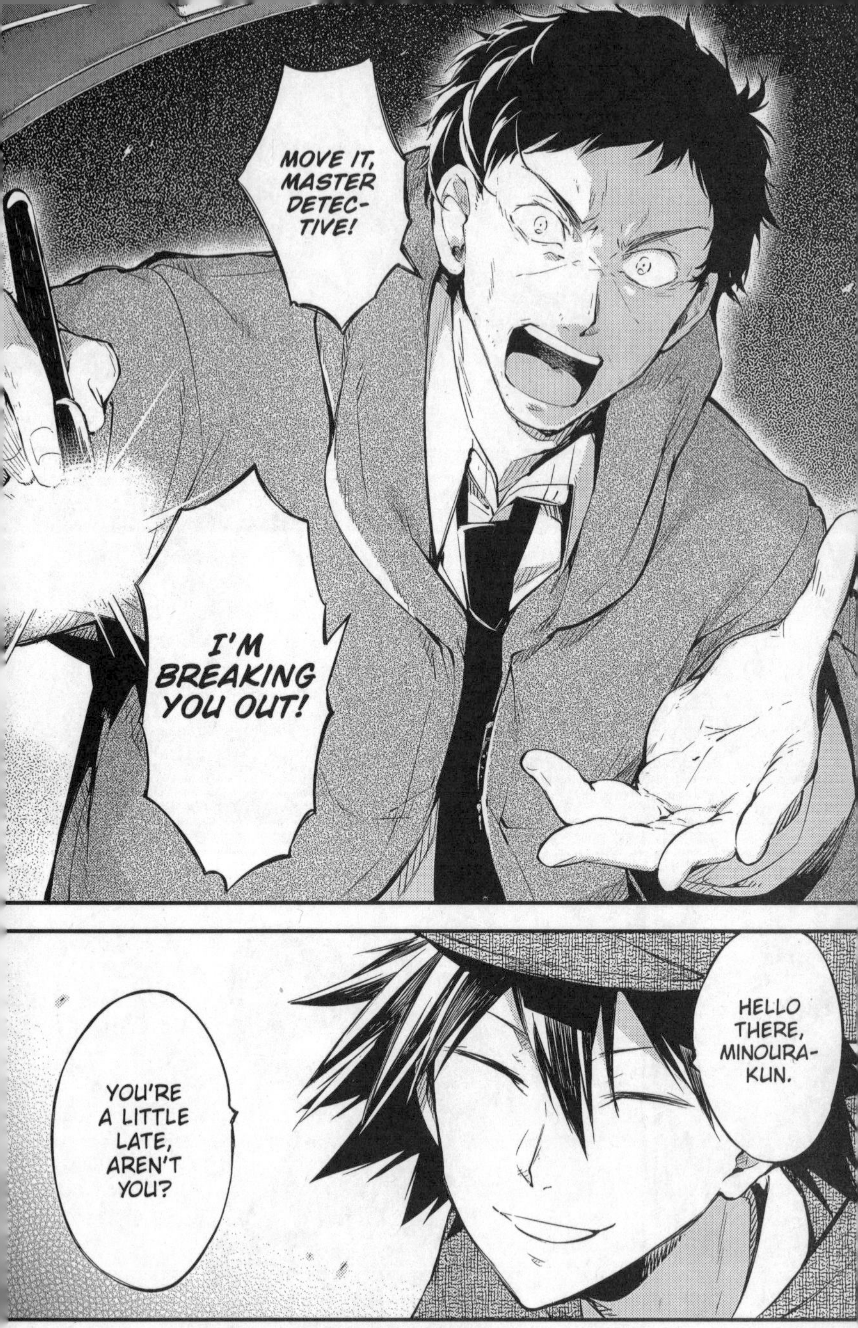
MOVE IT, MASTER DETECTIVE!
I'M BREAKING YOU OUT!
HELLO THERE, MINOURA-KUN.
YOU'RE A LITTLE LATE, AREN'T YOU?

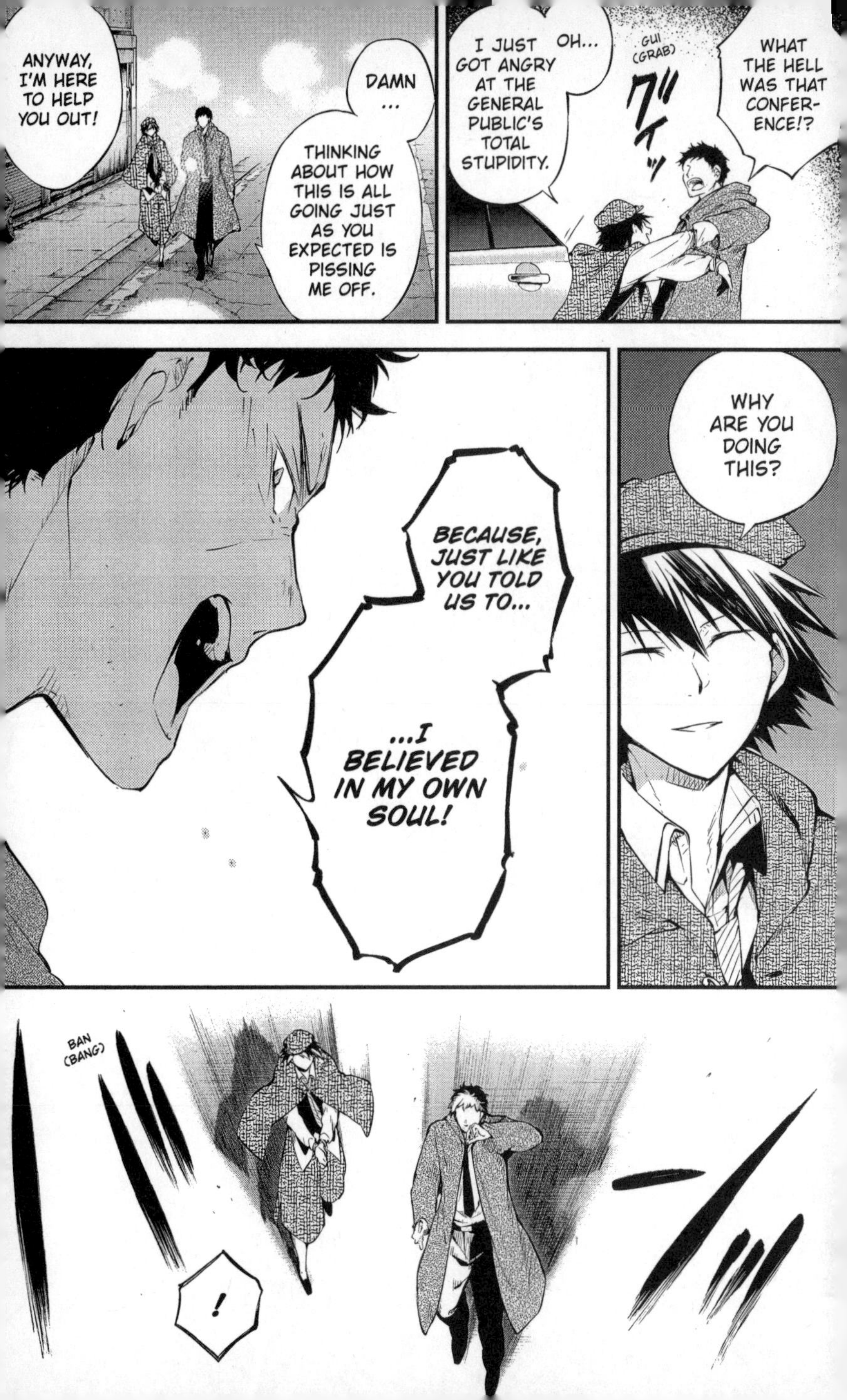
WHAT THE HELL WAS THAT CONFERENCE!?
GUI (GRAB)
OH... I JUST GOT ANGRY AT THE GENERAL PUBLIC'S TOTAL STUPIDITY.
DAMN ... THINKING ABOUT HOW THIS IS ALL GOING JUST AS YOU EXPECTED IS PISSING ME OFF.
ANYWAY, I'M HERE TO HELP YOU OUT!
WHY ARE YOU DOING THIS?
BECAUSE, JUST LIKE YOU TOLD US TO...
...I BELIEVED IN MY OWN SOUL!
BAN (BANG)
!

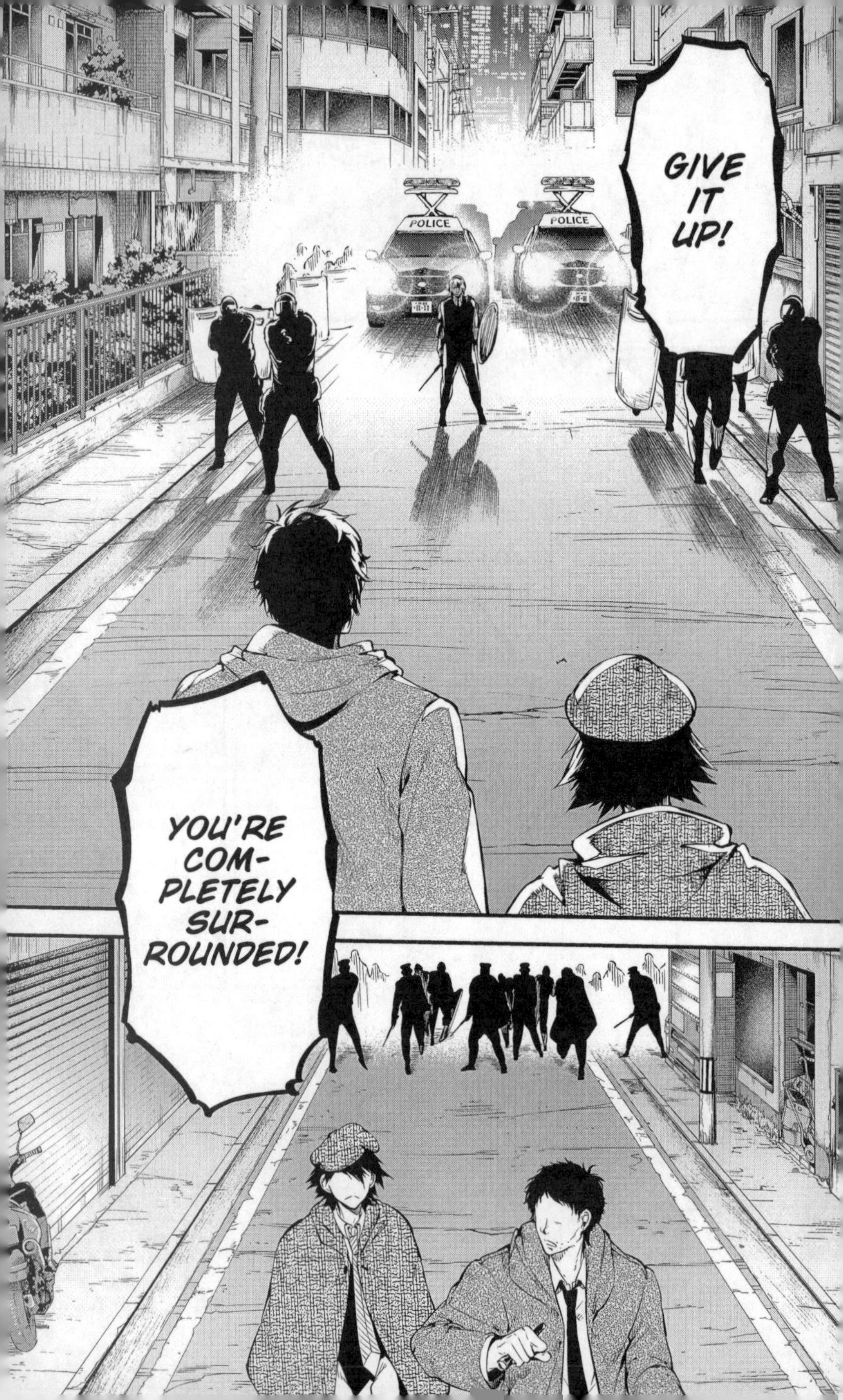
GIVE IT UP!
POLICE
POLICE
YOU'RE COM-PLETELY SUR-ROUNDED!

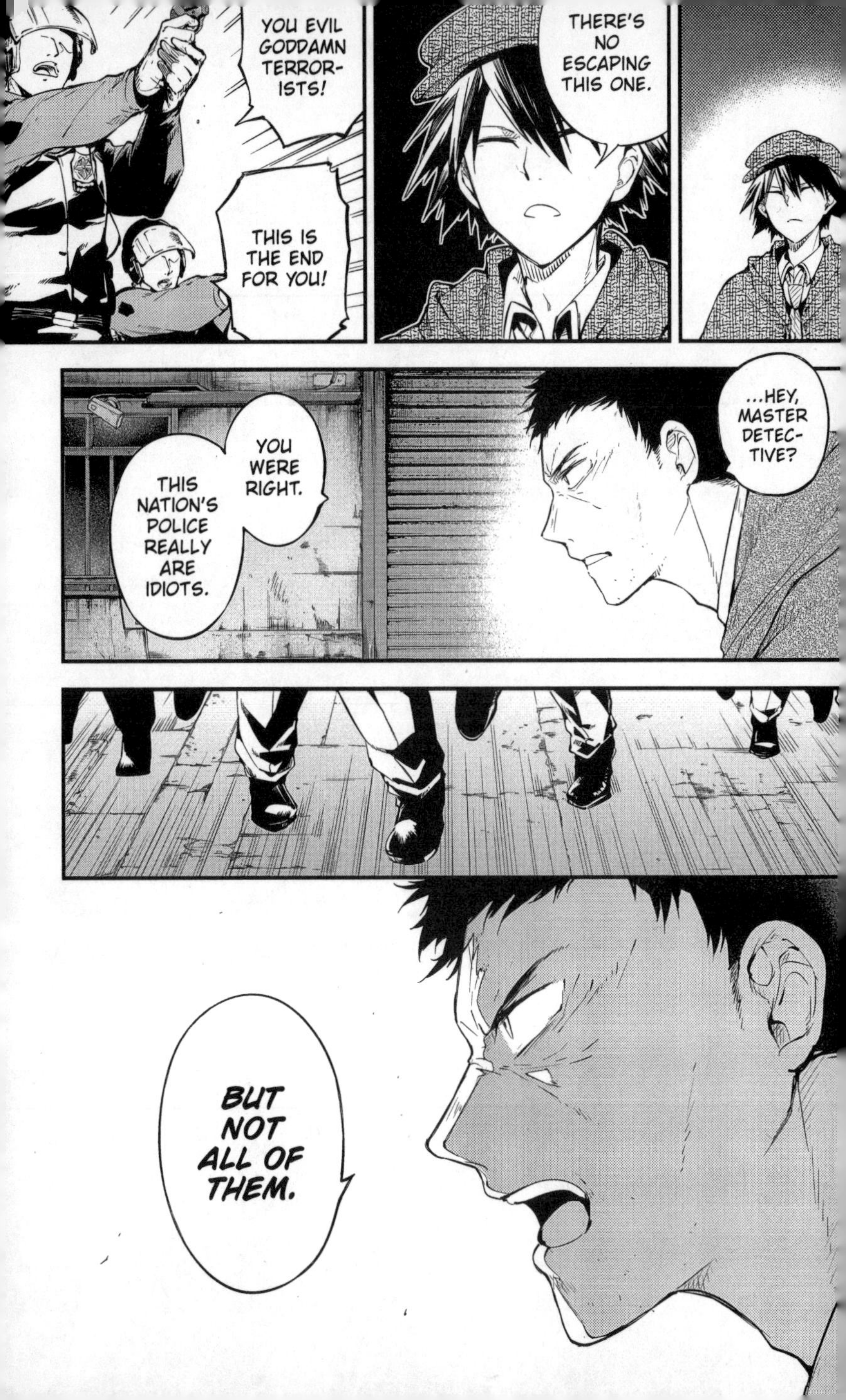
THERE'S NO ESCAPING THIS ONE.
YOU EVIL GODDAMN TERROR-ISTS!
THIS IS THE END FOR YOU!
...HEY, MASTER DETEC-TIVE?
YOU WERE RIGHT.
THIS NATION'S POLICE REALLY ARE IDIOTS.
BUT NOT ALL OF THEM.

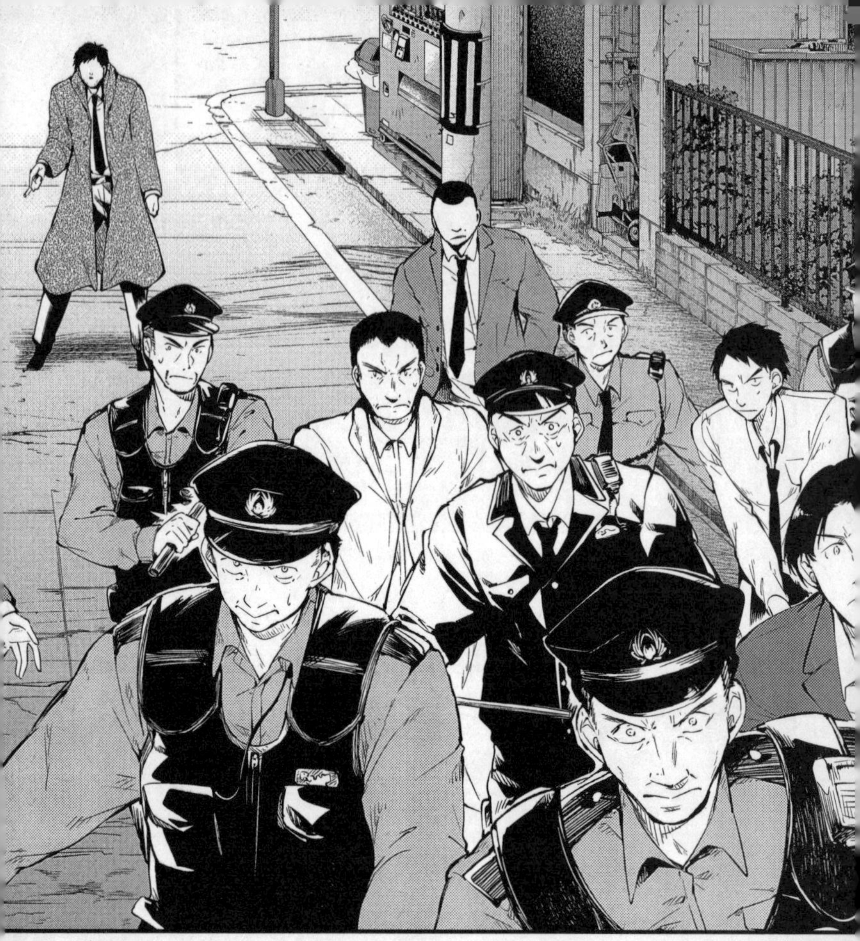

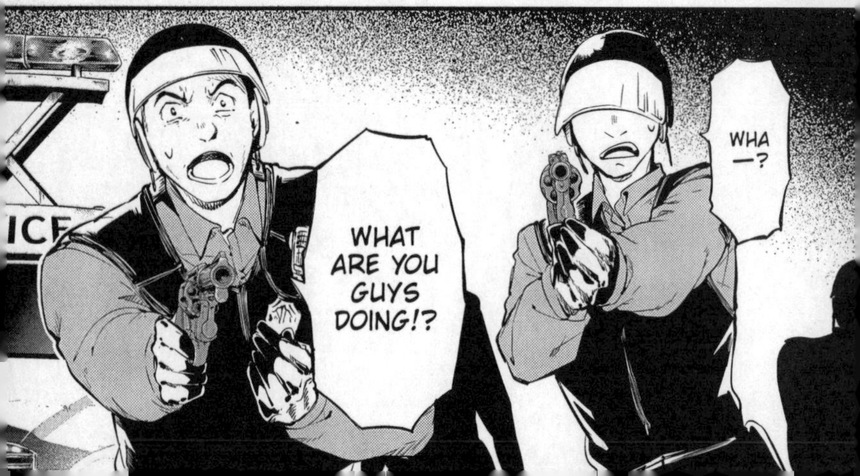
WHA—?
WHAT ARE YOU GUYS DOING!?

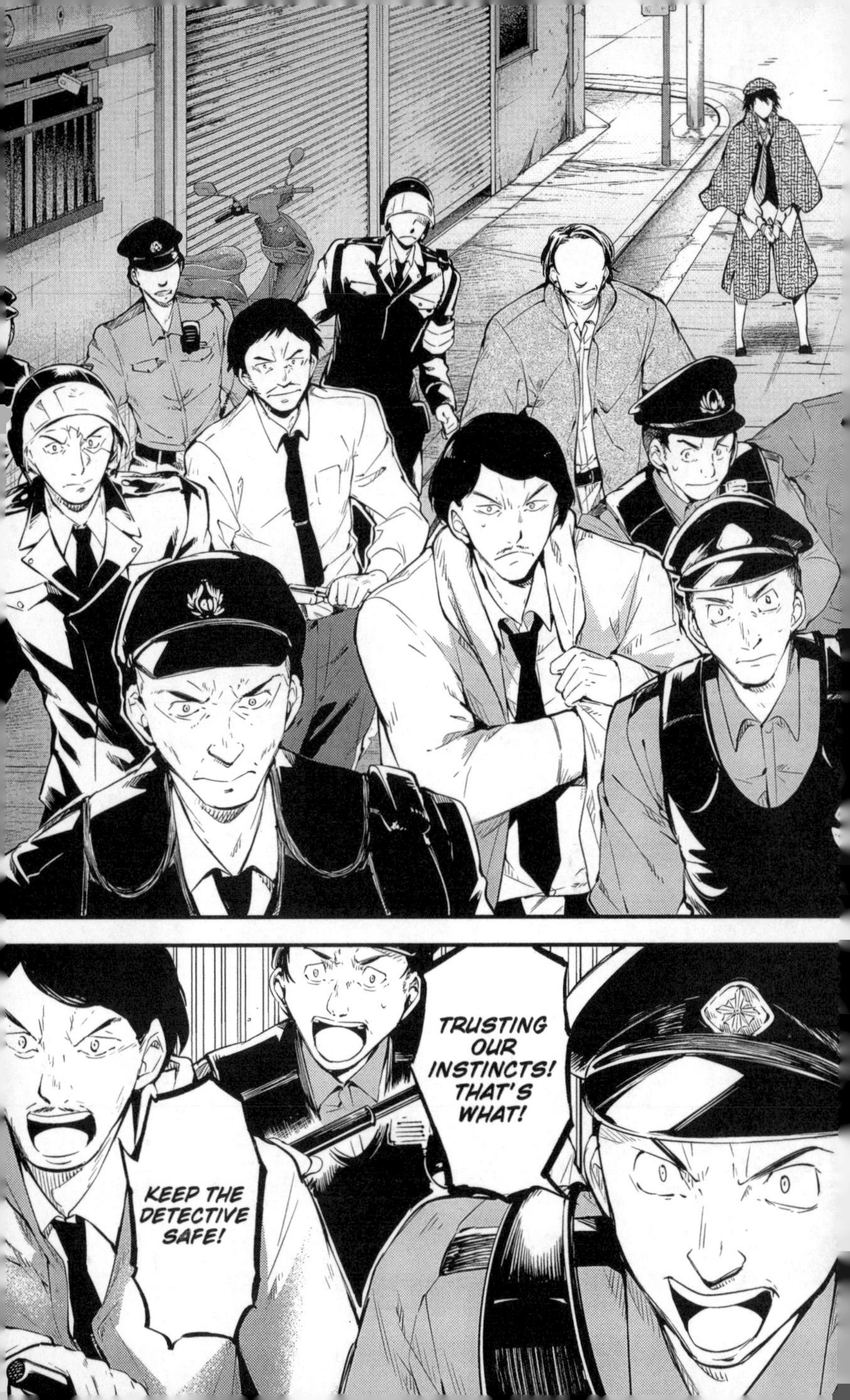
TRUSTING OUR INSTINCTS! THAT'S WHAT!
KEEP THE DETECTIVE SAFE!

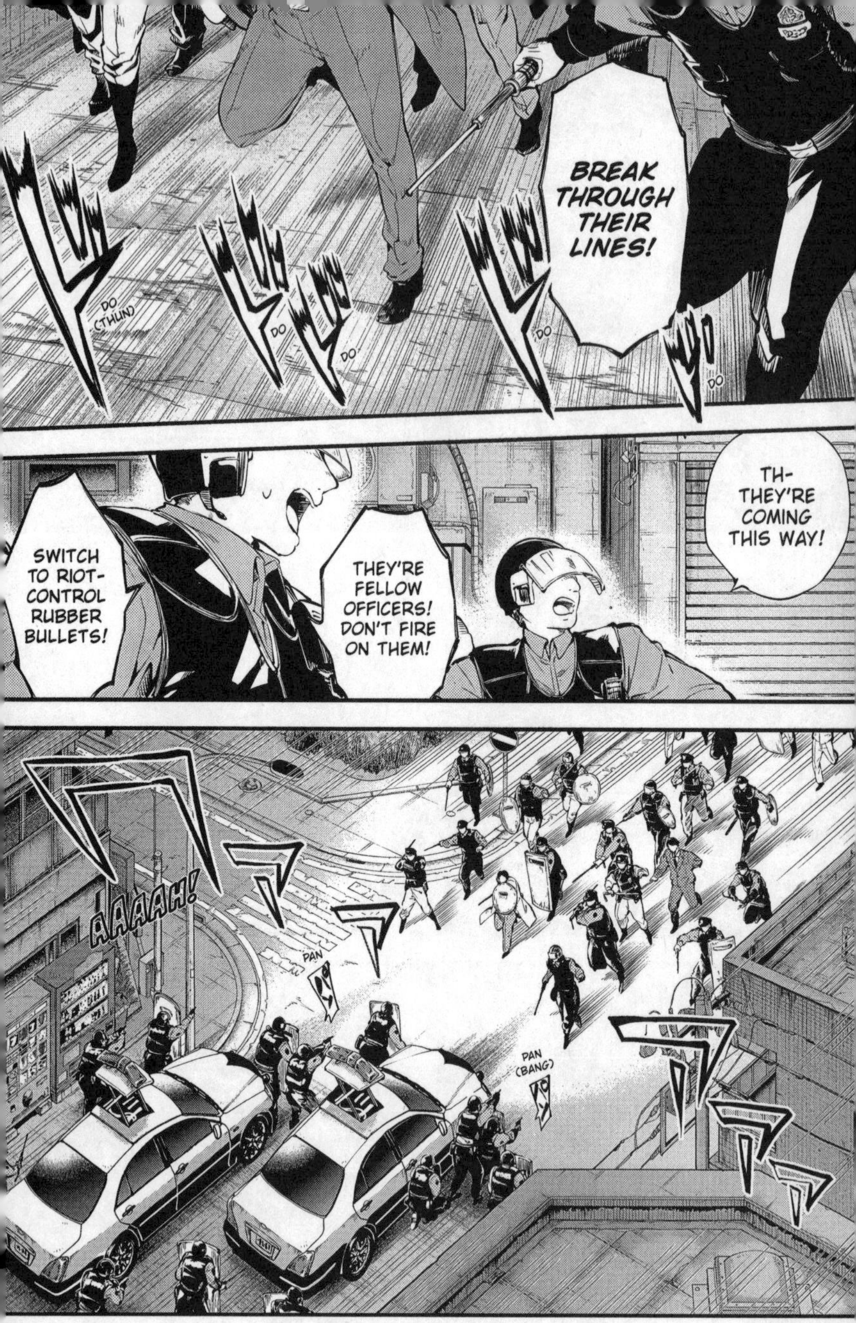
BREAK THROUGH THEIR LINES!
DO
DO
DO
DO
DO (THUD)
TH- THEY'RE COMING THIS WAY!
THEY'RE FELLOW OFFICERS! DON'T FIRE ON THEM!
SWITCH TO RIOT-CONTROL RUBBER BULLETS!
PAN (BANG)
PAN
AAAAH!

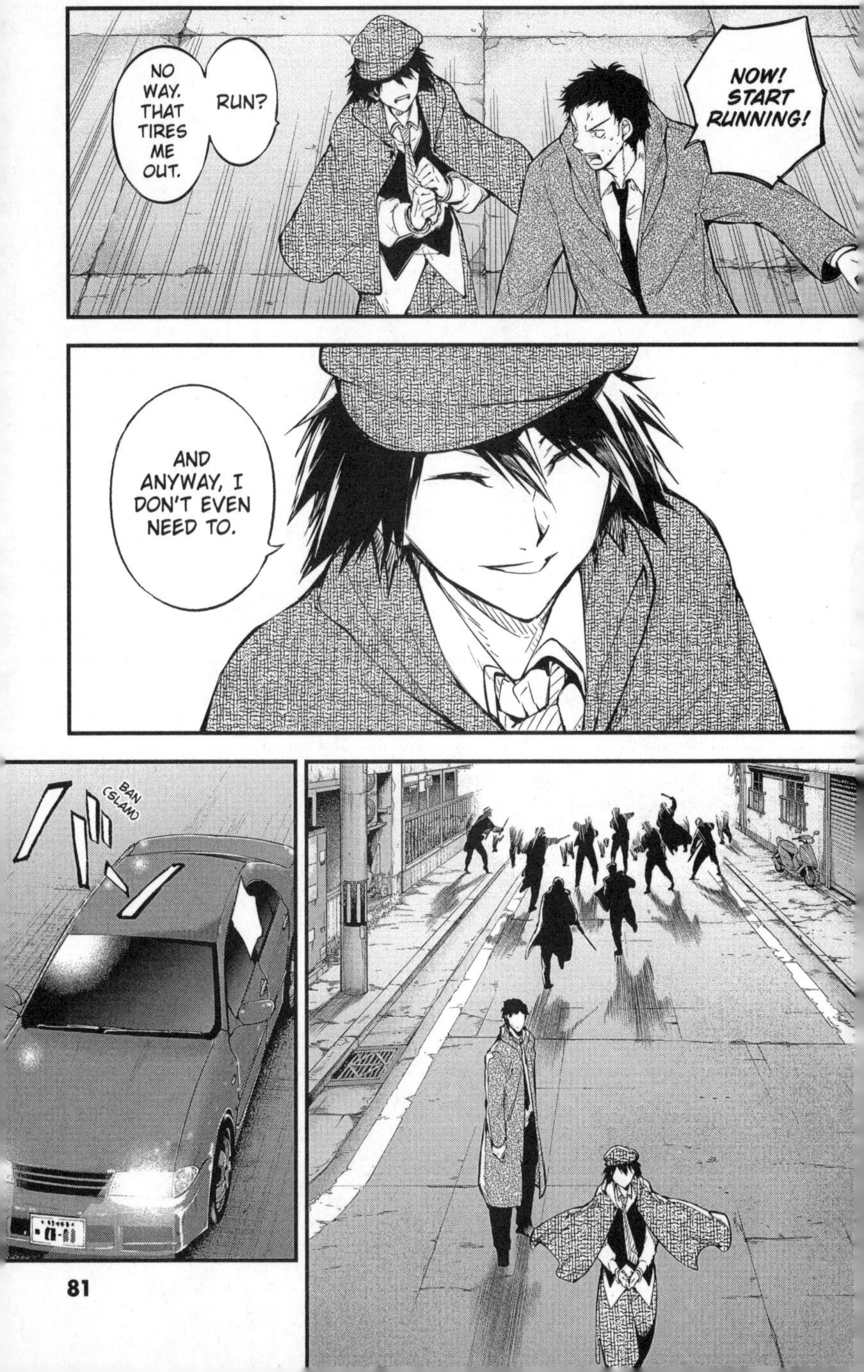
NOW! START RUNNING!
RUN?
NO WAY. THAT TIRES ME OUT.
AND ANYWAY, I DON'T EVEN NEED TO.
BAN (SLAM)

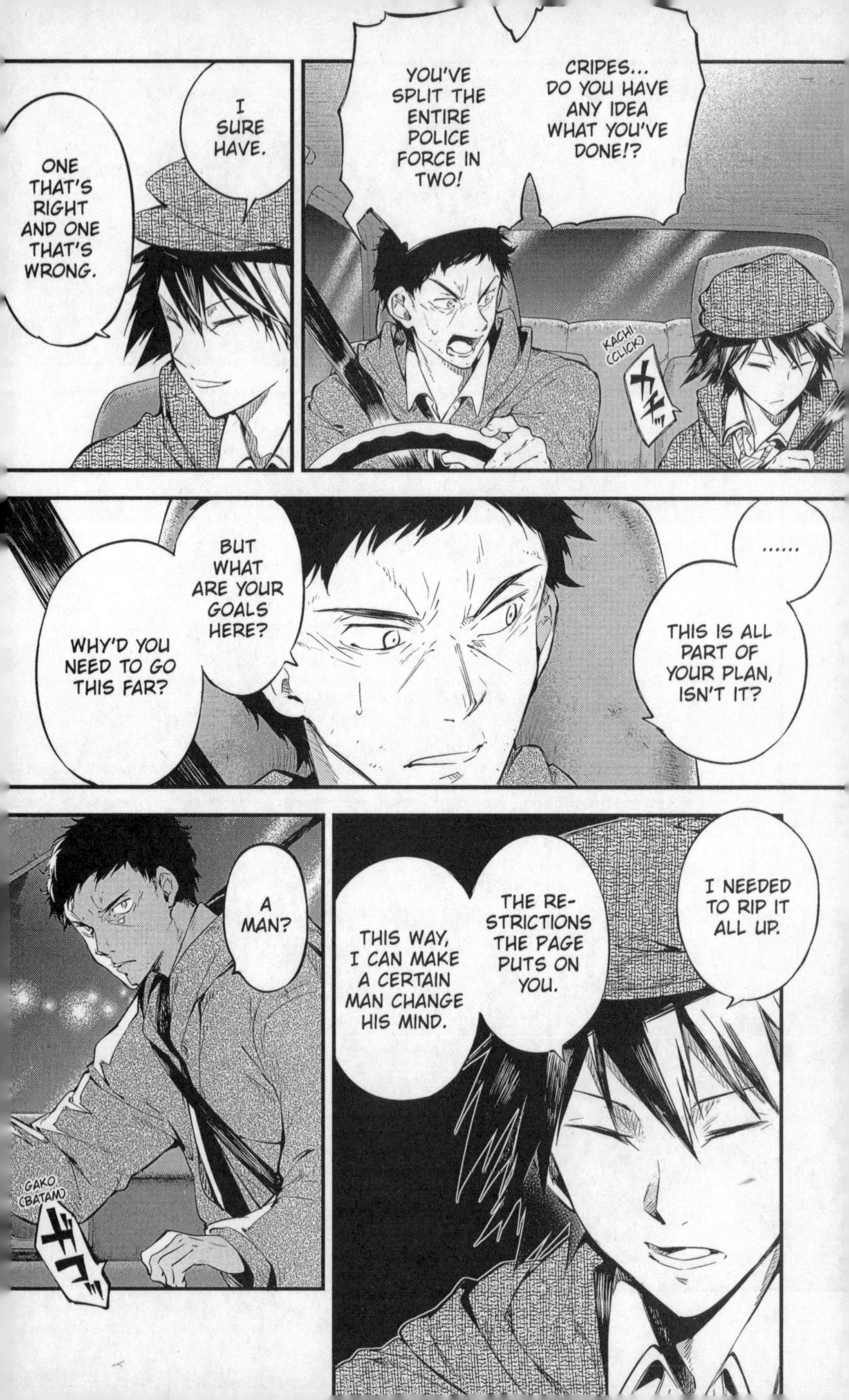
CRIPES... DO YOU HAVE ANY IDEA WHAT YOU'VE DONE!?
YOU'VE SPLIT THE ENTIRE POLICE FORCE IN TWO!
KACHI (CLICK)
I SURE HAVE.
ONE THAT'S RIGHT AND ONE THAT'S WRONG.
......
THIS IS ALL PART OF YOUR PLAN, ISN'T IT?
BUT WHAT ARE YOUR GOALS HERE?
WHY'D YOU NEED TO GO THIS FAR?
I NEEDED TO RIP IT ALL UP.
THE RE-STRICTIONS THE PAGE PUTS ON YOU.
THIS WAY, I CAN MAKE A CERTAIN MAN CHANGE HIS MIND.
A MAN?
GAKO (BATAM)

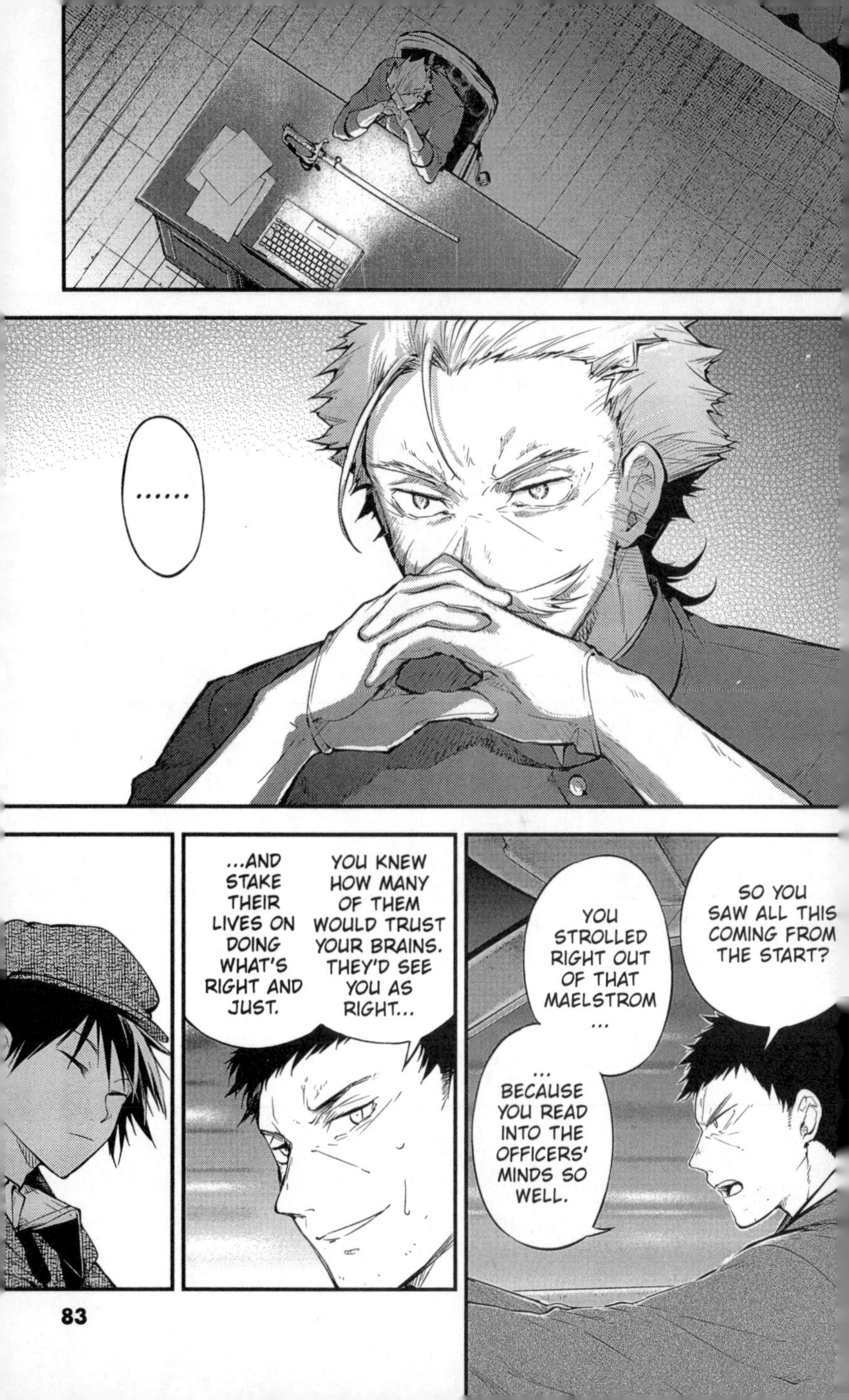
……
SO YOU SAW ALL THIS COMING FROM THE START?
YOU STROLLED RIGHT OUT OF THAT MAELSTROM ...
... BECAUSE YOU READ INTO THE OFFICERS' MINDS SO WELL.
YOU KNEW HOW MANY OF THEM WOULD TRUST YOUR BRAINS. THEY'D SEE YOU AS RIGHT...
...AND STAKE THEIR LIVES ON DOING WHAT'S RIGHT AND JUST.

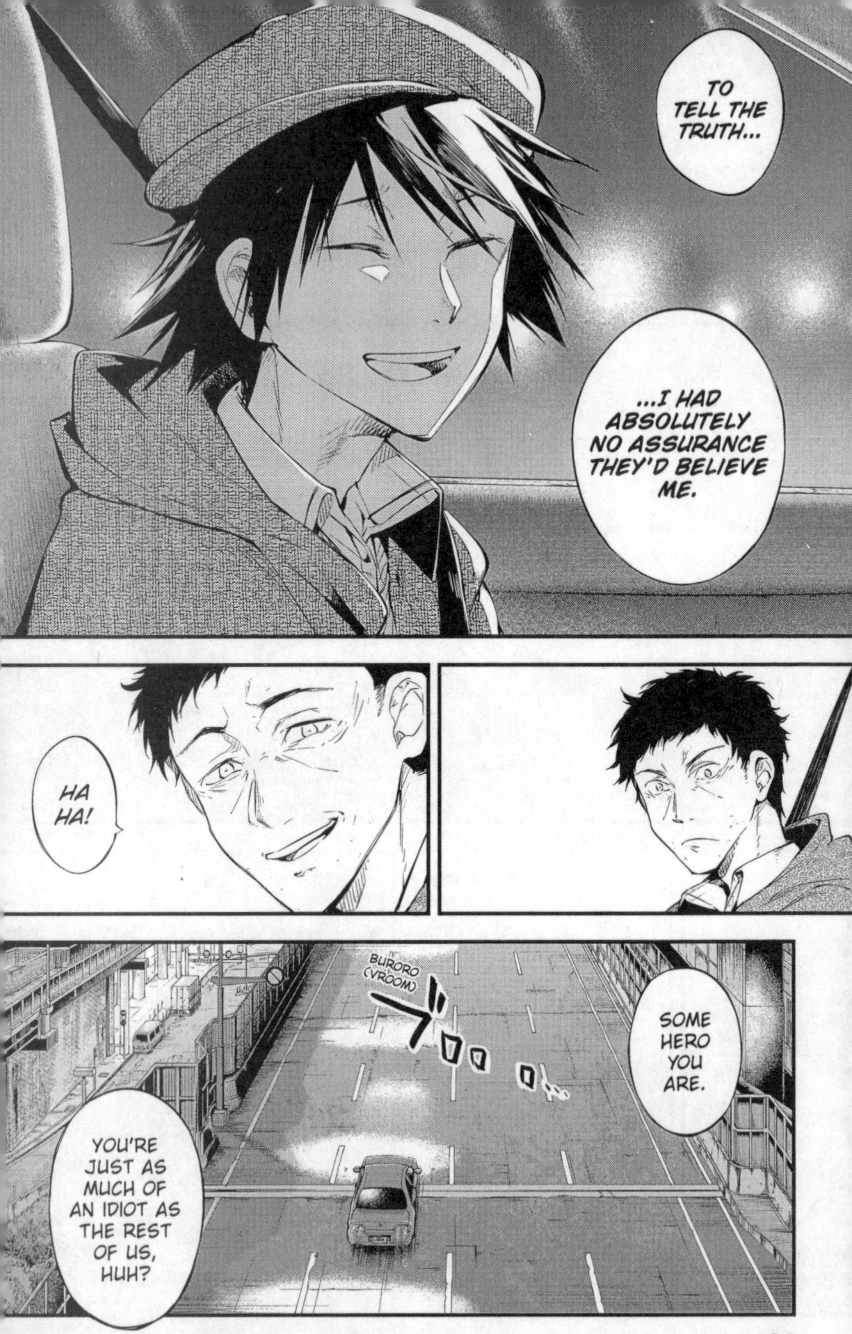
TO TELL THE TRUTH...
...I HAD ABSOLUTELY NO ASSURANCE THEY'D BELIEVE ME.
HA HA!
BURORO (VROOM)
SOME HERO YOU ARE.
YOU'RE JUST AS MUCH OF AN IDIOT AS THE REST OF US, HUH?

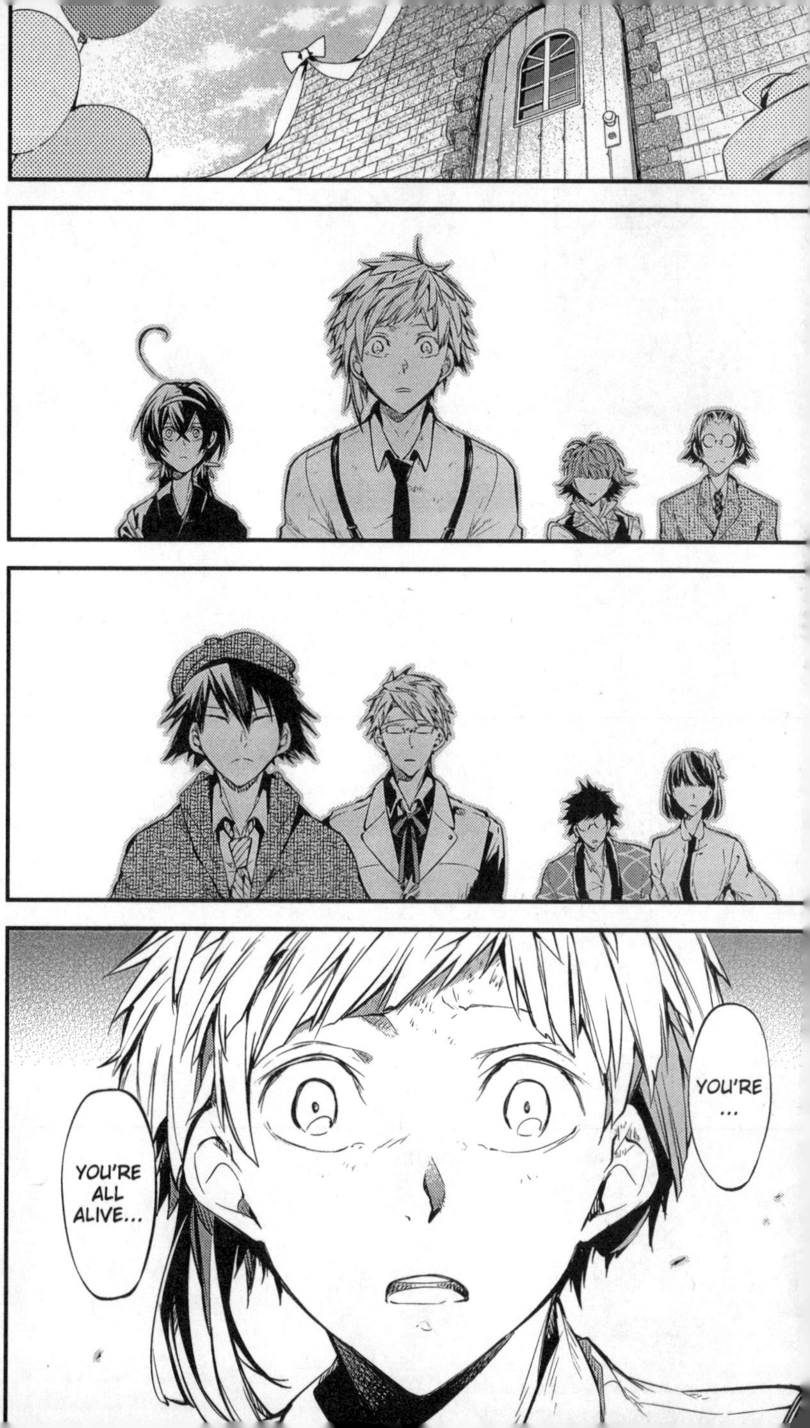
YOU'RE ...
YOU'RE ALL ALIVE...

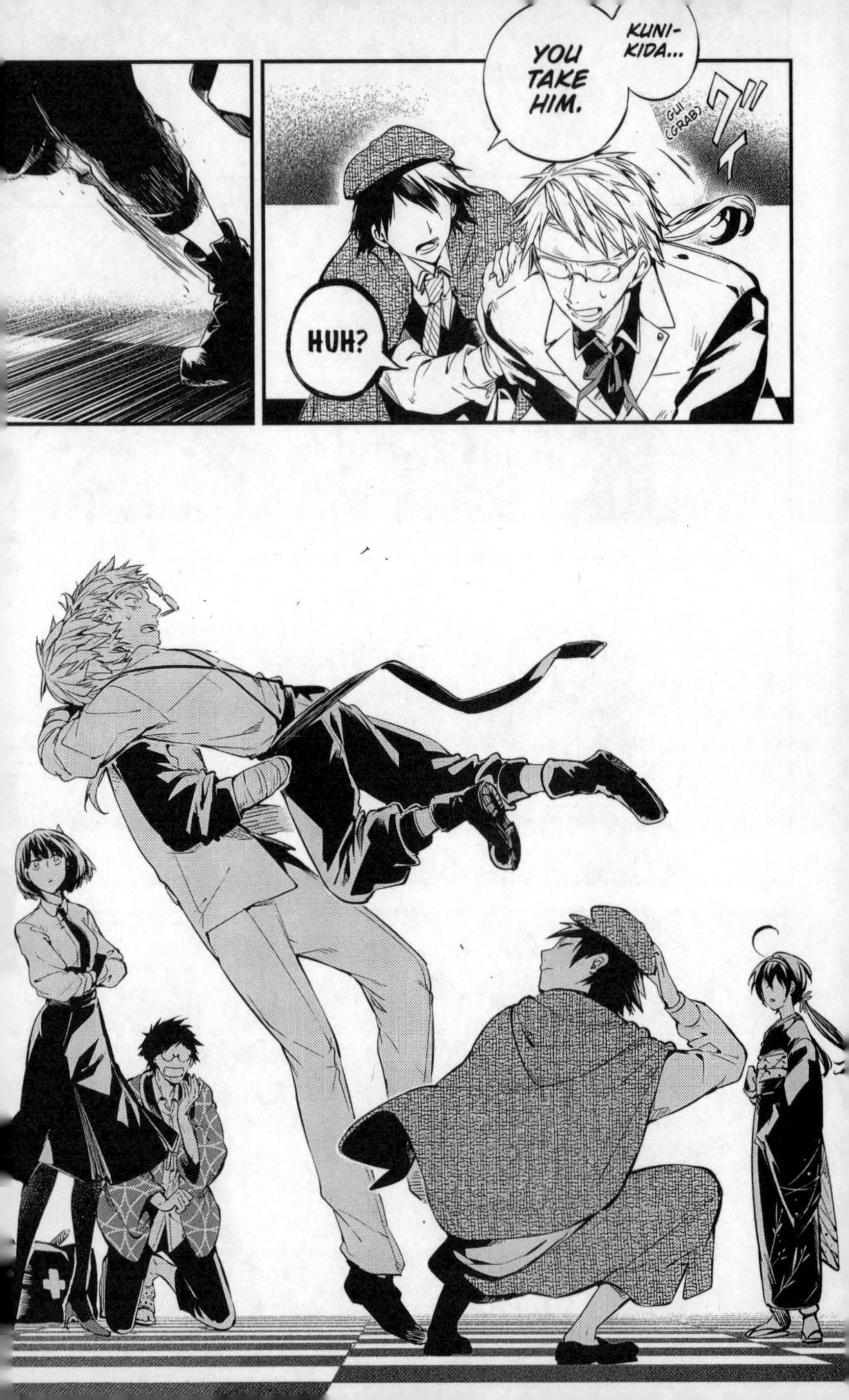
KUNI-KIDA... YOU TAKE HIM.
GUI... (GRAB)
HUH?

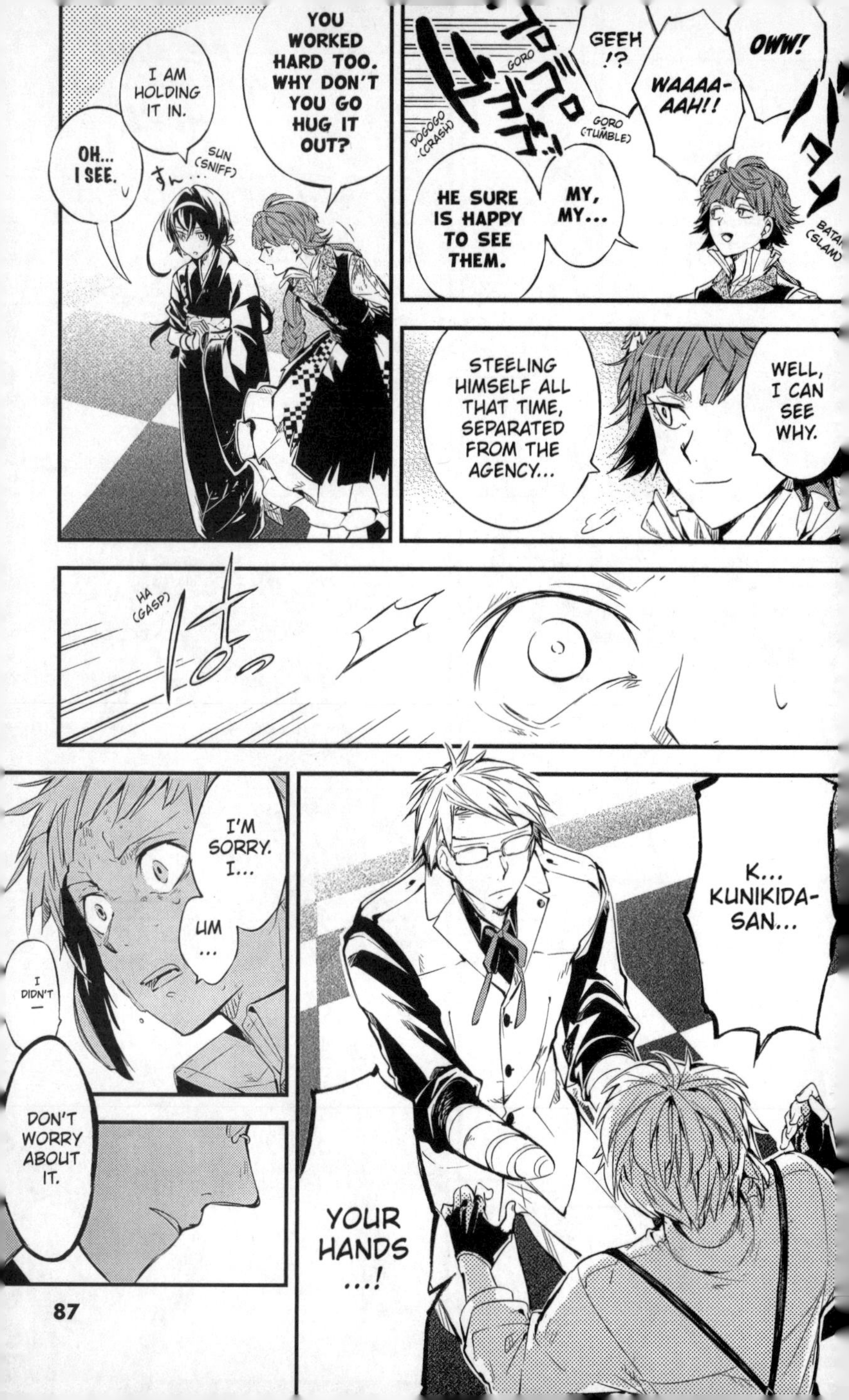
OWW!
WAAAA-AAH!!
BATAN (SLAM)
GEEH !?
GORO
GORO (TUMBLE)
MY, MY...
HE SURE IS HAPPY TO SEE THEM.
DOGOGO (CRASH)
WELL, I CAN SEE WHY.
STEELING HIMSELF ALL THAT TIME, SEPARATED FROM THE AGENCY...
YOU WORKED HARD TOO. WHY DON'T YOU GO HUG IT OUT?
I AM HOLDING IT IN.
SUN (SNIFF)
すん…
OH... I SEE.
HA (GASP)
は
K... KUNIKIDA-SAN...
YOUR HANDS ...!
I'M SORRY. I...
UM ...
I DIDN'T —
DON'T WORRY ABOUT IT.

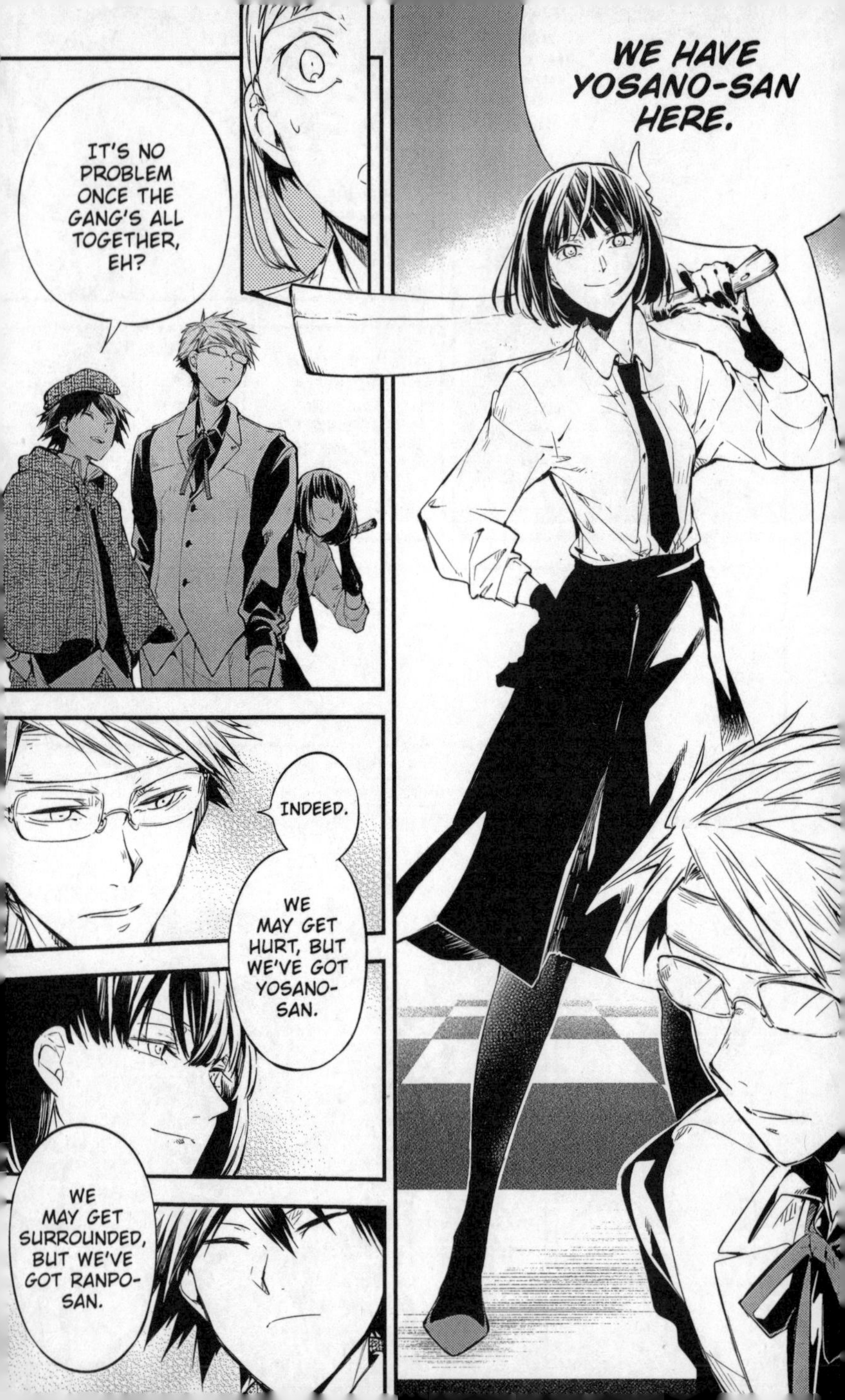
WE HAVE YOSANO-SAN HERE.
IT'S NO PROBLEM ONCE THE GANG'S ALL TOGETHER, EH?
INDEED.
WE MAY GET HURT, BUT WE'VE GOT YOSANO-SAN.
WE MAY GET SURROUNDED, BUT WE'VE GOT RANPO-SAN.

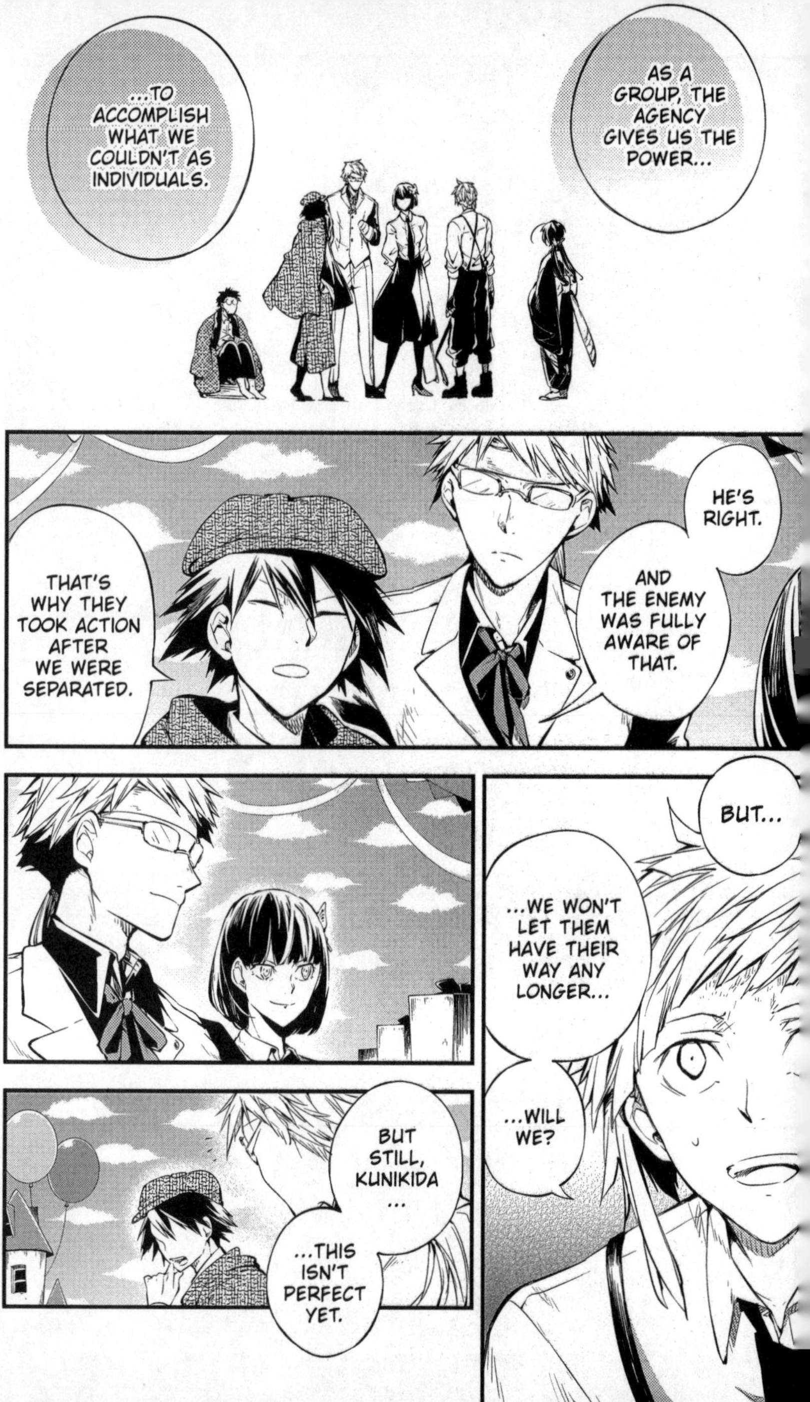
AS A GROUP, THE AGENCY GIVES US THE POWER...
...TO ACCOMPLISH WHAT WE COULDN'T AS INDIVIDUALS.
HE'S RIGHT.
AND THE ENEMY WAS FULLY AWARE OF THAT.
THAT'S WHY THEY TOOK ACTION AFTER WE WERE SEPARATED.
BUT...
...WE WON'T LET THEM HAVE THEIR WAY ANY LONGER...
...WILL WE?
BUT STILL, KUNIKIDA ...
...THIS ISN'T PERFECT YET.

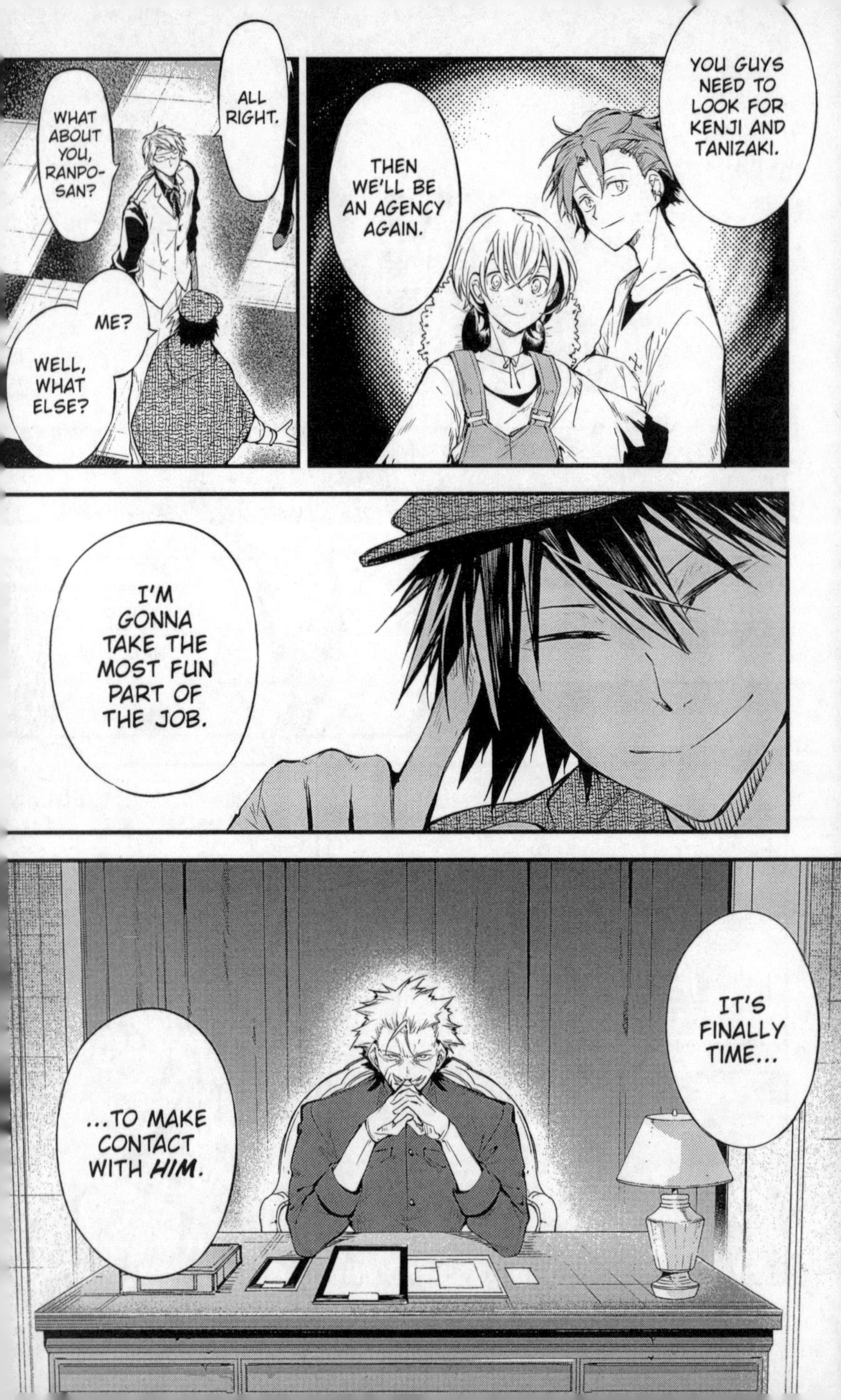
YOU GUYS NEED TO LOOK FOR KENJI AND TANIZAKI.
THEN WE'LL BE AN AGENCY AGAIN.
ALL RIGHT.
WHAT ABOUT YOU, RANPO-SAN?
ME?
WELL, WHAT ELSE?
I'M GONNA TAKE THE MOST FUN PART OF THE JOB.
IT'S FINALLY TIME...
...TO MAKE CONTACT WITH *HIM*.

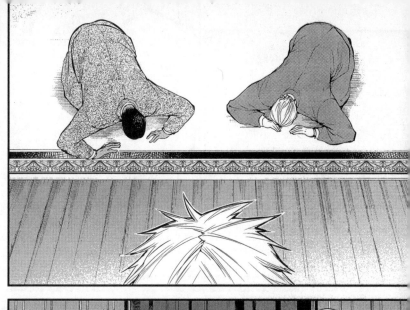

WE BEG YOU...

FUKUCHI-DONO...

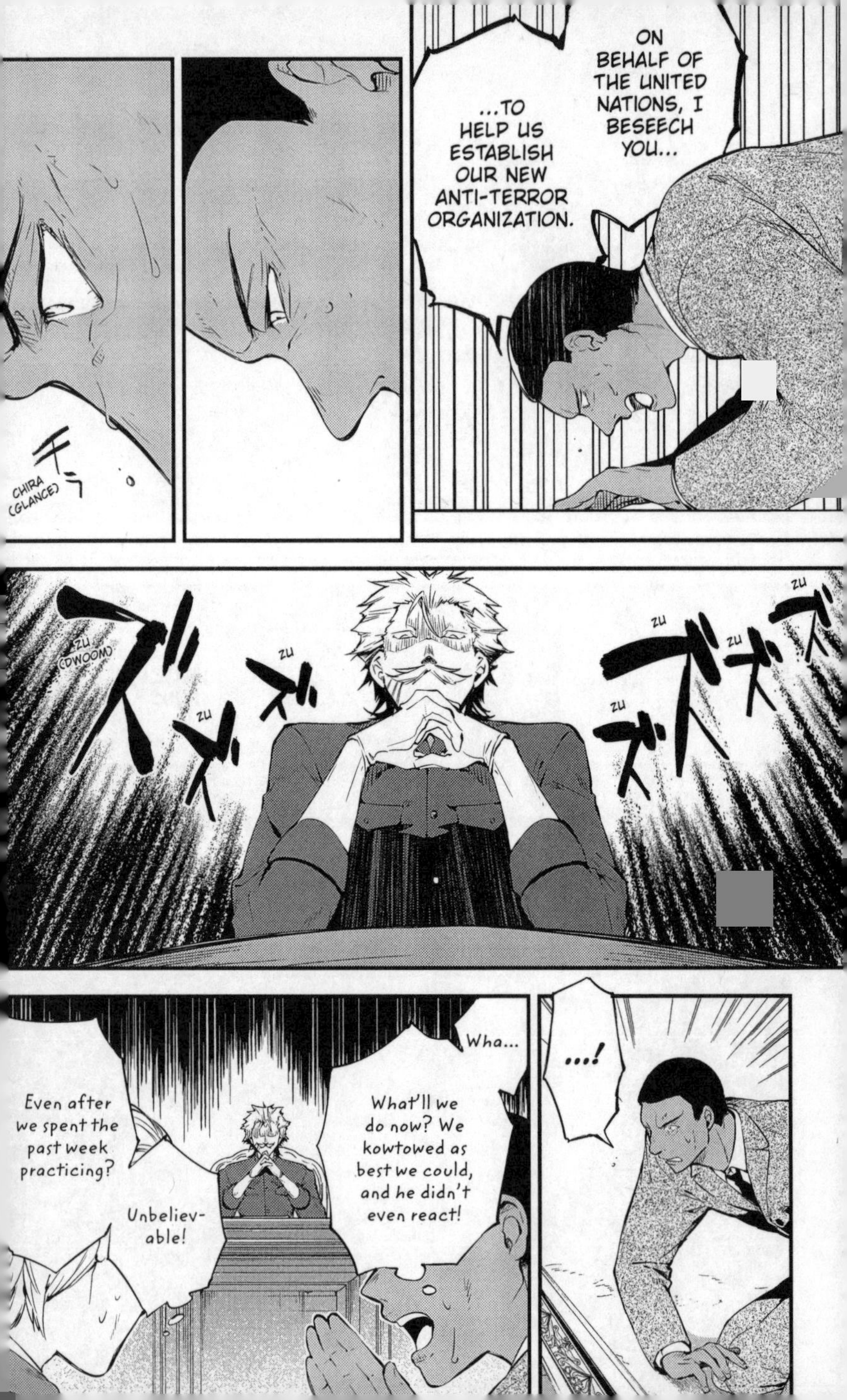
ON BEHALF OF THE UNITED NATIONS, I BESEECH YOU...
...TO HELP US ESTABLISH OUR NEW ANTI-TERROR ORGANIZATION.
CHIRA (GLANCE)
ZU
ZU
ZU
ZU
ZU (DWOOM)
ZU
ZU
...!
Wha...
What'll we do now? We kowtowed as best we could, and he didn't even react!
Even after we spent the past week practicing?
Unbeliev-able!

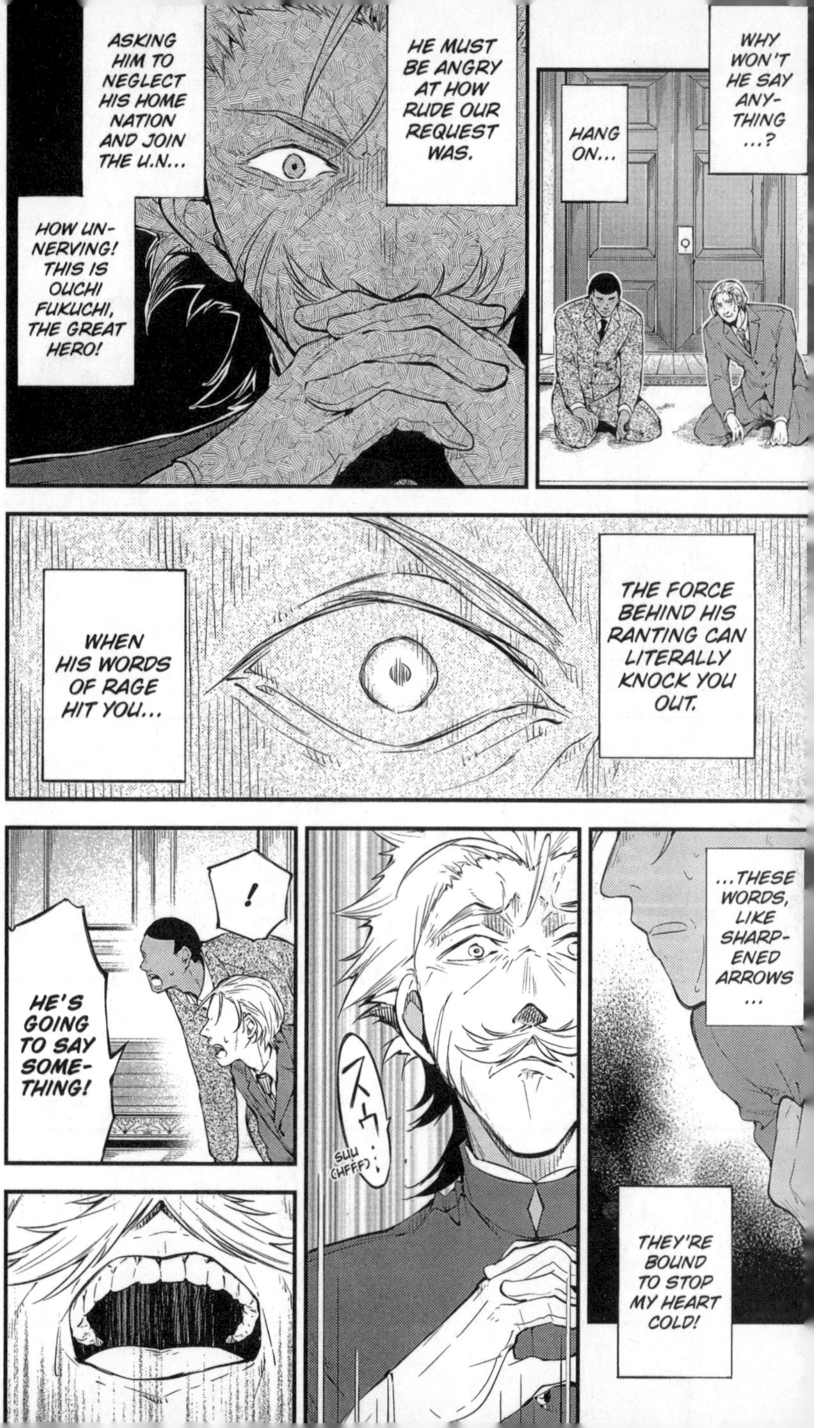
WHY WON'T HE SAY ANYTHING ...?
HANG ON...
HE MUST BE ANGRY AT HOW RUDE OUR REQUEST WAS.
ASKING HIM TO NEGLECT HIS HOME NATION AND JOIN THE U.N...
HOW UNNERVING! THIS IS OUCHI FUKUCHI, THE GREAT HERO!
THE FORCE BEHIND HIS RANTING CAN LITERALLY KNOCK YOU OUT.
WHEN HIS WORDS OF RAGE HIT YOU...
...THESE WORDS, LIKE SHARPENED ARROWS...
THEY'RE BOUND TO STOP MY HEART COLD!
スゥ…
SUU (HFFF)
!
HE'S GOING TO SAY SOMETHING!

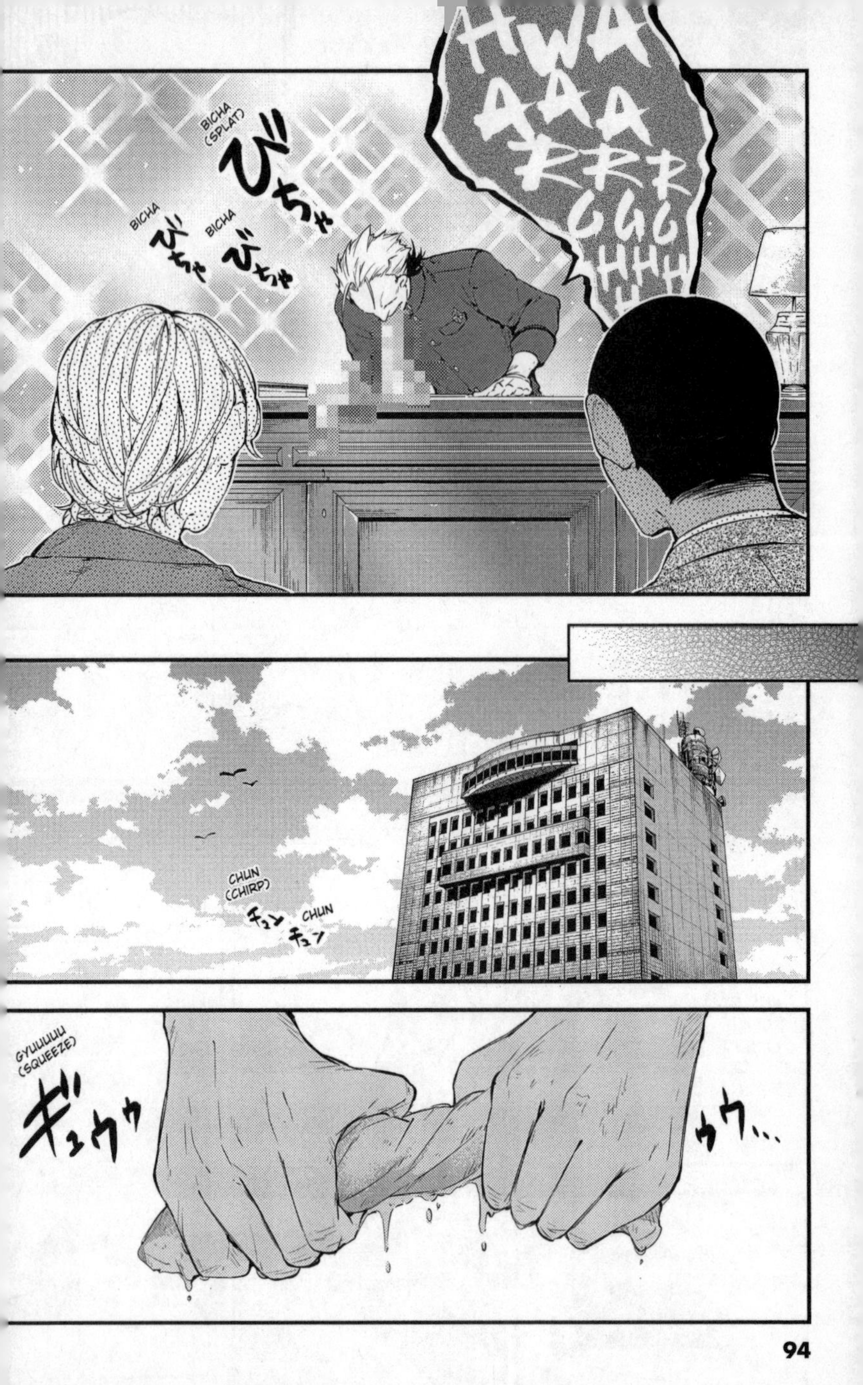
HWAAAARRRGUGHHHH
BICHA (SPLAT)
びちゃ
BICHA
びちゃ
BICHA
びちゃ
CHUN (CHIRP)
チュン
CHUN
チュン
GYUUUUU (SQUEEZE)
ギュウウ
ウウ...

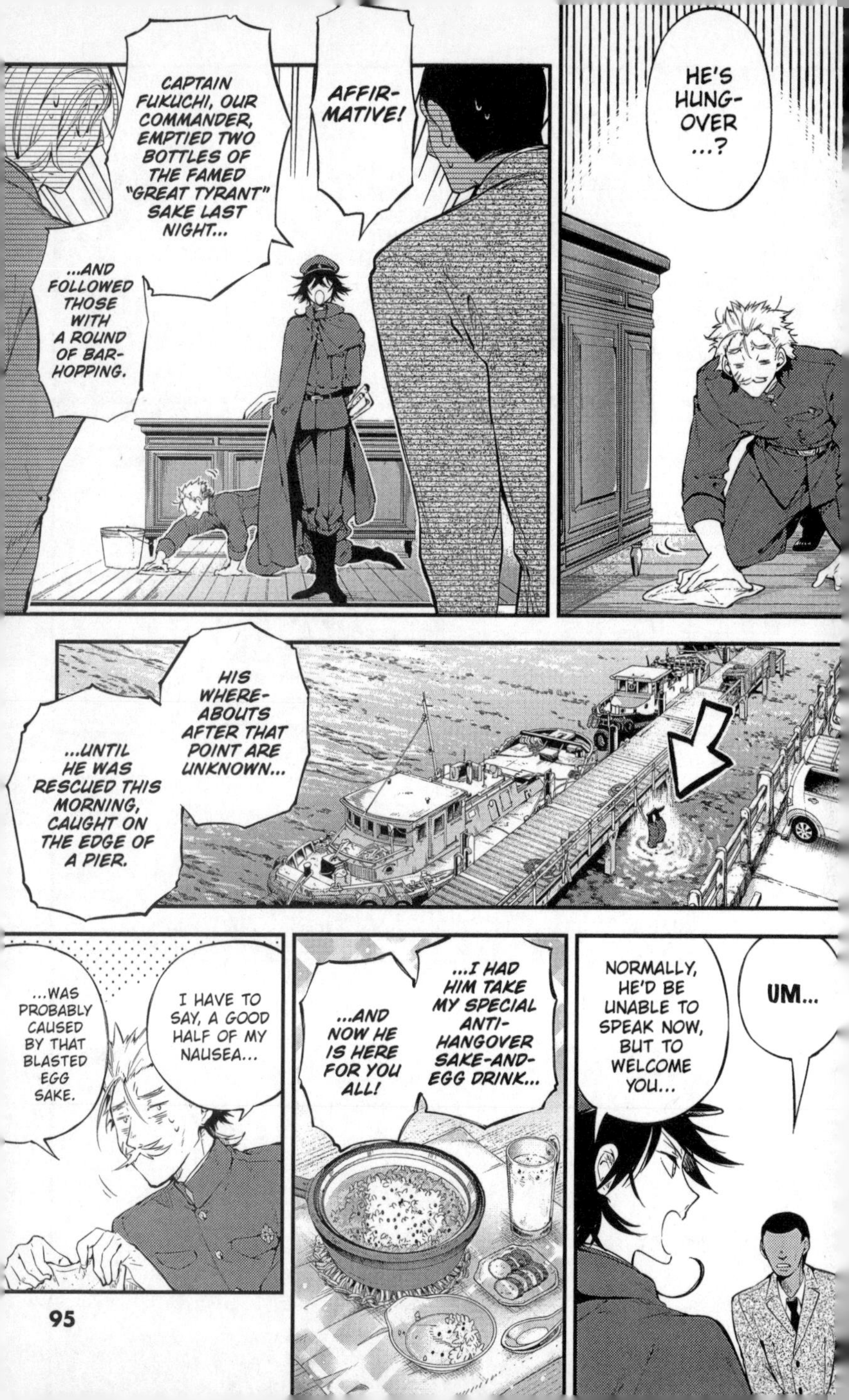
HE'S HUNG-OVER ...?
AFFIR-MATIVE!
CAPTAIN FUKUCHI, OUR COMMANDER, EMPTIED TWO BOTTLES OF THE FAMED "GREAT TYRANT" SAKE LAST NIGHT...
...AND FOLLOWED THOSE WITH A ROUND OF BAR-HOPPING.
HIS WHERE-ABOUTS AFTER THAT POINT ARE UNKNOWN...
...UNTIL HE WAS RESCUED THIS MORNING, CAUGHT ON THE EDGE OF A PIER.
UM...
NORMALLY, HE'D BE UNABLE TO SPEAK NOW, BUT TO WELCOME YOU...
...I HAD HIM TAKE MY SPECIAL ANTI-HANGOVER SAKE-AND-EGG DRINK...
...AND NOW HE IS HERE FOR YOU ALL!
I HAVE TO SAY, A GOOD HALF OF MY NAUSEA...
...WAS PROBABLY CAUSED BY THAT BLASTED EGG SAKE.

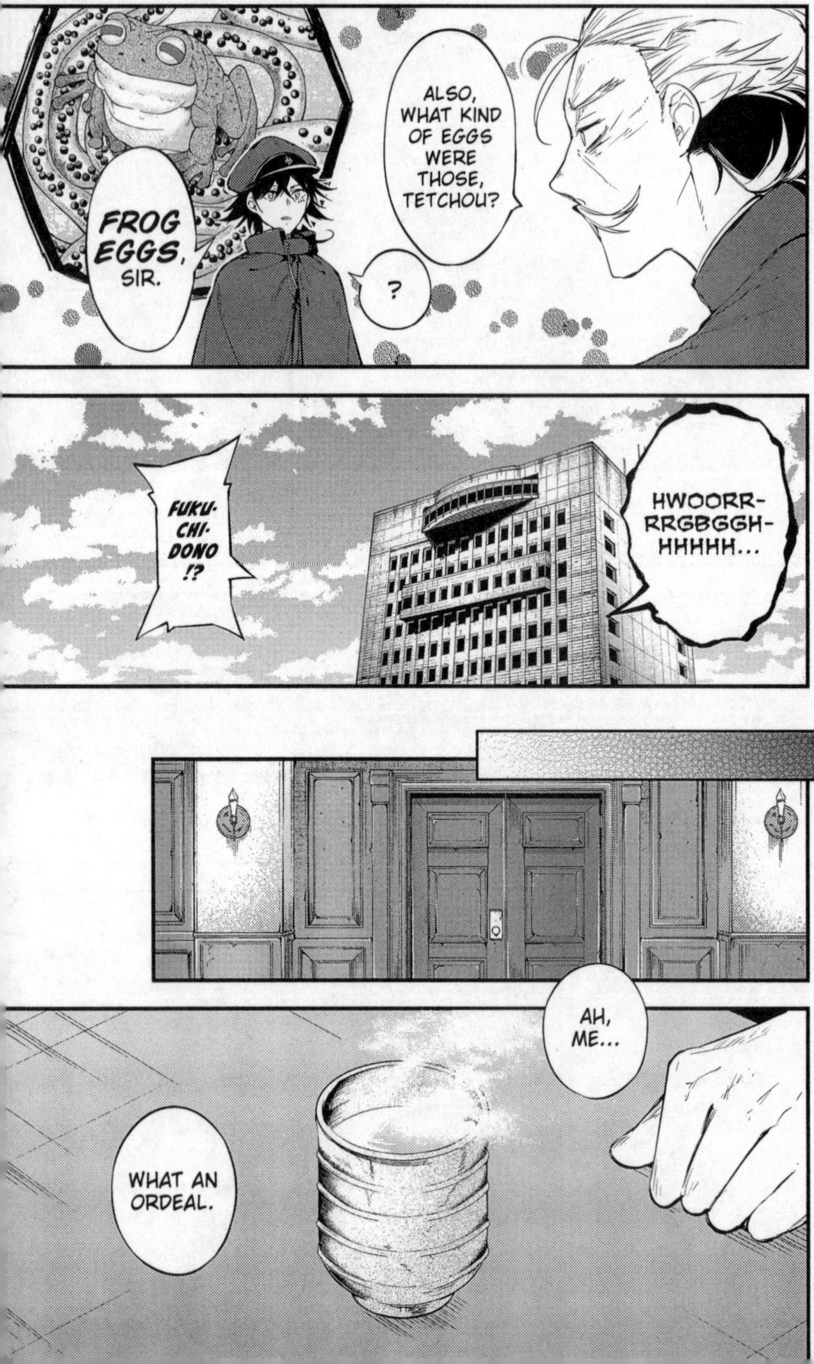
ALSO, WHAT KIND OF EGGS WERE THOSE, TETCHOU?
?
FROG EGGS, SIR.
HWOORR-RRGBGGH-HHHHH...
FUKU-CHI-DONO!?
AH, ME...
WHAT AN ORDEAL.

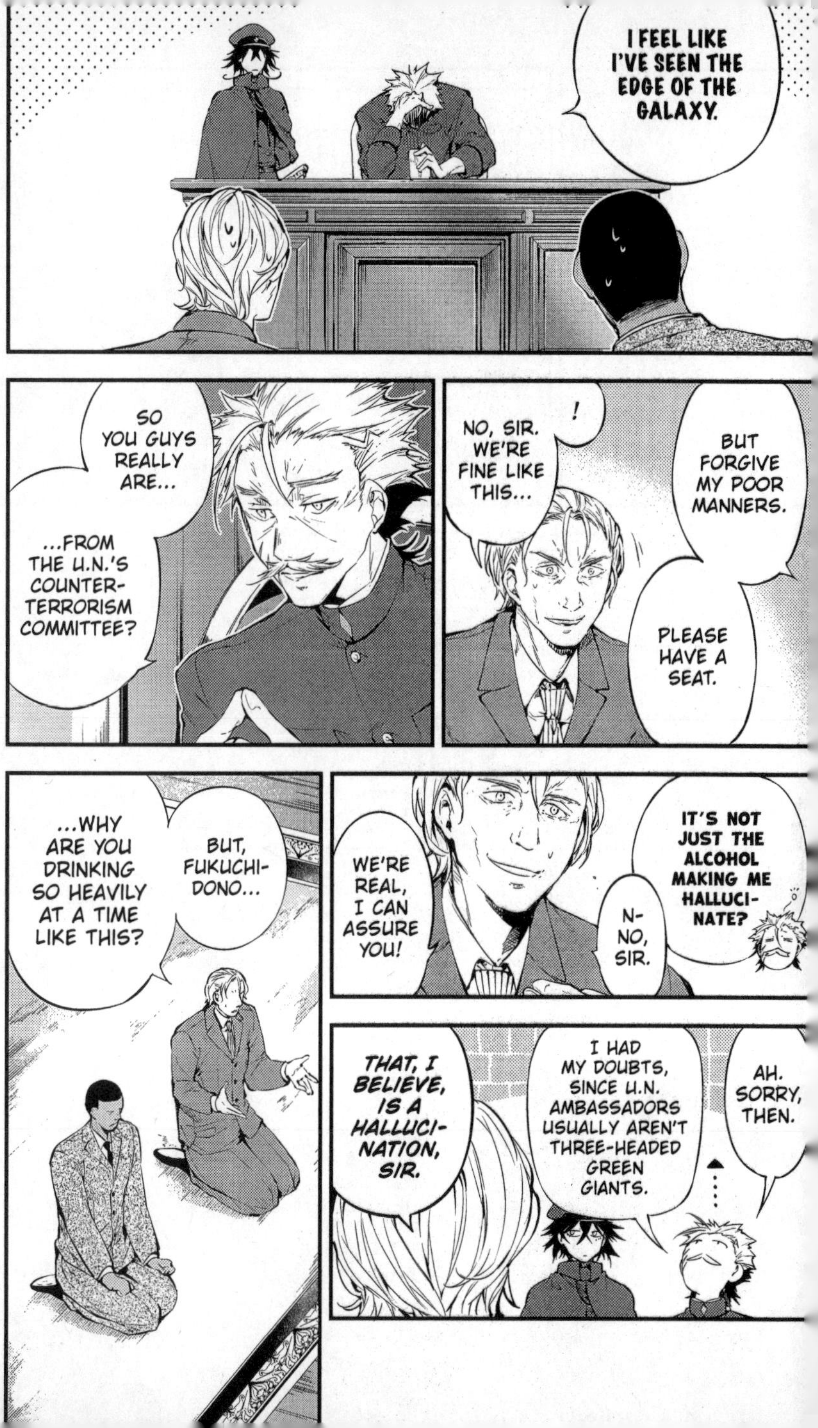
I FEEL LIKE I'VE SEEN THE EDGE OF THE GALAXY.
BUT FORGIVE MY POOR MANNERS.
!
NO, SIR. WE'RE FINE LIKE THIS...
PLEASE HAVE A SEAT.
SO YOU GUYS REALLY ARE...
...FROM THE U.N.'S COUNTER-TERRORISM COMMITTEE?
IT'S NOT JUST THE ALCOHOL MAKING ME HALLUCINATE?
N-NO, SIR.
WE'RE REAL, I CAN ASSURE YOU!
AH. SORRY, THEN.
I HAD MY DOUBTS, SINCE U.N. AMBASSADORS USUALLY AREN'T THREE-HEADED GREEN GIANTS.
THAT, I BELIEVE, IS A HALLUCINATION, SIR.
BUT, FUKUCHI-DONO...
...WHY ARE YOU DRINKING SO HEAVILY AT A TIME LIKE THIS?

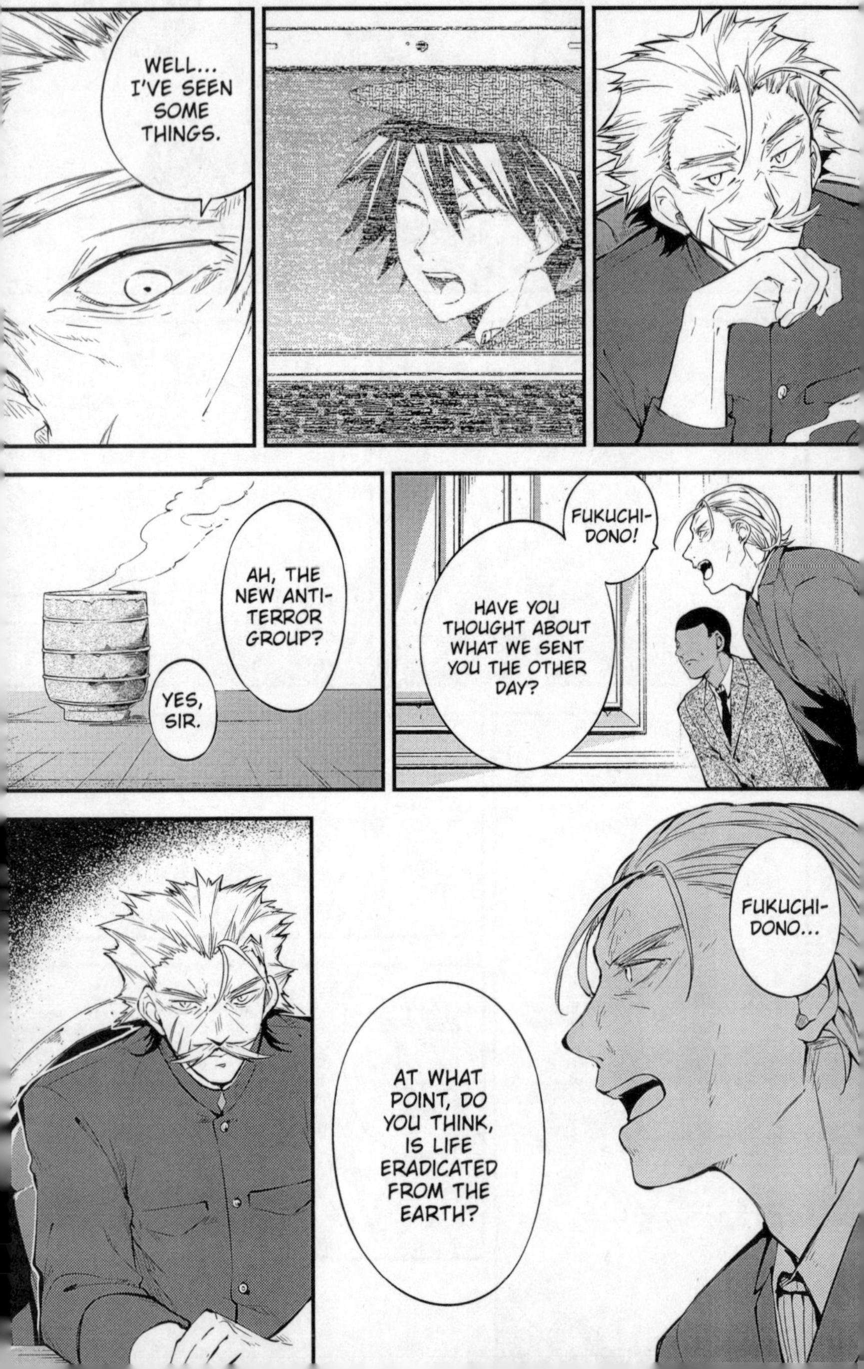
WELL... I'VE SEEN SOME THINGS.
FUKUCHI-DONO!
HAVE YOU THOUGHT ABOUT WHAT WE SENT YOU THE OTHER DAY?
AH, THE NEW ANTI-TERROR GROUP?
YES, SIR.
FUKUCHI-DONO...
AT WHAT POINT, DO YOU THINK, IS LIFE ERADICATED FROM THE EARTH?

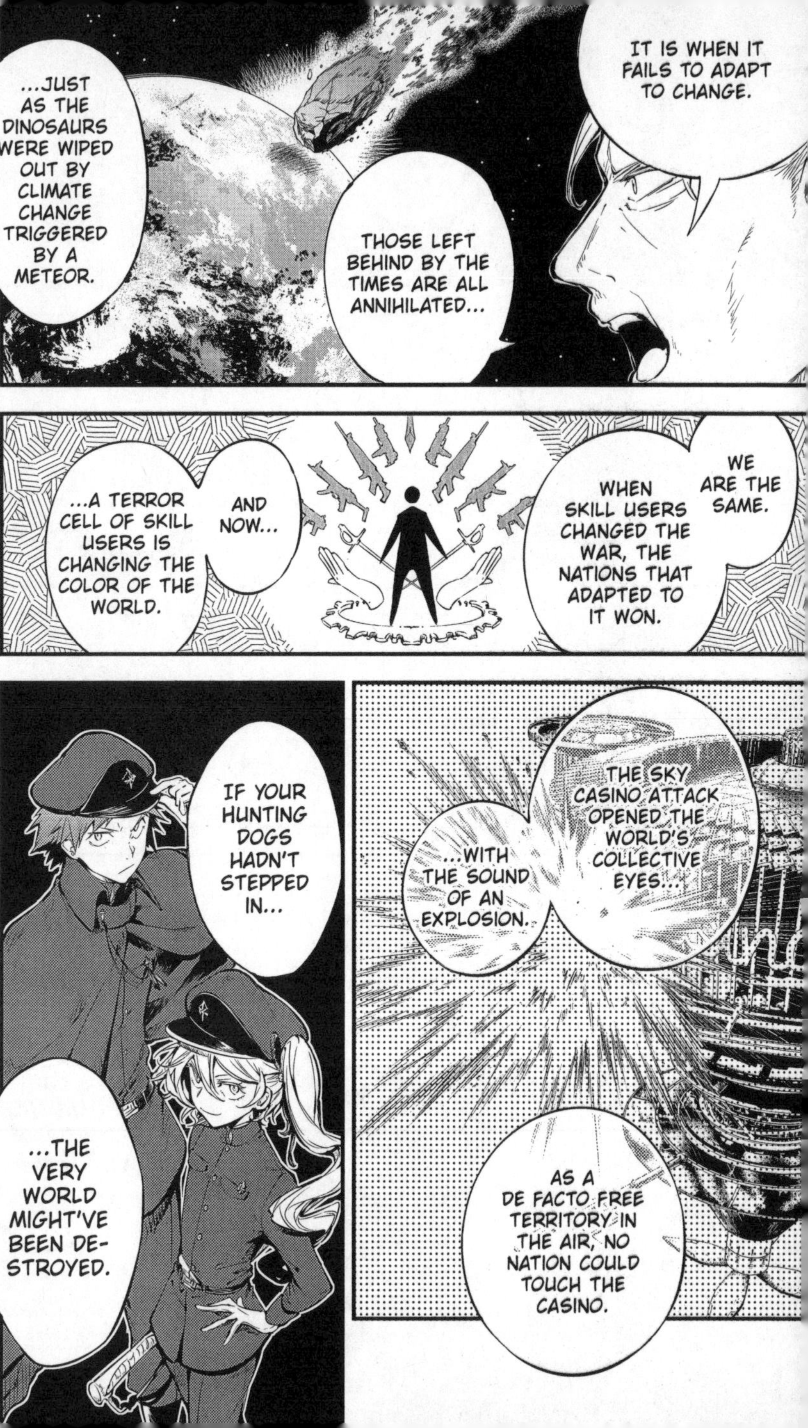
IT IS WHEN IT FAILS TO ADAPT TO CHANGE.
THOSE LEFT BEHIND BY THE TIMES ARE ALL ANNIHILATED...
...JUST AS THE DINOSAURS WERE WIPED OUT BY CLIMATE CHANGE TRIGGERED BY A METEOR.
WE ARE THE SAME.
WHEN SKILL USERS CHANGED THE WAR, THE NATIONS THAT ADAPTED TO IT WON.
AND NOW...
...A TERROR CELL OF SKILL USERS IS CHANGING THE COLOR OF THE WORLD.
THE SKY CASINO ATTACK OPENED THE WORLD'S COLLECTIVE EYES...
...WITH THE SOUND OF AN EXPLOSION.
AS A DE FACTO FREE TERRITORY IN THE AIR, NO NATION COULD TOUCH THE CASINO.
IF YOUR HUNTING DOGS HADN'T STEPPED IN...
...THE VERY WORLD MIGHT'VE BEEN DE-STROYED.

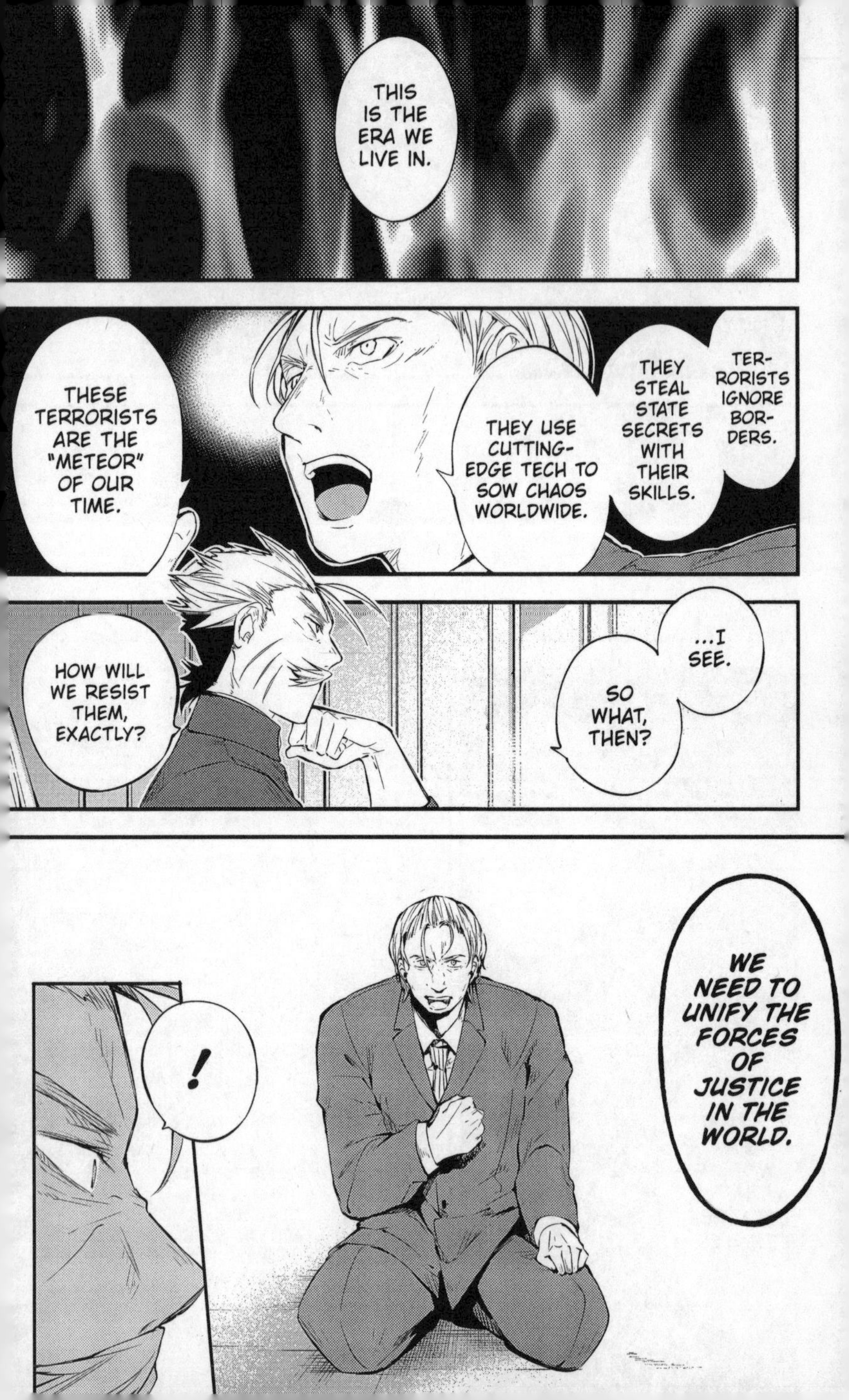
THIS IS THE ERA WE LIVE IN.
TER-RORISTS IGNORE BOR-DERS.
THEY STEAL STATE SECRETS WITH THEIR SKILLS.
THEY USE CUTTING-EDGE TECH TO SOW CHAOS WORLDWIDE.
THESE TERRORISTS ARE THE "METEOR" OF OUR TIME.
...I SEE.
SO WHAT, THEN?
HOW WILL WE RESIST THEM, EXACTLY?
WE NEED TO UNIFY THE FORCES OF JUSTICE IN THE WORLD.
!

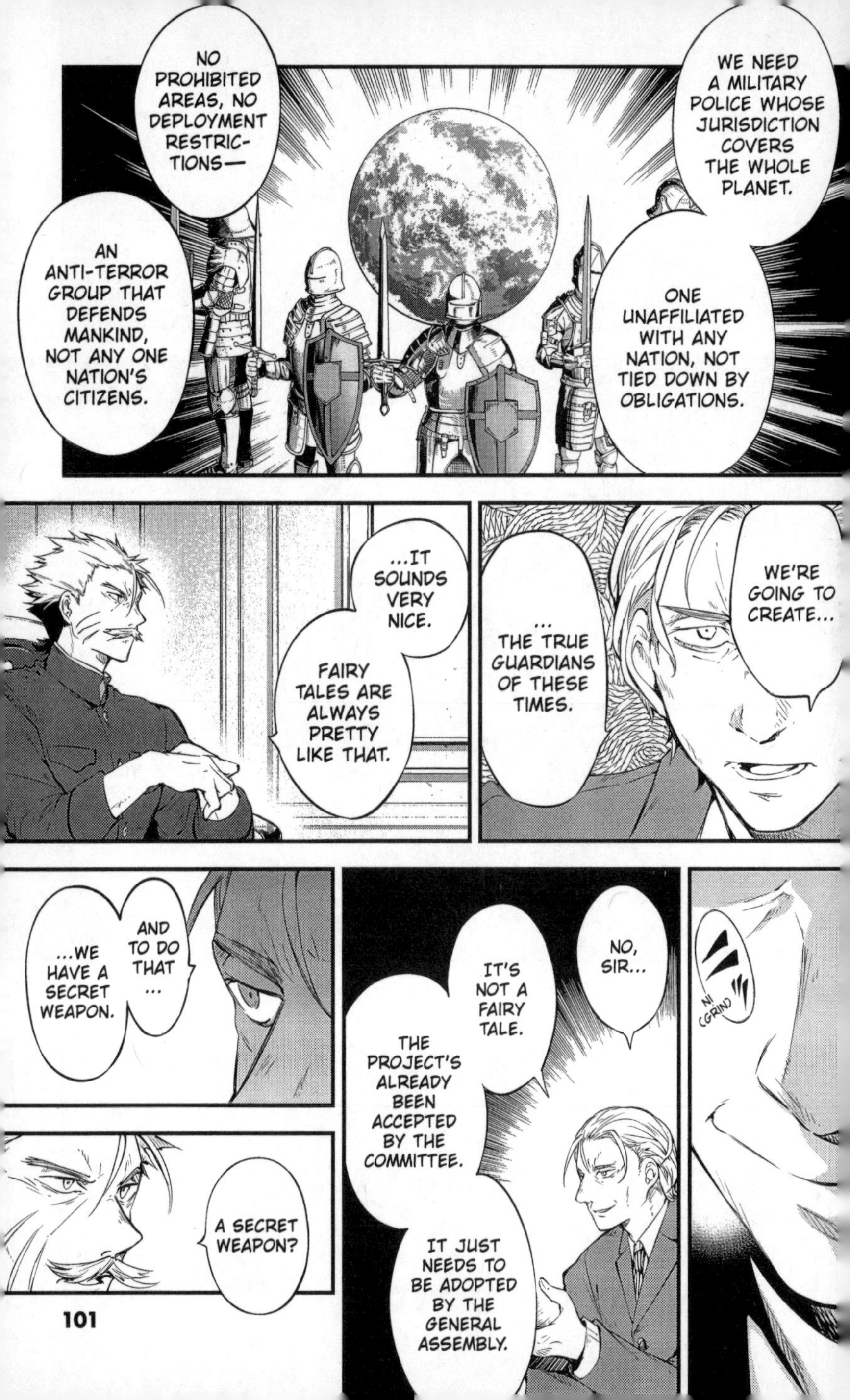
WE NEED A MILITARY POLICE WHOSE JURISDICTION COVERS THE WHOLE PLANET.
NO PROHIBITED AREAS, NO DEPLOYMENT RESTRIC-TIONS—
ONE UNAFFILIATED WITH ANY NATION, NOT TIED DOWN BY OBLIGATIONS.
AN ANTI-TERROR GROUP THAT DEFENDS MANKIND, NOT ANY ONE NATION'S CITIZENS.
WE'RE GOING TO CREATE...
...THE TRUE GUARDIANS OF THESE TIMES.
...IT SOUNDS VERY NICE.
FAIRY TALES ARE ALWAYS PRETTY LIKE THAT.
NI (GRIN)
NO, SIR...
IT'S NOT A FAIRY TALE.
THE PROJECT'S ALREADY BEEN ACCEPTED BY THE COMMITTEE.
IT JUST NEEDS TO BE ADOPTED BY THE GENERAL ASSEMBLY.
AND TO DO THAT...
...WE HAVE A SECRET WEAPON.
A SECRET WEAPON?

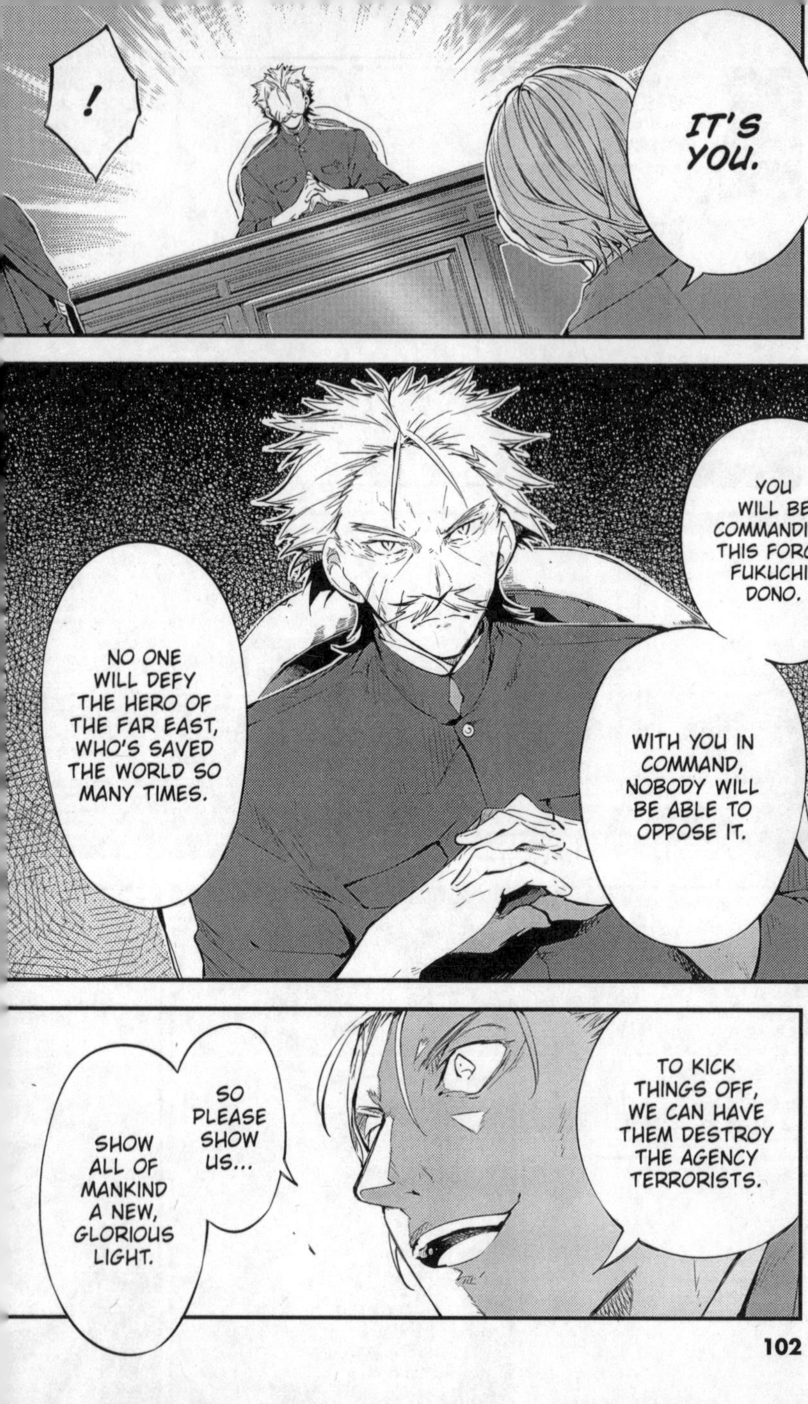
IT'S YOU.
!
YOU WILL BE COMMANDING THIS FORCE, FUKUCHI-DONO.
WITH YOU IN COMMAND, NOBODY WILL BE ABLE TO OPPOSE IT.
NO ONE WILL DEFY THE HERO OF THE FAR EAST, WHO'S SAVED THE WORLD SO MANY TIMES.
TO KICK THINGS OFF, WE CAN HAVE THEM DESTROY THE AGENCY TERRORISTS.
SO PLEASE SHOW US...
SHOW ALL OF MANKIND A NEW, GLORIOUS LIGHT.

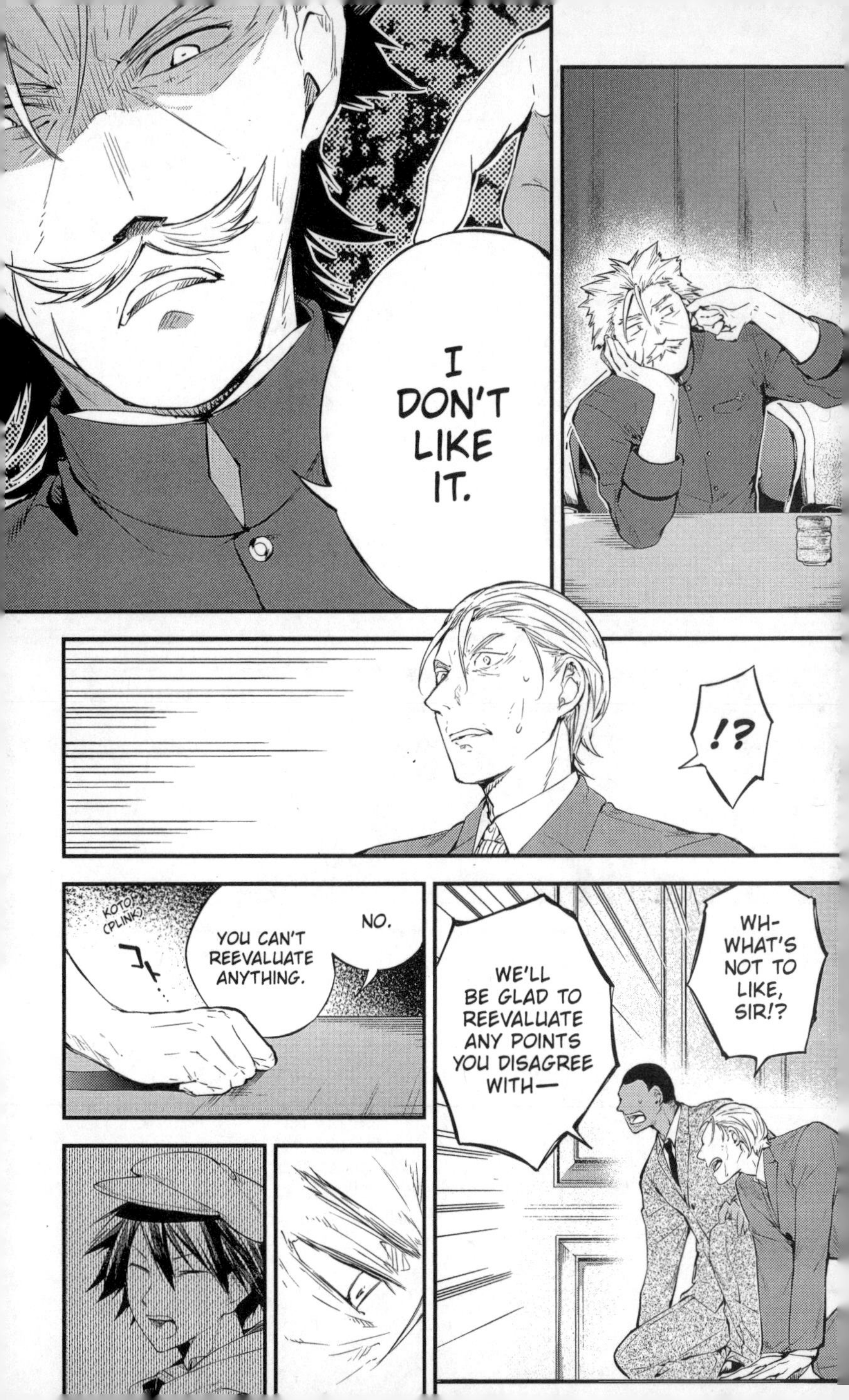
I DON'T LIKE IT.
!?
WH-WHAT'S NOT TO LIKE, SIR!?
WE'LL BE GLAD TO REEVALUATE ANY POINTS YOU DISAGREE WITH—
NO.
YOU CAN'T REEVALUATE ANYTHING.
KOTO (PLINK)

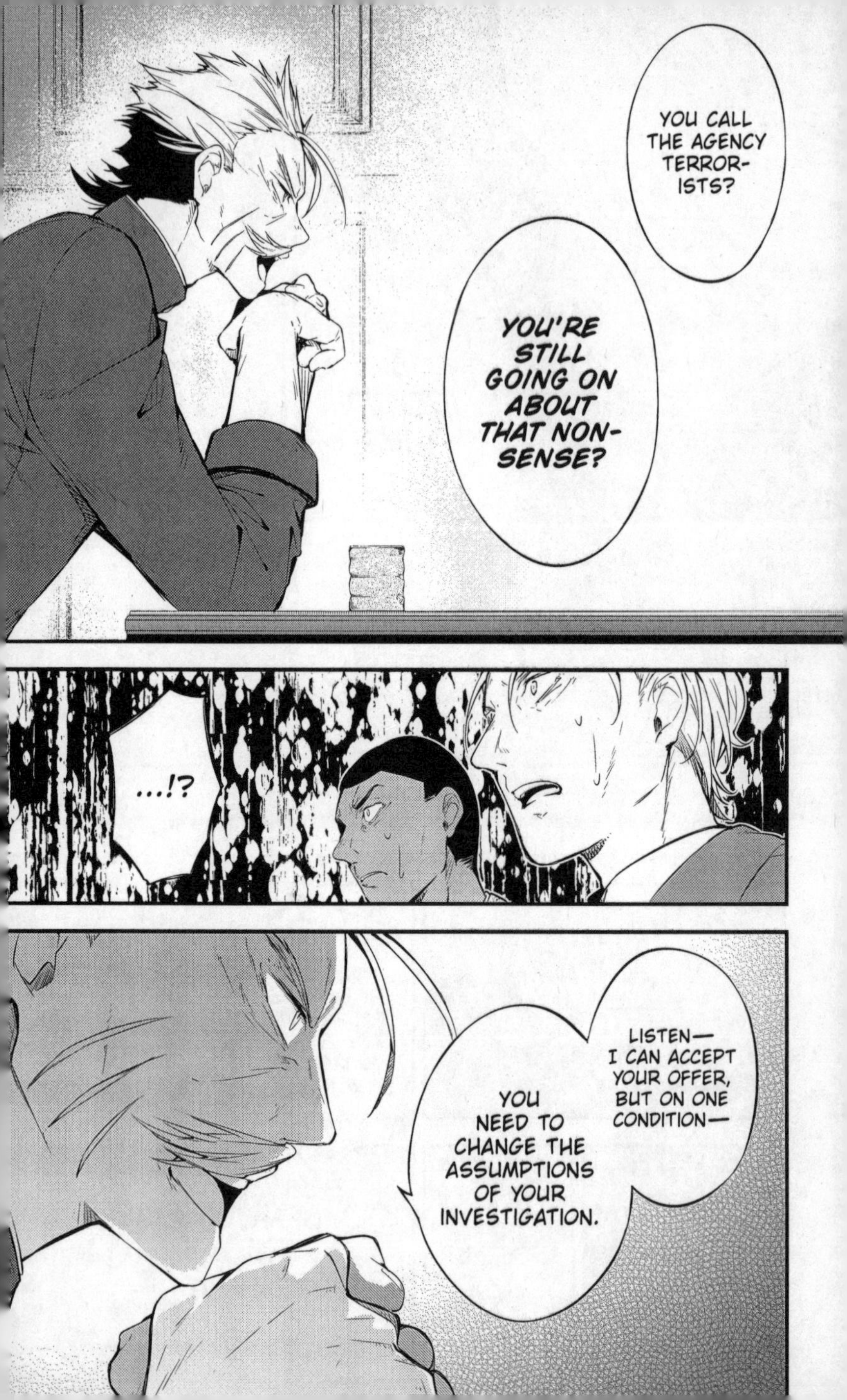
YOU CALL THE AGENCY TERROR-ISTS?
YOU'RE STILL GOING ON ABOUT THAT NON-SENSE?
...!?
LISTEN— I CAN ACCEPT YOUR OFFER, BUT ON ONE CONDITION—
YOU NEED TO CHANGE THE ASSUMPTIONS OF YOUR INVESTIGATION.

SANTOUKA TANEDA

SKILL: **Hail in the Begging Bowl**
If a skill is invoked near him, he can instantly grasp the nature of it.

AGE: *50*

BIRTH DATE: *December 3*

HEIGHT: *185cm*

WEIGHT: *98kg*

BLOOD TYPE: *O*

LIKES: *Sake, hot springs, staying up late*

DISLIKES: *Treating things badly*

BUNGO
STRAY DOGS

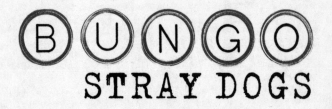

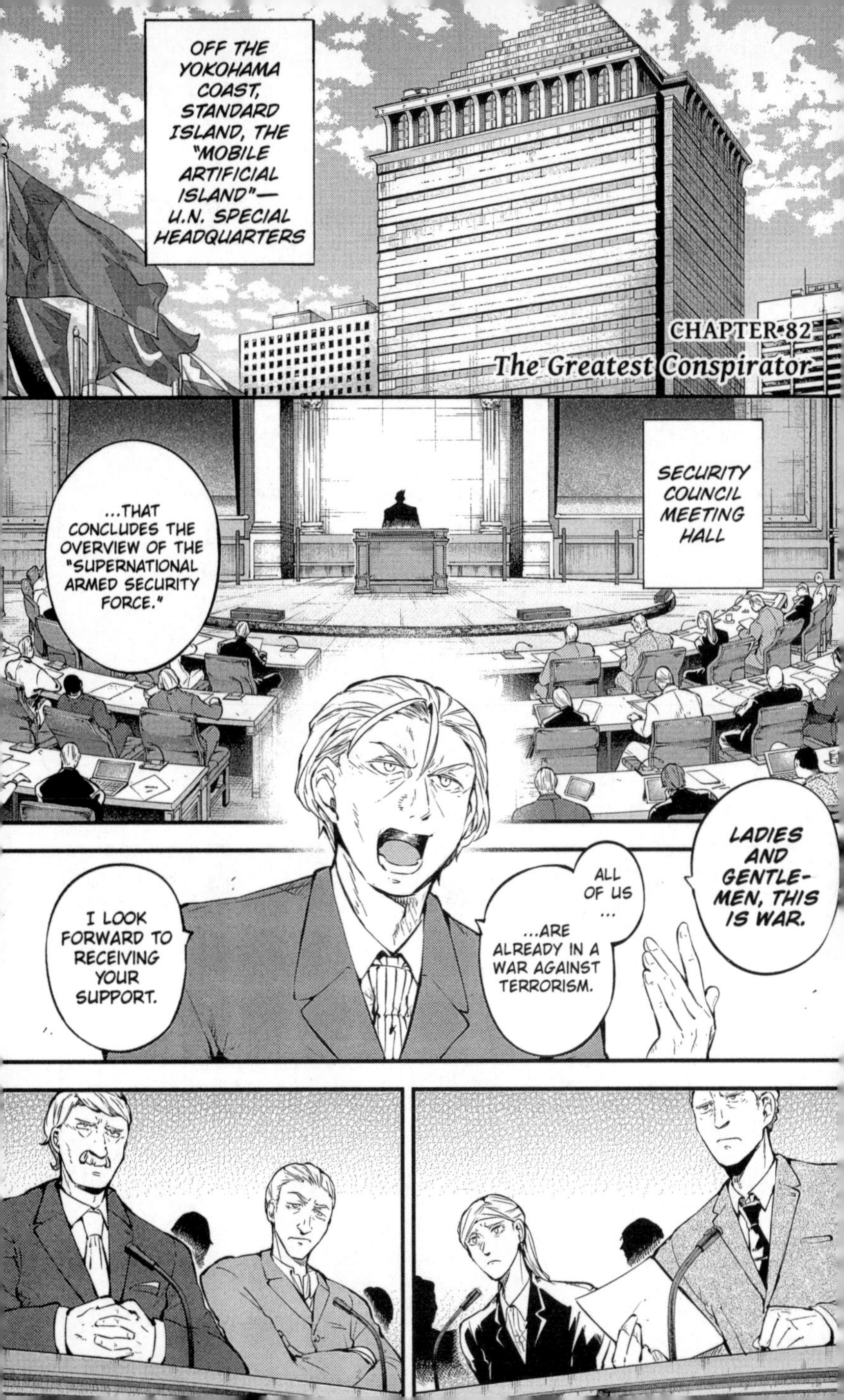
OFF THE YOKOHAMA COAST, STANDARD ISLAND, THE "MOBILE ARTIFICIAL ISLAND"— U.N. SPECIAL HEADQUARTERS
CHAPTER 82
The Greatest Conspirator
SECURITY COUNCIL MEETING HALL
...THAT CONCLUDES THE OVERVIEW OF THE "SUPERNATIONAL ARMED SECURITY FORCE."
LADIES AND GENTLE-MEN, THIS IS WAR.
ALL OF US ...
...ARE ALREADY IN A WAR AGAINST TERRORISM.
I LOOK FORWARD TO RECEIVING YOUR SUPPORT.

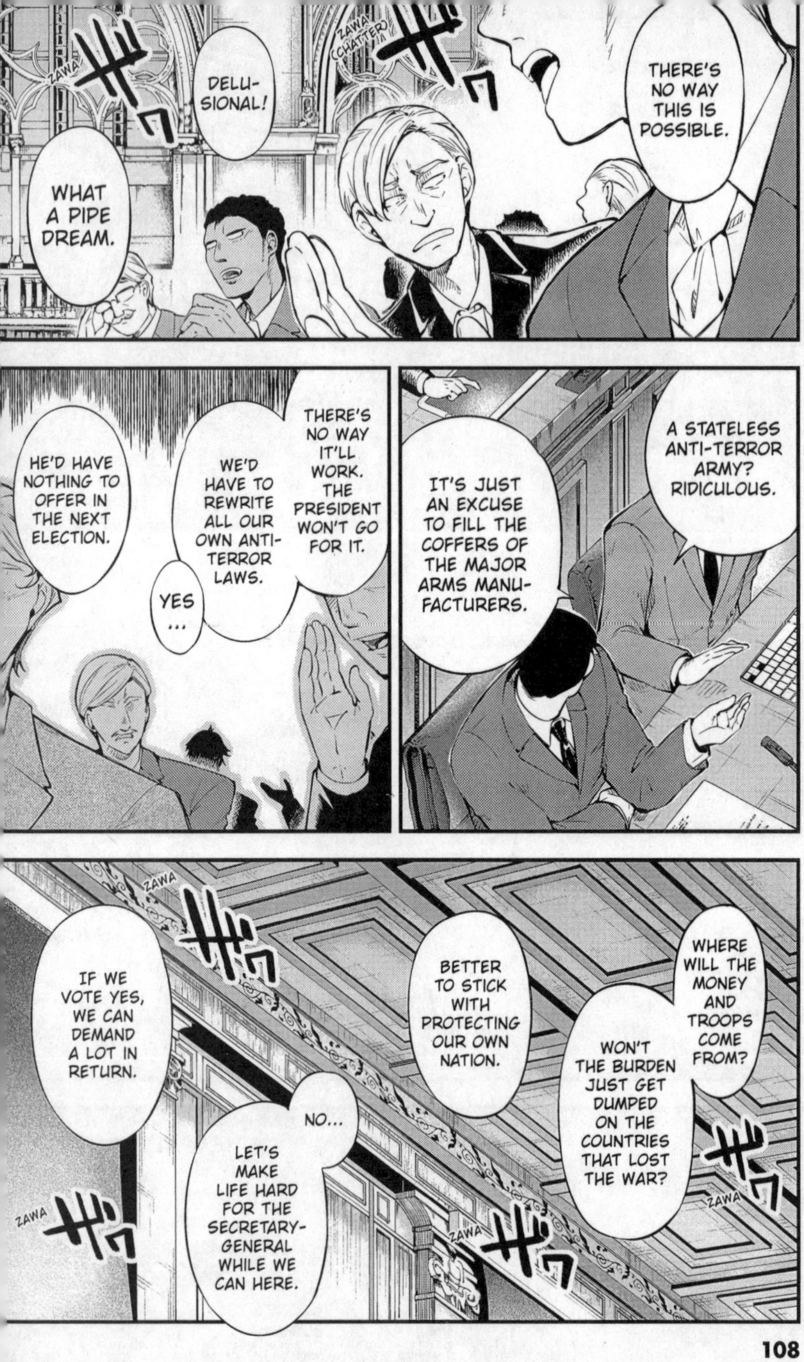
THERE'S NO WAY THIS IS POSSIBLE.
ZAWA (CHATTER)
DELUSIONAL!
ZAWA
WHAT A PIPE DREAM.
A STATELESS ANTI-TERROR ARMY? RIDICULOUS.
IT'S JUST AN EXCUSE TO FILL THE COFFERS OF THE MAJOR ARMS MANUFACTURERS.
THERE'S NO WAY IT'LL WORK. THE PRESIDENT WON'T GO FOR IT.
WE'D HAVE TO REWRITE ALL OUR OWN ANTI-TERROR LAWS.
YES ...
HE'D HAVE NOTHING TO OFFER IN THE NEXT ELECTION.
WHERE WILL THE MONEY AND TROOPS COME FROM?
WON'T THE BURDEN JUST GET DUMPED ON THE COUNTRIES THAT LOST THE WAR?
ZAWA
BETTER TO STICK WITH PROTECTING OUR OWN NATION.
ZAWA
NO...
LET'S MAKE LIFE HARD FOR THE SECRETARY-GENERAL WHILE WE CAN HERE.
ZAWA
IF WE VOTE YES, WE CAN DEMAND A LOT IN RETURN.
ZAWA

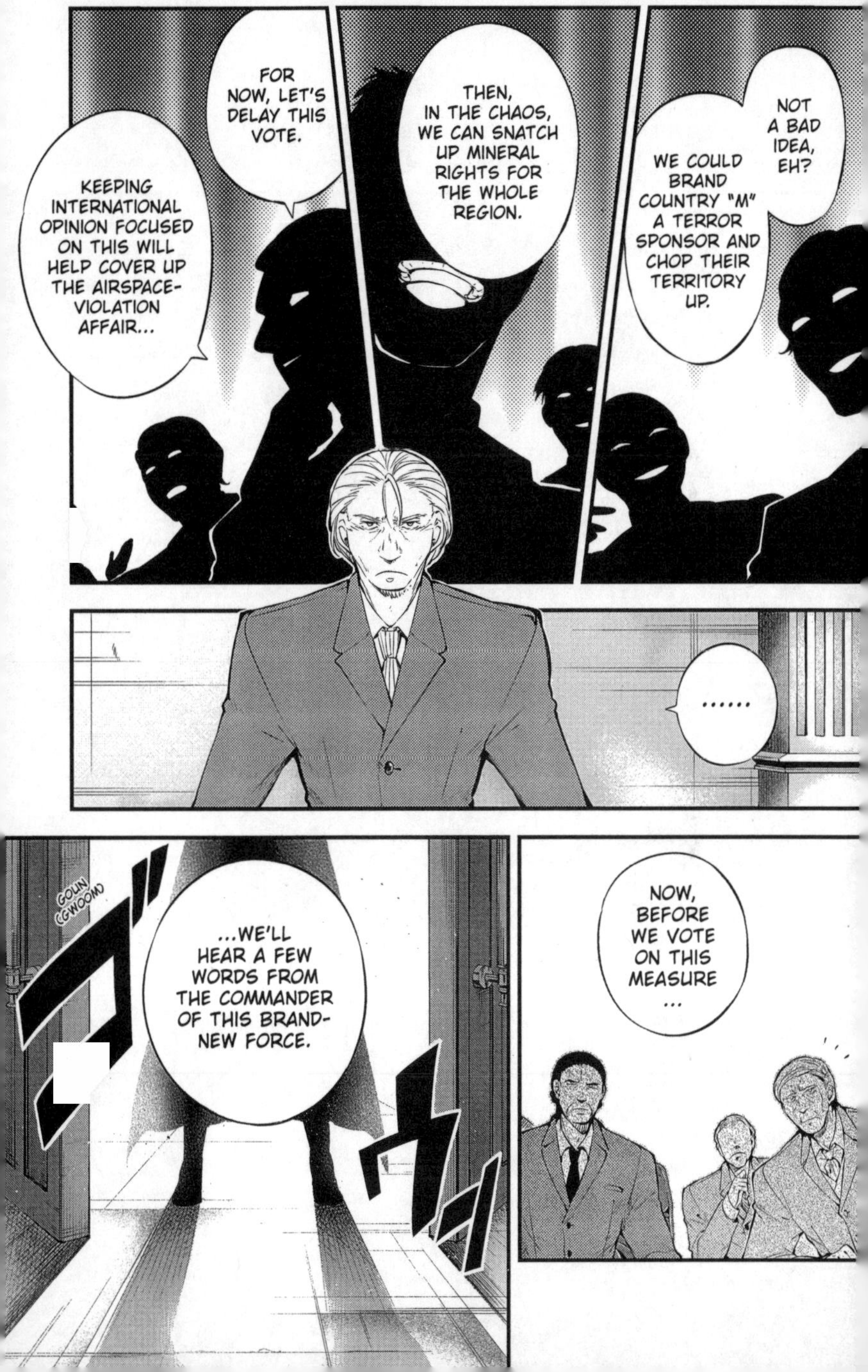
NOT A BAD IDEA, EH?
WE COULD BRAND COUNTRY "M" A TERROR SPONSOR AND CHOP THEIR TERRITORY UP.
THEN, IN THE CHAOS, WE CAN SNATCH UP MINERAL RIGHTS FOR THE WHOLE REGION.
FOR NOW, LET'S DELAY THIS VOTE.
KEEPING INTERNATIONAL OPINION FOCUSED ON THIS WILL HELP COVER UP THE AIRSPACE-VIOLATION AFFAIR...
......
NOW, BEFORE WE VOTE ON THIS MEASURE...
GOUN (GWOOM)
...WE'LL HEAR A FEW WORDS FROM THE COMMANDER OF THIS BRAND-NEW FORCE.

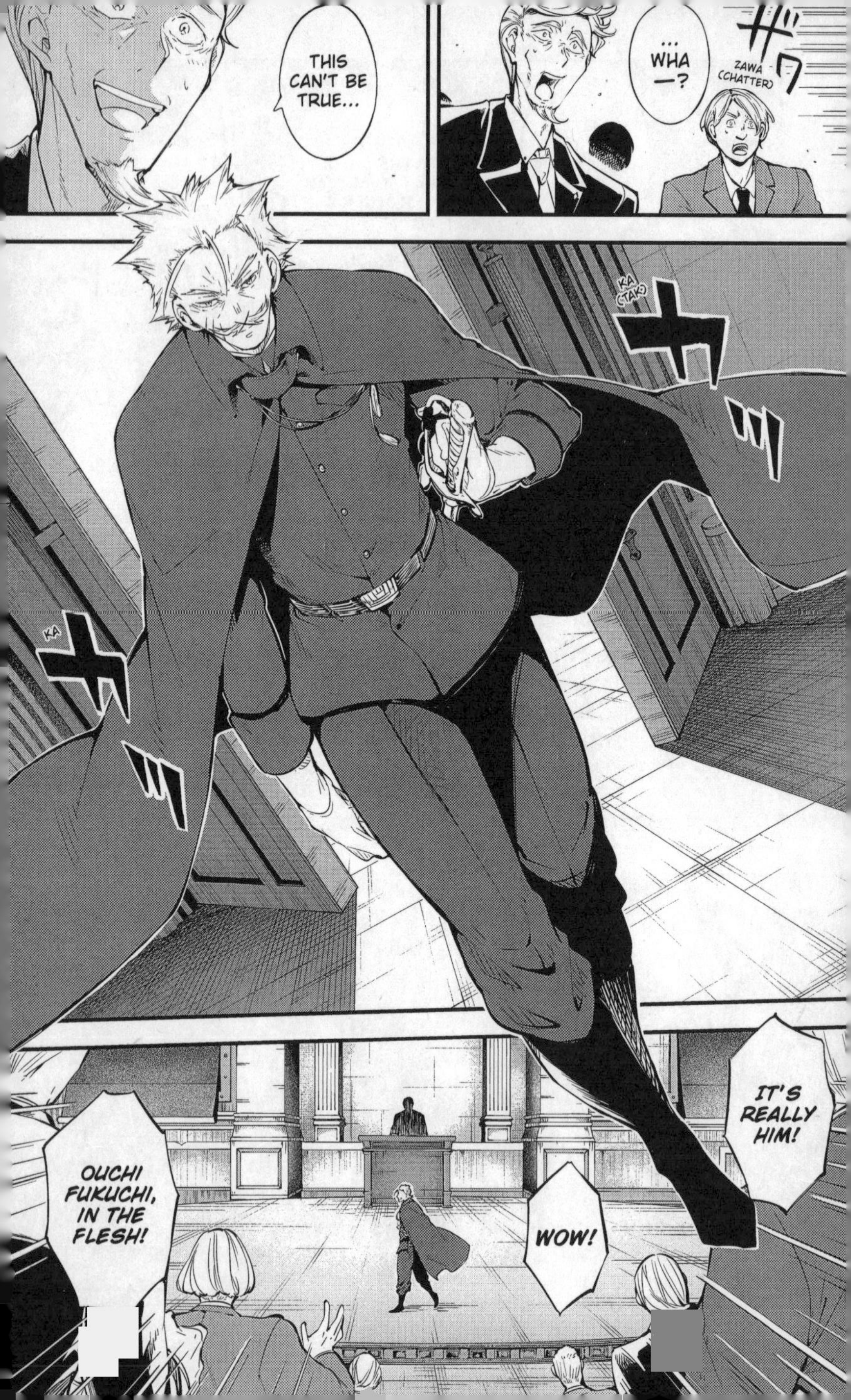

... WHA —?
ZAWA (CHATTER)
THIS CAN'T BE TRUE...
KA (TAK)
KA
IT'S REALLY HIM!
WOW!
OUCHI FUKUCHI, IN THE FLESH!

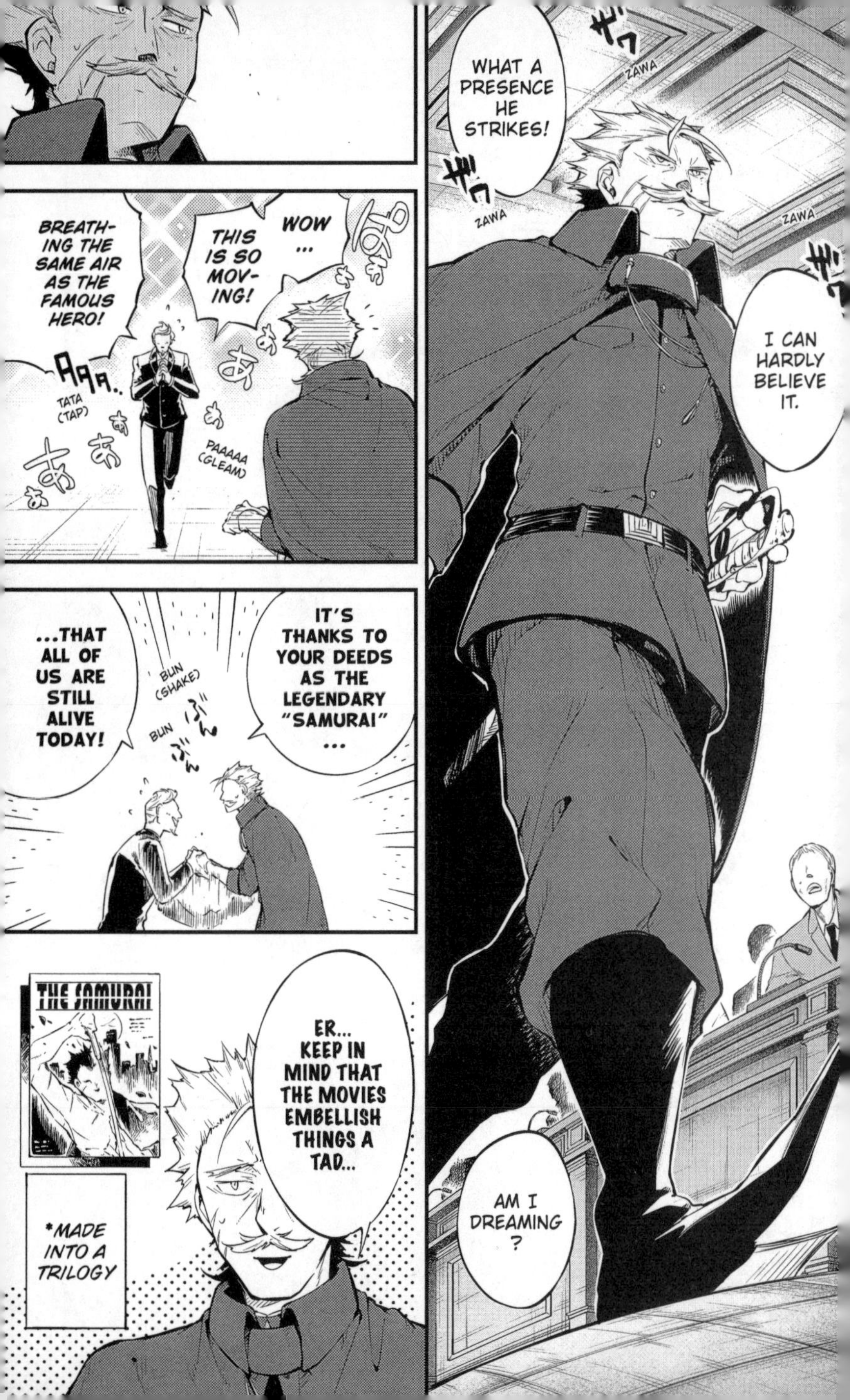

WHAT A PRESENCE HE STRIKES!
ZAWA
ZAWA
ZAWA
I CAN HARDLY BELIEVE IT.
AM I DREAMING?
WOW...
THIS IS SO MOVING!
BREATHING THE SAME AIR AS THE FAMOUS HERO!
TATA (TAP)
PAAAAA (GLEAM)
IT'S THANKS TO YOUR DEEDS AS THE LEGENDARY "SAMURAI"...
BUN (SHAKE)
BUN
...THAT ALL OF US ARE STILL ALIVE TODAY!
ER... KEEP IN MIND THAT THE MOVIES EMBELLISH THINGS A TAD...
THE SAMURAI
*MADE INTO A TRILOGY

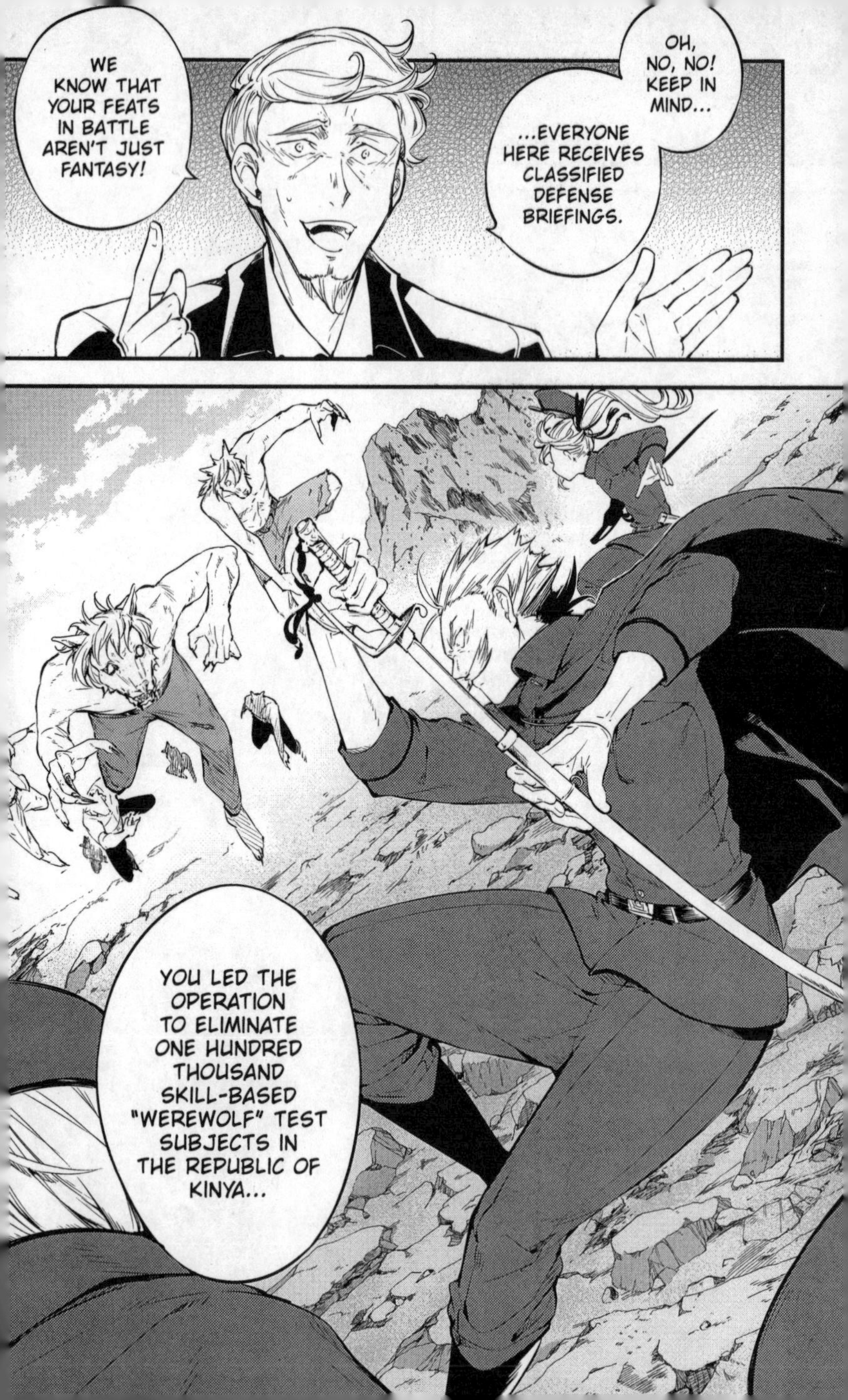
OH, NO, NO! KEEP IN MIND...
...EVERYONE HERE RECEIVES CLASSIFIED DEFENSE BRIEFINGS.
WE KNOW THAT YOUR FEATS IN BATTLE AREN'T JUST FANTASY!
YOU LED THE OPERATION TO ELIMINATE ONE HUNDRED THOUSAND SKILL-BASED "WEREWOLF" TEST SUBJECTS IN THE REPUBLIC OF KINYA...

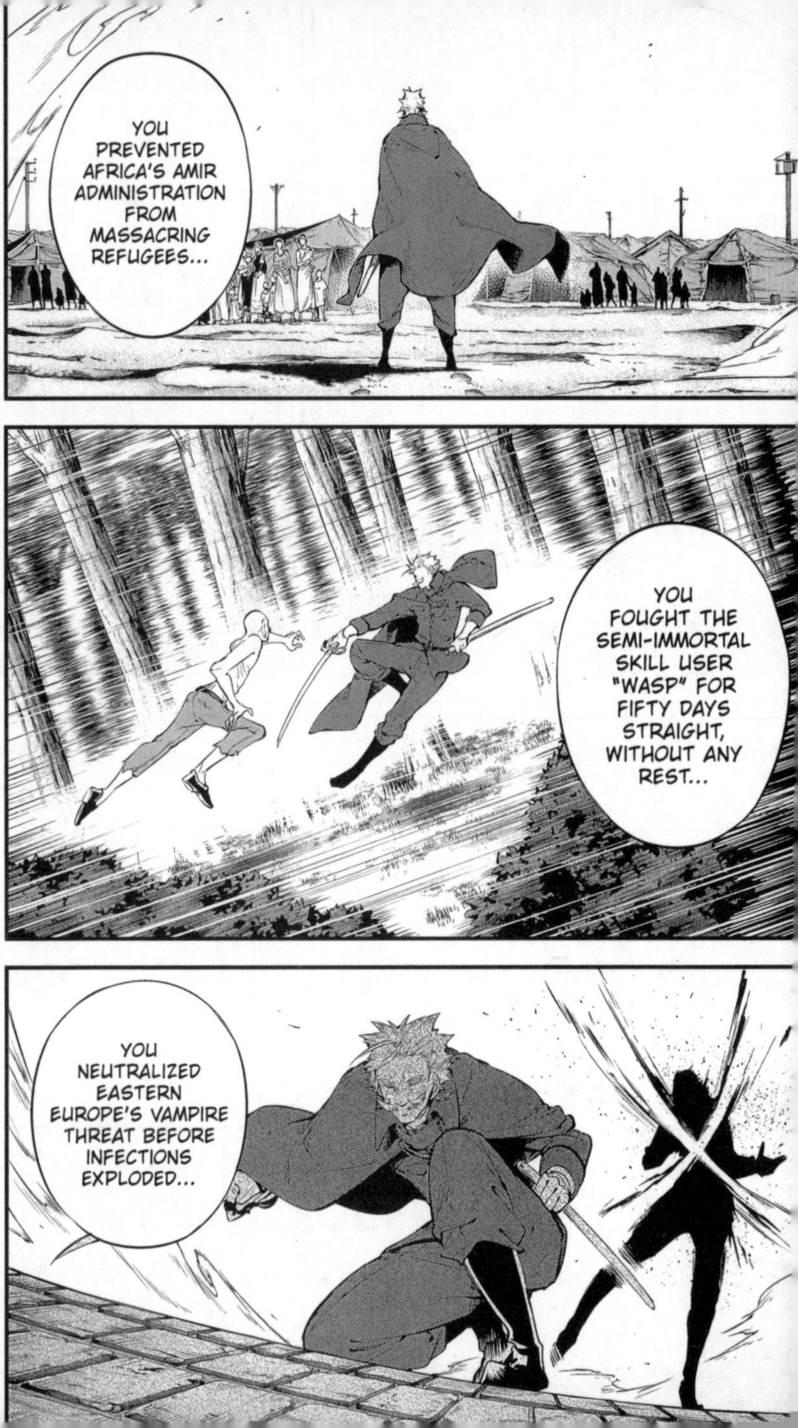
YOU PREVENTED AFRICA'S AMIR ADMINISTRATION FROM MASSACRING REFUGEES...
YOU FOUGHT THE SEMI-IMMORTAL SKILL USER "WASP" FOR FIFTY DAYS STRAIGHT, WITHOUT ANY REST...
YOU NEUTRALIZED EASTERN EUROPE'S VAMPIRE THREAT BEFORE INFECTIONS EXPLODED...

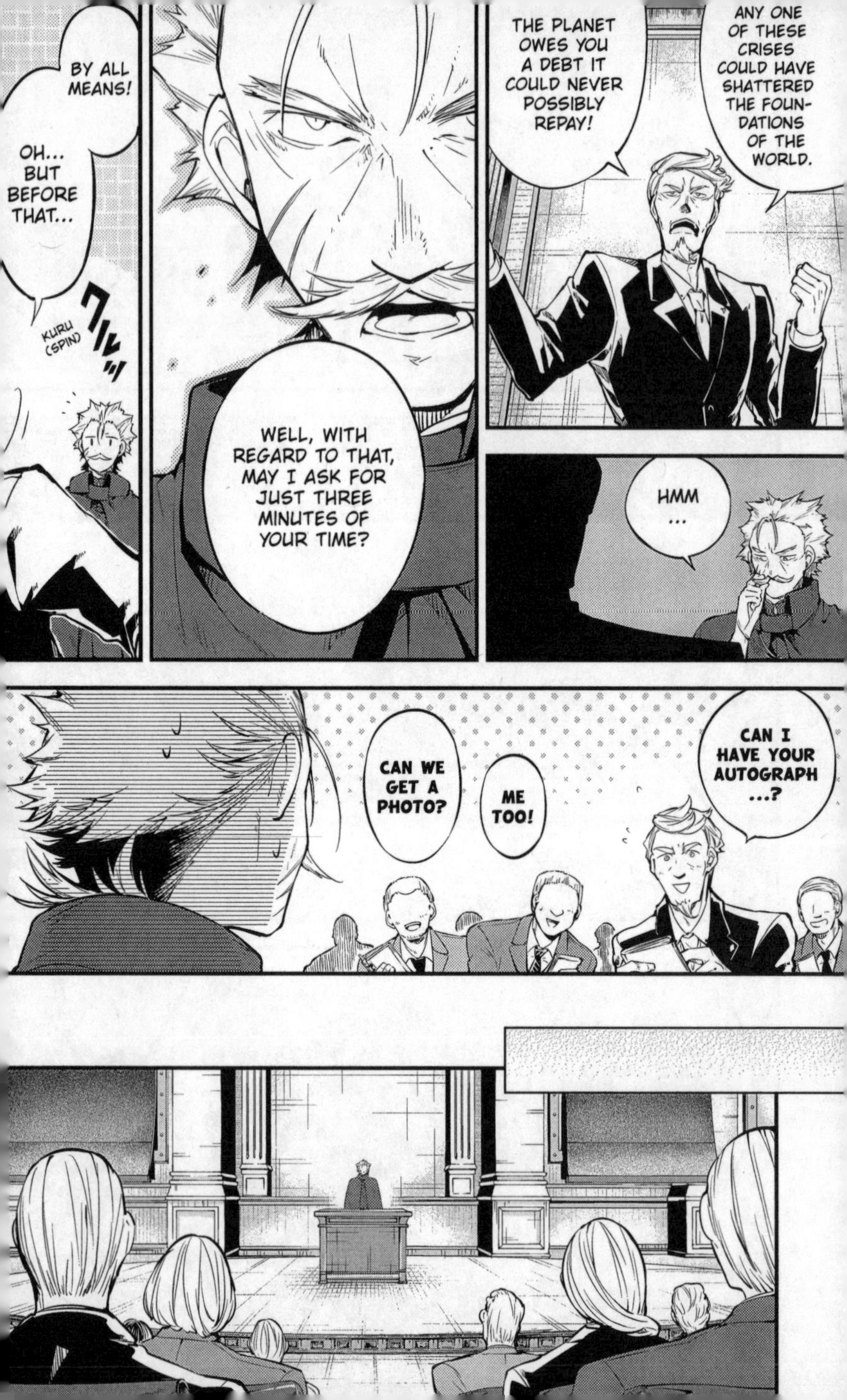
ANY ONE OF THESE CRISES COULD HAVE SHATTERED THE FOUN-DATIONS OF THE WORLD.
THE PLANET OWES YOU A DEBT IT COULD NEVER POSSIBLY REPAY!
HMM ...
WELL, WITH REGARD TO THAT, MAY I ASK FOR JUST THREE MINUTES OF YOUR TIME?
BY ALL MEANS!
OH... BUT BEFORE THAT...
KURU (SPIN)
CAN I HAVE YOUR AUTOGRAPH ...?
ME TOO!
CAN WE GET A PHOTO?

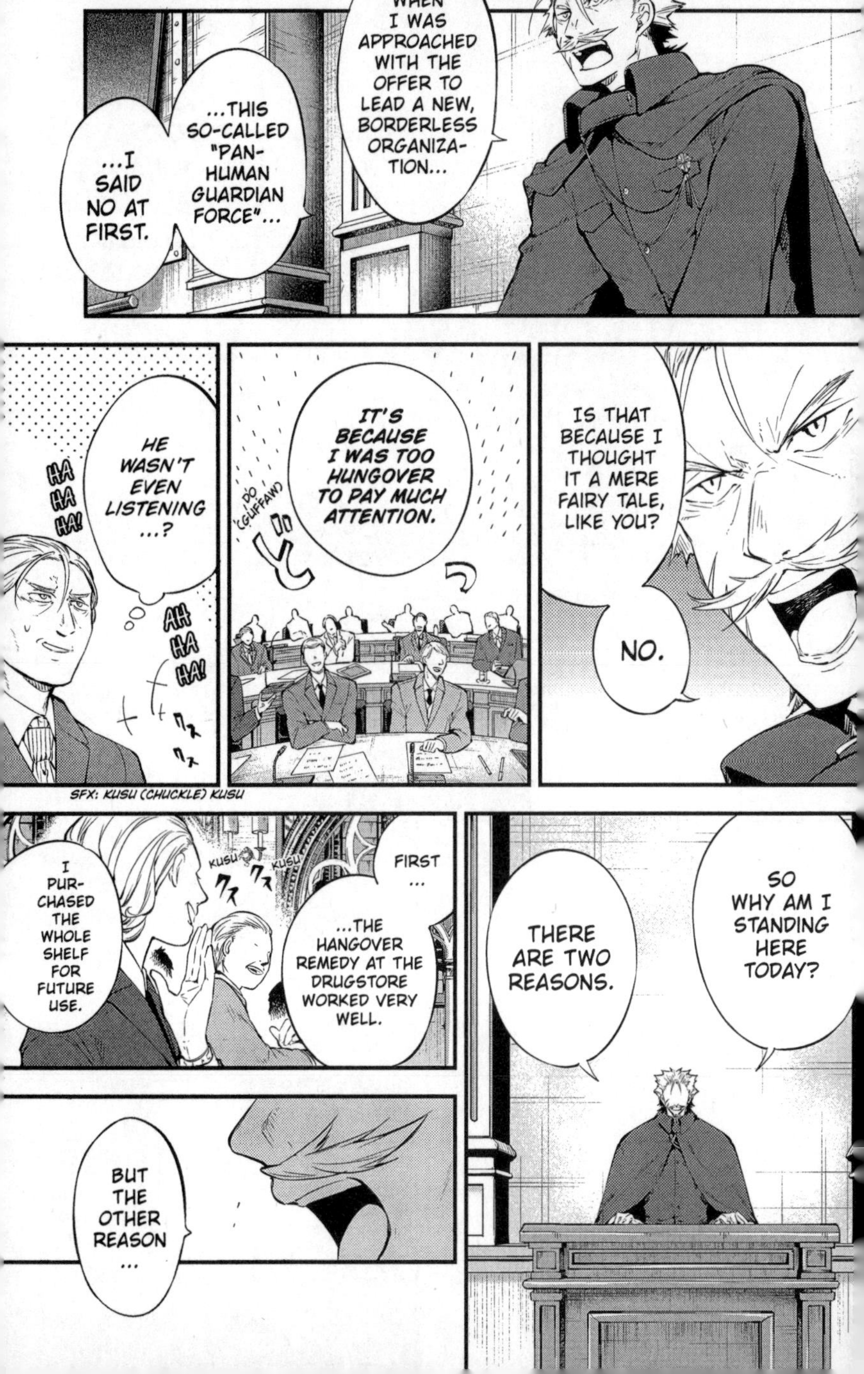
WHEN I WAS APPROACHED WITH THE OFFER TO LEAD A NEW, BORDERLESS ORGANIZA-TION...
...THIS SO-CALLED "PAN-HUMAN GUARDIAN FORCE"...
...I SAID NO AT FIRST.
IS THAT BECAUSE I THOUGHT IT A MERE FAIRY TALE, LIKE YOU?
NO.
IT'S BECAUSE I WAS TOO HUNGOVER TO PAY MUCH ATTENTION.
DO (GUFFAW)
HA HA HA!
HE WASN'T EVEN LISTENING ...?
AH HA HA!
SFX: KUSU (CHUCKLE) KUSU
SO WHY AM I STANDING HERE TODAY?
THERE ARE TWO REASONS.
FIRST ...
...THE HANGOVER REMEDY AT THE DRUGSTORE WORKED VERY WELL.
KUSU
KUSU
I PUR-CHASED THE WHOLE SHELF FOR FUTURE USE.
BUT THE OTHER REASON ...

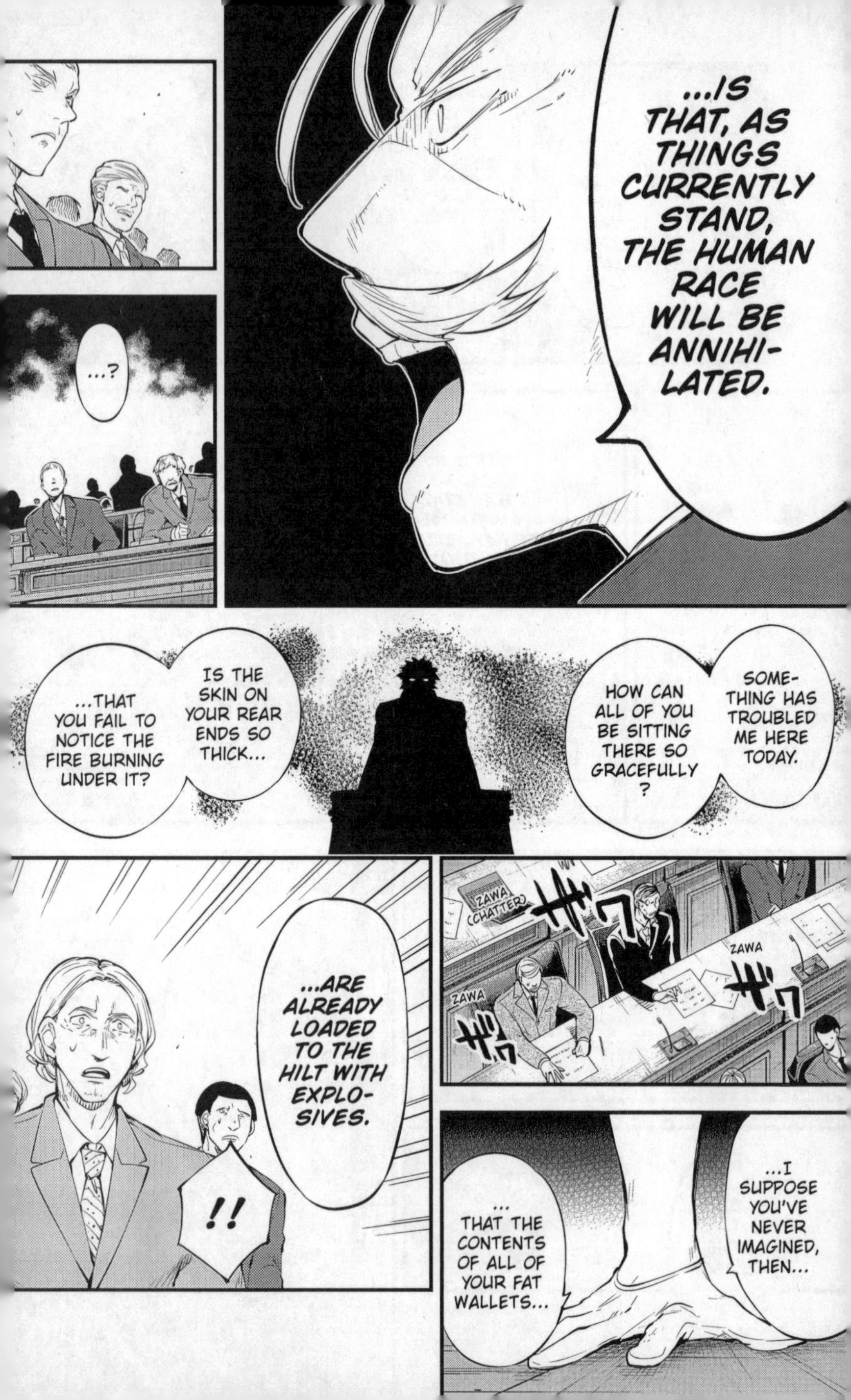
...IS THAT, AS THINGS CURRENTLY STAND, THE HUMAN RACE WILL BE ANNIHILATED.
...?
SOMETHING HAS TROUBLED ME HERE TODAY.
HOW CAN ALL OF YOU BE SITTING THERE SO GRACEFULLY?
IS THE SKIN ON YOUR REAR ENDS SO THICK...
...THAT YOU FAIL TO NOTICE THE FIRE BURNING UNDER IT?
ZAWA (CHATTER)
ZAWA
ZAWA
...I SUPPOSE YOU'VE NEVER IMAGINED, THEN...
...THAT THE CONTENTS OF ALL OF YOUR FAT WALLETS...
...ARE ALREADY LOADED TO THE HILT WITH EXPLOSIVES.
!!

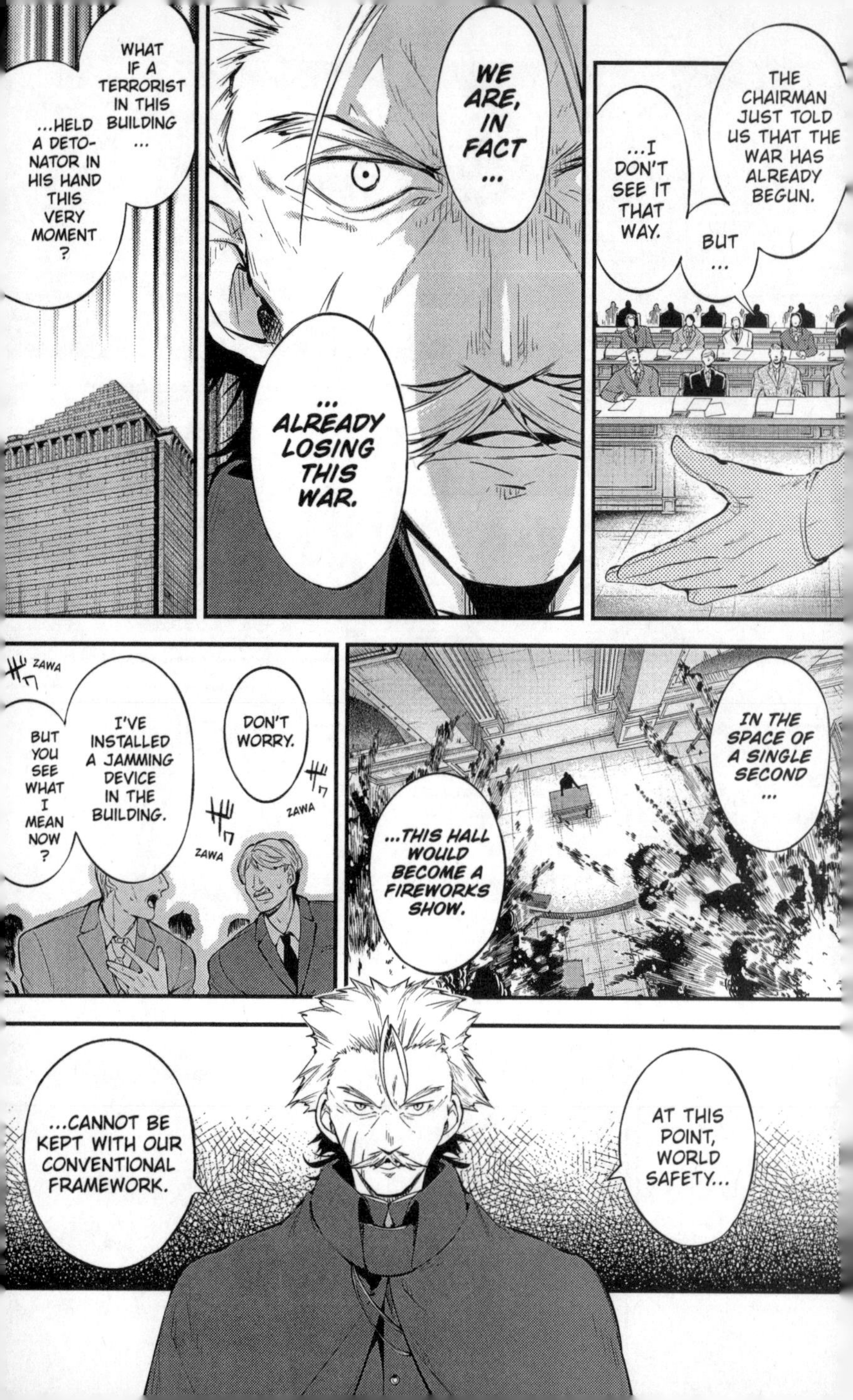
THE CHAIRMAN JUST TOLD US THAT THE WAR HAS ALREADY BEGUN.
BUT ...
...I DON'T SEE IT THAT WAY.
WE ARE, IN FACT ...
... ALREADY LOSING THIS WAR.
WHAT IF A TERRORIST IN THIS BUILDING ...
...HELD A DETONATOR IN HIS HAND THIS VERY MOMENT ?
IN THE SPACE OF A SINGLE SECOND ...
...THIS HALL WOULD BECOME A FIREWORKS SHOW.
ZAWA
DON'T WORRY.
ZAWA
I'VE INSTALLED A JAMMING DEVICE IN THE BUILDING.
ZAWA
BUT YOU SEE WHAT I MEAN NOW ?
AT THIS POINT, WORLD SAFETY...
...CANNOT BE KEPT WITH OUR CONVENTIONAL FRAMEWORK.

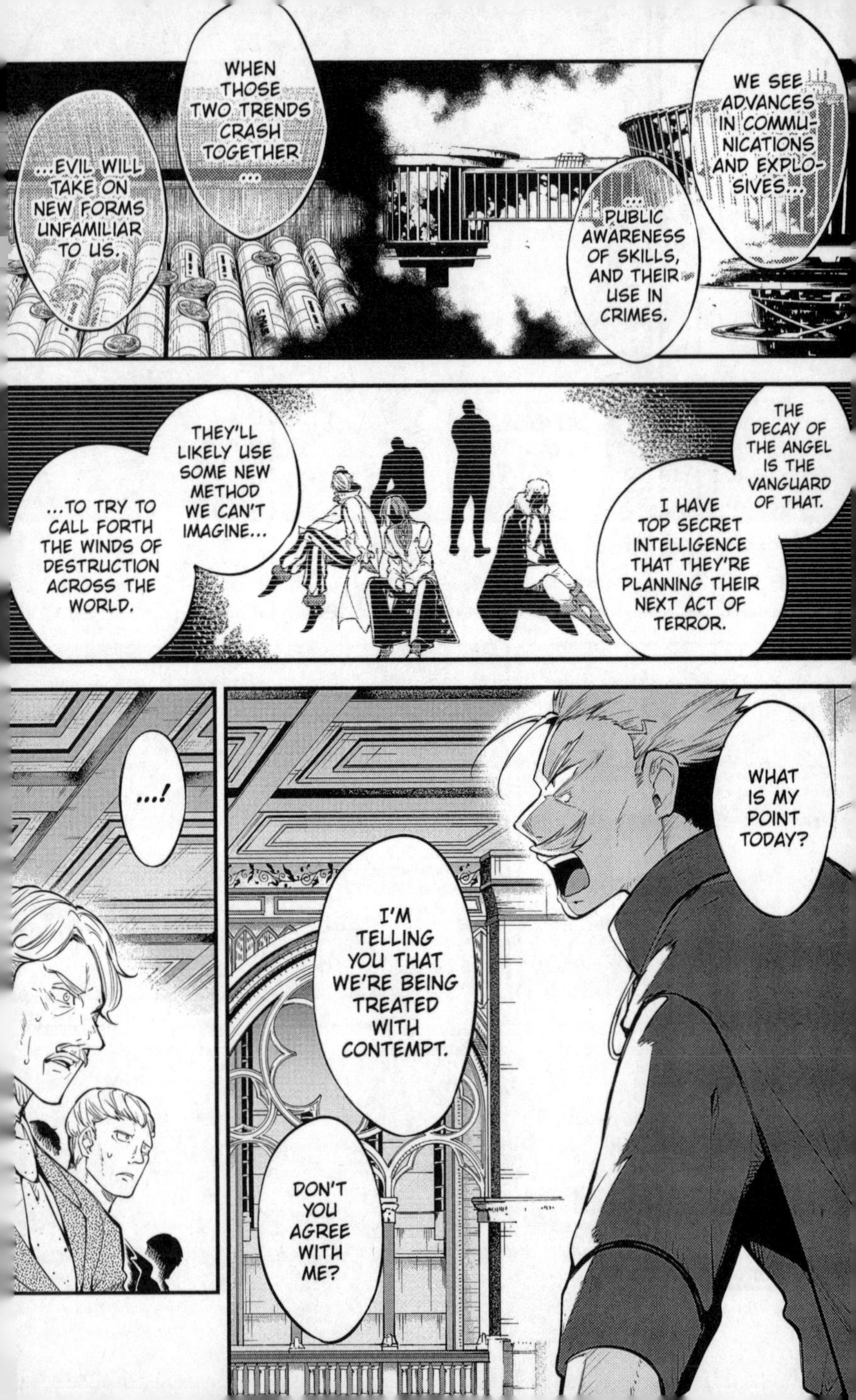
WE SEE ADVANCES IN COMMUNICATIONS AND EXPLOSIVES...
...PUBLIC AWARENESS OF SKILLS, AND THEIR USE IN CRIMES.
WHEN THOSE TWO TRENDS CRASH TOGETHER...
...EVIL WILL TAKE ON NEW FORMS UNFAMILIAR TO US.
THE DECAY OF THE ANGEL IS THE VANGUARD OF THAT.
I HAVE TOP SECRET INTELLIGENCE THAT THEY'RE PLANNING THEIR NEXT ACT OF TERROR.
THEY'LL LIKELY USE SOME NEW METHOD WE CAN'T IMAGINE...
...TO TRY TO CALL FORTH THE WINDS OF DESTRUCTION ACROSS THE WORLD.
WHAT IS MY POINT TODAY?
I'M TELLING YOU THAT WE'RE BEING TREATED WITH CONTEMPT.
DON'T YOU AGREE WITH ME?
...!

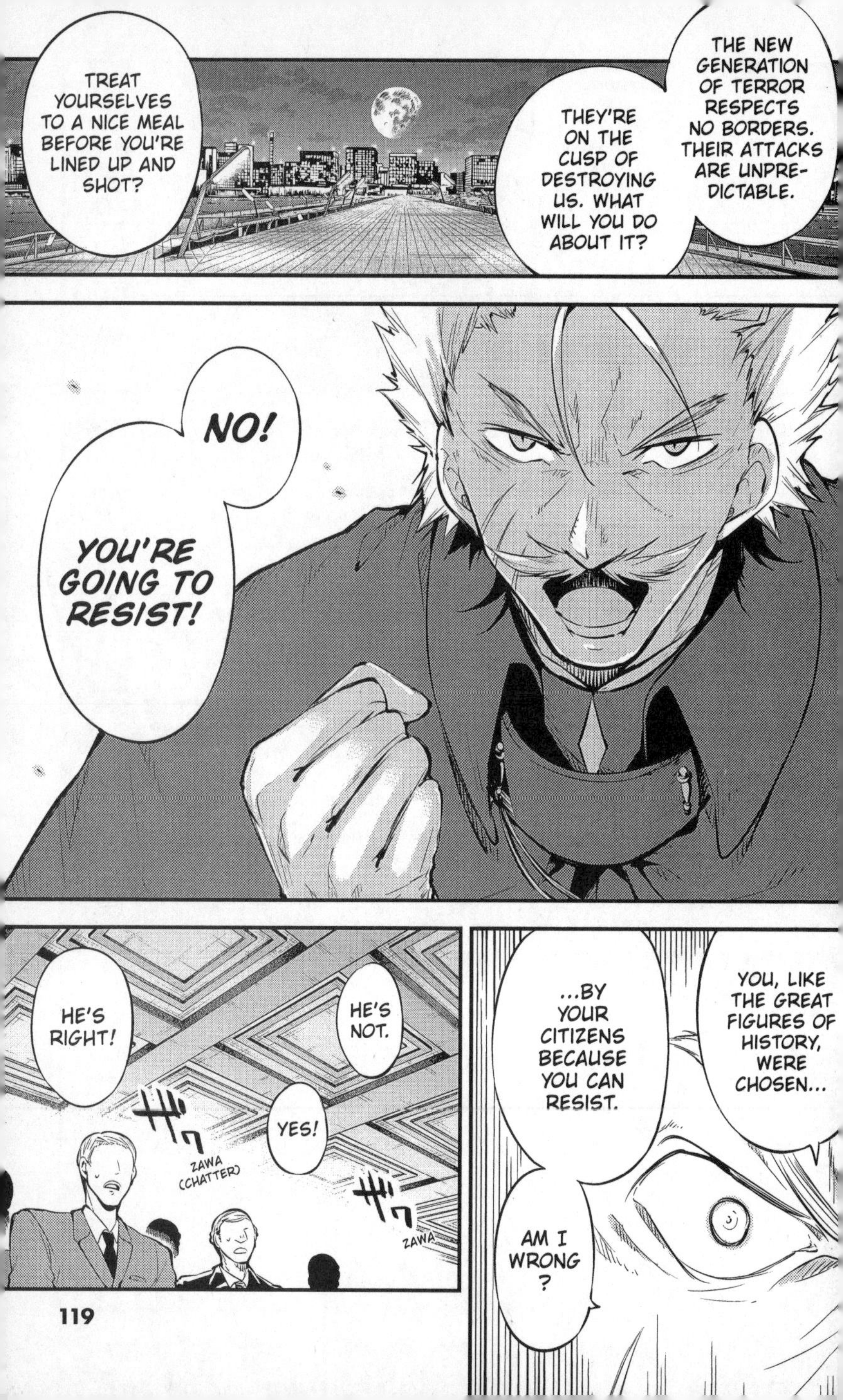

THE NEW GENERATION OF TERROR RESPECTS NO BORDERS. THEIR ATTACKS ARE UNPRE-DICTABLE.
THEY'RE ON THE CUSP OF DESTROYING US. WHAT WILL YOU DO ABOUT IT?
TREAT YOURSELVES TO A NICE MEAL BEFORE YOU'RE LINED UP AND SHOT?
NO!
YOU'RE GOING TO RESIST!
YOU, LIKE THE GREAT FIGURES OF HISTORY, WERE CHOSEN...
...BY YOUR CITIZENS BECAUSE YOU CAN RESIST.
AM I WRONG?
HE'S NOT.
HE'S RIGHT!
YES!
ZAWA (CHATTER)
ZAWA

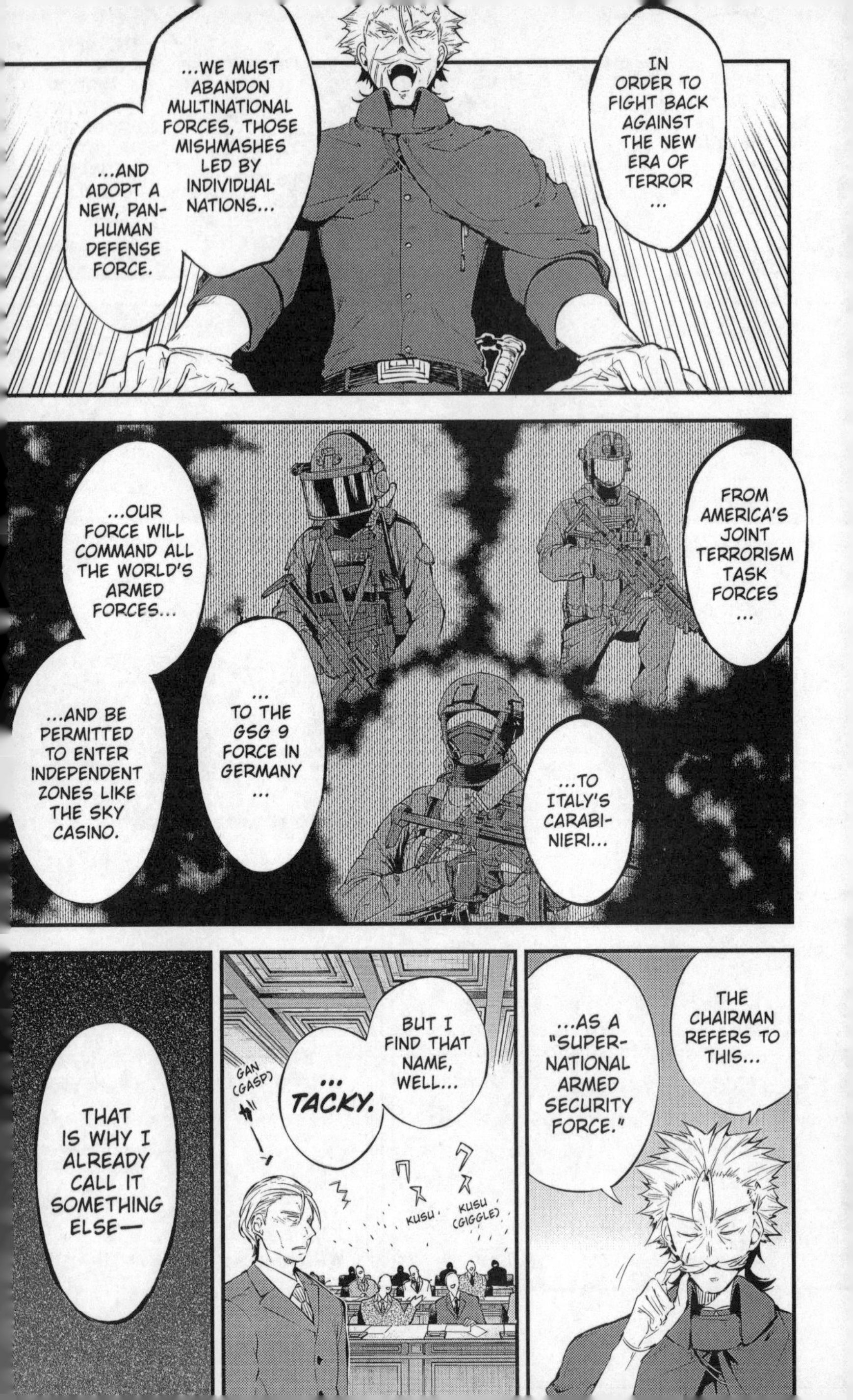
IN ORDER TO FIGHT BACK AGAINST THE NEW ERA OF TERROR...
...WE MUST ABANDON MULTINATIONAL FORCES, THOSE MISHMASHES LED BY INDIVIDUAL NATIONS...
...AND ADOPT A NEW, PAN-HUMAN DEFENSE FORCE.
FROM AMERICA'S JOINT TERRORISM TASK FORCES...
...TO ITALY'S CARABINIERI...
...TO THE GSG 9 FORCE IN GERMANY...
...OUR FORCE WILL COMMAND ALL THE WORLD'S ARMED FORCES...
...AND BE PERMITTED TO ENTER INDEPENDENT ZONES LIKE THE SKY CASINO.
THE CHAIRMAN REFERS TO THIS...
...AS A "SUPER-NATIONAL ARMED SECURITY FORCE."
BUT I FIND THAT NAME, WELL...
...TACKY.
GAN (GASP)
KUSU
KUSU (GIGGLE)
THAT IS WHY I ALREADY CALL IT SOMETHING ELSE—

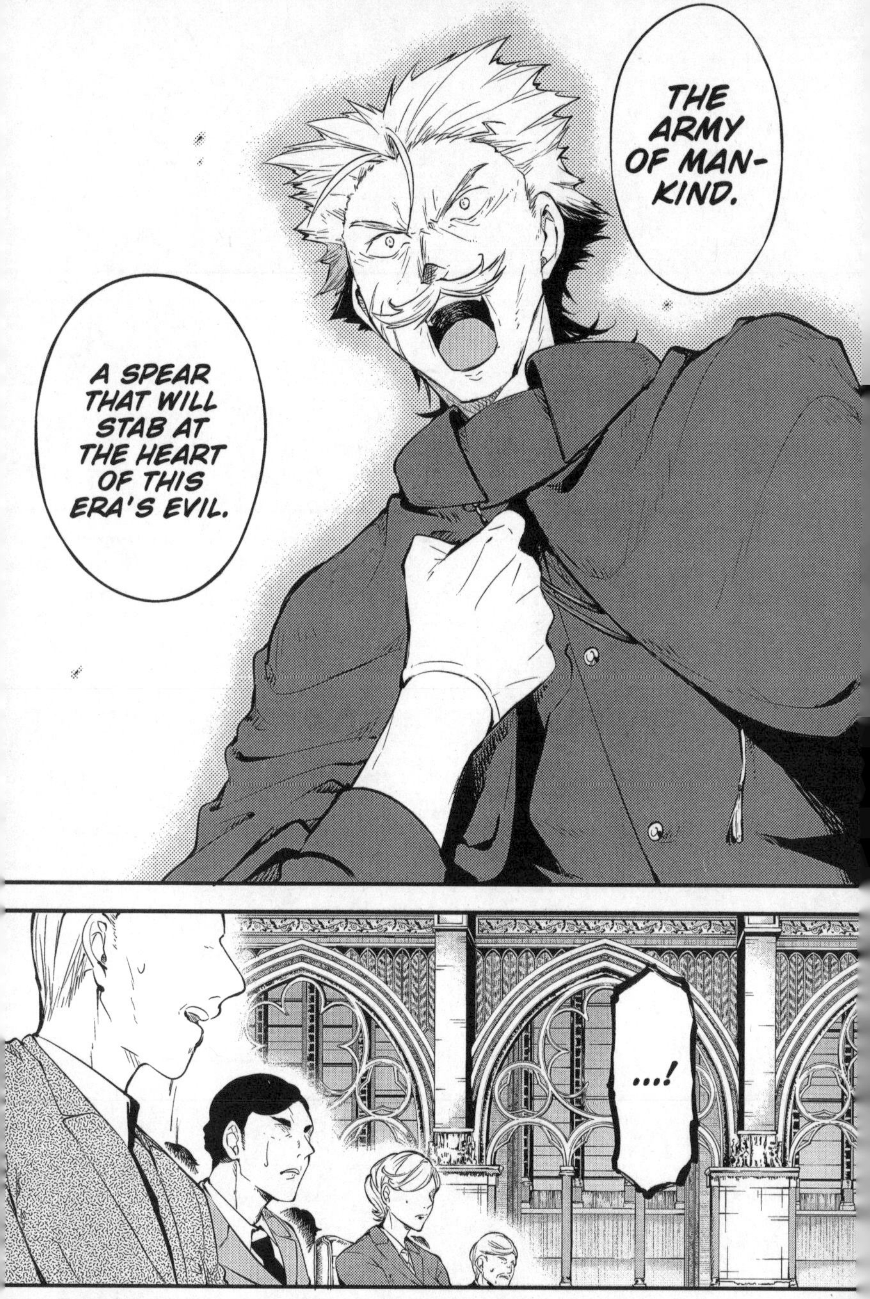
THE ARMY OF MAN-KIND.
A SPEAR THAT WILL STAB AT THE HEART OF THIS ERA'S EVIL.
...!

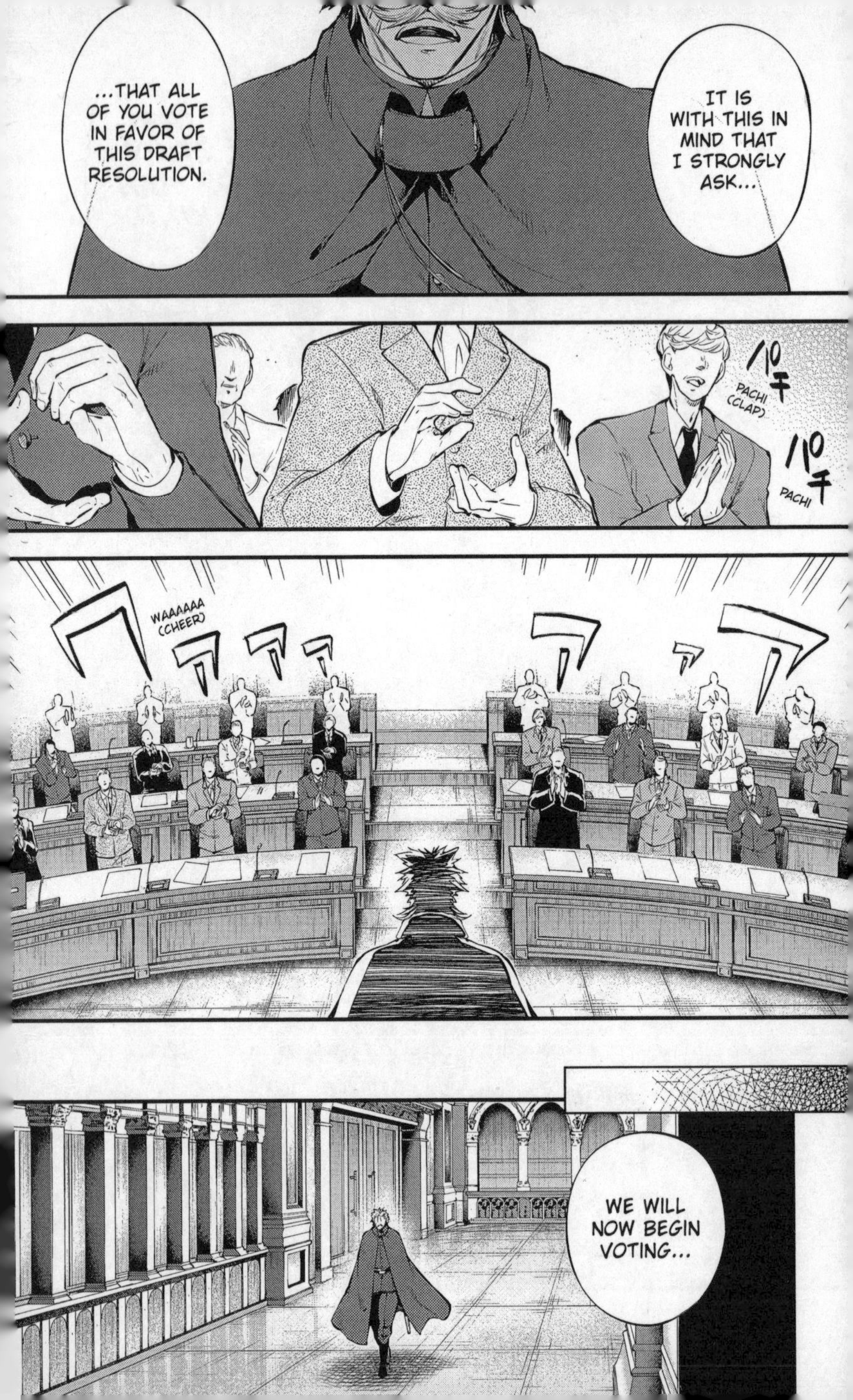
IT IS WITH THIS IN MIND THAT I STRONGLY ASK...
...THAT ALL OF YOU VOTE IN FAVOR OF THIS DRAFT RESOLUTION.
パチ
PACHI (CLAP)
パチ
PACHI
WAAAAAA (CHEER)
WE WILL NOW BEGIN VOTING...

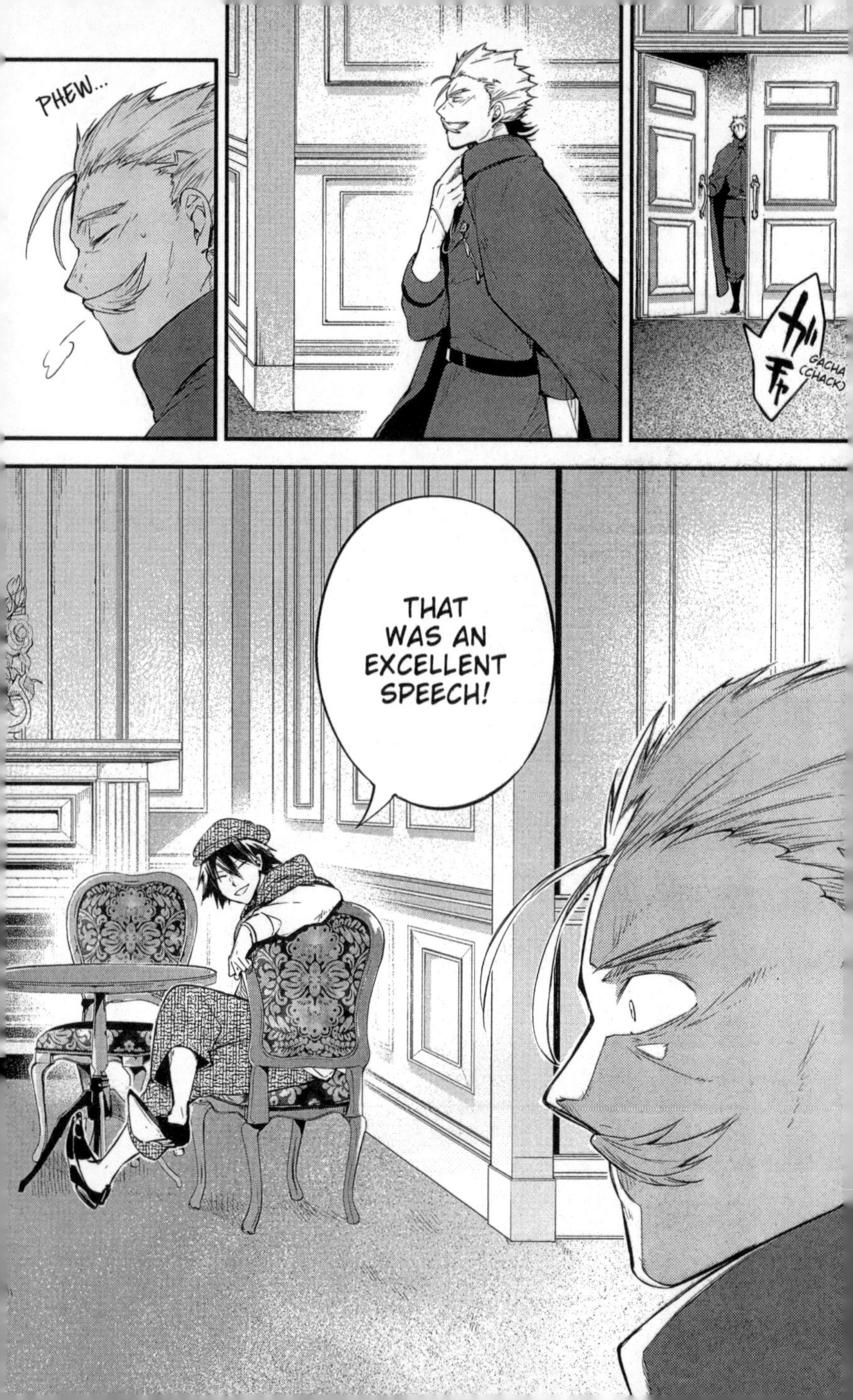
GACHA (CHACK)
PHEW...
THAT WAS AN EXCELLENT SPEECH!

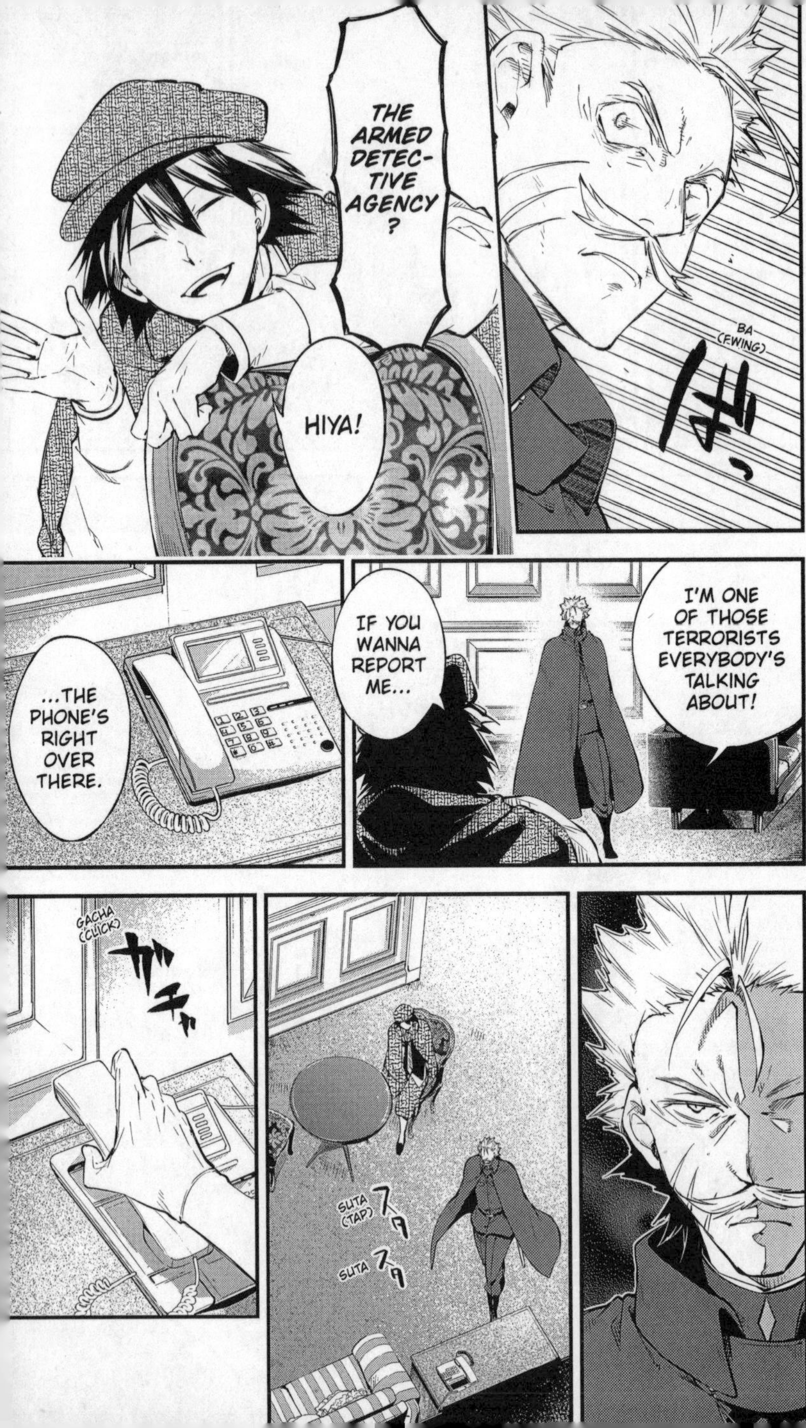
BA (FWING)
THE ARMED DETECTIVE AGENCY?
HIYA!
I'M ONE OF THOSE TERRORISTS EVERYBODY'S TALKING ABOUT!
IF YOU WANNA REPORT ME...
...THE PHONE'S RIGHT OVER THERE.
SUTA (TAP)
SUTA
GACHA (CLICK)

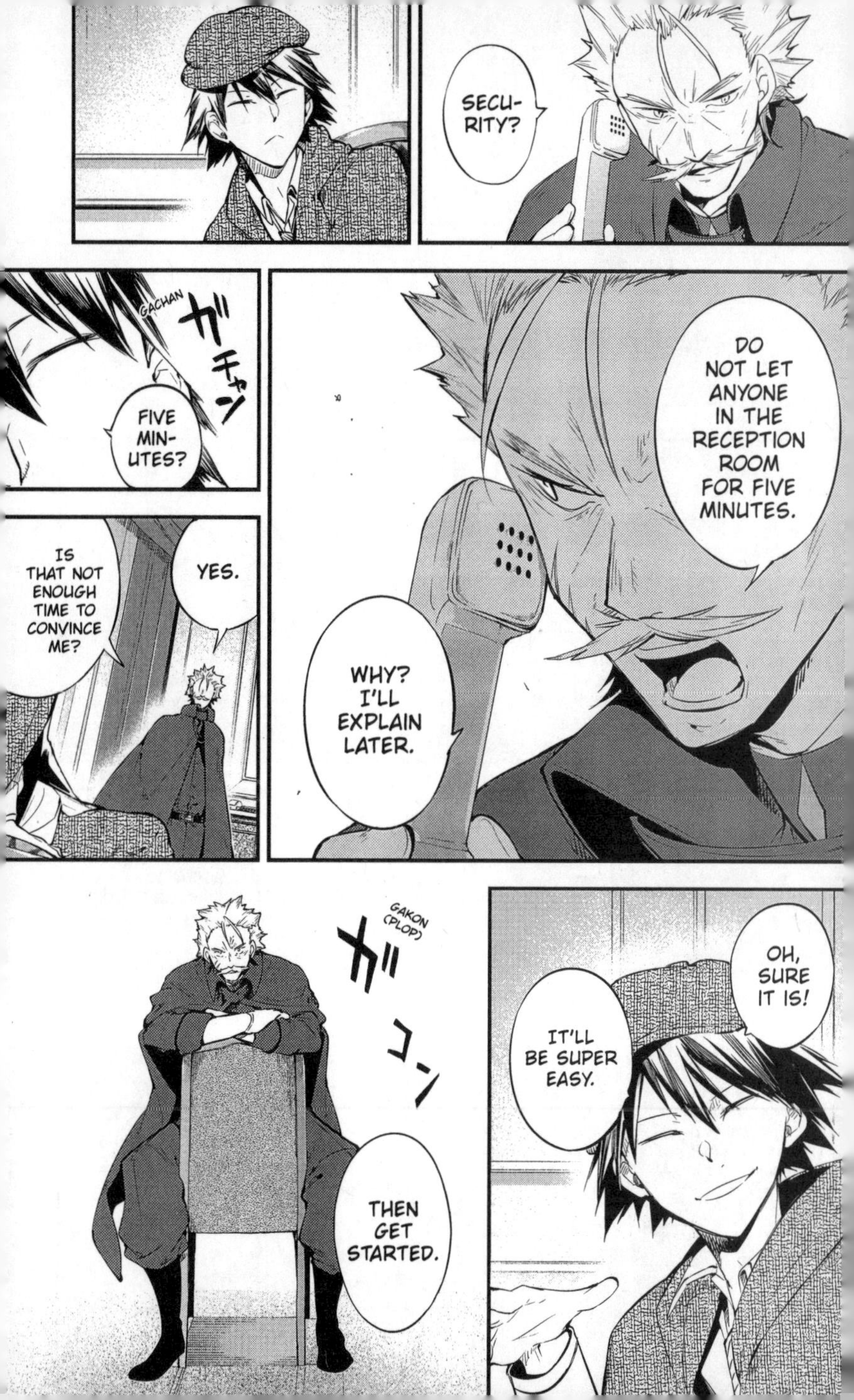
SECU-RITY?
DO NOT LET ANYONE IN THE RECEPTION ROOM FOR FIVE MINUTES.
WHY? I'LL EXPLAIN LATER.
GACHAN
ガチャン
FIVE MIN-UTES?
YES.
IS THAT NOT ENOUGH TIME TO CONVINCE ME?
OH, SURE IT IS!
IT'LL BE SUPER EASY.
GAKON (PLOP)
ガコン
THEN GET STARTED.

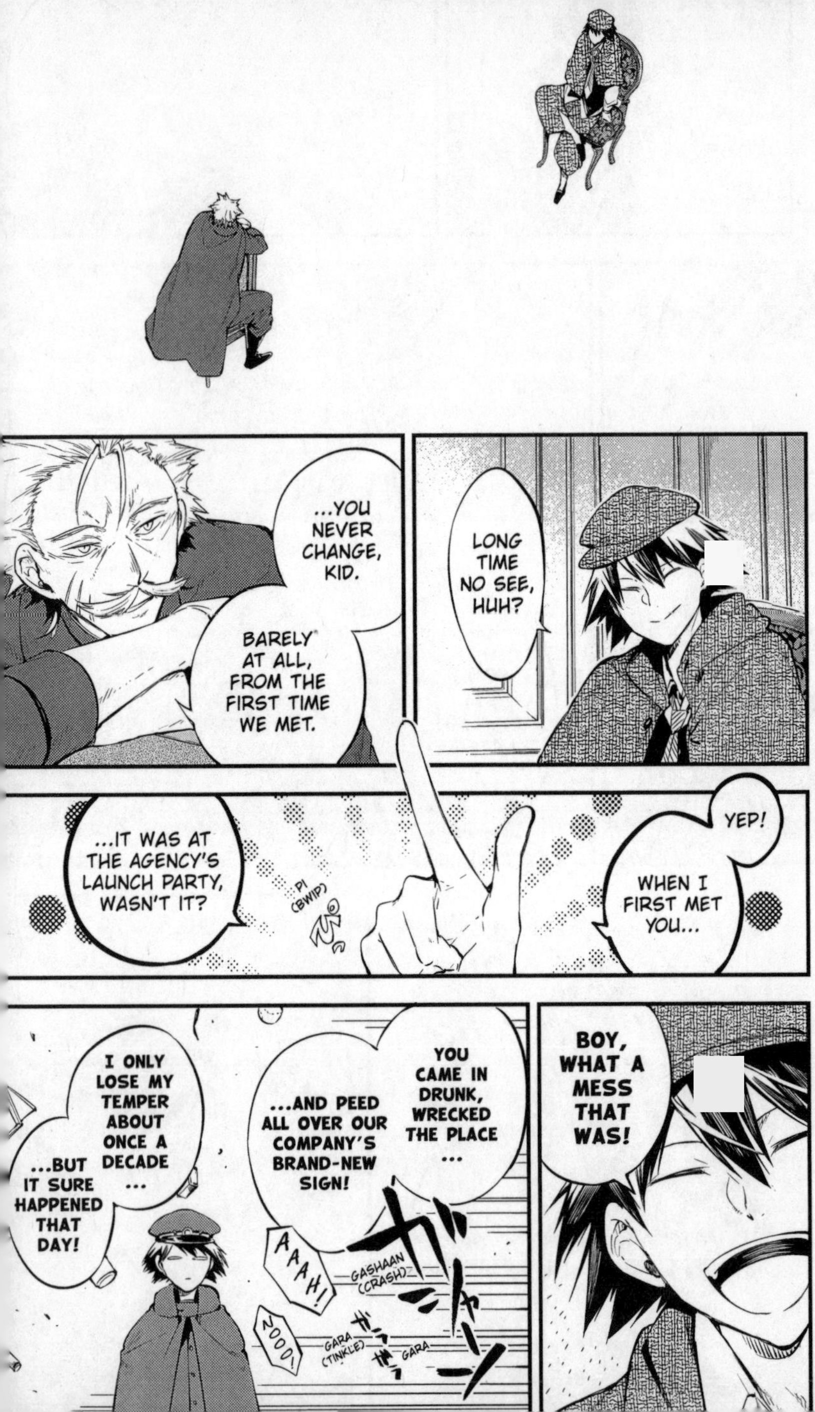
LONG TIME NO SEE, HUH?
...YOU NEVER CHANGE, KID.
BARELY AT ALL, FROM THE FIRST TIME WE MET.
YEP!
WHEN I FIRST MET YOU...
PI (BWIP)
...IT WAS AT THE AGENCY'S LAUNCH PARTY, WASN'T IT?
BOY, WHAT A MESS THAT WAS!
YOU CAME IN DRUNK, WRECKED THE PLACE...
...AND PEED ALL OVER OUR COMPANY'S BRAND-NEW SIGN!
GASHAAN (CRASH)
AAAH!
GARA (TINKLE) GARA
NOOO!
I ONLY LOSE MY TEMPER ABOUT ONCE A DECADE...
...BUT IT SURE HAPPENED THAT DAY!

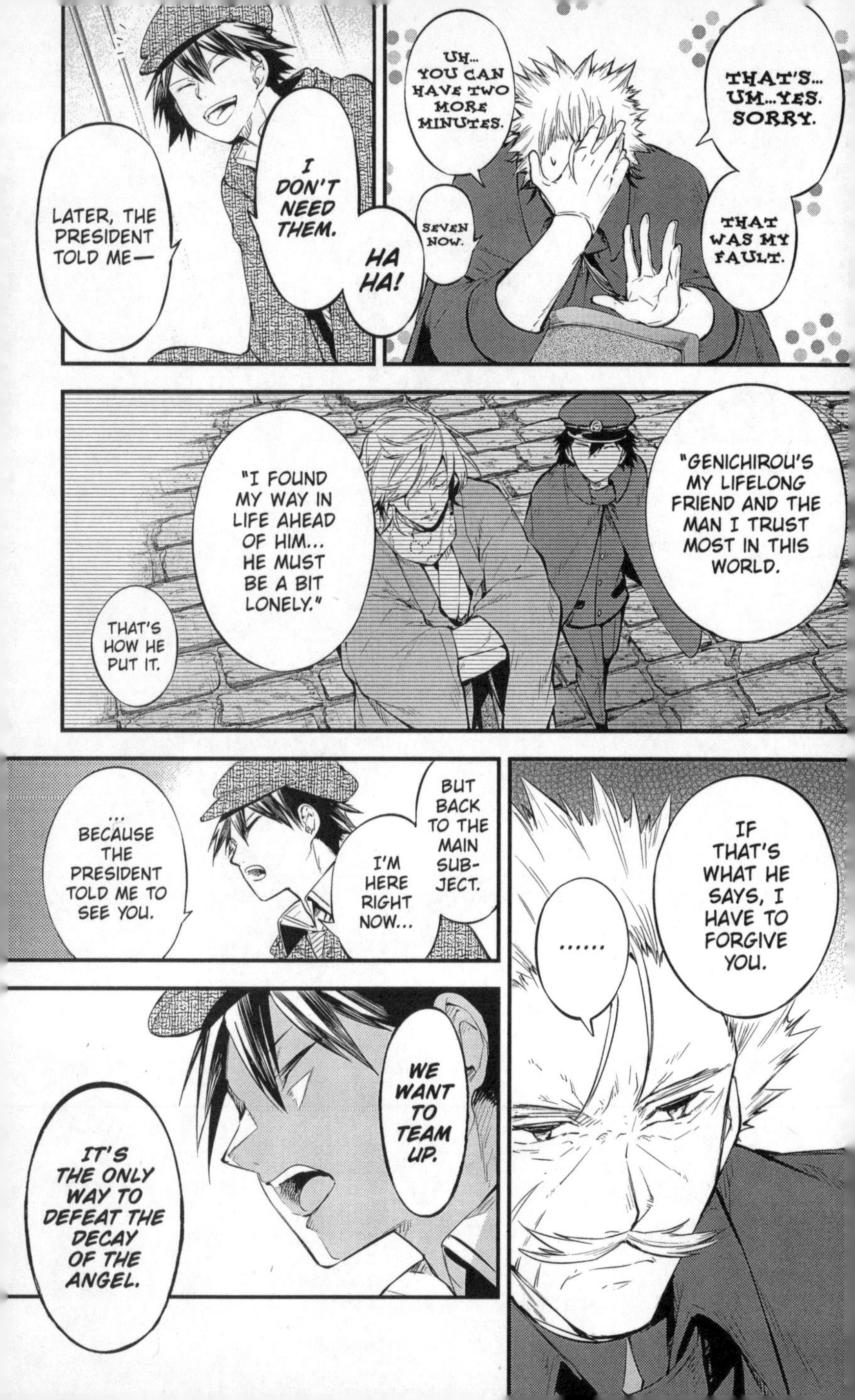
THAT'S... UM...YES. SORRY.
THAT WAS MY FAULT.
UH... YOU CAN HAVE TWO MORE MINUTES.
SEVEN NOW.
HA HA!
I DON'T NEED THEM.
LATER, THE PRESIDENT TOLD ME—
"GENICHIROU'S MY LIFELONG FRIEND AND THE MAN I TRUST MOST IN THIS WORLD.
"I FOUND MY WAY IN LIFE AHEAD OF HIM... HE MUST BE A BIT LONELY."
THAT'S HOW HE PUT IT.
IF THAT'S WHAT HE SAYS, I HAVE TO FORGIVE YOU.
......
BUT BACK TO THE MAIN SUB-JECT.
I'M HERE RIGHT NOW...
...BECAUSE THE PRESIDENT TOLD ME TO SEE YOU.
WE WANT TO TEAM UP.
IT'S THE ONLY WAY TO DEFEAT THE DECAY OF THE ANGEL.

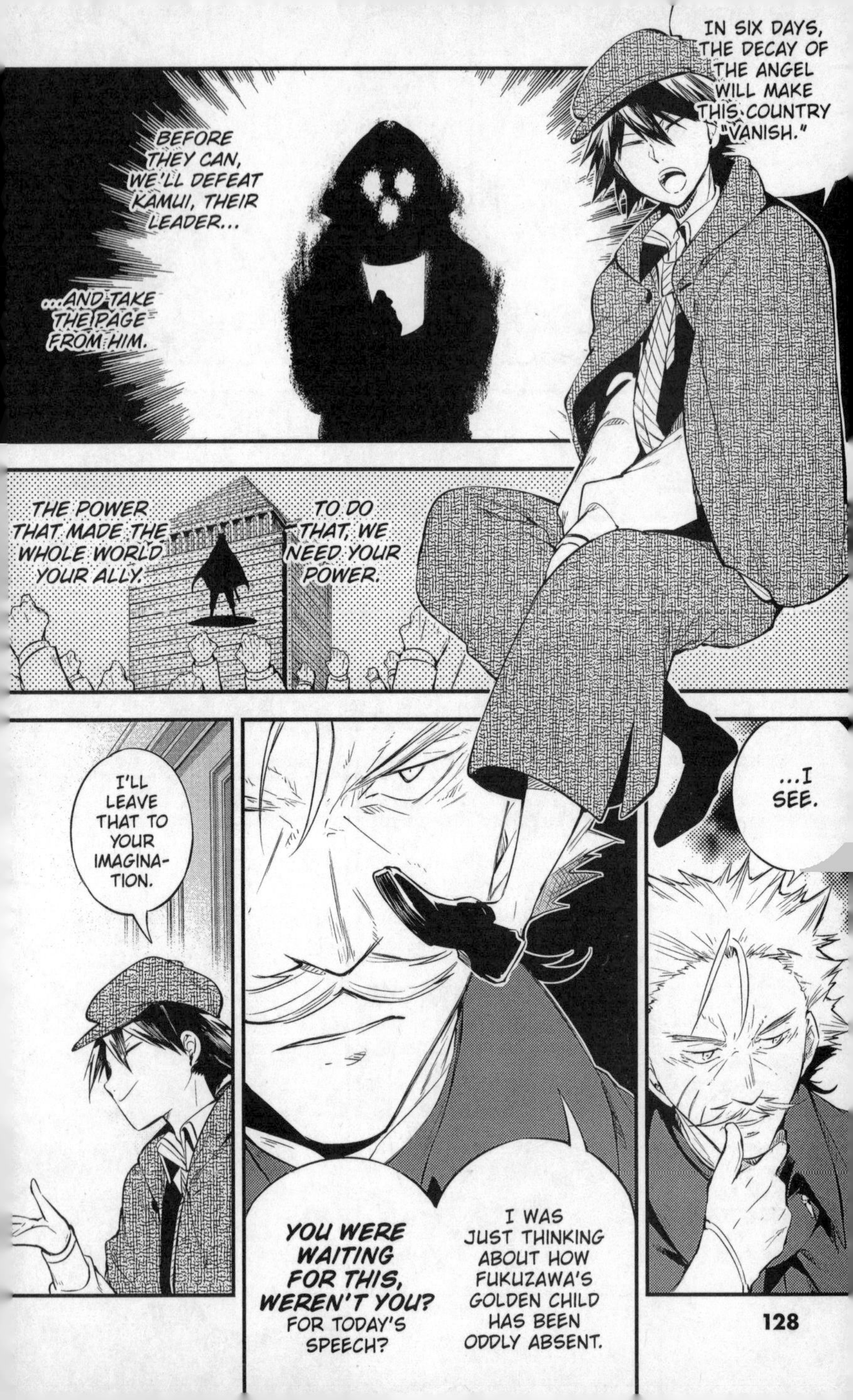
IN SIX DAYS, THE DECAY OF THE ANGEL WILL MAKE THIS COUNTRY "VANISH."
BEFORE THEY CAN, WE'LL DEFEAT KAMUI, THEIR LEADER...
...AND TAKE THE PAGE FROM HIM.
TO DO THAT, WE NEED YOUR POWER.
THE POWER THAT MADE THE WHOLE WORLD YOUR ALLY.
...I SEE.
I WAS JUST THINKING ABOUT HOW FUKUZAWA'S GOLDEN CHILD HAS BEEN ODDLY ABSENT.
YOU WERE WAITING FOR THIS, WEREN'T YOU? FOR TODAY'S SPEECH?
I'LL LEAVE THAT TO YOUR IMAGINATION.

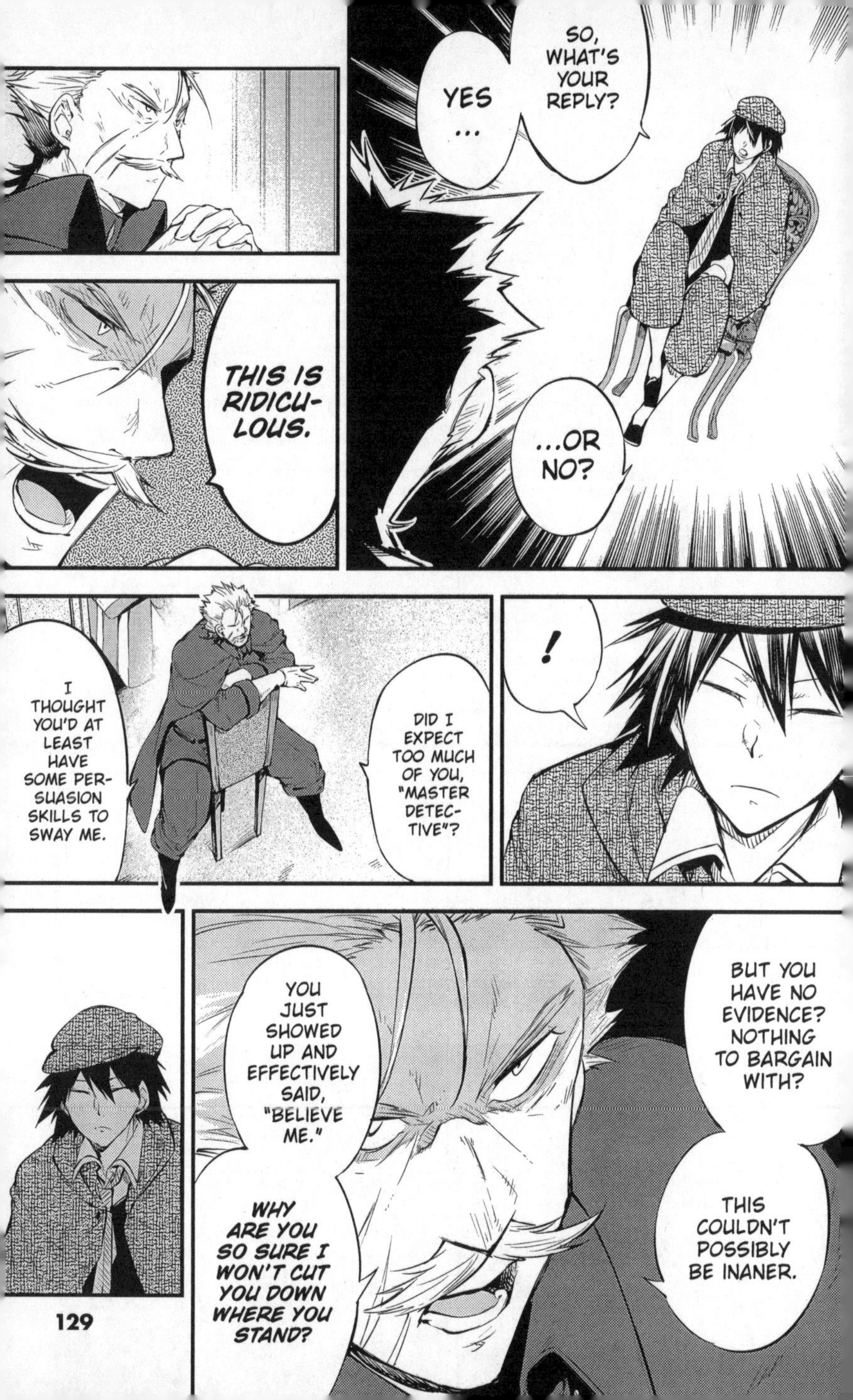
SO, WHAT'S YOUR REPLY?
YES ...
...OR NO?
THIS IS RIDICU-LOUS.
!
DID I EXPECT TOO MUCH OF YOU, "MASTER DETEC-TIVE"?
I THOUGHT YOU'D AT LEAST HAVE SOME PER-SUASION SKILLS TO SWAY ME.
BUT YOU HAVE NO EVIDENCE? NOTHING TO BARGAIN WITH?
YOU JUST SHOWED UP AND EFFECTIVELY SAID, "BELIEVE ME."
THIS COULDN'T POSSIBLY BE INANER.
WHY ARE YOU SO SURE I WON'T CUT YOU DOWN WHERE YOU STAND?

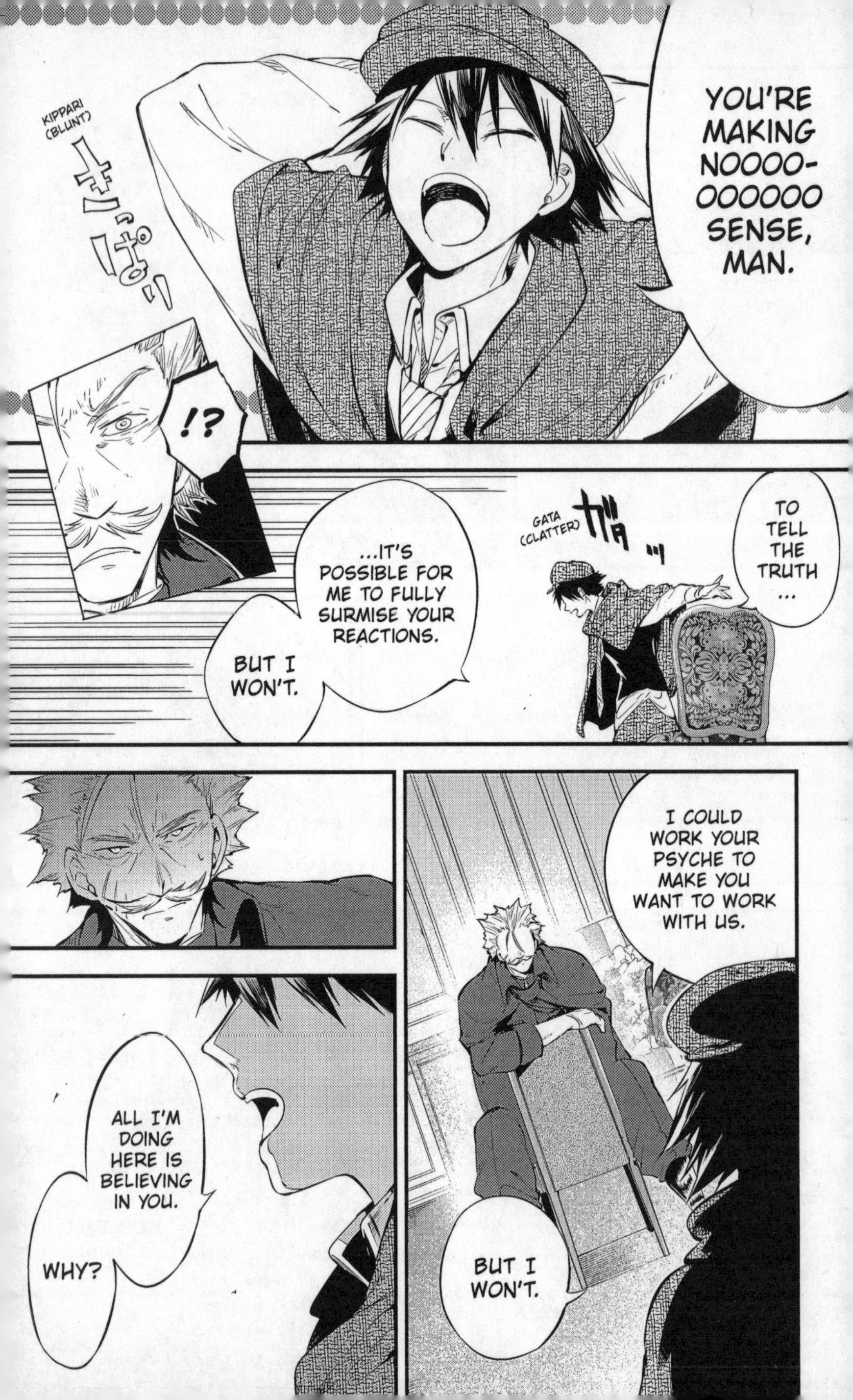
YOU'RE MAKING NOOOO-OOOOOO SENSE, MAN.
KIPPARI (BLUNT)
!?
TO TELL THE TRUTH...
GATA (CLATTER)
...IT'S POSSIBLE FOR ME TO FULLY SURMISE YOUR REACTIONS.
BUT I WON'T.
I COULD WORK YOUR PSYCHE TO MAKE YOU WANT TO WORK WITH US.
BUT I WON'T.
ALL I'M DOING HERE IS BELIEVING IN YOU.
WHY?

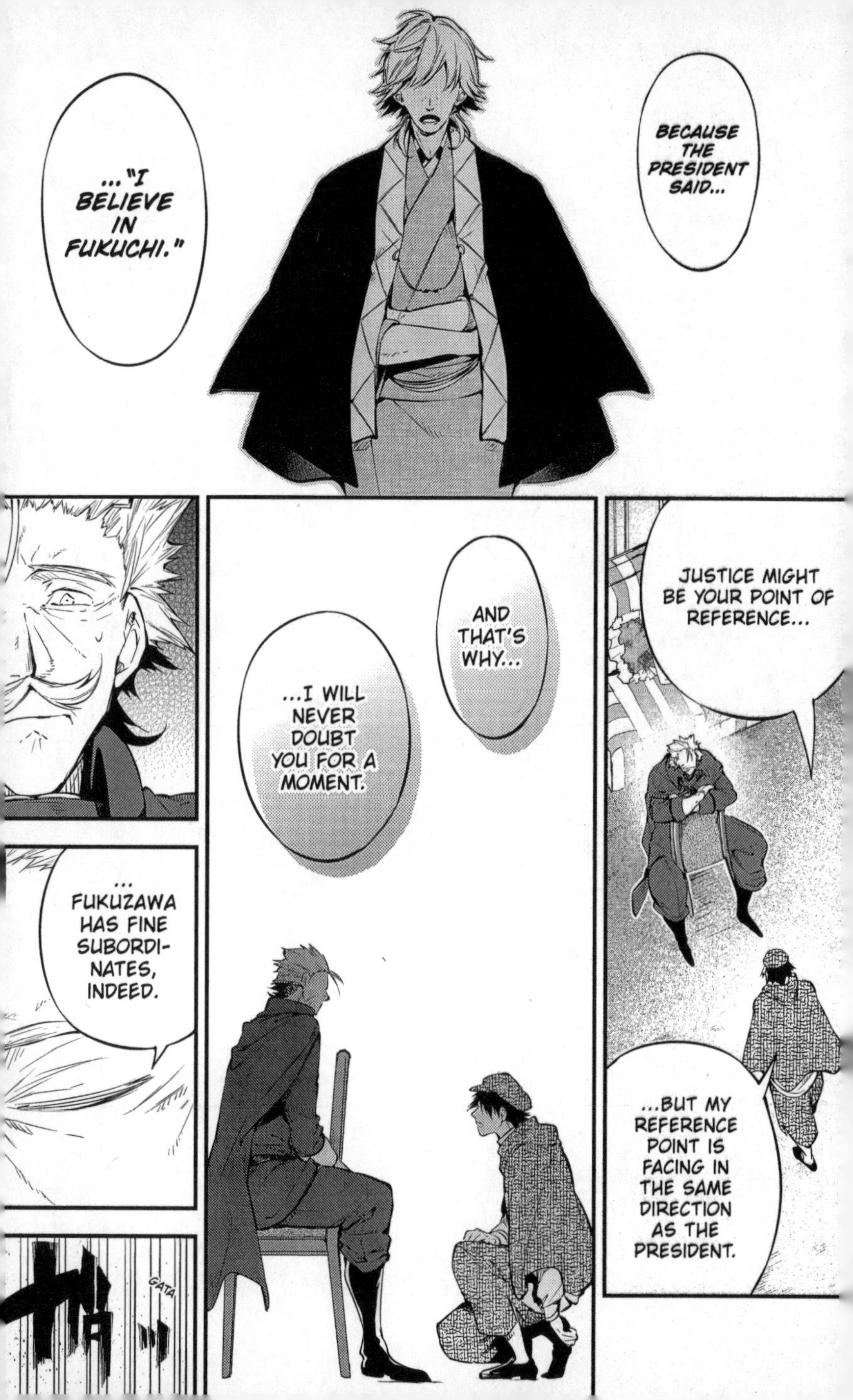
BECAUSE THE PRESIDENT SAID...
..."I BELIEVE IN FUKUCHI."
JUSTICE MIGHT BE YOUR POINT OF REFERENCE...
...BUT MY REFERENCE POINT IS FACING IN THE SAME DIRECTION AS THE PRESIDENT.
AND THAT'S WHY...
...I WILL NEVER DOUBT YOU FOR A MOMENT.
... FUKUZAWA HAS FINE SUBORDI-NATES, INDEED.
GATA

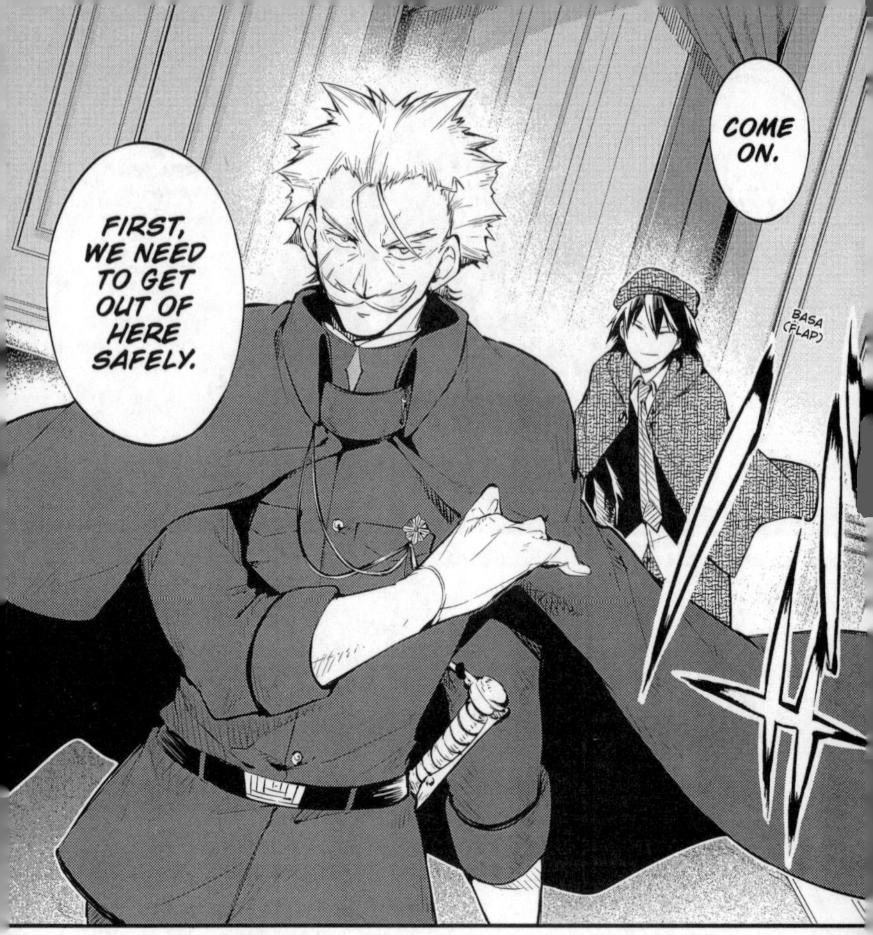
COME ON.
BASA (FLAP)
FIRST, WE NEED TO GET OUT OF HERE SAFELY.

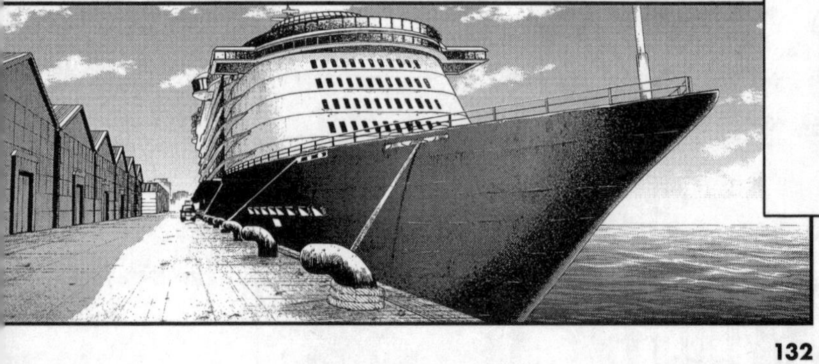

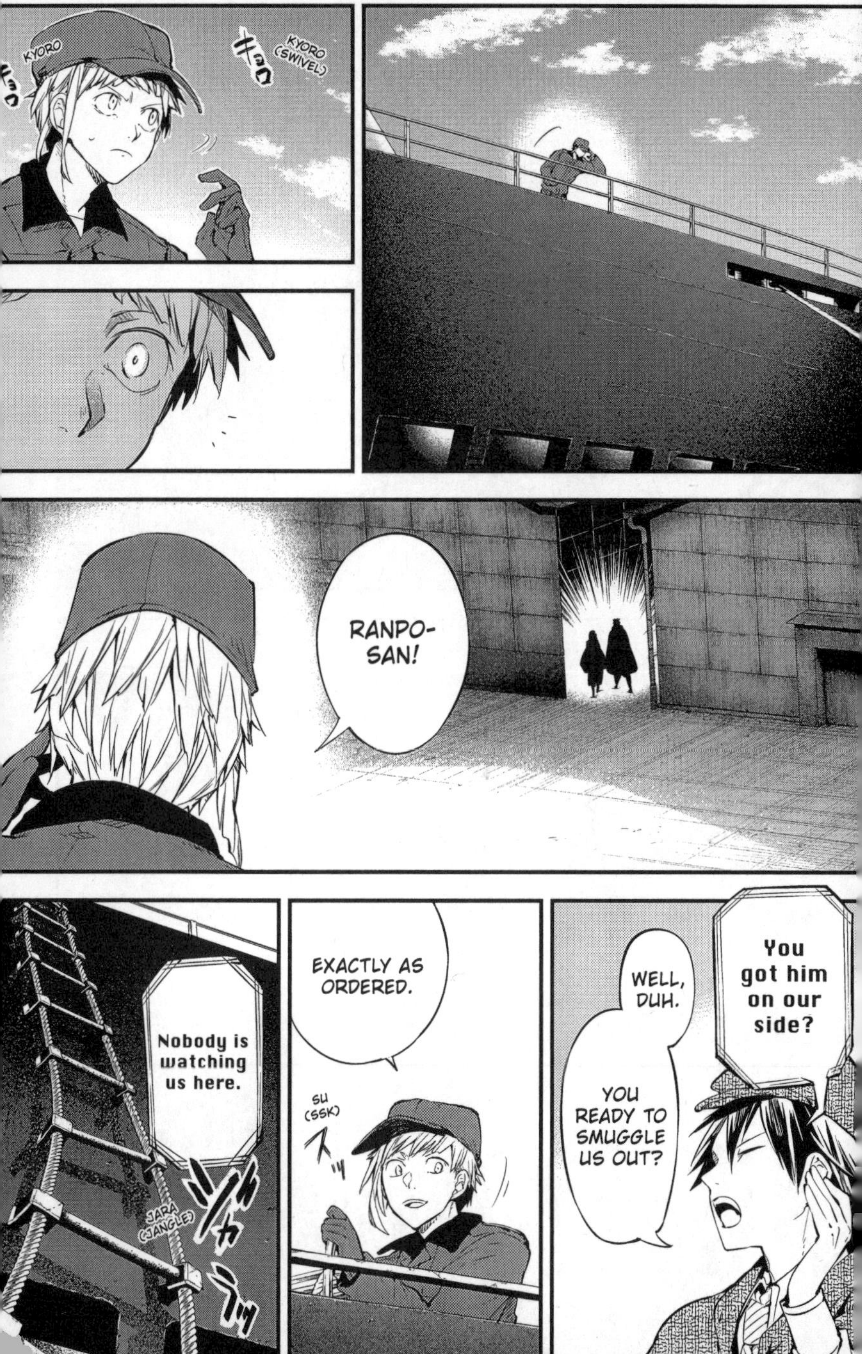
KYORO (SWIVEL)
キョロ
KYORO
RANPO-SAN!
You got him on our side?
WELL, DUH.
YOU READY TO SMUGGLE US OUT?
EXACTLY AS ORDERED.
SU (SSK)
Nobody is watching us here.
JARA (JANGLE)

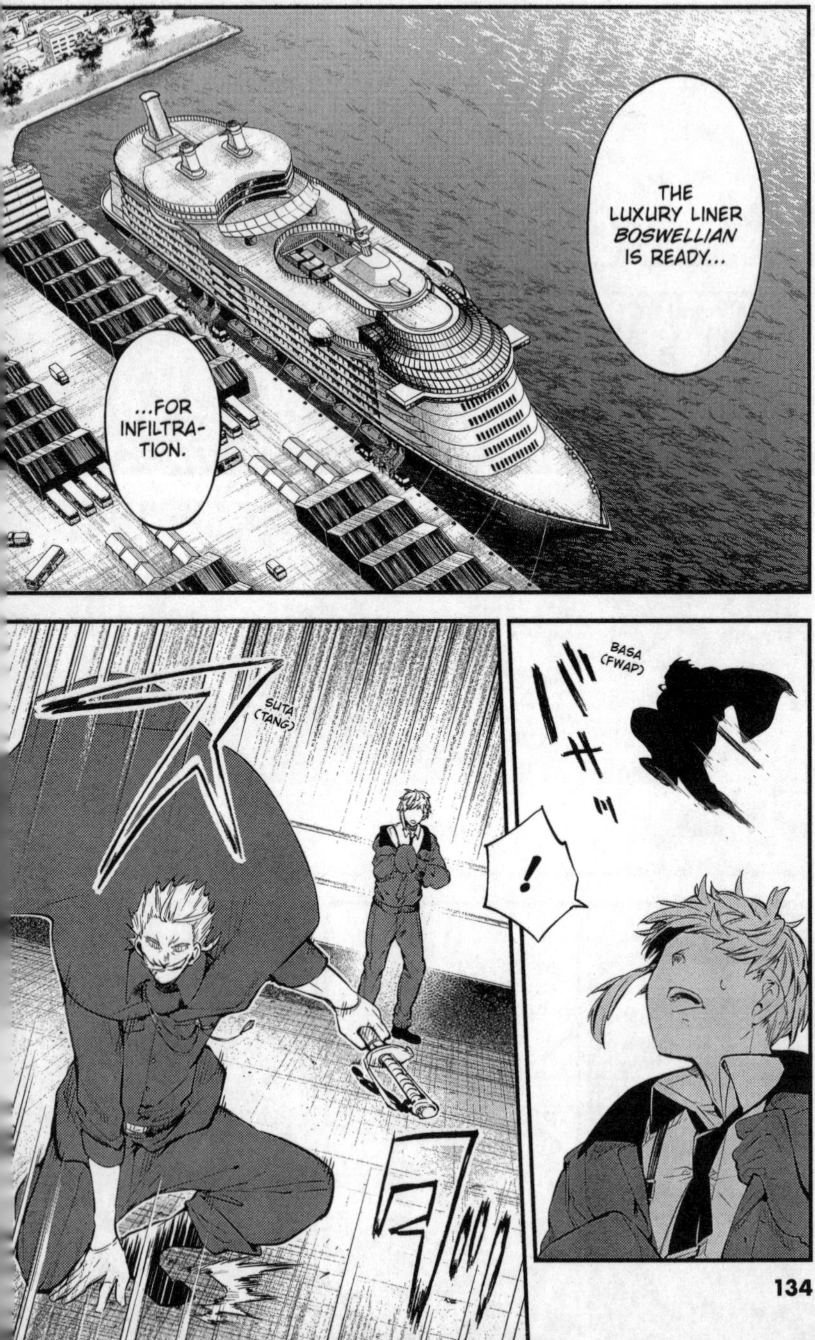
THE LUXURY LINER *BOSWELLIAN* IS READY...
...FOR INFILTRATION.
BASA (FWAP)
!
SUTA (TANG)

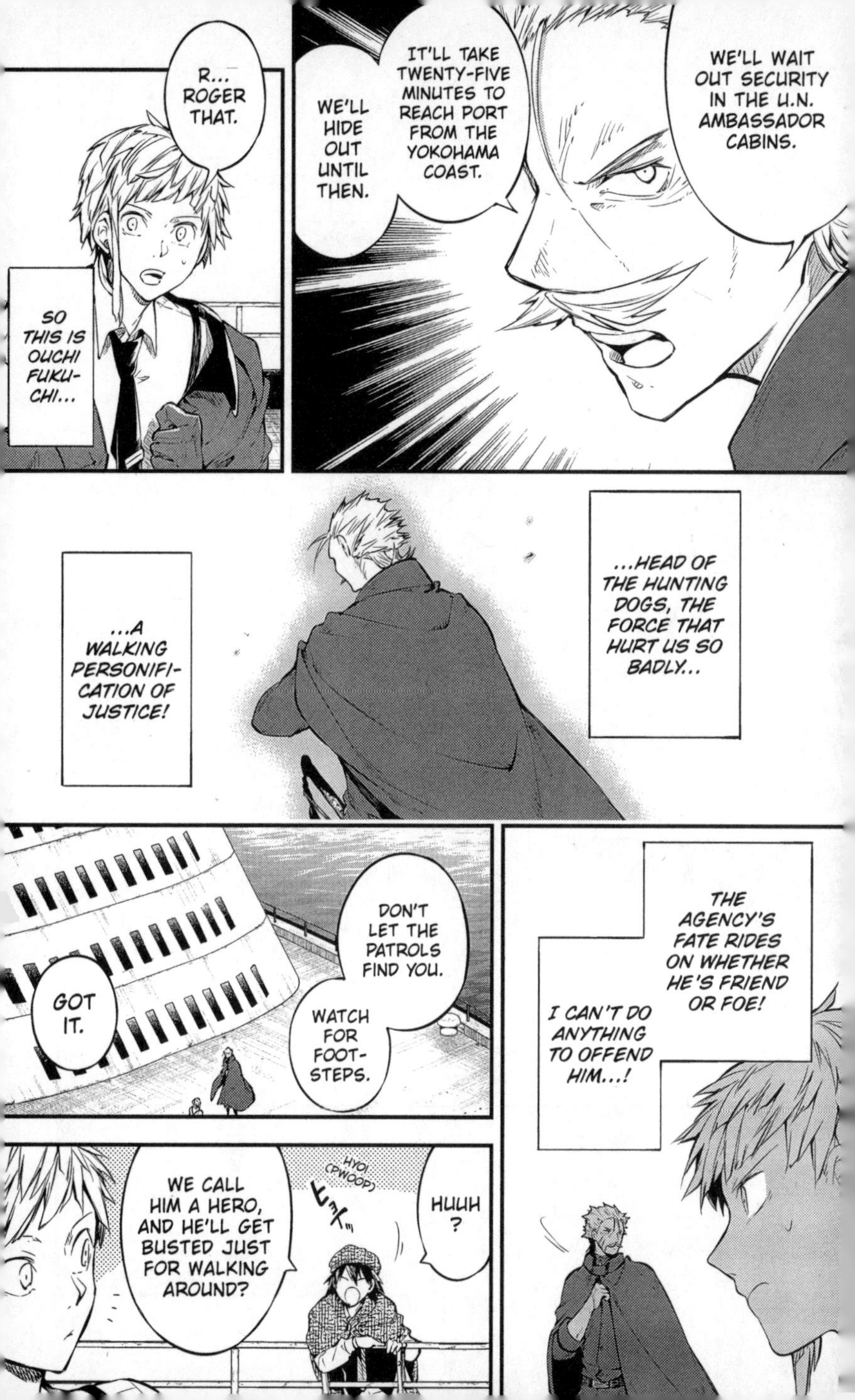
WE'LL WAIT OUT SECURITY IN THE U.N. AMBASSADOR CABINS.
IT'LL TAKE TWENTY-FIVE MINUTES TO REACH PORT FROM THE YOKOHAMA COAST.
WE'LL HIDE OUT UNTIL THEN.
R... ROGER THAT.
SO THIS IS OUCHI FUKU-CHI...
...HEAD OF THE HUNTING DOGS, THE FORCE THAT HURT US SO BADLY...
...A WALKING PERSONIFI-CATION OF JUSTICE!
THE AGENCY'S FATE RIDES ON WHETHER HE'S FRIEND OR FOE!
I CAN'T DO ANYTHING TO OFFEND HIM...!
DON'T LET THE PATROLS FIND YOU.
WATCH FOR FOOT-STEPS.
GOT IT.
HUUH?
HYOI (PWOOP)
WE CALL HIM A HERO, AND HE'LL GET BUSTED JUST FOR WALKING AROUND?

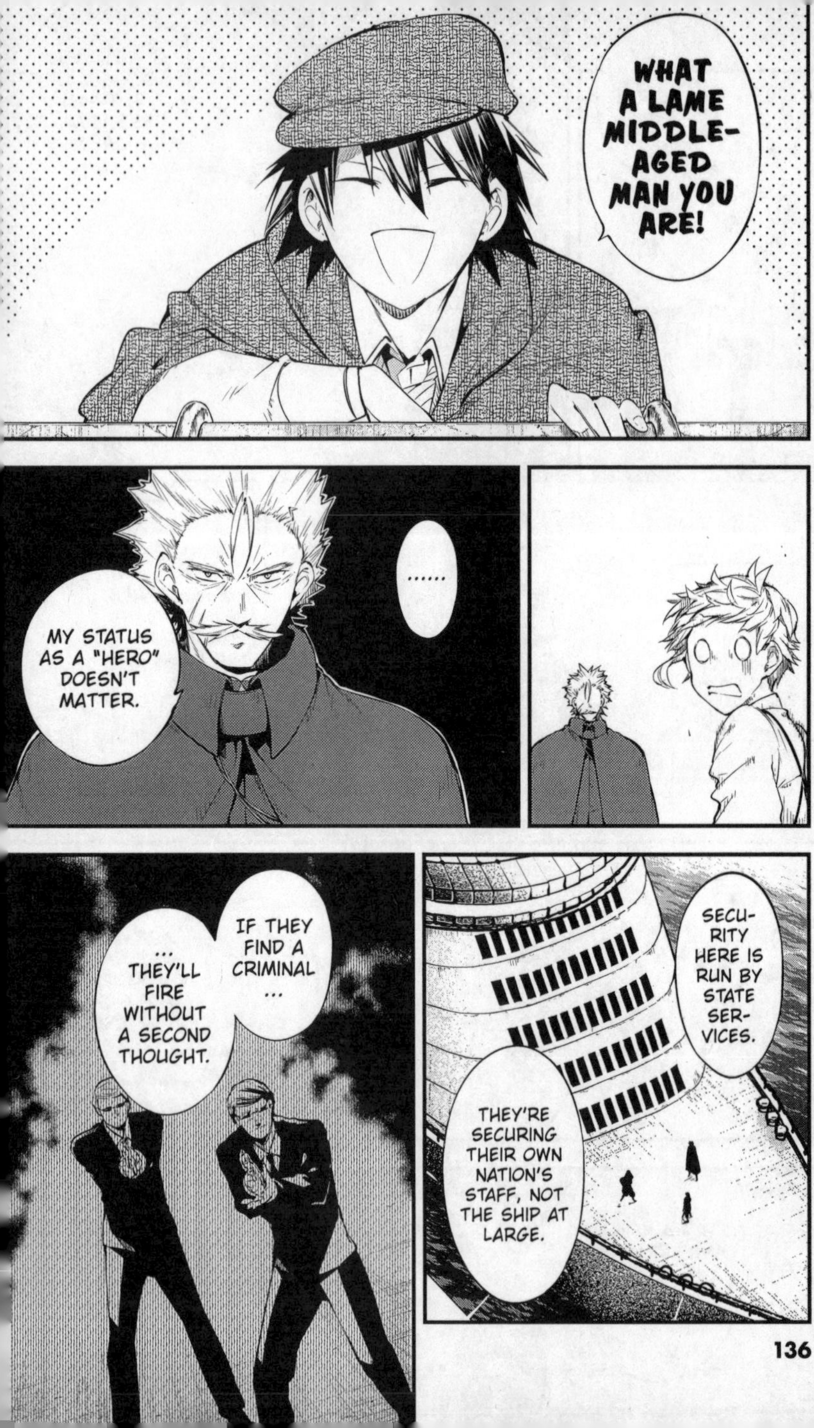
WHAT A LAME MIDDLE-AGED MAN YOU ARE!
......
MY STATUS AS A "HERO" DOESN'T MATTER.
SECU-RITY HERE IS RUN BY STATE SER-VICES.
THEY'RE SECURING THEIR OWN NATION'S STAFF, NOT THE SHIP AT LARGE.
IF THEY FIND A CRIMINAL ...
... THEY'LL FIRE WITHOUT A SECOND THOUGHT.

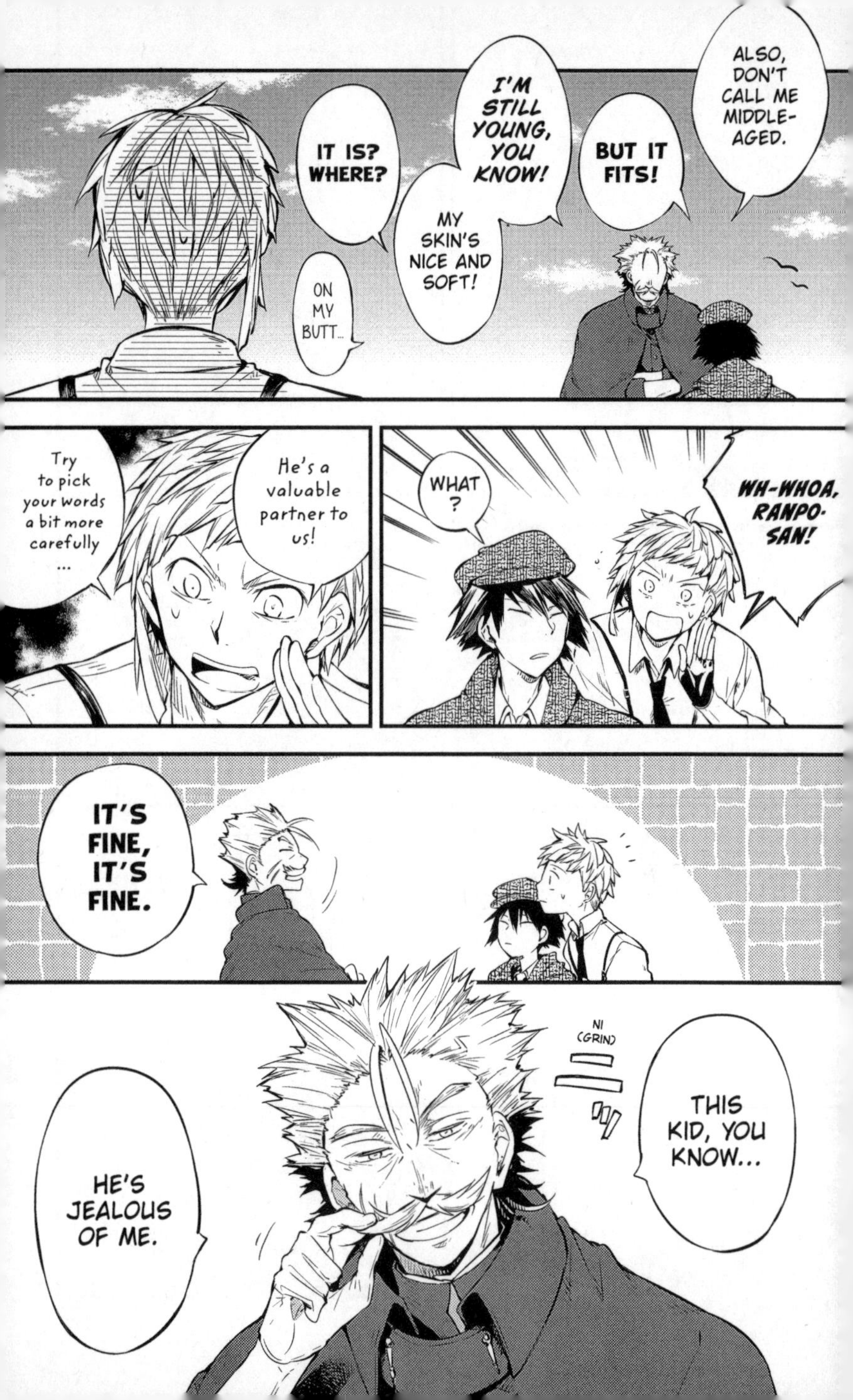
ALSO, DON'T CALL ME MIDDLE-AGED.
BUT IT FITS!
I'M STILL YOUNG, YOU KNOW!
MY SKIN'S NICE AND SOFT!
IT IS? WHERE?
ON MY BUTT...
WH-WHOA, RANPO-SAN!
WHAT?
He's a valuable partner to us!
Try to pick your words a bit more carefully...
IT'S FINE, IT'S FINE.
NI (GRIN)
THIS KID, YOU KNOW...
HE'S JEALOUS OF ME.

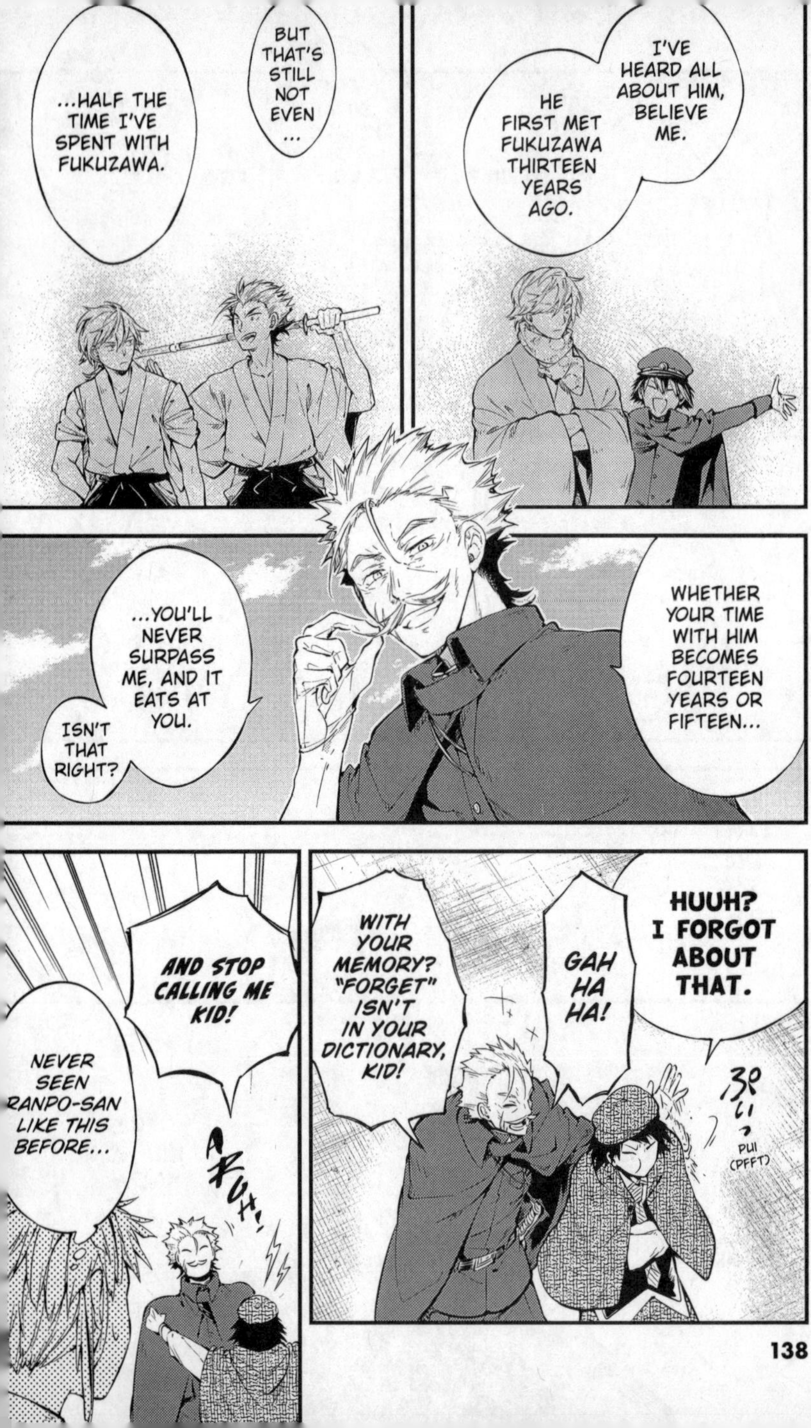
I'VE HEARD ALL ABOUT HIM, BELIEVE ME.
HE FIRST MET FUKUZAWA THIRTEEN YEARS AGO.
BUT THAT'S STILL NOT EVEN ...
...HALF THE TIME I'VE SPENT WITH FUKUZAWA.
WHETHER YOUR TIME WITH HIM BECOMES FOURTEEN YEARS OR FIFTEEN...
...YOU'LL NEVER SURPASS ME, AND IT EATS AT YOU.
ISN'T THAT RIGHT?
HUUH? I FORGOT ABOUT THAT.
GAH HA HA!
WITH YOUR MEMORY? "FORGET" ISN'T IN YOUR DICTIONARY, KID!
PUI (PFFT)
AND STOP CALLING ME KID!
NEVER SEEN RANPO-SAN LIKE THIS BEFORE...

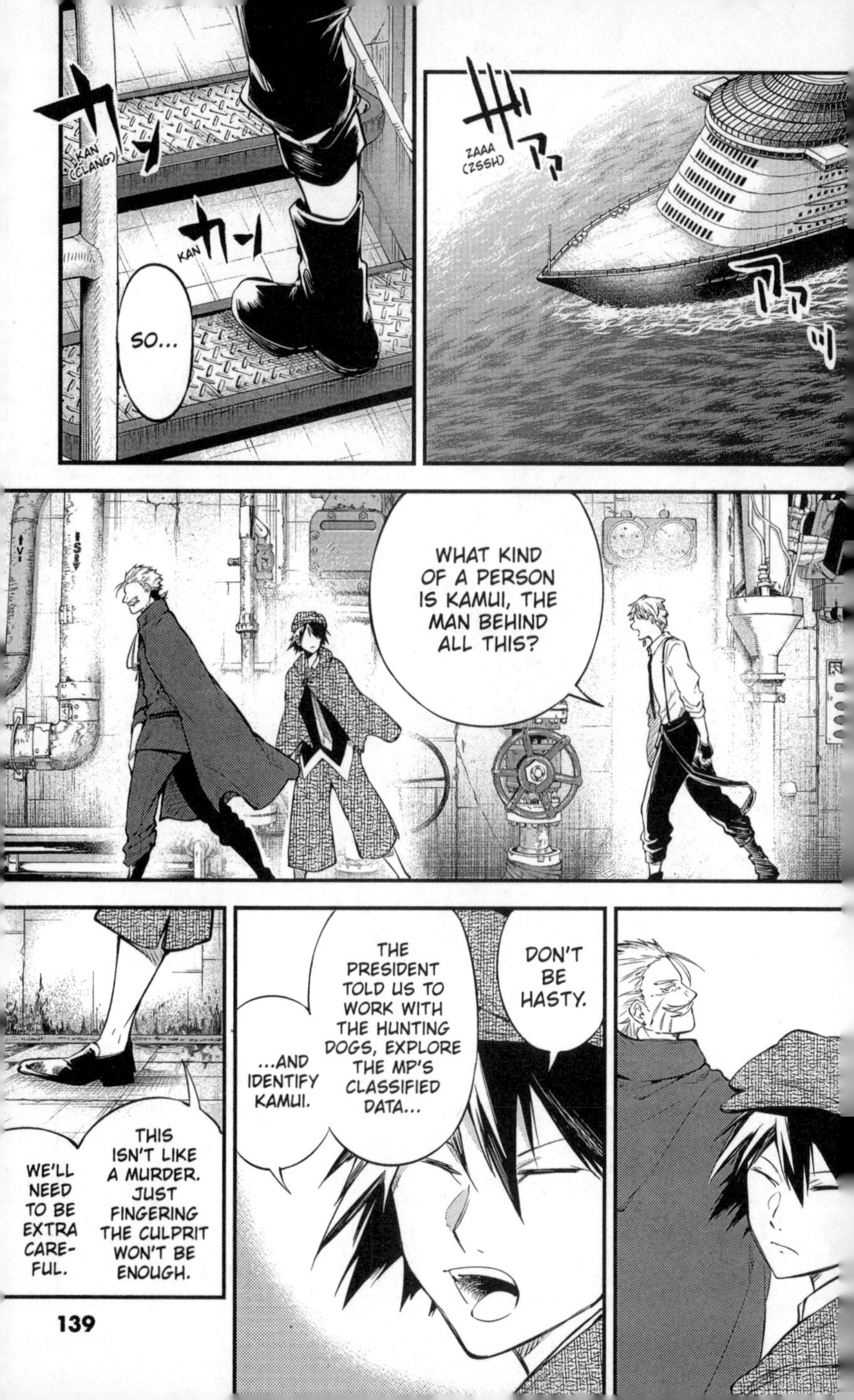
ZAAA (ZSSH)
KAN (CLANG)
KAN
SO...
WHAT KIND OF A PERSON IS KAMUI, THE MAN BEHIND ALL THIS?
DON'T BE HASTY.
THE PRESIDENT TOLD US TO WORK WITH THE HUNTING DOGS, EXPLORE THE MP'S CLASSIFIED DATA...
...AND IDENTIFY KAMUI.
THIS ISN'T LIKE A MURDER. JUST FINGERING THE CULPRIT WON'T BE ENOUGH.
WE'LL NEED TO BE EXTRA CARE-FUL.

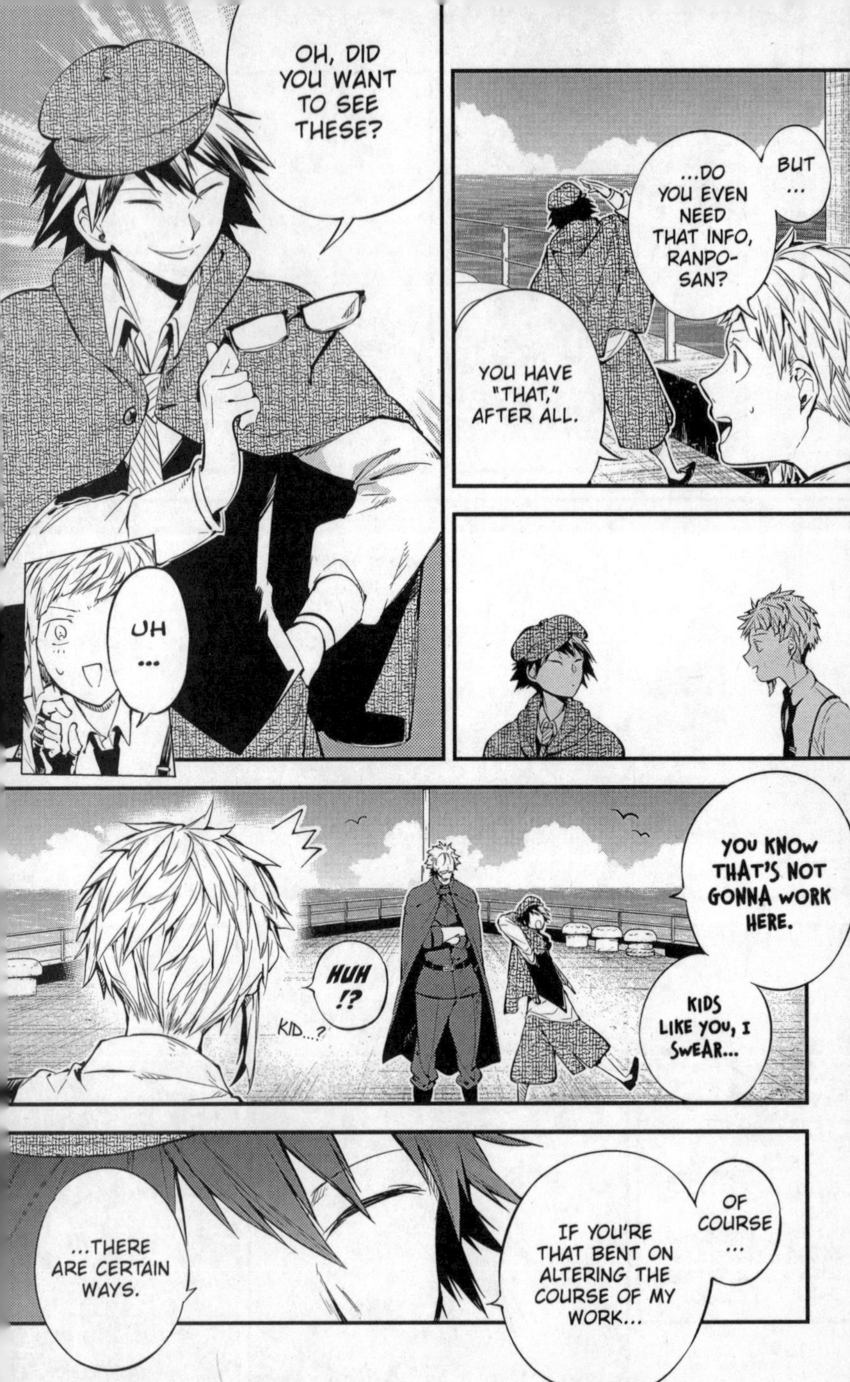
BUT ...
...DO YOU EVEN NEED THAT INFO, RANPO-SAN?
YOU HAVE "THAT," AFTER ALL.
OH, DID YOU WANT TO SEE THESE?
UH ...
YOU KNOW THAT'S NOT GONNA WORK HERE.
KIDS LIKE YOU, I SWEAR...
HUH !?
KID...?
OF COURSE ...
IF YOU'RE THAT BENT ON ALTERING THE COURSE OF MY WORK...
...THERE ARE CERTAIN WAYS.

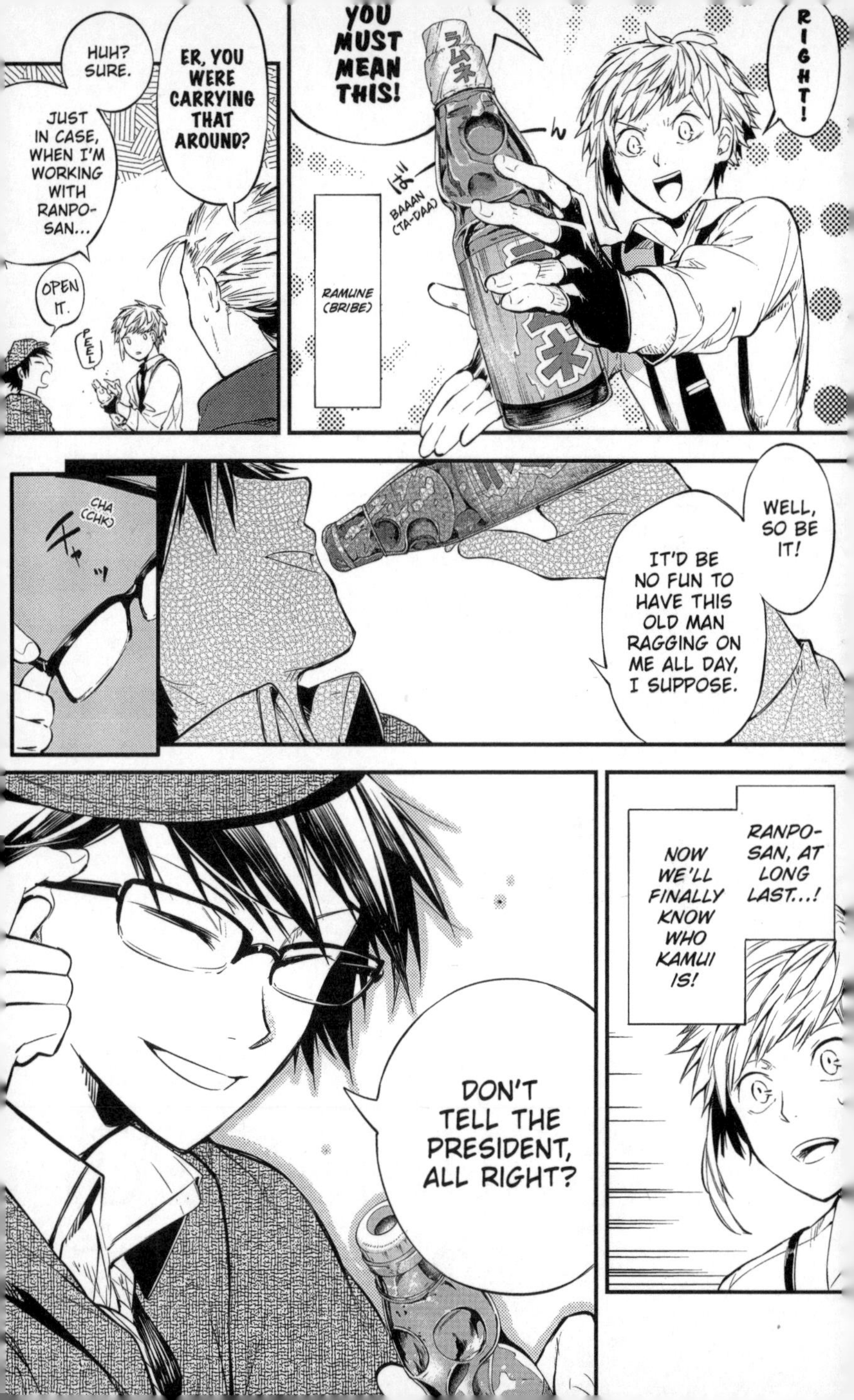

RIGHT!
YOU MUST MEAN THIS!
BAAAN (TA-DAA)
RAMUNE (BRIBE)
ER, YOU WERE CARRYING THAT AROUND?
HUH? SURE.
JUST IN CASE, WHEN I'M WORKING WITH RANPO-SAN...
OPEN IT.
PEEL
WELL, SO BE IT!
IT'D BE NO FUN TO HAVE THIS OLD MAN RAGGING ON ME ALL DAY, I SUPPOSE.
CHA (CHK)
RANPO-SAN, AT LONG LAST...!
NOW WE'LL FINALLY KNOW WHO KAMUI IS!
DON'T TELL THE PRESIDENT, ALL RIGHT?

BUNGO
STRAY DOGS

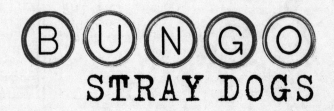

CHAPTER 83
Toward the Complete Answer

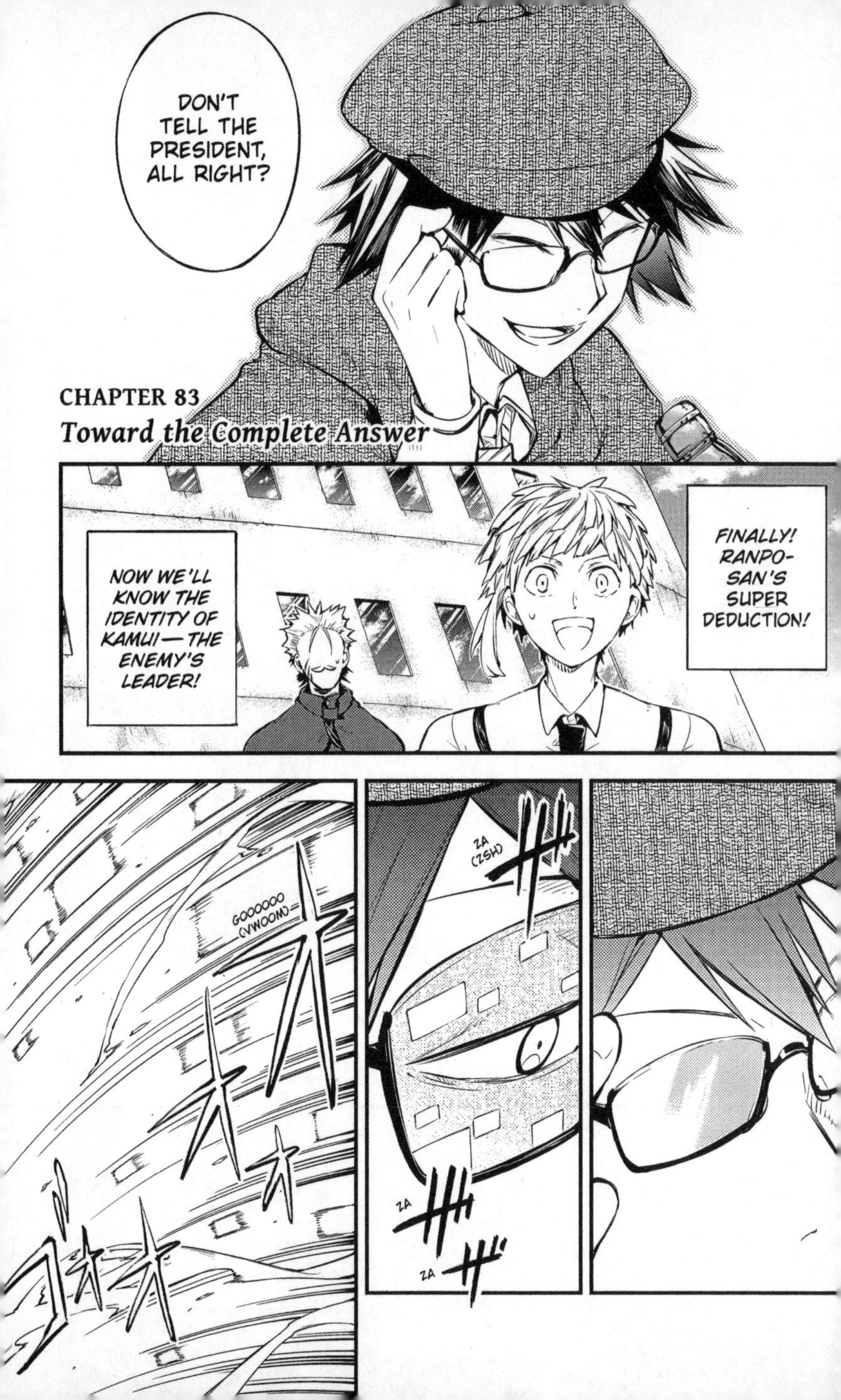
DON'T TELL THE PRESIDENT, ALL RIGHT?
FINALLY! RANPO-SAN'S SUPER DEDUCTION!
NOW WE'LL KNOW THE IDENTITY OF KAMUI— THE ENEMY'S LEADER!
ZA (ZSH)
ZA
ZA
GOOOOOO (VWOOM)

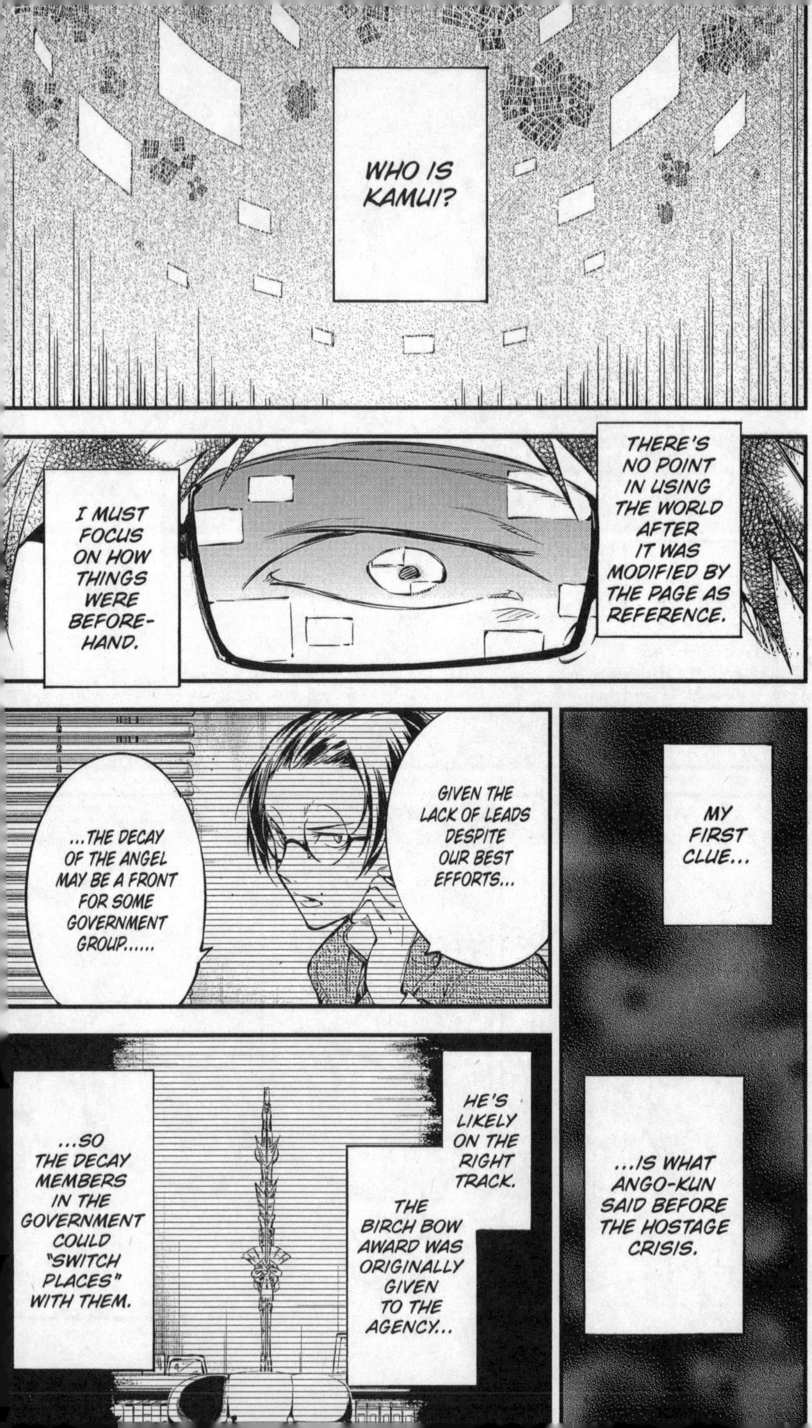
WHO IS KAMUI?
THERE'S NO POINT IN USING THE WORLD AFTER IT WAS MODIFIED BY THE PAGE AS REFERENCE.
I MUST FOCUS ON HOW THINGS WERE BEFORE-HAND.
MY FIRST CLUE...
...IS WHAT ANGO-KUN SAID BEFORE THE HOSTAGE CRISIS.
GIVEN THE LACK OF LEADS DESPITE OUR BEST EFFORTS...
...THE DECAY OF THE ANGEL MAY BE A FRONT FOR SOME GOVERNMENT GROUP......
HE'S LIKELY ON THE RIGHT TRACK.
THE BIRCH BOW AWARD WAS ORIGINALLY GIVEN TO THE AGENCY...
...SO THE DECAY MEMBERS IN THE GOVERNMENT COULD "SWITCH PLACES" WITH THEM.

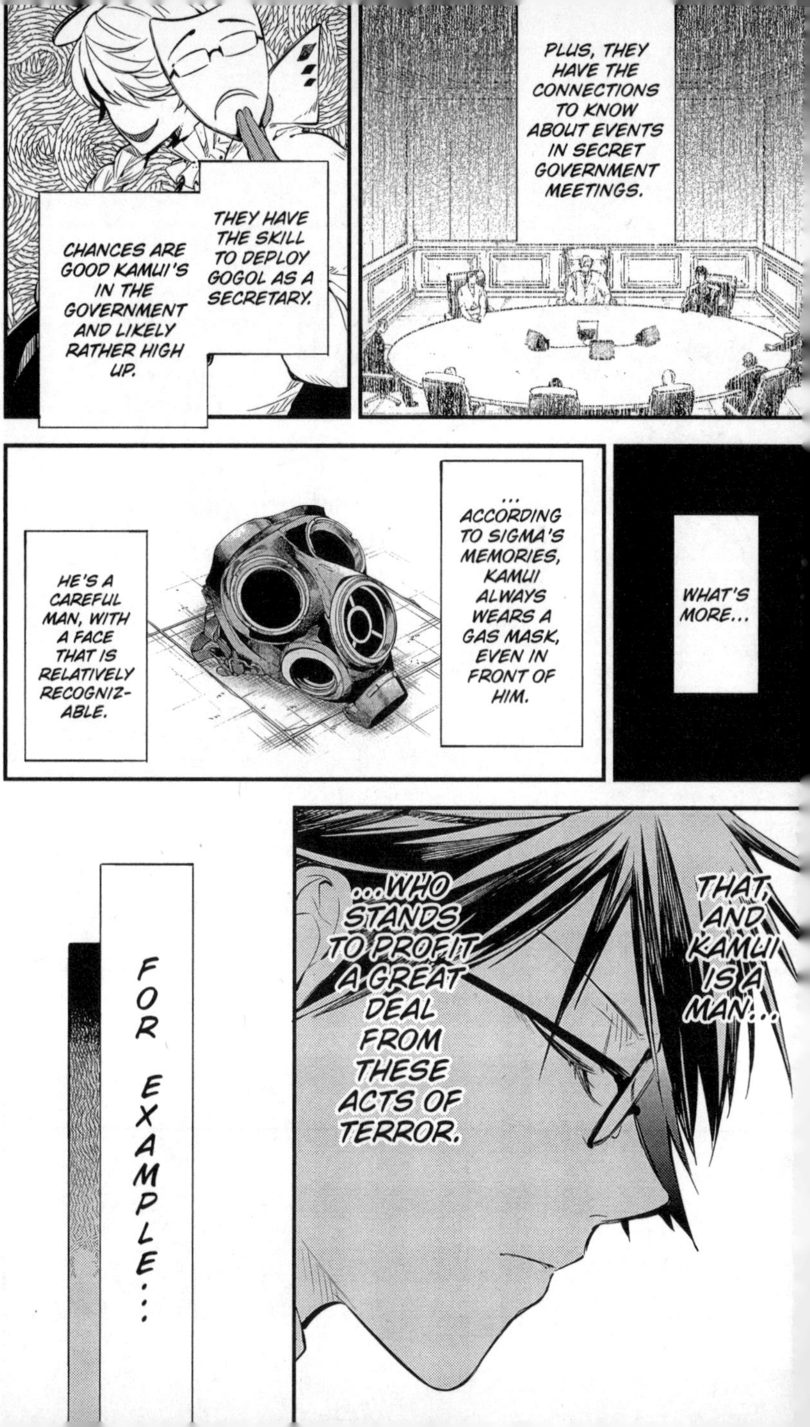
PLUS, THEY HAVE THE CONNECTIONS TO KNOW ABOUT EVENTS IN SECRET GOVERNMENT MEETINGS.
THEY HAVE THE SKILL TO DEPLOY GOGOL AS A SECRETARY.
CHANCES ARE GOOD KAMUI'S IN THE GOVERNMENT AND LIKELY RATHER HIGH UP.
WHAT'S MORE...
... ACCORDING TO SIGMA'S MEMORIES, KAMUI ALWAYS WEARS A GAS MASK, EVEN IN FRONT OF HIM.
HE'S A CAREFUL MAN, WITH A FACE THAT IS RELATIVELY RECOGNIZ-ABLE.
THAT, AND KAMUI IS A MAN...
...WHO STANDS TO PROFIT A GREAT DEAL FROM THESE ACTS OF TERROR.
FOR EXAMPLE...

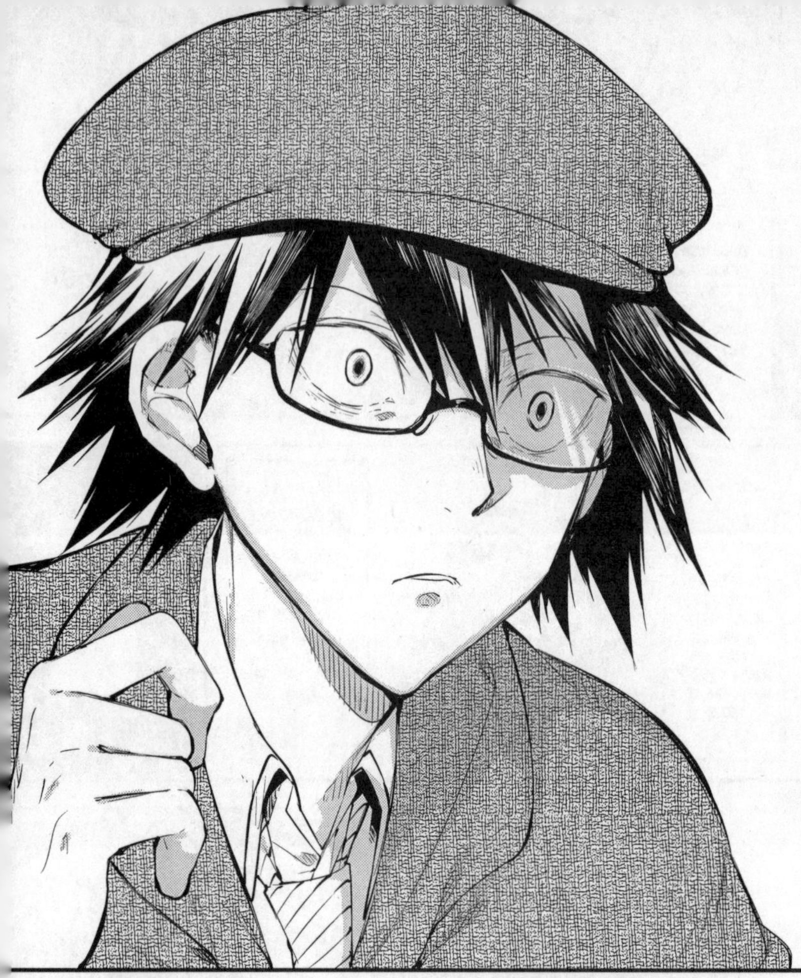

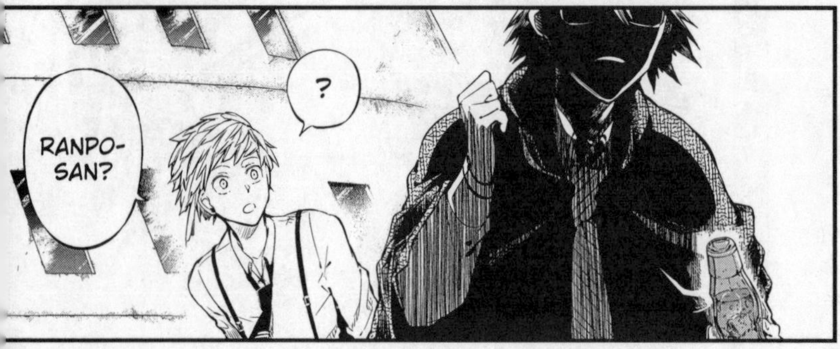
?
RANPO-SAN?

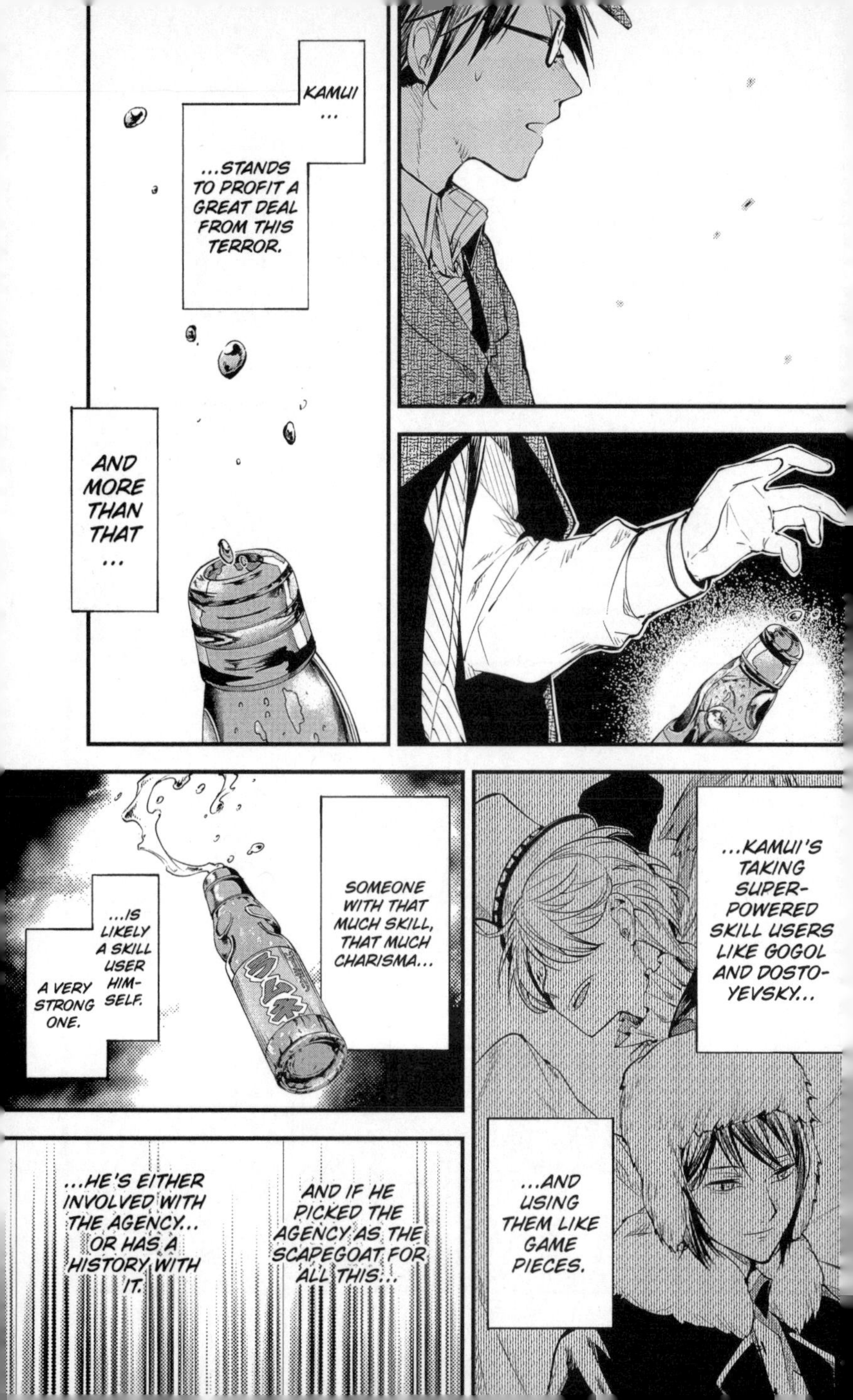
KAMUI ...
...STANDS TO PROFIT A GREAT DEAL FROM THIS TERROR.
AND MORE THAN THAT ...
...KAMUI'S TAKING SUPER-POWERED SKILL USERS LIKE GOGOL AND DOSTO-YEVSKY...
...AND USING THEM LIKE GAME PIECES.
SOMEONE WITH THAT MUCH SKILL, THAT MUCH CHARISMA...
...IS LIKELY A SKILL USER HIM-SELF.
A VERY STRONG ONE.
AND IF HE PICKED THE AGENCY AS THE SCAPEGOAT FOR ALL THIS...
...HE'S EITHER INVOLVED WITH THE AGENCY... OR HAS A HISTORY WITH IT.

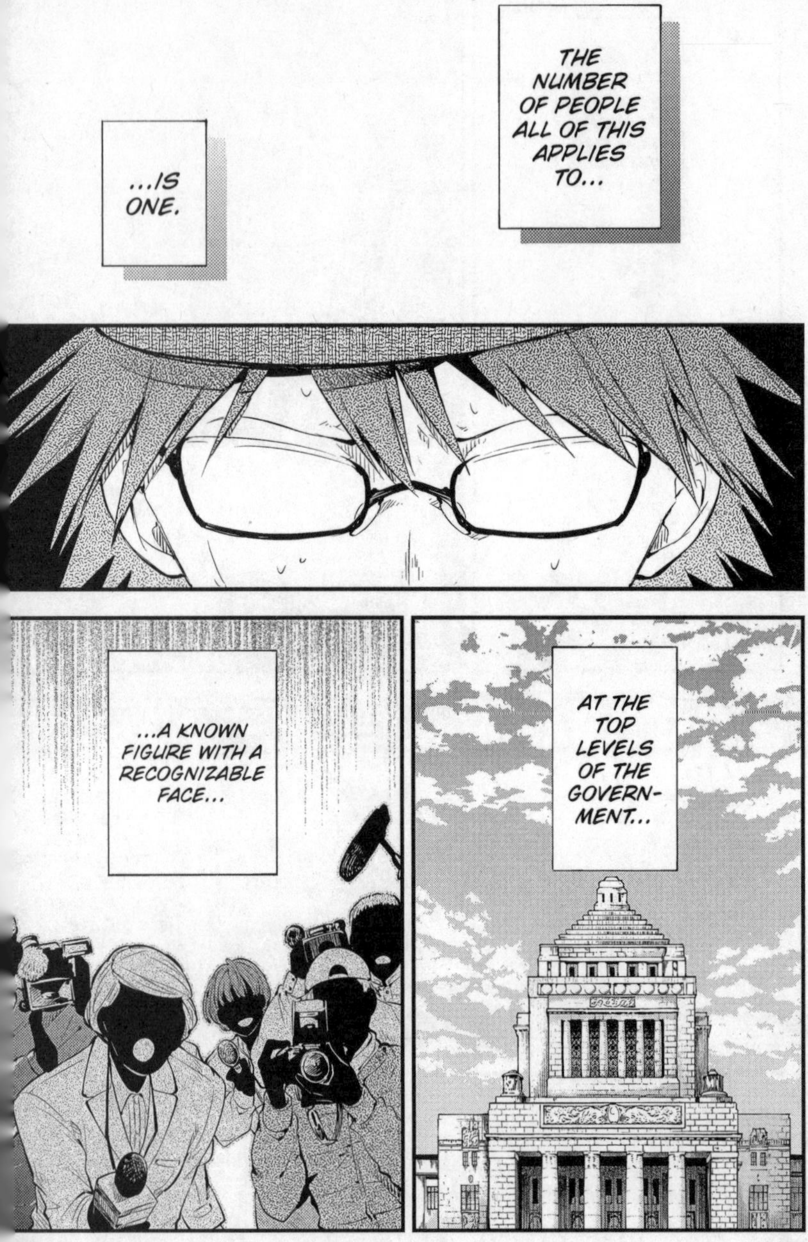
THE NUMBER OF PEOPLE ALL OF THIS APPLIES TO...
...IS ONE.
AT THE TOP LEVELS OF THE GOVERN-MENT...
...A KNOWN FIGURE WITH A RECOGNIZABLE FACE...

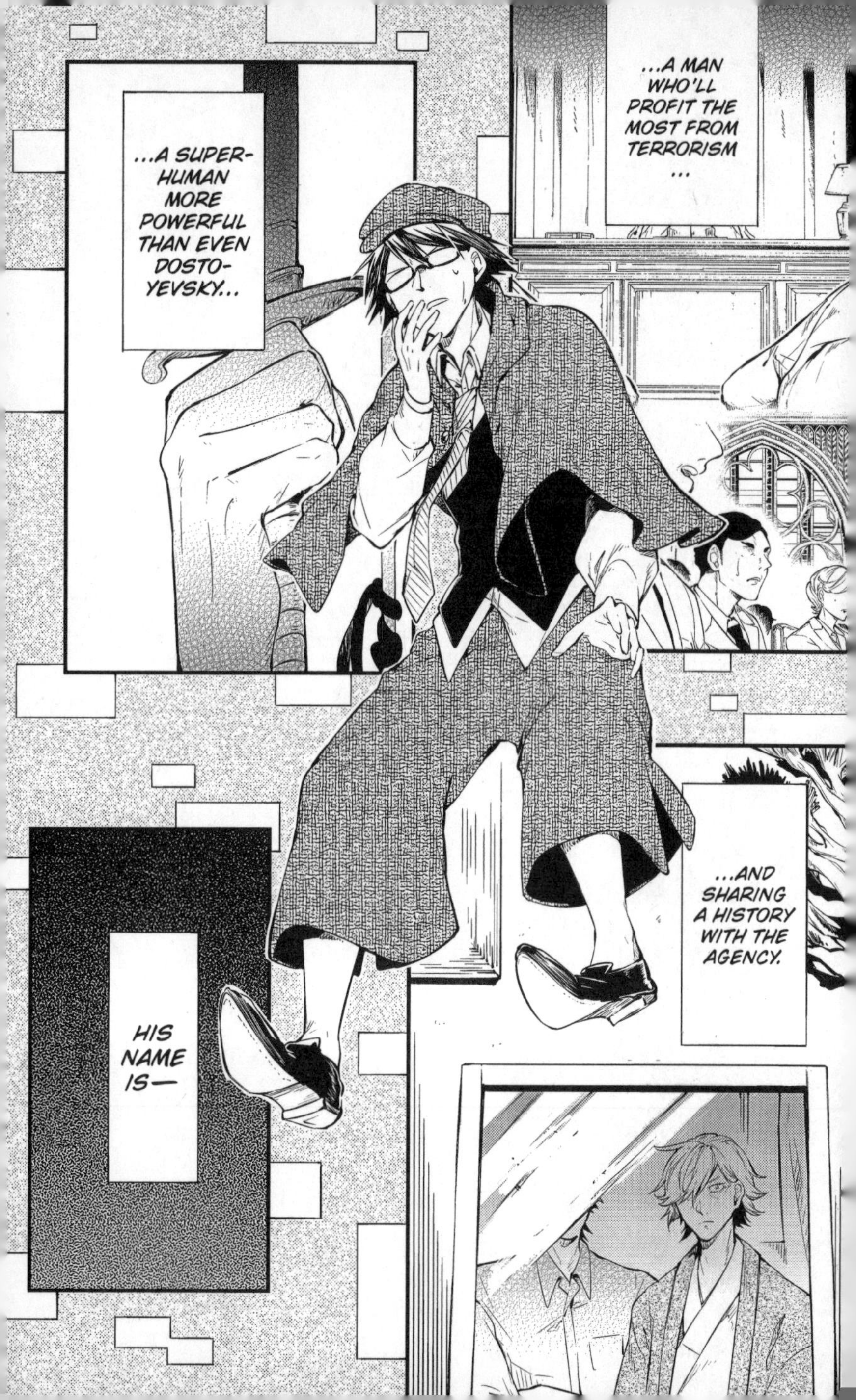
...A MAN WHO'LL PROFIT THE MOST FROM TERRORISM...
...A SUPER-HUMAN MORE POWERFUL THAN EVEN DOSTO-YEVSKY...
...AND SHARING A HISTORY WITH THE AGENCY.
HIS NAME IS—

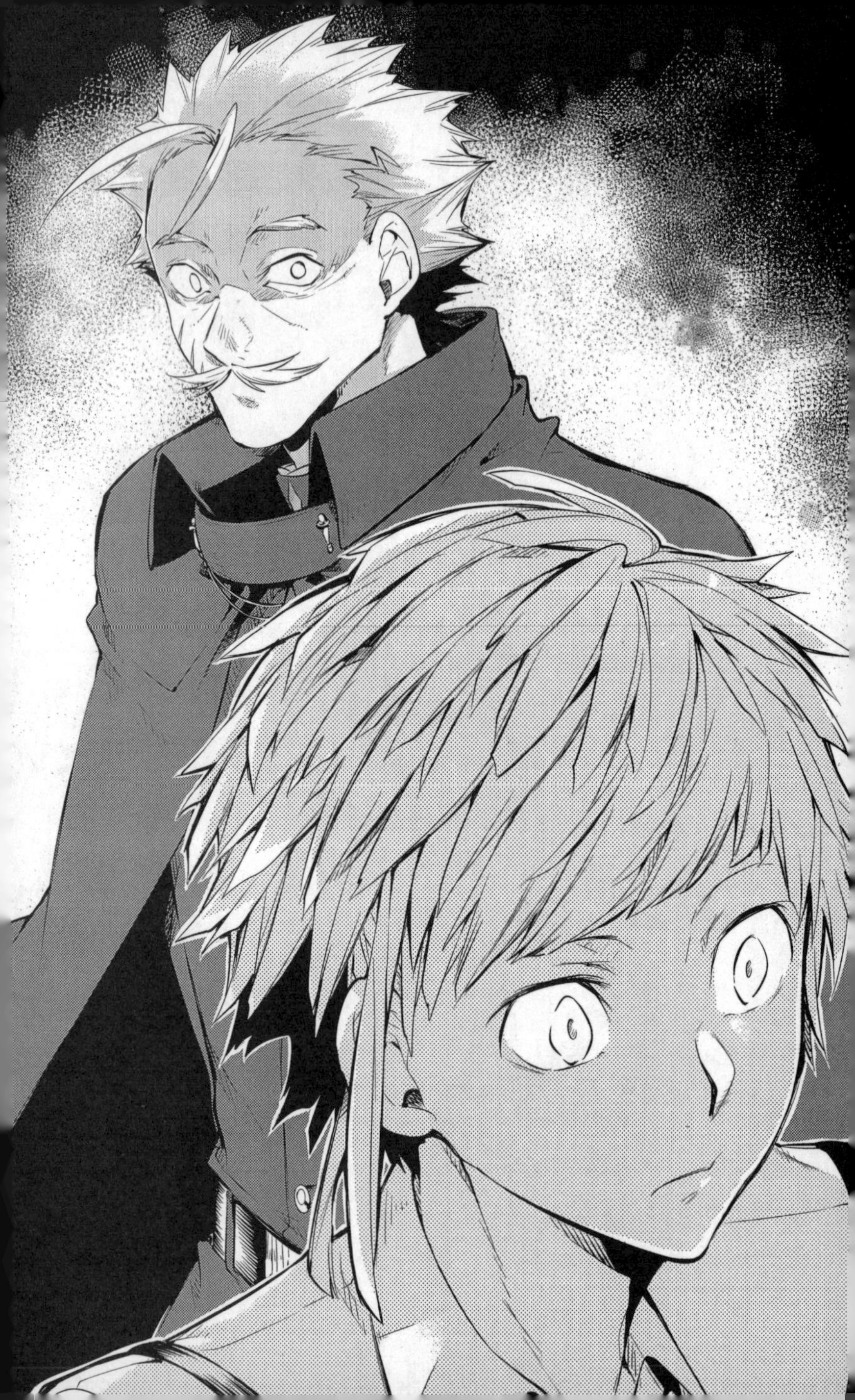

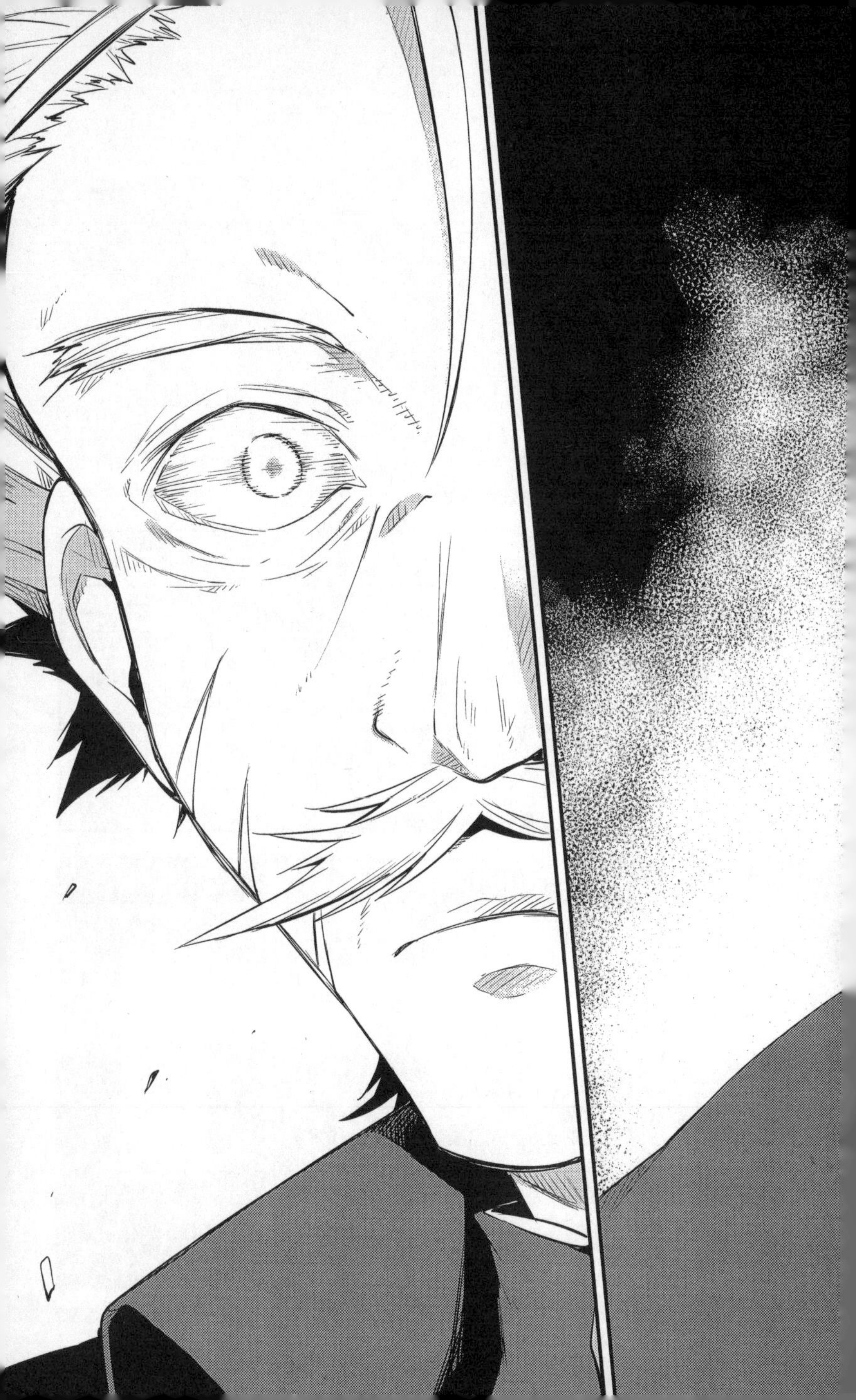

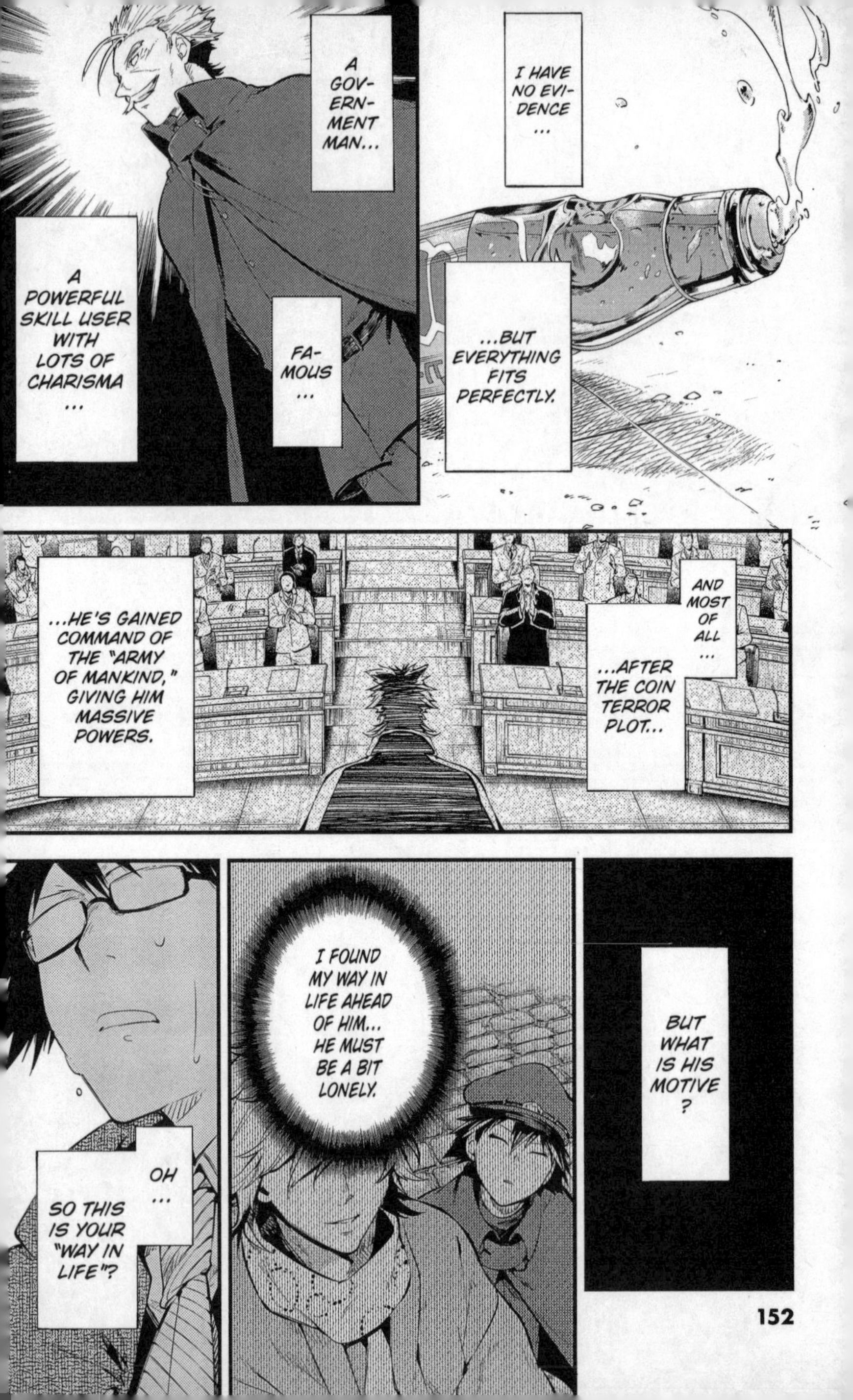
I HAVE NO EVIDENCE...
...BUT EVERYTHING FITS PERFECTLY.
A GOVERNMENT MAN...
FAMOUS...
A POWERFUL SKILL USER WITH LOTS OF CHARISMA...
AND MOST OF ALL...
...AFTER THE COIN TERROR PLOT...
...HE'S GAINED COMMAND OF THE "ARMY OF MANKIND," GIVING HIM MASSIVE POWERS.
BUT WHAT IS HIS MOTIVE?
I FOUND MY WAY IN LIFE AHEAD OF HIM... HE MUST BE A BIT LONELY.
OH...
SO THIS IS YOUR "WAY IN LIFE"?

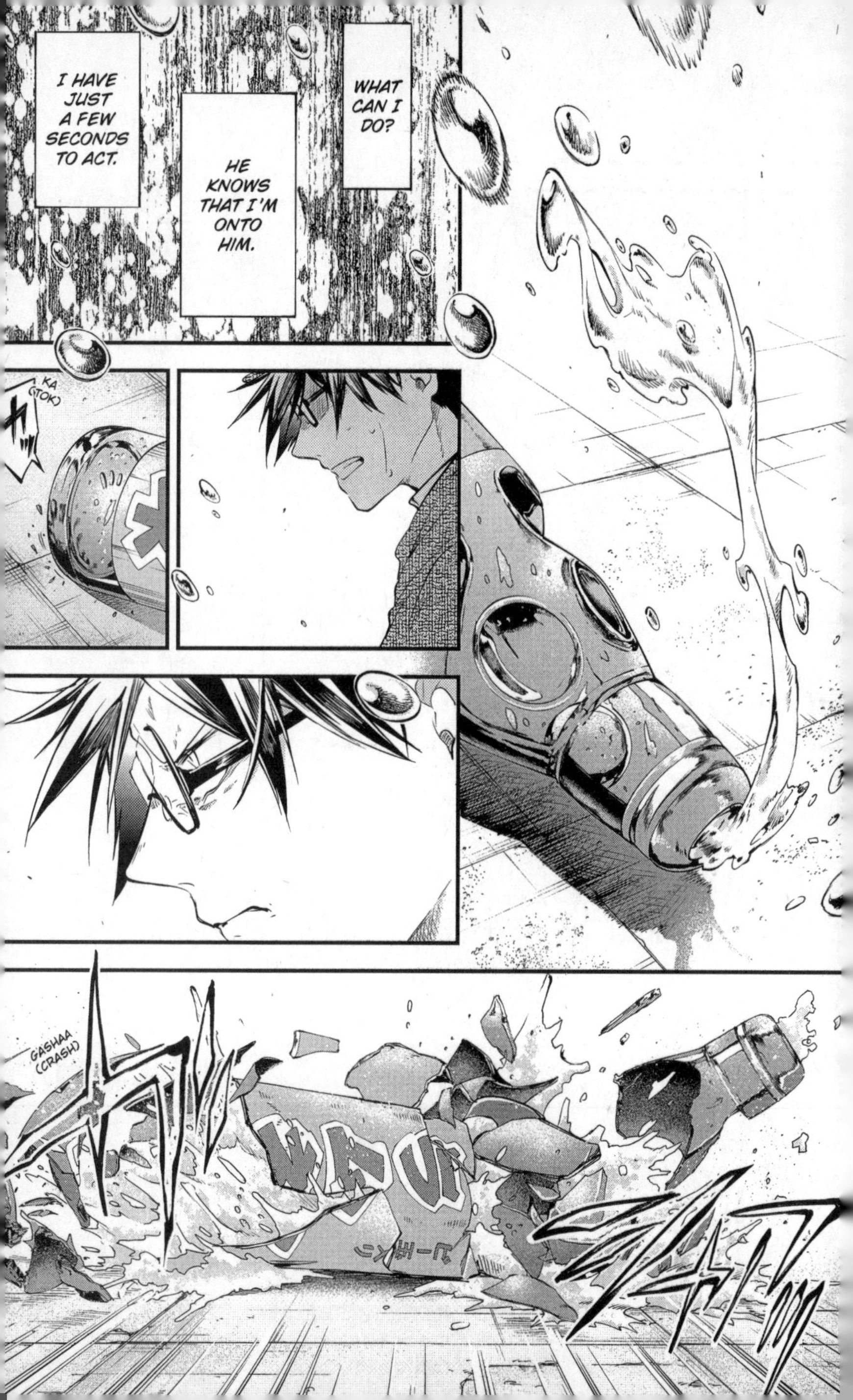
WHAT CAN I DO?
HE KNOWS THAT I'M ONTO HIM.
I HAVE JUST A FEW SECONDS TO ACT.
KA (TOK)
GASHAA (CRASH)

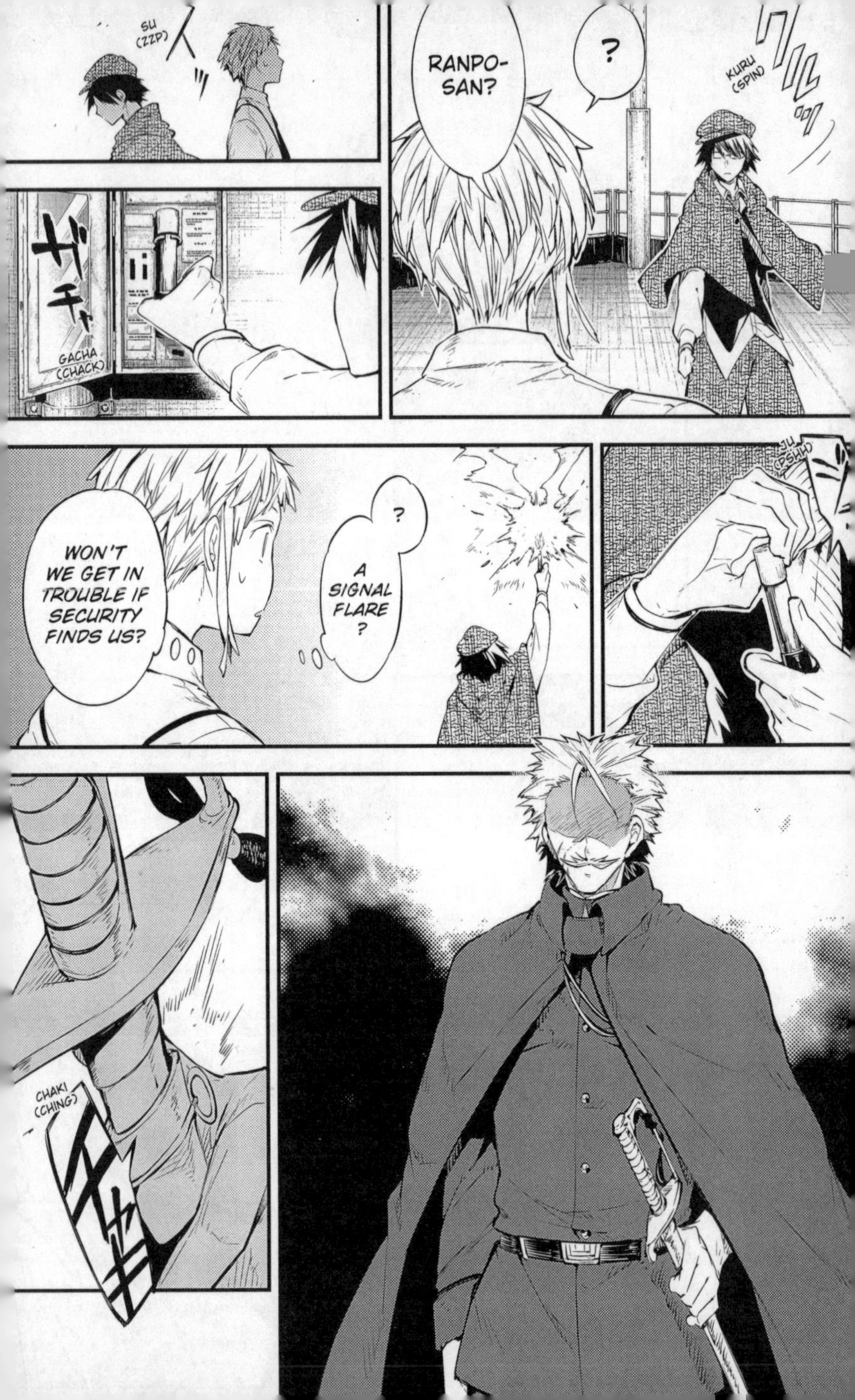
RANPO-SAN?
?
KURU (SPIN)
SU (ZZP)
GACHA (CHACK)
JU (PSHH)
?
A SIGNAL FLARE ?
WON'T WE GET IN TROUBLE IF SECURITY FINDS US?
CHAKI (CHING)

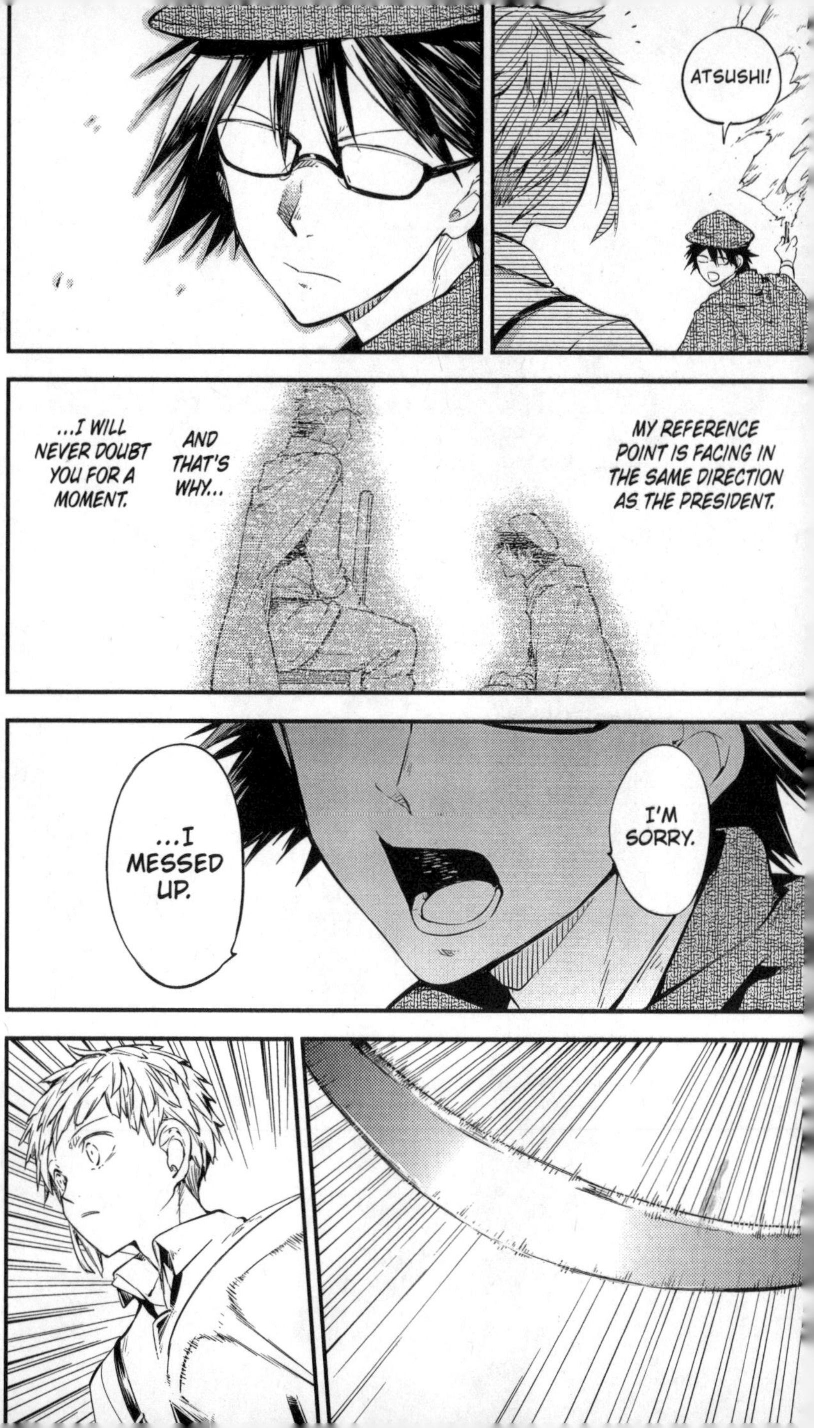
ATSUSHI!
MY REFERENCE POINT IS FACING IN THE SAME DIRECTION AS THE PRESIDENT.
AND THAT'S WHY...
...I WILL NEVER DOUBT YOU FOR A MOMENT.
I'M SORRY.
...I MESSED UP.

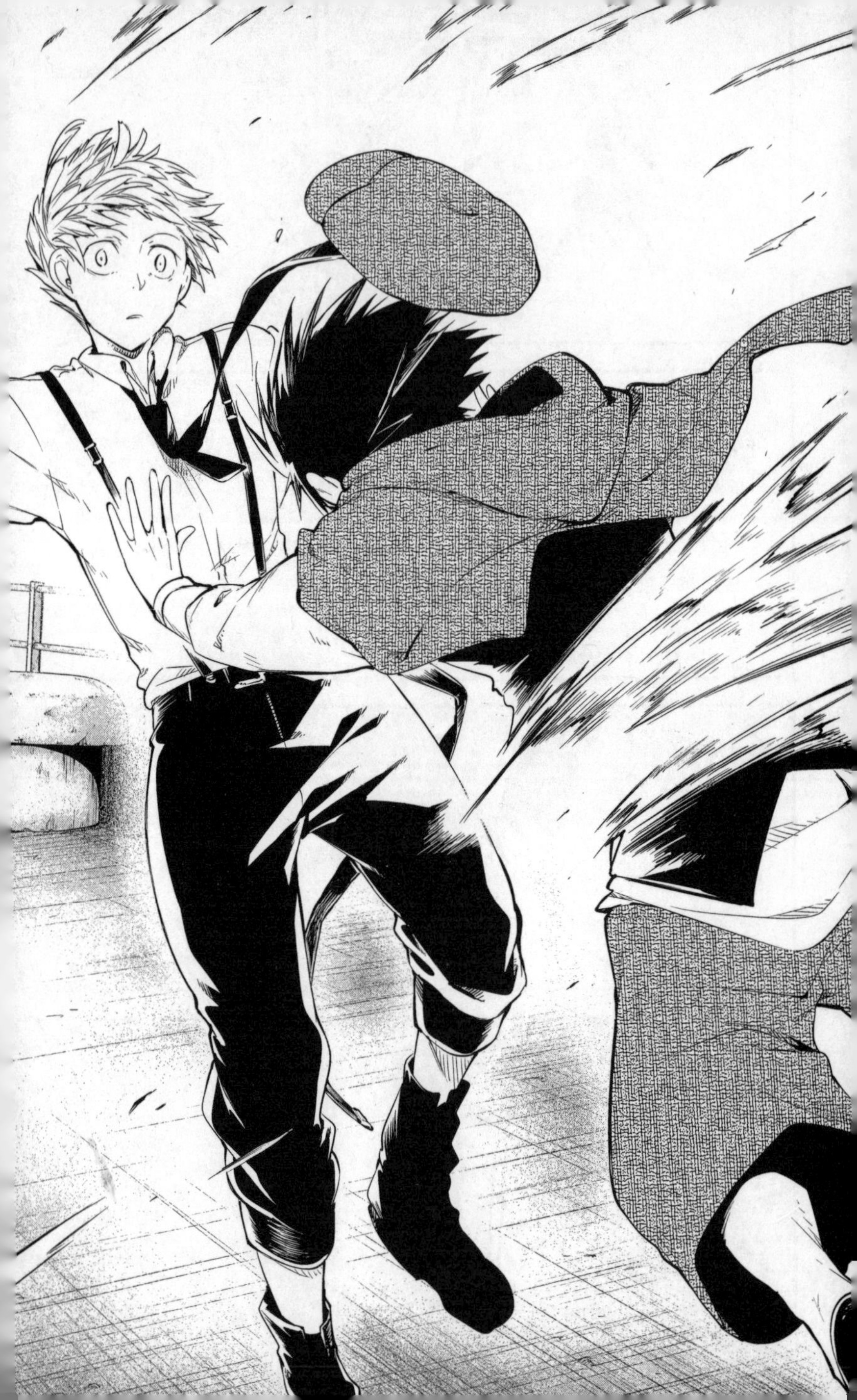

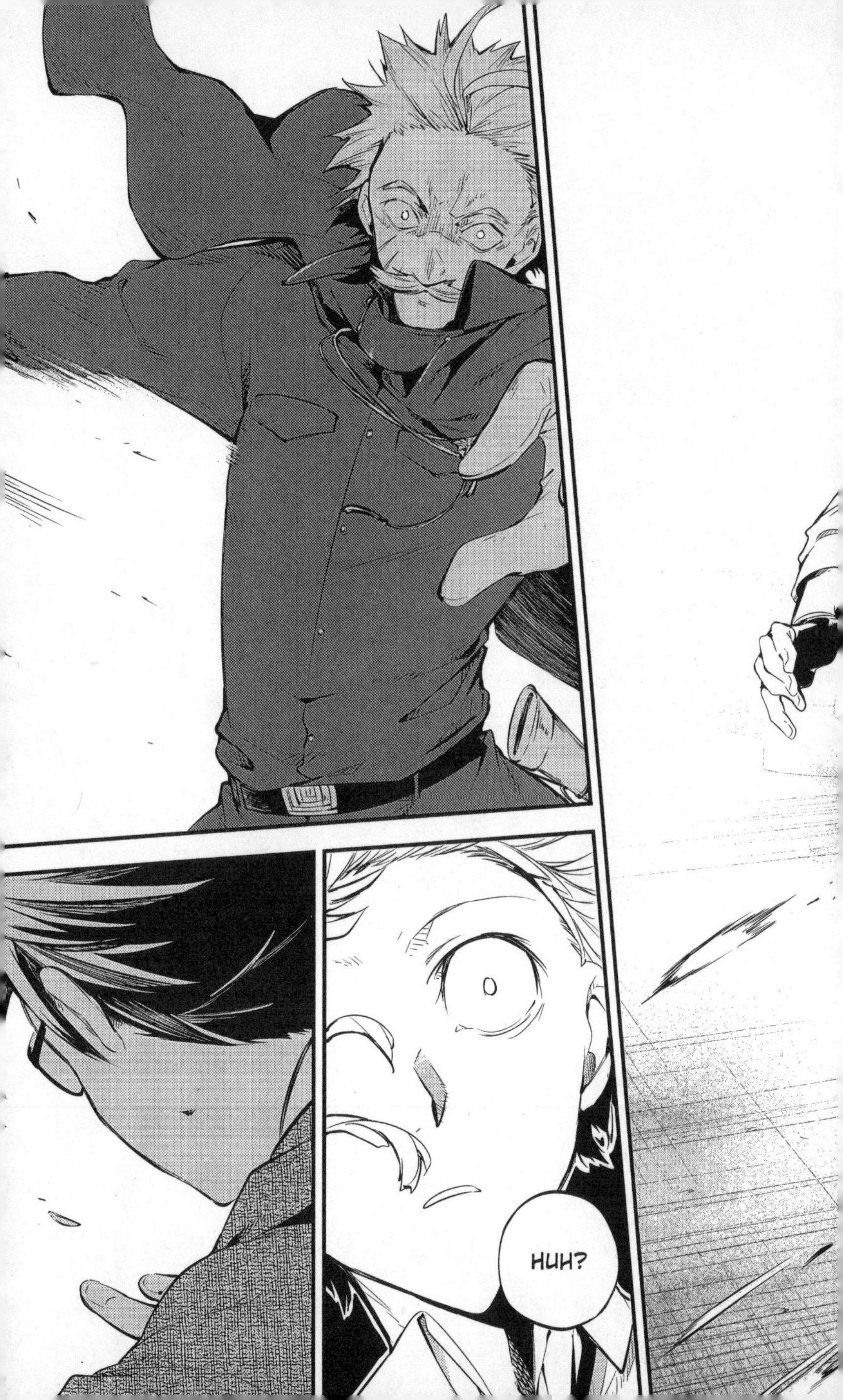
HUH?

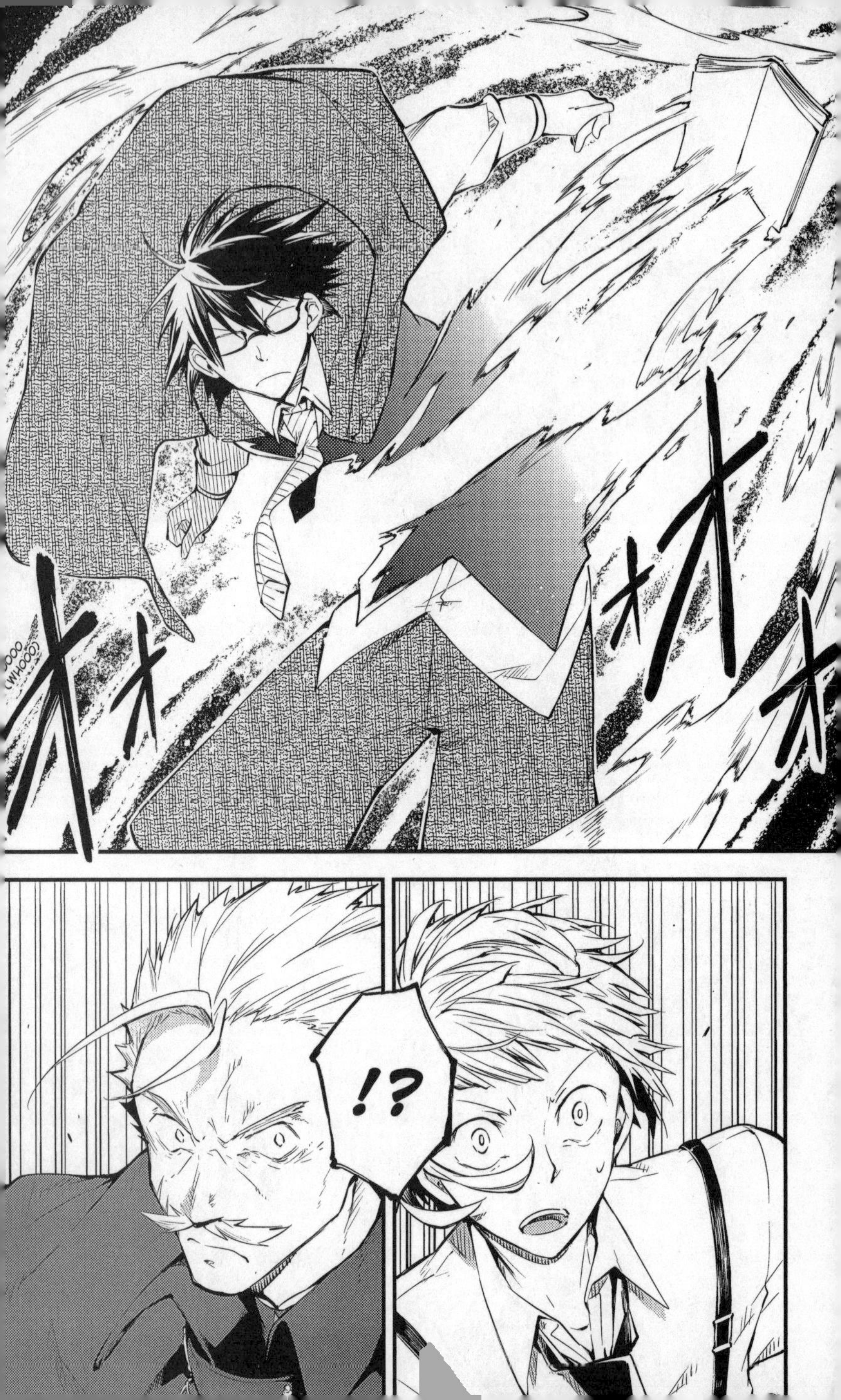
(WHOOOO)
!?

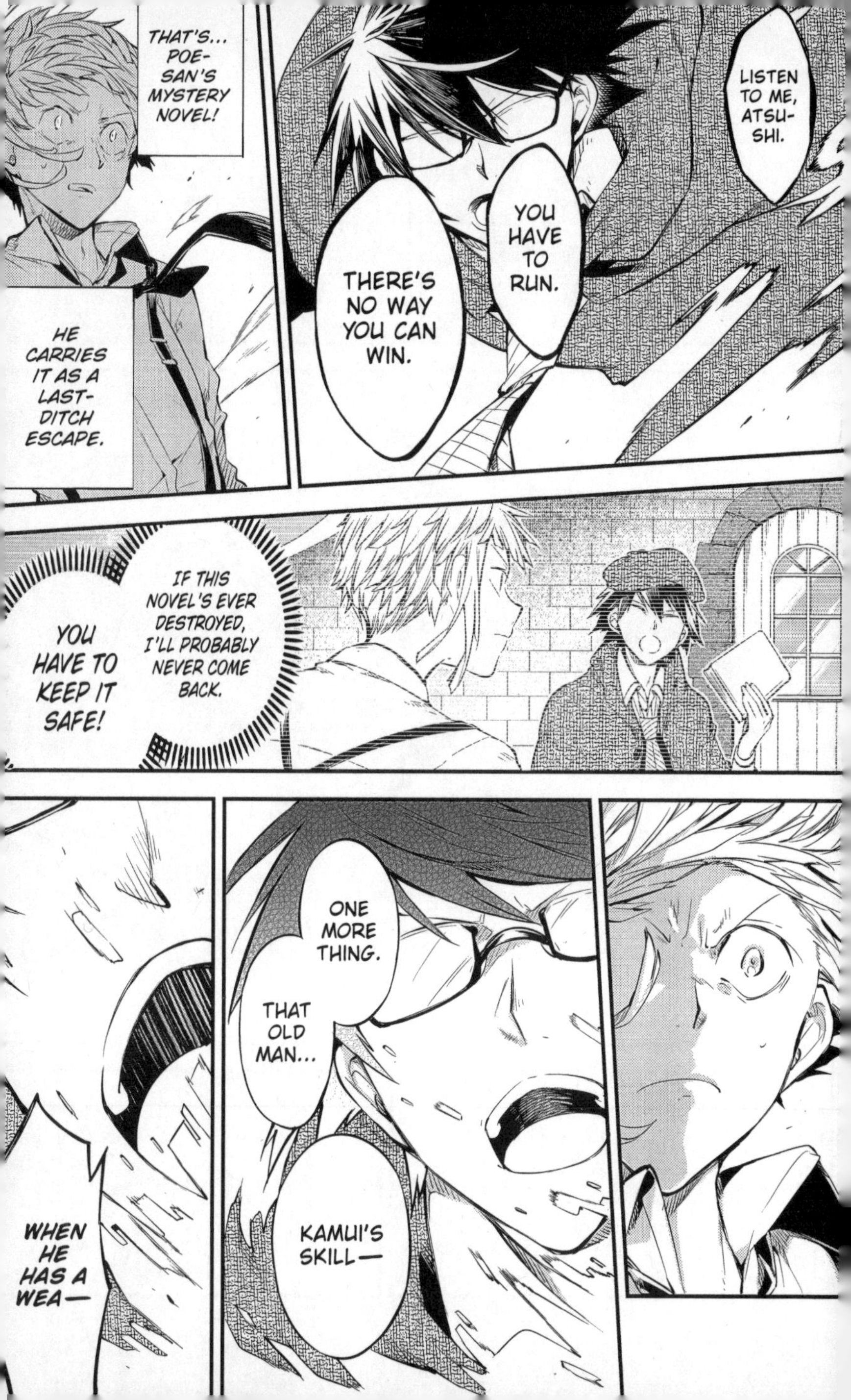

LISTEN TO ME, ATSUSHI.
YOU HAVE TO RUN.
THERE'S NO WAY YOU CAN WIN.
THAT'S... POE-SAN'S MYSTERY NOVEL!
HE CARRIES IT AS A LAST-DITCH ESCAPE.
IF THIS NOVEL'S EVER DESTROYED, I'LL PROBABLY NEVER COME BACK.
YOU HAVE TO KEEP IT SAFE!
ONE MORE THING.
THAT OLD MAN...
KAMUI'S SKILL—
WHEN HE HAS A WEA—

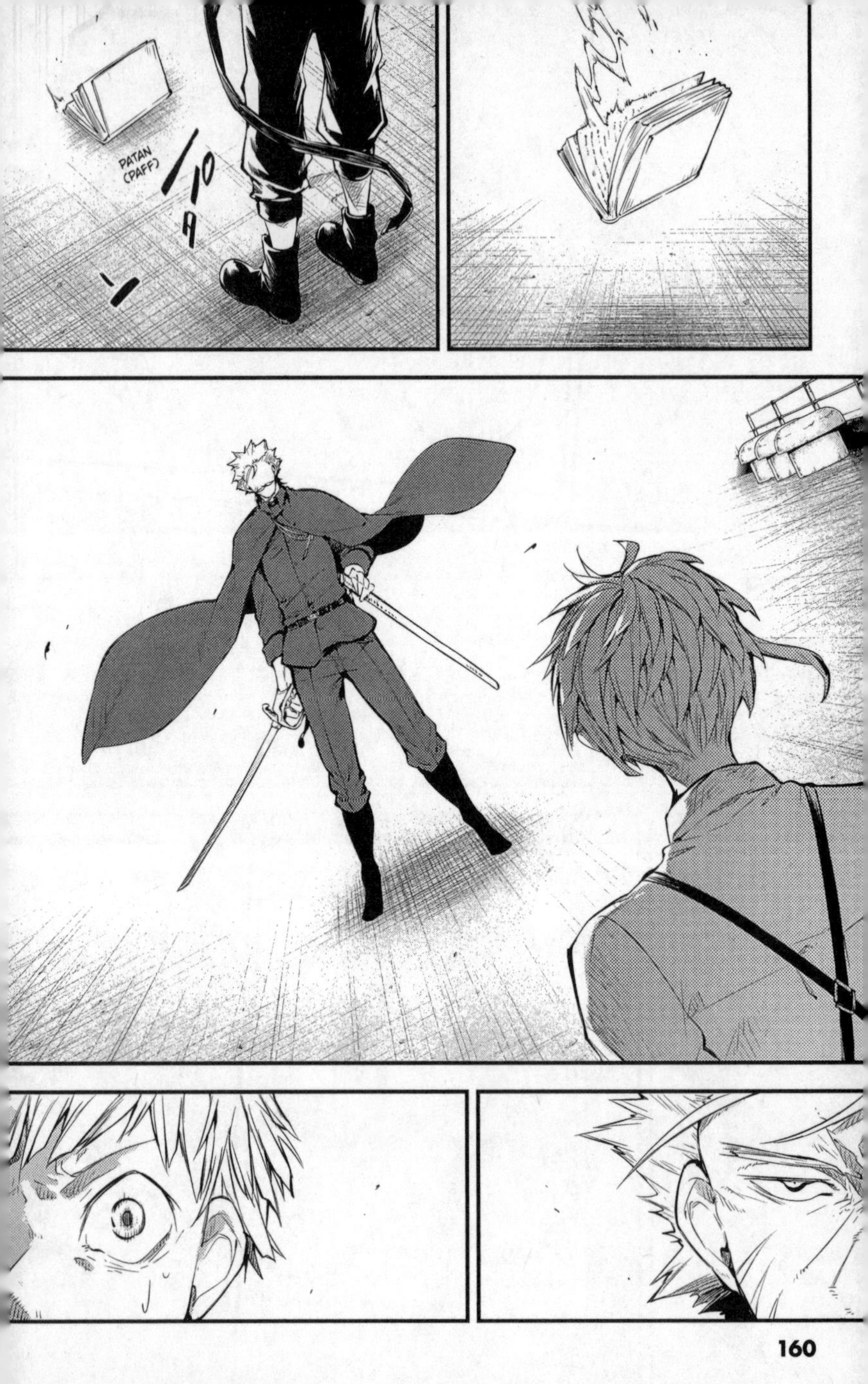
PATAN
(PAFF)

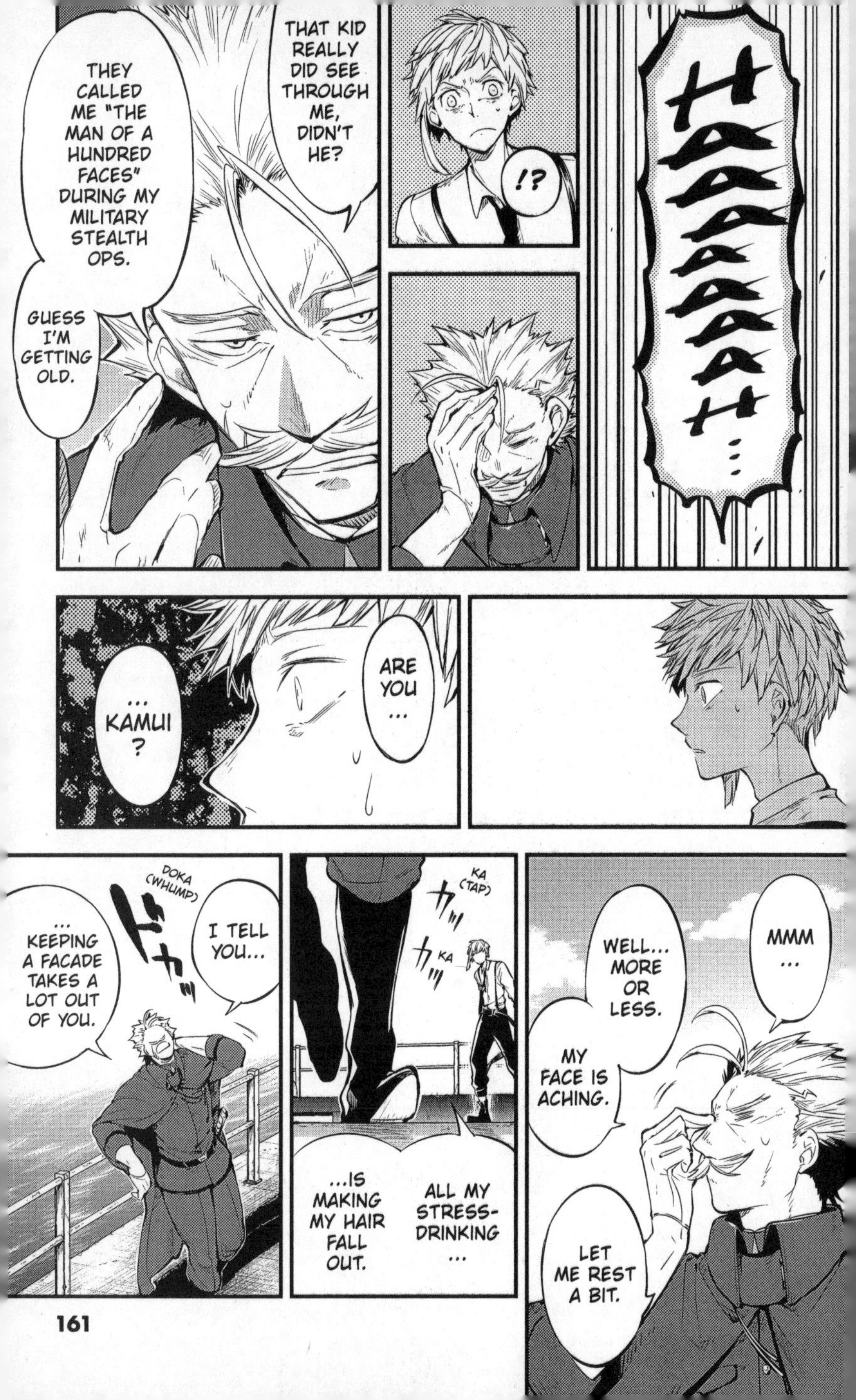
HAAAAAAH...
!?
THAT KID REALLY DID SEE THROUGH ME, DIDN'T HE?
THEY CALLED ME "THE MAN OF A HUNDRED FACES" DURING MY MILITARY STEALTH OPS.
GUESS I'M GETTING OLD.
ARE YOU...
...KAMUI?
MMM...
WELL... MORE OR LESS.
MY FACE IS ACHING.
LET ME REST A BIT.
KA (TAP)
KA
ALL MY STRESS-DRINKING...
...IS MAKING MY HAIR FALL OUT.
DOKA (WHUMP)
I TELL YOU...
...KEEPING A FACADE TAKES A LOT OUT OF YOU.

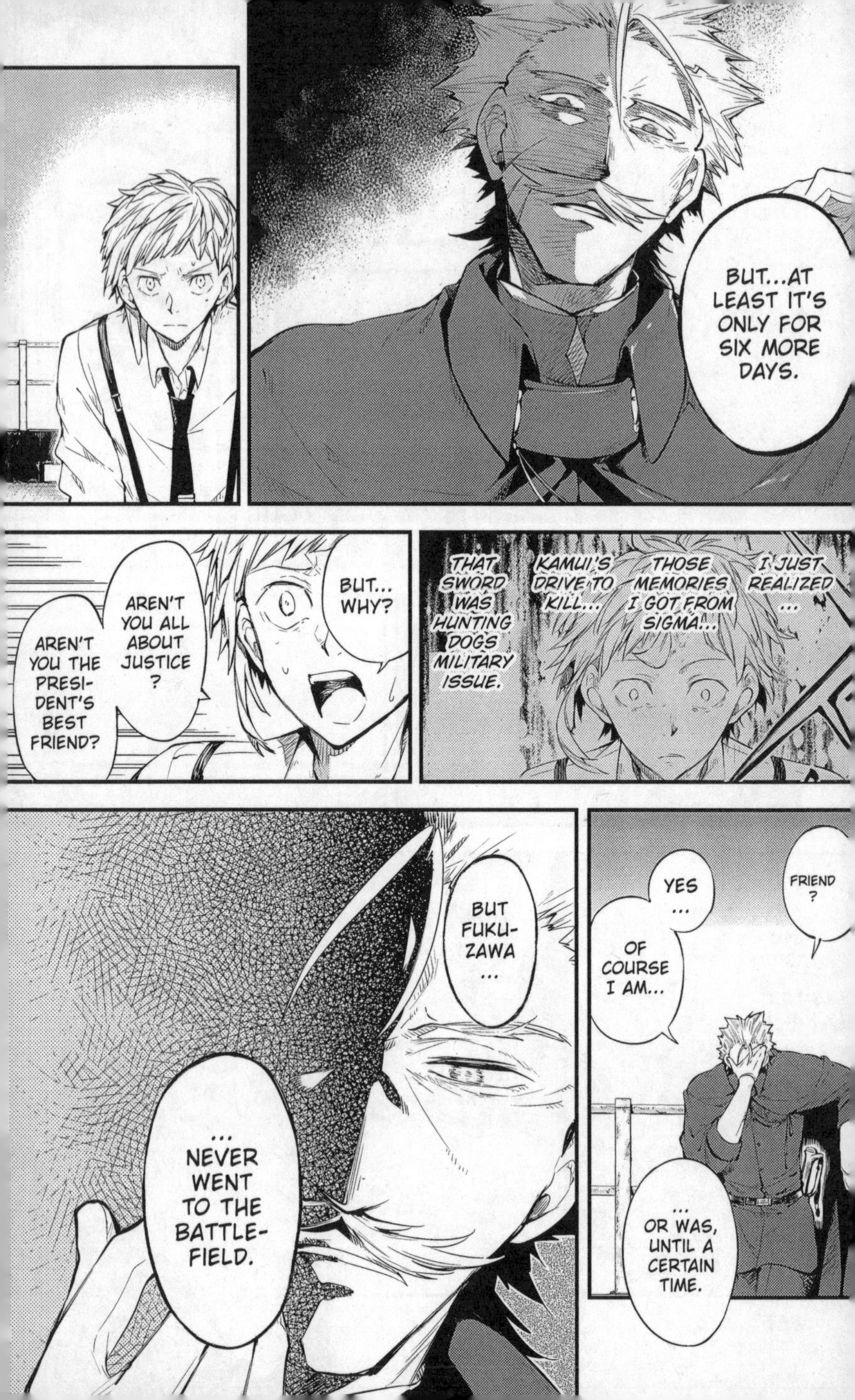
BUT...AT LEAST IT'S ONLY FOR SIX MORE DAYS.
I JUST REALIZED...
THOSE MEMORIES I GOT FROM SIGMA...
KAMUI'S DRIVE TO KILL...
THAT SWORD WAS HUNTING DOGS MILITARY ISSUE.
BUT... WHY?
AREN'T YOU ALL ABOUT JUSTICE?
AREN'T YOU THE PRESIDENT'S BEST FRIEND?
FRIEND?
YES...
OF COURSE I AM...
...OR WAS, UNTIL A CERTAIN TIME.
BUT FUKUZAWA...
...NEVER WENT TO THE BATTLEFIELD.

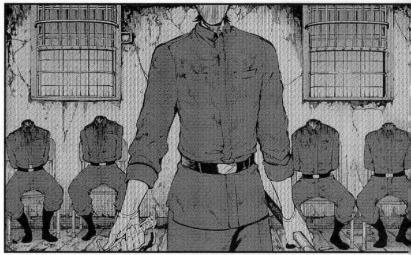

THAT'S WHERE OUR PATHS SPLIT...

...FOR ALL TIME.

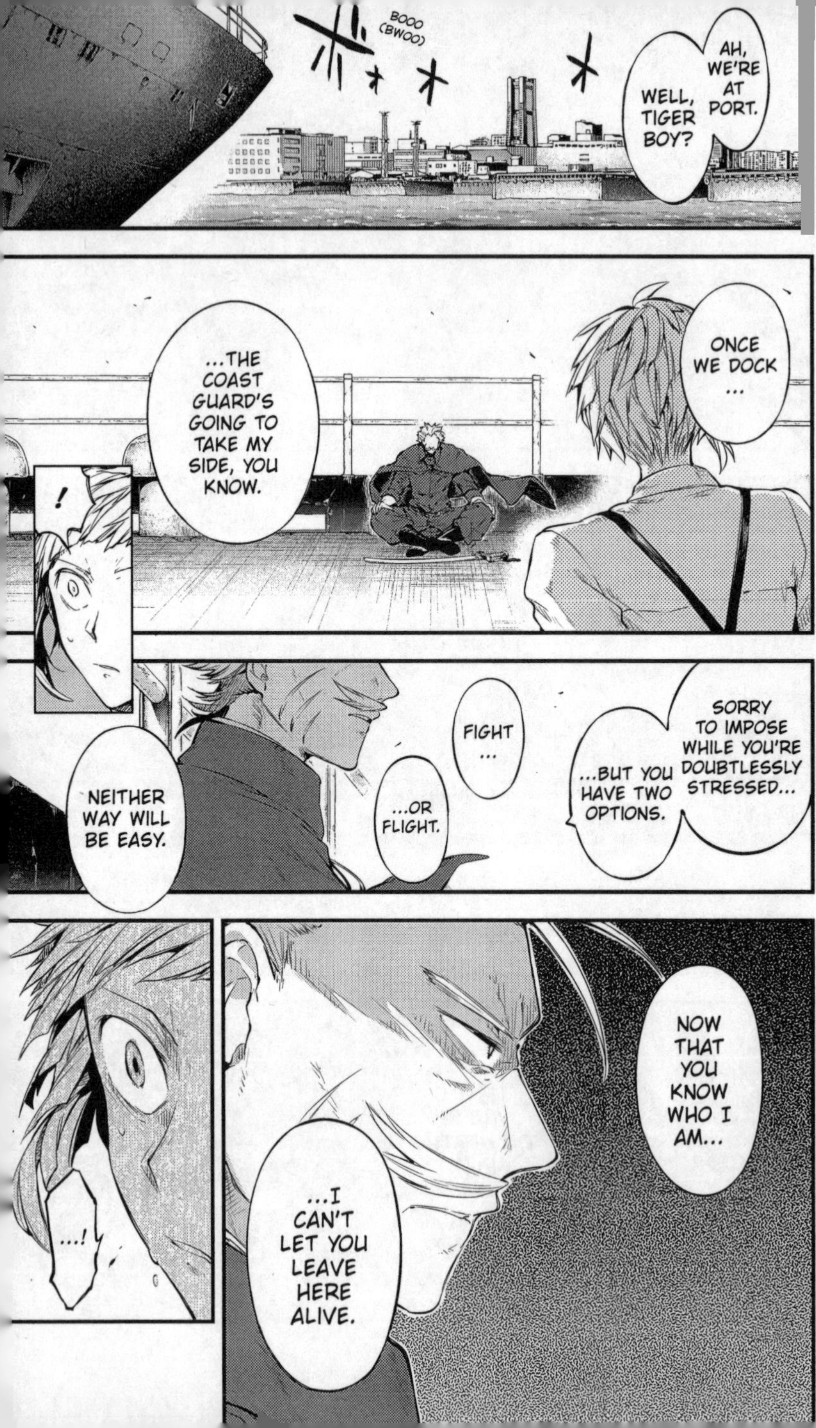
BOOO (BWOO)
AH, WE'RE AT PORT.
WELL, TIGER BOY?
ONCE WE DOCK ...
...THE COAST GUARD'S GOING TO TAKE MY SIDE, YOU KNOW.
!
SORRY TO IMPOSE WHILE YOU'RE DOUBTLESSLY STRESSED...
...BUT YOU HAVE TWO OPTIONS.
FIGHT ...
...OR FLIGHT.
NEITHER WAY WILL BE EASY.
NOW THAT YOU KNOW WHO I AM...
...I CAN'T LET YOU LEAVE HERE ALIVE.
...!

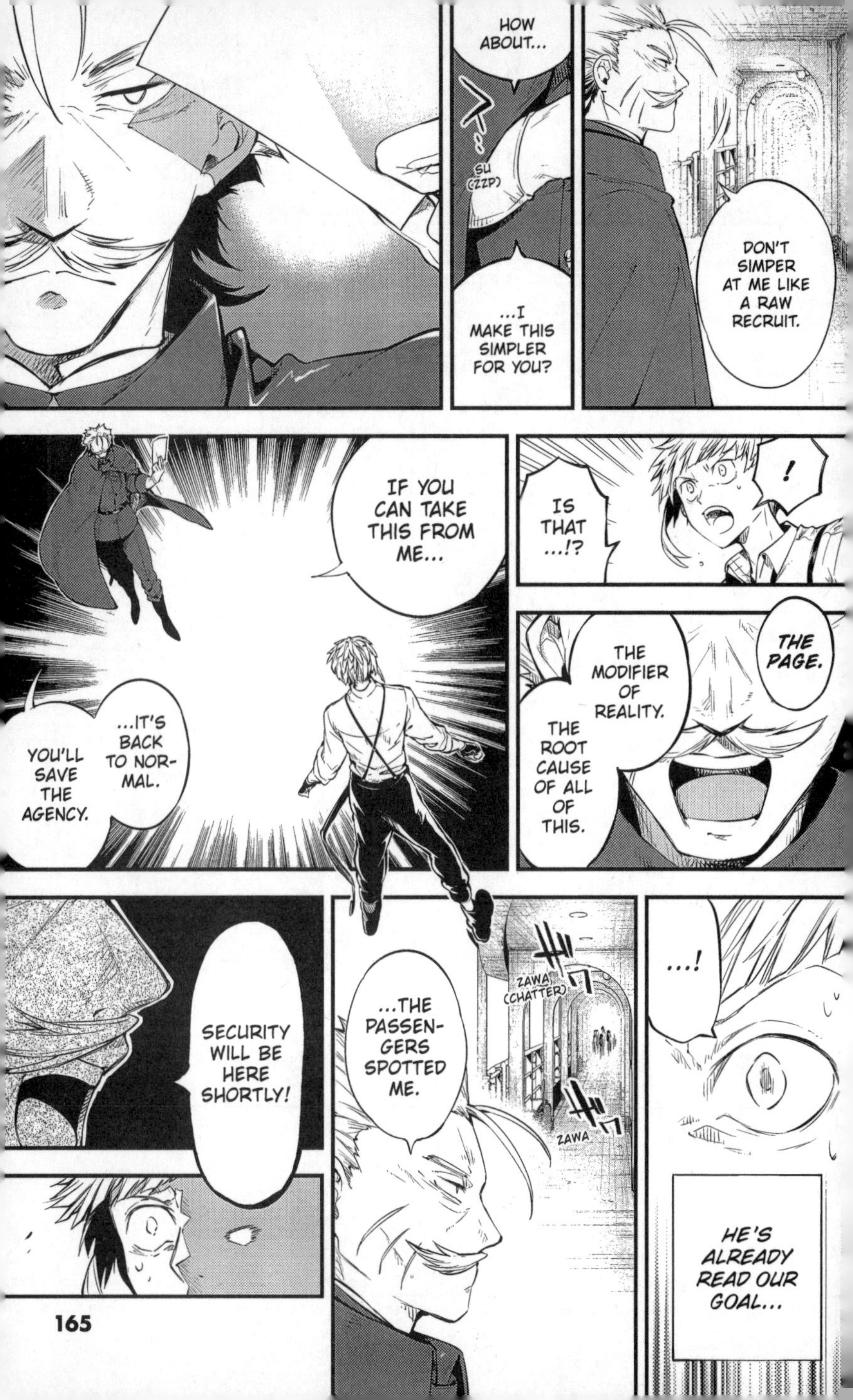

DON'T SIMPER AT ME LIKE A RAW RECRUIT.
HOW ABOUT...
SU (ZZP)
...I MAKE THIS SIMPLER FOR YOU?
!
IS THAT ...!?
THE PAGE.
THE MODIFIER OF REALITY.
THE ROOT CAUSE OF ALL OF THIS.
IF YOU CAN TAKE THIS FROM ME...
...IT'S BACK TO NORMAL.
YOU'LL SAVE THE AGENCY.
...!
HE'S ALREADY READ OUR GOAL...
ZAWA (CHATTER)
ZAWA
...THE PASSENGERS SPOTTED ME.
SECURITY WILL BE HERE SHORTLY!

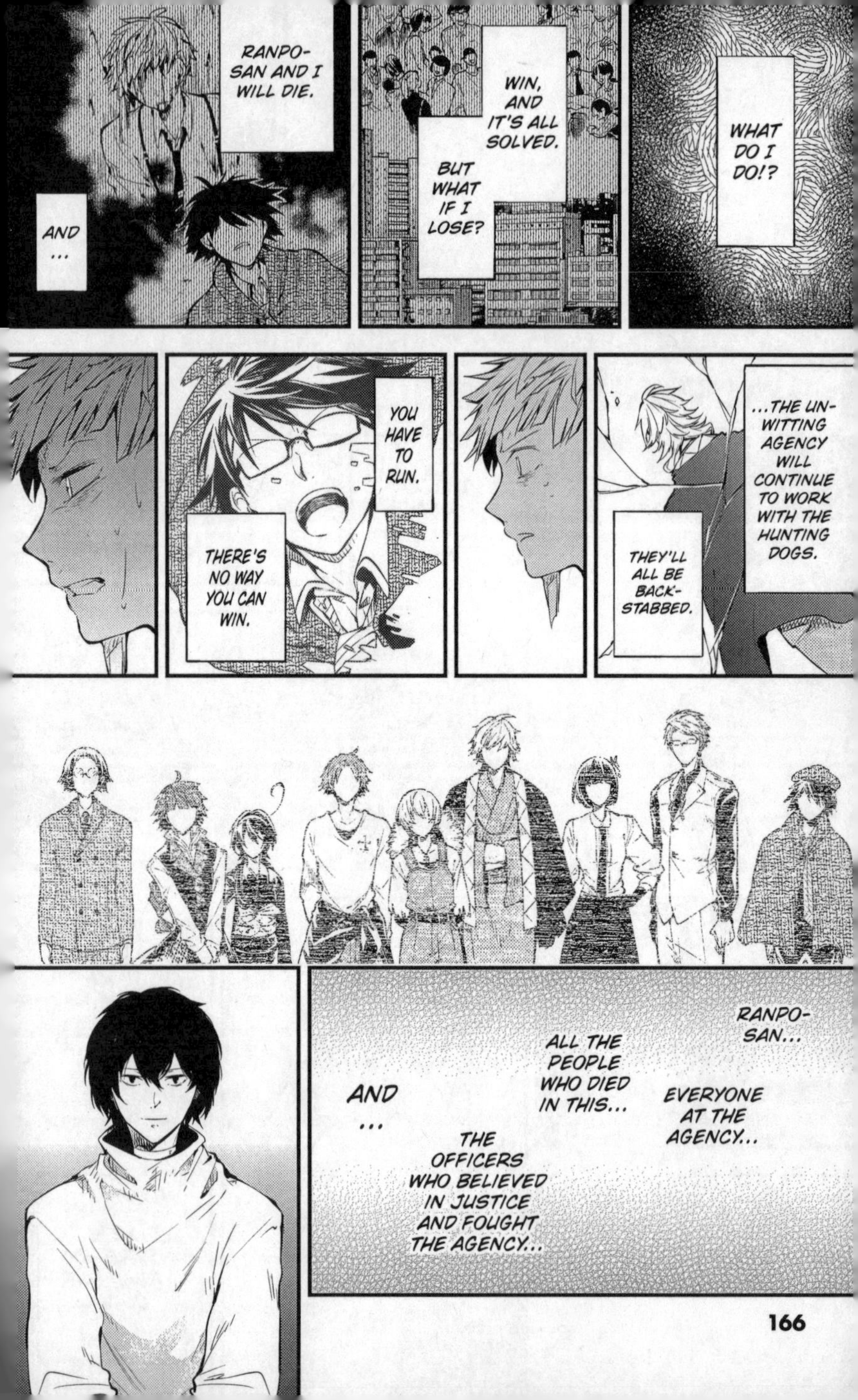
WHAT DO I DO!?
WIN, AND IT'S ALL SOLVED.
BUT WHAT IF I LOSE?
RANPO-SAN AND I WILL DIE.
AND ...
...THE UN-WITTING AGENCY WILL CONTINUE TO WORK WITH THE HUNTING DOGS.
THEY'LL ALL BE BACK-STABBED.
YOU HAVE TO RUN.
THERE'S NO WAY YOU CAN WIN.
RANPO-SAN...
EVERYONE AT THE AGENCY...
ALL THE PEOPLE WHO DIED IN THIS...
THE OFFICERS WHO BELIEVED IN JUSTICE AND FOUGHT THE AGENCY...
AND ...

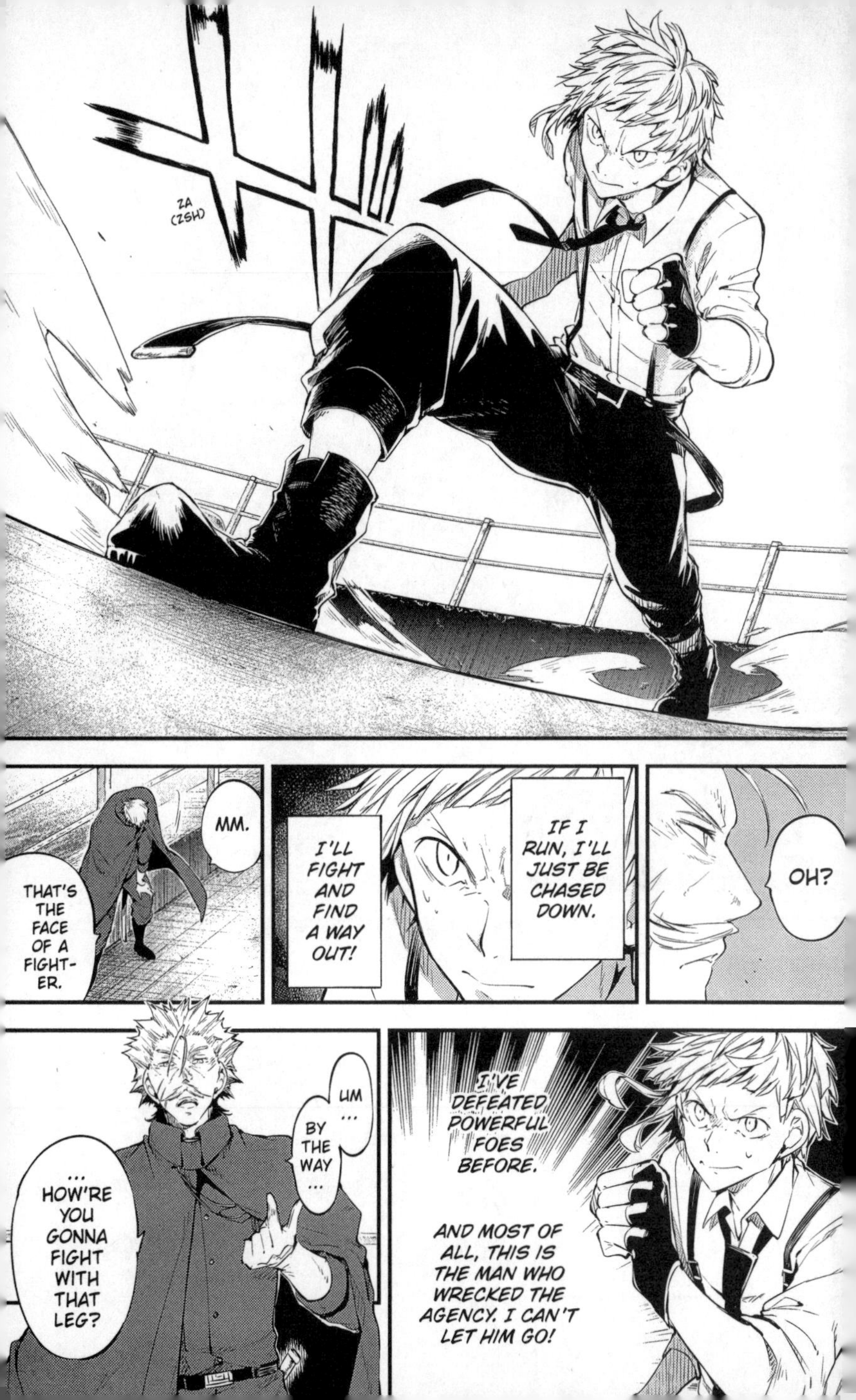
ZA (ZSH)
OH?
IF I RUN, I'LL JUST BE CHASED DOWN.
I'LL FIGHT AND FIND A WAY OUT!
MM.
THAT'S THE FACE OF A FIGHT-ER.
I'VE DEFEATED POWERFUL FOES BEFORE.
AND MOST OF ALL, THIS IS THE MAN WHO WRECKED THE AGENCY. I CAN'T LET HIM GO!
UM ...
BY THE WAY ...
... HOW'RE YOU GONNA FIGHT WITH THAT LEG?

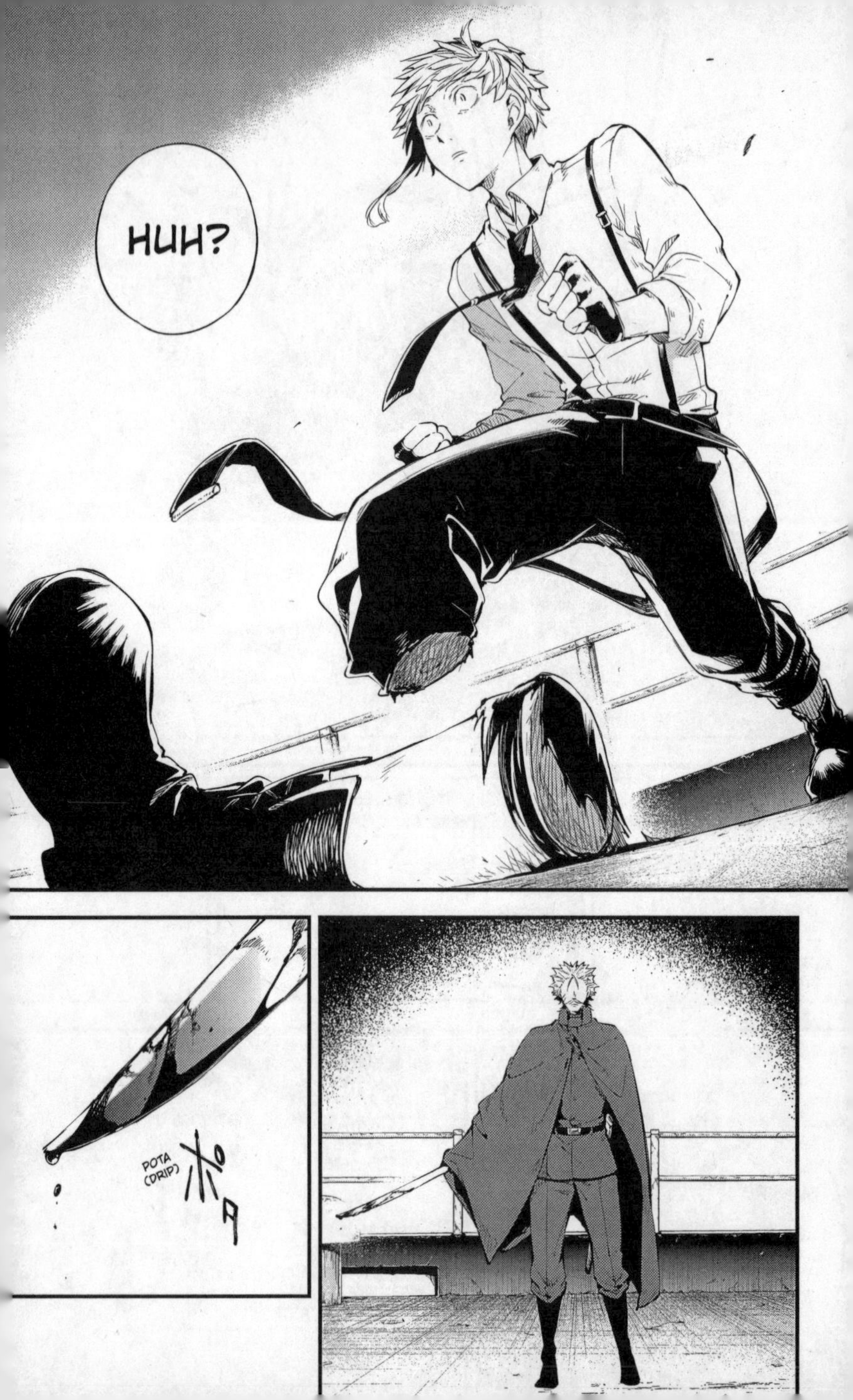
HUH?
POTA (DRIP)
ポタ

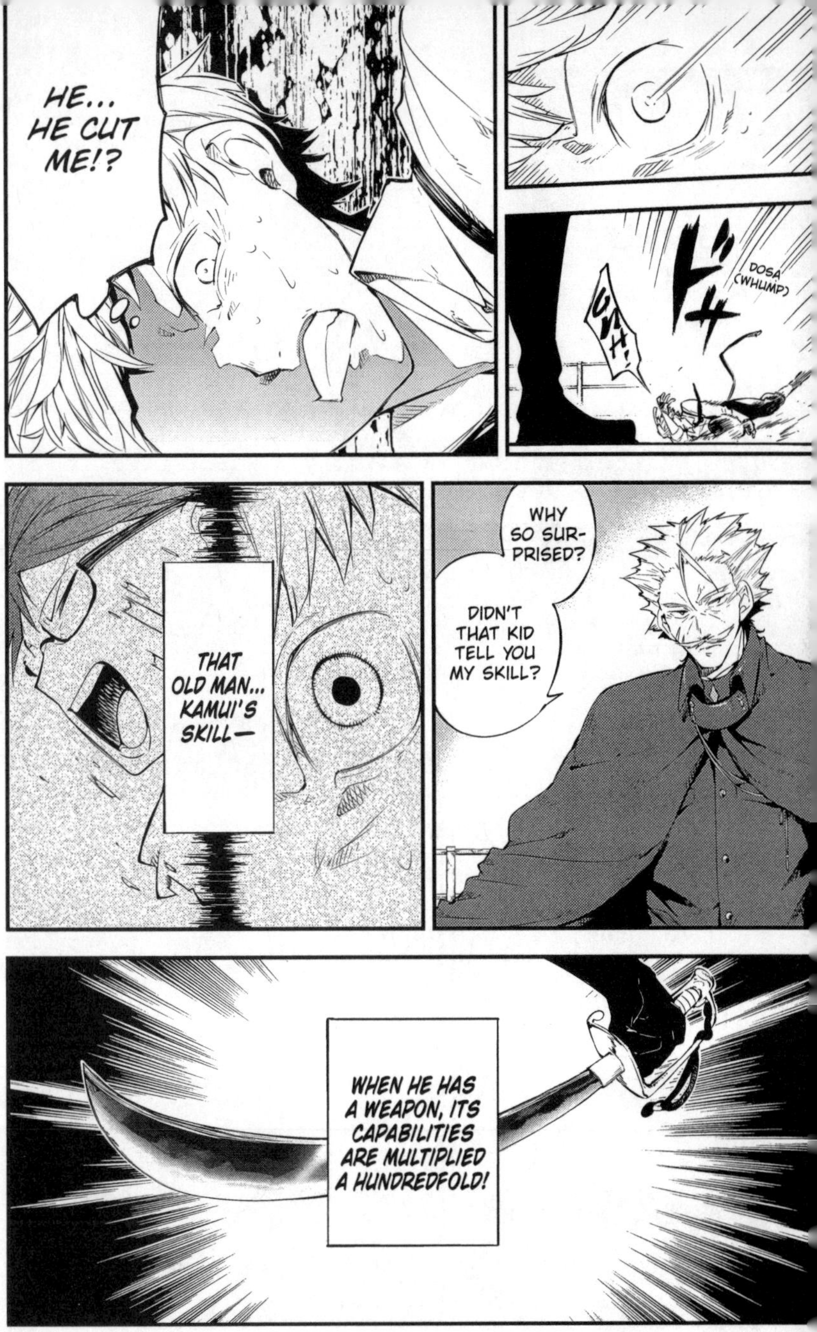
DOSA (WHUMP)
ドサ
UNH!
HE... HE CUT ME!?
WHY SO SURPRISED?
DIDN'T THAT KID TELL YOU MY SKILL?
THAT OLD MAN... KAMUI'S SKILL—
WHEN HE HAS A WEAPON, ITS CAPABILITIES ARE MULTIPLIED A HUNDREDFOLD!

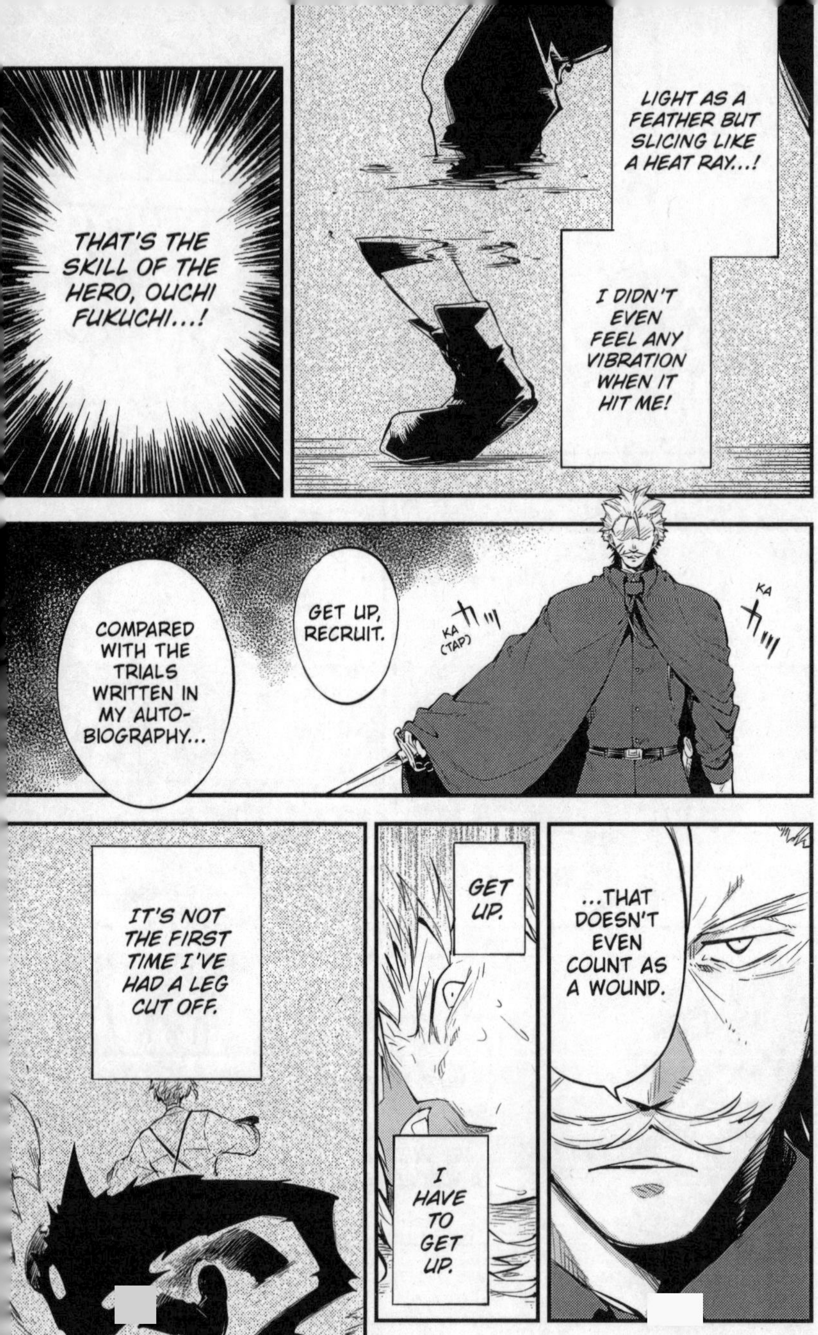
LIGHT AS A FEATHER BUT SLICING LIKE A HEAT RAY...!
I DIDN'T EVEN FEEL ANY VIBRATION WHEN IT HIT ME!
THAT'S THE SKILL OF THE HERO, OUCHI FUKUCHI...!
KA
KA (TAP)
GET UP, RECRUIT.
COMPARED WITH THE TRIALS WRITTEN IN MY AUTO-BIOGRAPHY...
...THAT DOESN'T EVEN COUNT AS A WOUND.
GET UP.
I HAVE TO GET UP.
IT'S NOT THE FIRST TIME I'VE HAD A LEG CUT OFF.

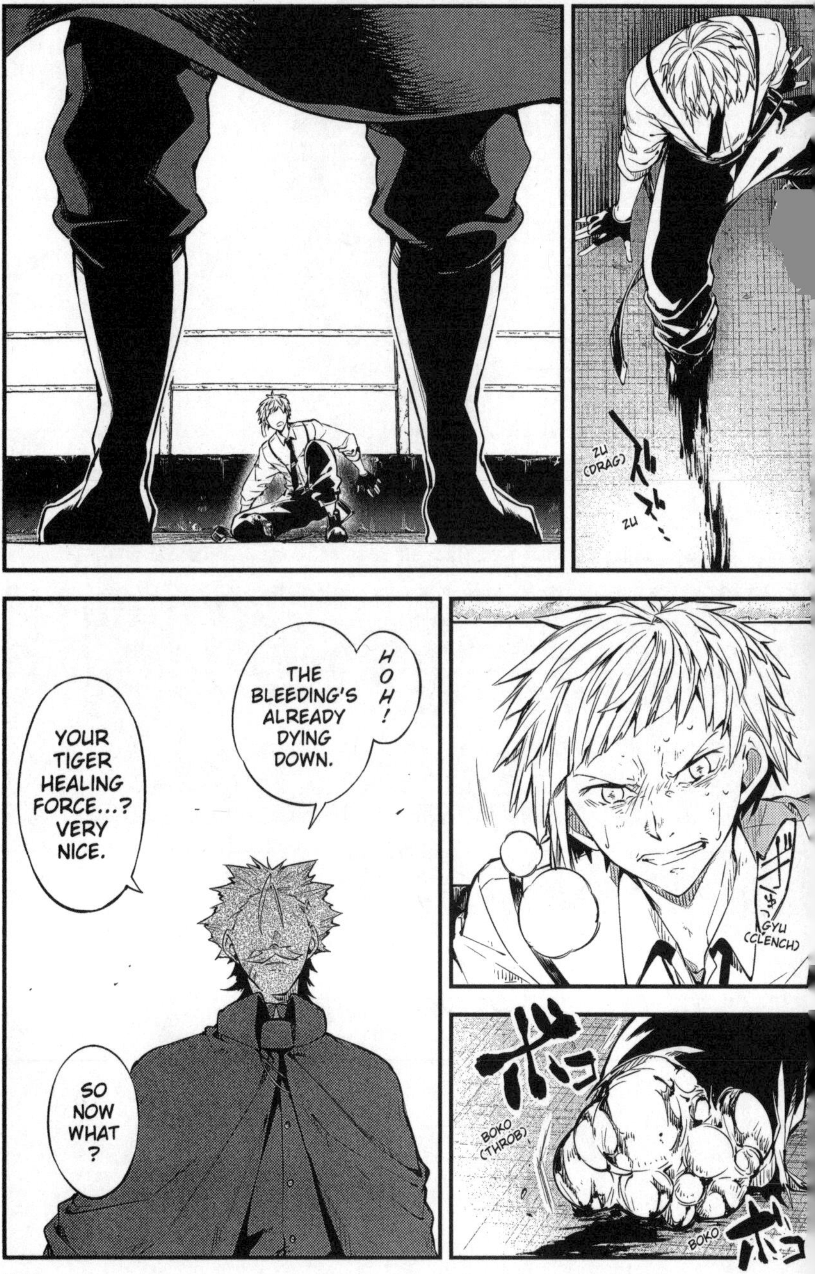
ZU (DRAG)
ZU
GYU (CLENCH)
BOKO (THROB)
BOKO
HOH!
THE BLEEDING'S ALREADY DYING DOWN.
YOUR TIGER HEALING FORCE...? VERY NICE.
SO NOW WHAT?

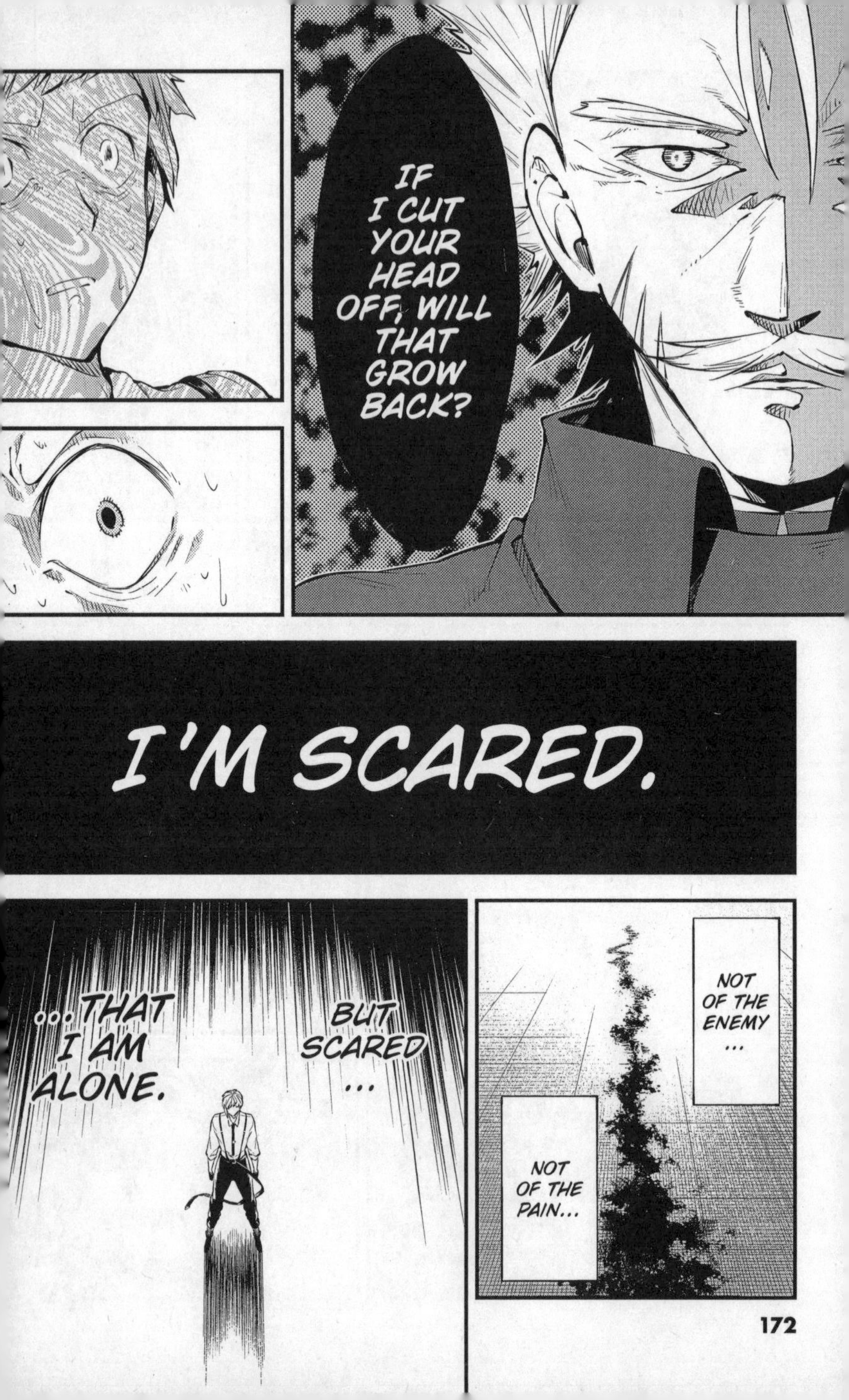
IF I CUT YOUR HEAD OFF, WILL THAT GROW BACK?
I'M SCARED.
NOT OF THE ENEMY...
NOT OF THE PAIN...
BUT SCARED...
...THAT I AM ALONE.

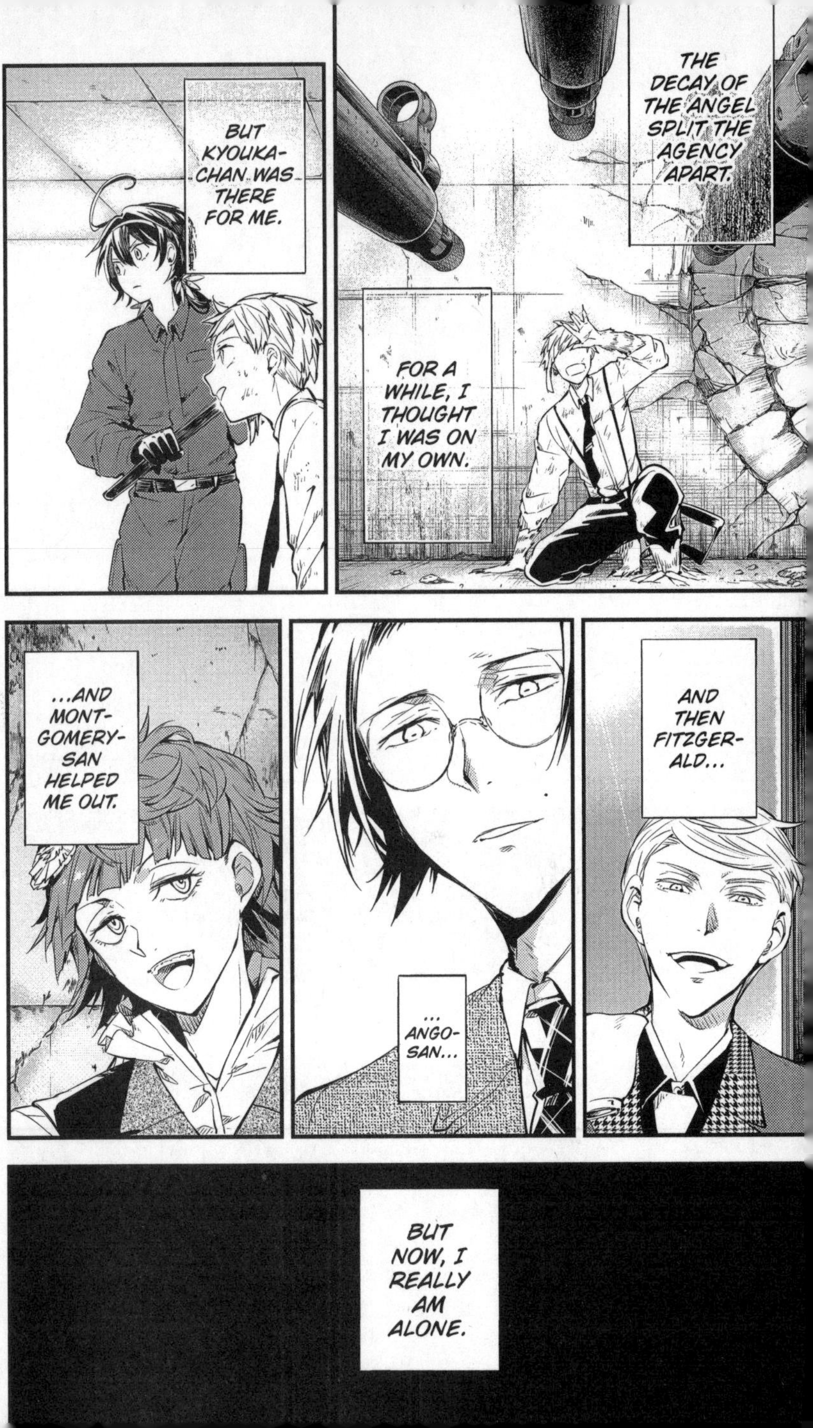
THE DECAY OF THE ANGEL SPLIT THE AGENCY APART.
FOR A WHILE, I THOUGHT I WAS ON MY OWN.
BUT KYOUKA-CHAN WAS THERE FOR ME.
AND THEN FITZGER-ALD...
...ANGO-SAN...
...AND MONT-GOMERY-SAN HELPED ME OUT.
BUT NOW, I REALLY AM ALONE.

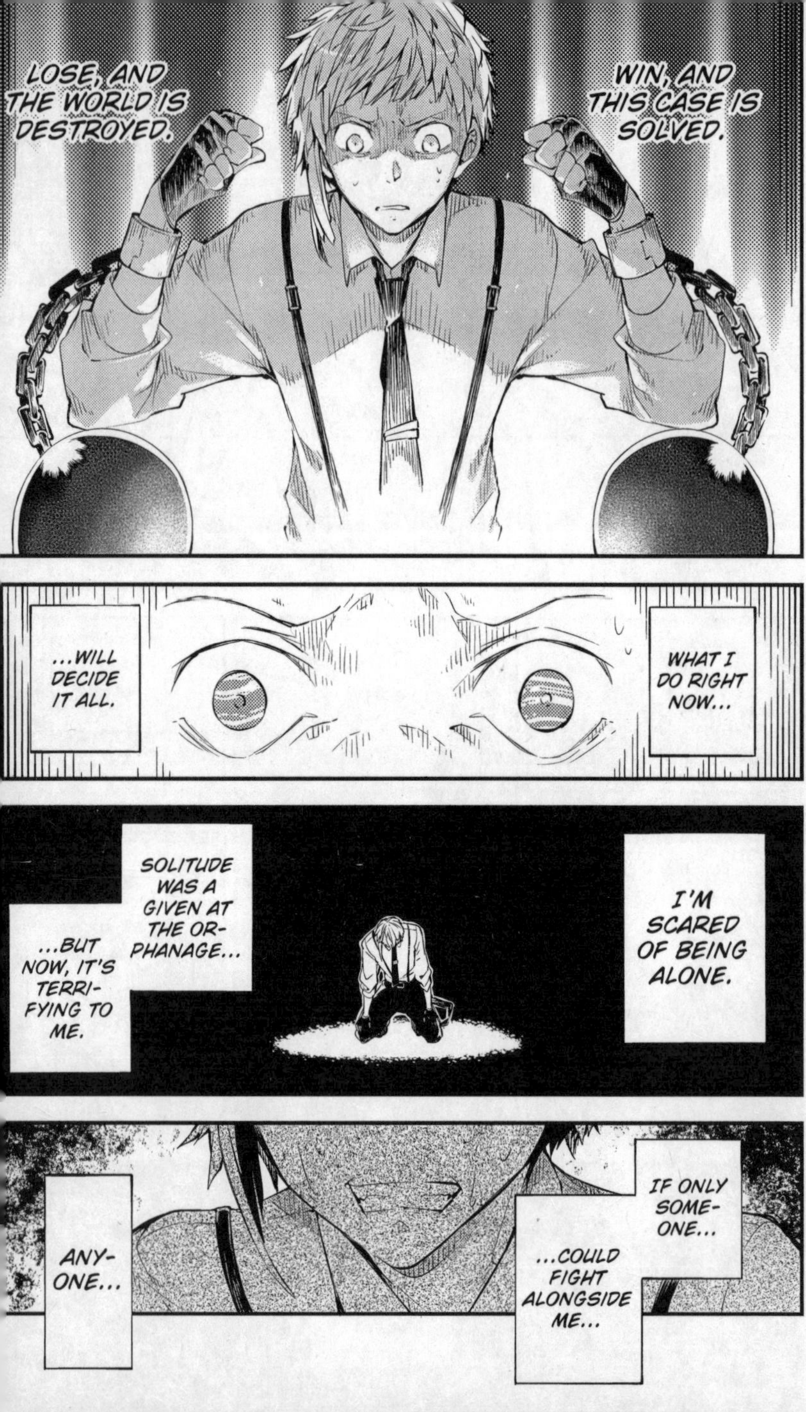
WIN, AND THIS CASE IS SOLVED.
LOSE, AND THE WORLD IS DESTROYED.
WHAT I DO RIGHT NOW...
...WILL DECIDE IT ALL.
I'M SCARED OF BEING ALONE.
SOLITUDE WAS A GIVEN AT THE OR-PHANAGE...
...BUT NOW, IT'S TERRI-FYING TO ME.
IF ONLY SOME-ONE...
...COULD FIGHT ALONGSIDE ME...
ANY-ONE...

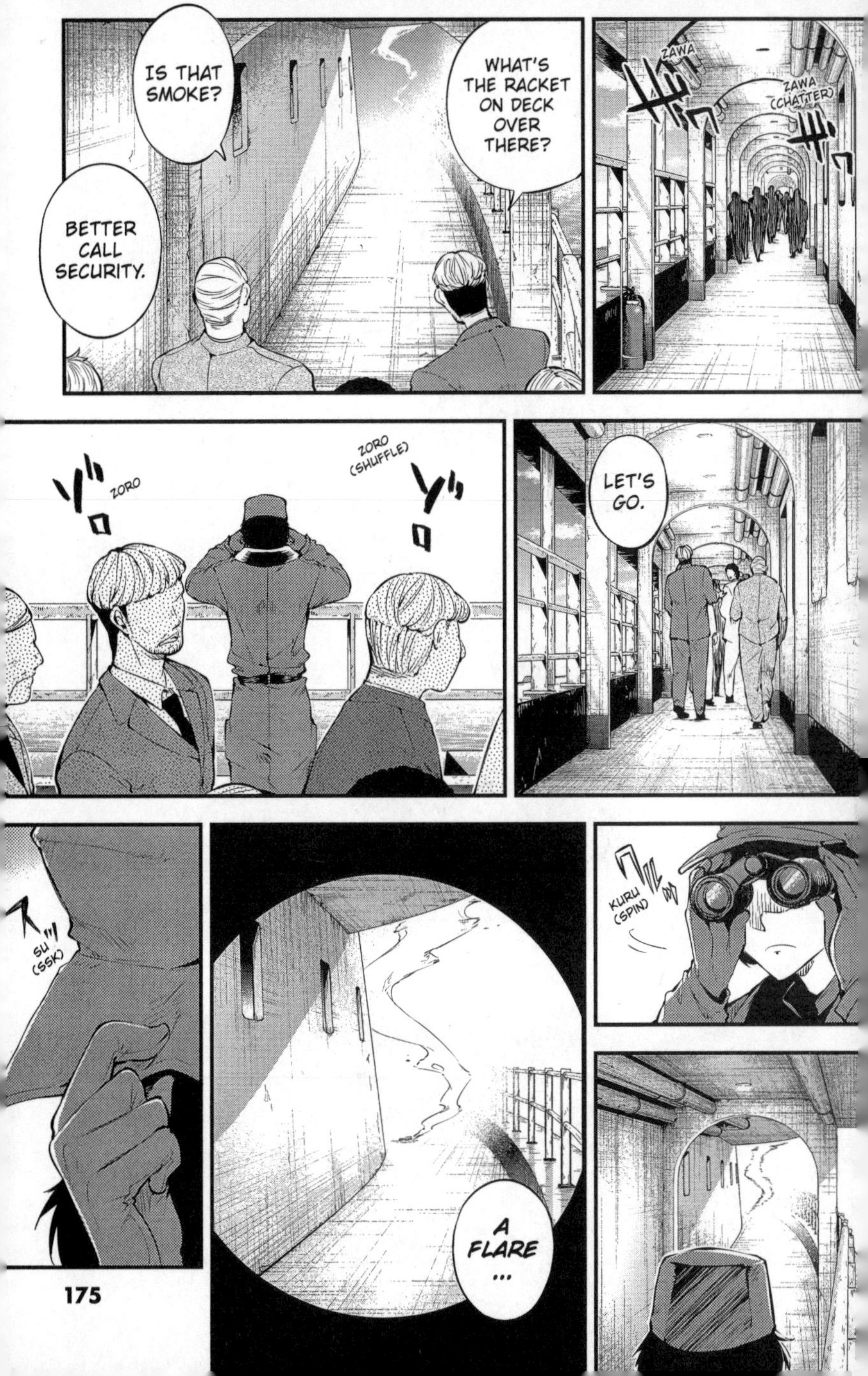
ZAWA
ZAWA (CHATTER)
WHAT'S THE RACKET ON DECK OVER THERE?
IS THAT SMOKE?
BETTER CALL SECURITY.
LET'S GO.
ZORO (SHUFFLE)
ZORO
KURU (SPIN)
A FLARE ...
SU (SSK)

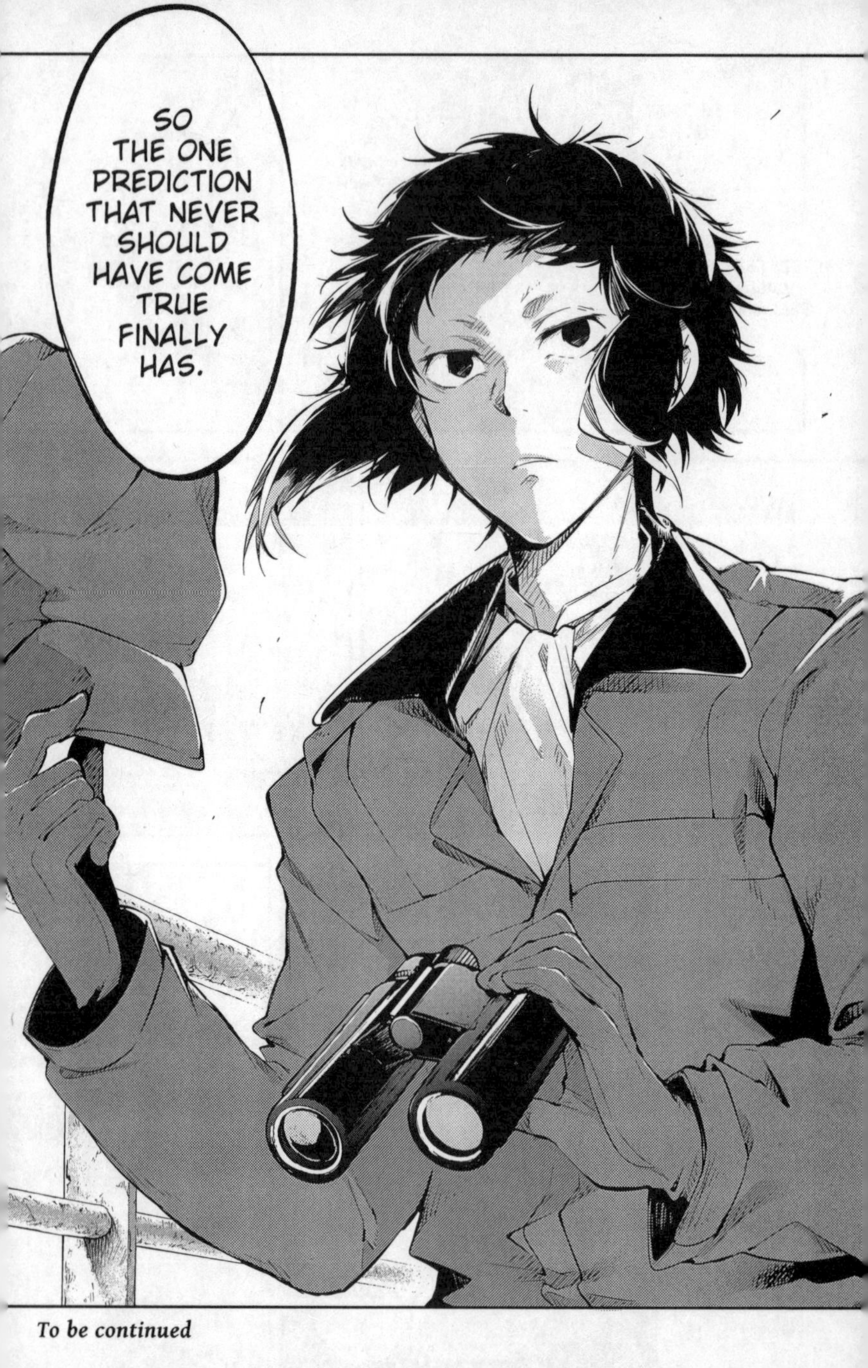
SO THE ONE PREDICTION THAT NEVER SHOULD HAVE COME TRUE FINALLY HAS.

To be continued

MICHIZOU TACHIHARA

SKILL: Midwinter Memento
A metal manipulation skill, capable of delicate work like safecracking and feats of strength like stopping a charging plane.

AGE: *19*

BIRTH DATE: *July 30*

HEIGHT: *176cm*

WEIGHT: *62kg*

BLOOD TYPE: *A*

LIKES: *Pencils, hyacinths*

DISLIKES: *The past, Teruko Ookura's craziness*

BUNGO STRAY DOGS

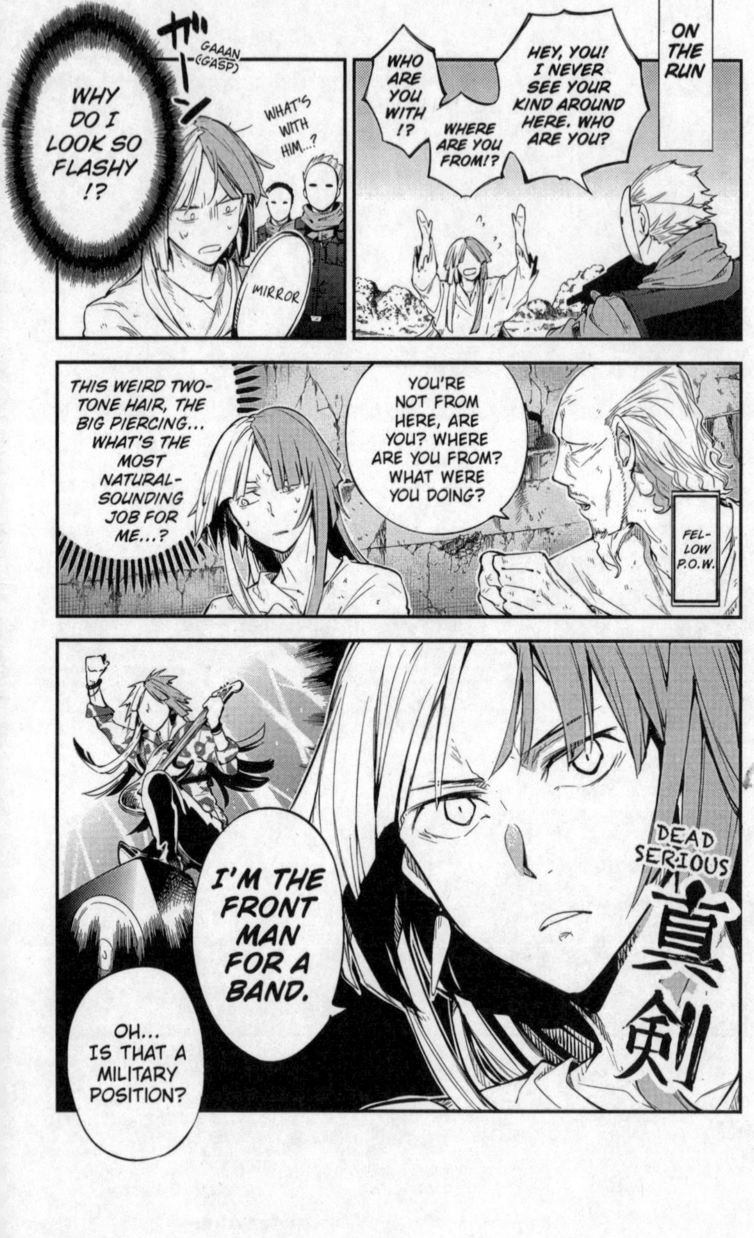
ON THE RUN
HEY, YOU! I NEVER SEE YOUR KIND AROUND HERE. WHO ARE YOU?
WHERE ARE YOU FROM!?
WHO ARE YOU WITH!?
ガーン
GAAAN (GASP)
WHY DO I LOOK SO FLASHY!?
WHAT'S WITH HIM...?
MIRROR
FEL-LOW P.O.W.
YOU'RE NOT FROM HERE, ARE YOU? WHERE ARE YOU FROM? WHAT WERE YOU DOING?
THIS WEIRD TWO-TONE HAIR, THE BIG PIERCING... WHAT'S THE MOST NATURAL-SOUNDING JOB FOR ME...?
DEAD SERIOUS
真剣
I'M THE FRONT MAN FOR A BAND.
OH... IS THAT A MILITARY POSITION?

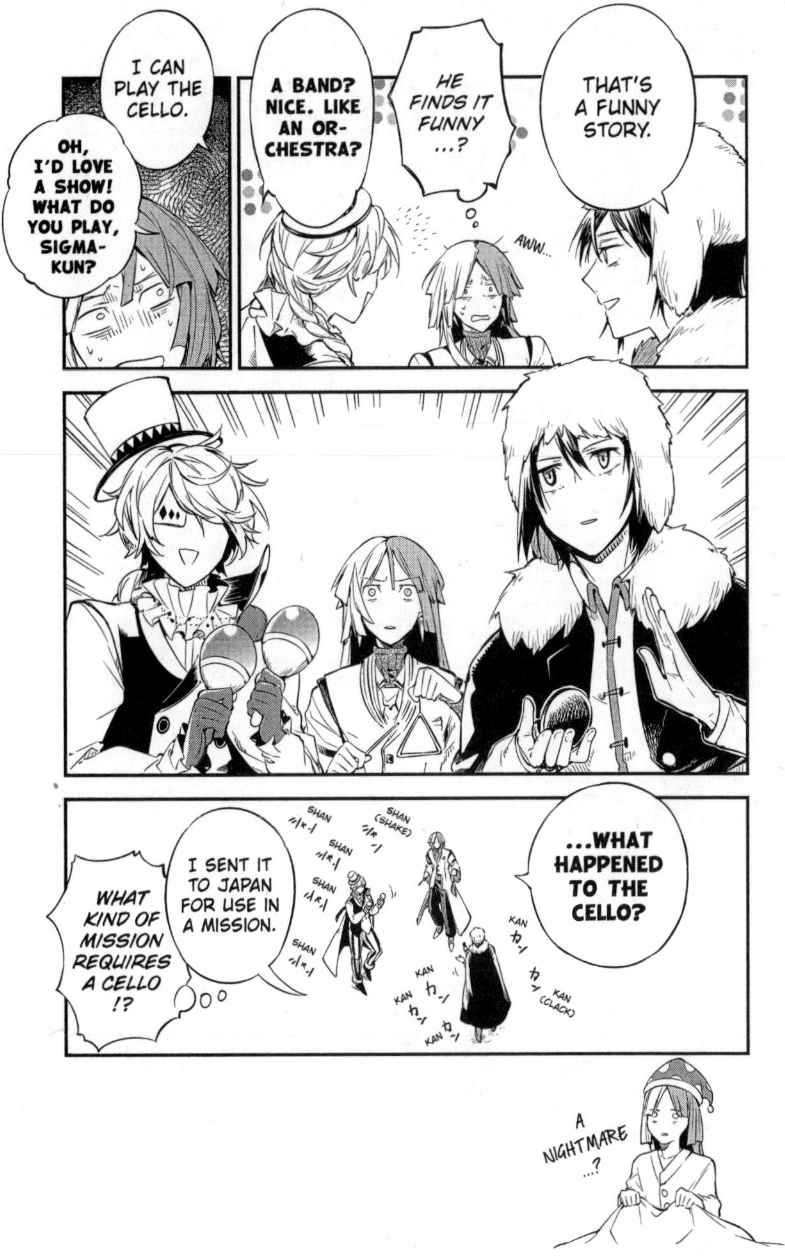
THAT'S A FUNNY STORY.
AWW...
HE FINDS IT FUNNY ...?
A BAND? NICE. LIKE AN ORCHESTRA?
I CAN PLAY THE CELLO.
OH, I'D LOVE A SHOW! WHAT DO YOU PLAY, SIGMA-KUN?
...WHAT HAPPENED TO THE CELLO?
KAN
KAN (CLACK)
KAN
KAN
KAN
SHAN (SHAKE)
SHAN
SHAN
SHAN
SHAN
I SENT IT TO JAPAN FOR USE IN A MISSION.
WHAT KIND OF MISSION REQUIRES A CELLO !?
A NIGHTMARE ...?

BUNGO STRAY DOGS

Story: *Kafka Asagiri*   Art: *Sango Harukawa*

Translation: Kevin Gifford   †   Lettering: Bianca Pistillo

BUNGO STRAY DOGS Volume 19
©Kafka Asagiri 2020
©Sango Harukawa 2020
First published in Japan in 2020 by KADOKAWA CORPORATION, Tokyo.
English translation rights arranged with KADOKAWA CORPORATION, Tokyo through TUTTLE-MORI AGENCY, INC., Tokyo.

English translation © 2021 by Yen Press, LLC

Yen Press
150 West 30th Street, 19th Floor
New York, NY 10001

Visit us at yenpress.com
facebook.com/yenpress
twitter.com/yenpress
yenpress.tumblr.com
instagram.com/yenpress

First Yen Press Edition: June 2021

Yen Press is an imprint of Yen Press, LLC.
The Yen Press name and logo are trademarks of Yen Press, LLC.

Library of Congress Control Number: 2016956681

ISBNs: 978-1-9753-2246-5 (paperback)
        978-1-9753-2247-2 (ebook)

10 9 8 7 6 5 4 3 2 1

BVG

Printed in the United States of America